PASS THE SIE™

A PLAIN ENGLISH EXPLANATION TO HELP YOU PASS
THE SECURITIES INDUSTRY ESSENTIALS EXAM

EXAMZONE, INC.

PASS THE SIE™ - A PLAIN ENGLISH EXPLANATION TO HELP YOU PASS THE SECURITIES INDUSTRY ESSENTIALS EXAM

By Robert M. Walker

1st Edition – January, 2018

NASAA Statements of Policy and Model Rules reprinted with permission.

FINRA rules and definitions from the FINRA manual reprinted with permission from FINRA; ©2018 Financial Industry Regulatory Authority (FINRA).

MSRB General Rules reprinted with permission from MSRB.

www.examzone.com

Pass The SIE™, 1st Edition ISBN-13 978-0-9985176-7-4

Publisher: Examzone, Inc., Chicago, IL

Printed in the U.S.A.

Table of Contents

How to Use This Book

We're happy you chose Examzone to help you pass the Securities Industry Essentials (SIE) Exam. Our **Pass the SIE™** Exam Manual (this textbook) is written in Plain English so you can learn concepts and assimilate the material quickly and easily. We hope you take advantage of our full **Pass The SIE Success Program™** (sold separately*), complete with test prep materials for each step of the learning process.

All of the Learning Components of the **Pass The SIE Success Program™** are sold separately and can be found at http://www.examzone.com/passthesie and include:

- Pass the SIE™ Exam Manual (this textbook)
- Pass the SIE™ Online Practice Question Bank
- Pass the SIE™ Online Training Videos
- Pass the SIE™ Streaming Audio Lessons
- Pass the SIE™ Digital Study Plan

Our research has shown that students who follow the entire **Pass The SIE Success Program™** have considerably higher pass rates than those who use only one or two of the Learning Components. Our Success Program integrates each of the Learning Components on a chapter-by-chapter basis. The sequence starts with each textbook exam manual chapter, followed by the requisite Review Exercise and Review Quiz and finally finishes with the streaming video and audio lessons for that chapter. You can see this sequence outlined at www.examzone.com/studyplan by signing up for the **free** Pass The SIE Success Program™ Digital Study Plan.

Additionally, our Pass the SIE™ Online Practice Question Bank are designed to test your readiness for the Securities Industry Essentials (SIE) Exam. We recommend you take the final practice exam at least two weeks prior to your scheduled test date. If you score an 80% or above, we think you're ready to take the Securities Industry Essentials (SIE) Exam.

All of the Success Program materials mentioned above are available for purchase at http://www.examzone.com/passthesie. Email us at support@examzone.com or call us toll free at 1-855-EXAM-CARE – 1 (855) 392-6227 with any questions.

Please visit www.examzone.com/studyplan to sign up for your free personalized Pass the SIE™ Digital Study Plan which will help guide you and track your progress ensuring your success in passing the SIE.

Thanks for studying with Examzone, and good luck!

* Pass the SIE™ Learning Components and Pass the SIE Success Program Online Only Bundle™ are sold separately at http://www.examzone.com/passthesie. **The Pass The SIE Success Program Online Only Bundle™** includes 6 Month subscription access to the Pass the SIE™ Online Practice Question Bank, Pass the SIE™ Online Training Videos, Pass the SIE™ Streaming Audio Lessons and may be purchased for an additional subscription fee.

Introduction To the Securities Industry Essentials (SIE) Exam

What is the Securities Industry Essentials (SIE) Exam?

The Securities Industry Essentials Exam is an exciting, new development from the industry regulator known as FINRA. Historically, those who wanted to become securities agents had to be hired by a broker-dealer before taking a license exam. Now, with the implementation of the Securities Industry Essentials (SIE) Exam, those interested in entering the industry can take a securities license exam on their own. Then, after being hired by a member firm, these individuals will take a top-off exam, such as the Series 6 or Series 7, to complete their FINRA licensing requirements.

The results of the SIE are good for four years. Therefore, an individual can take the exam long before he chooses his career path and begins his job search in the financial services industry. Those who have passed the Securities Industry Essentials (SIE) Exam are presumed to have an advantage over other candidates, as they have shown initiative and already cleared one hurdle in the process of getting a candidate registered with FINRA and the state securities regulators.

Why Do I Need to Pass the SIE?

To sell securities for compensation, individuals are required to pass either a Series 6 or Series 7 license exam. The Series 6 license allows the individual to sell packaged products such as mutual funds and variable annuities for compensation, while the Series 7 license allows the individual to sell these products plus common stock, bonds, options, and other securities. For years, candidates have taken either the 100-question Series 6 Exam or the 250-question Series 7 Exam, depending on the securities sold to customers.

With the implementation of the SIE, candidates will now take the 75-question Securities Industry Essentials (SIE) Exam, typically, while in college. Then, after being hired by a broker-dealer, the individual will be required to pass either the Series 6 or Series 7 top-off exam, down to 50 questions for the Series 6 and just 125 for the Series 7 exam going forward.

So, if you pass the Securities Industry Essentials (SIE) Exam and then get hired by a firm to sell only packaged products, you will complete your license exam requirements by passing the Series 6, and then passing the state-law exam called the Series 63. If you will sell these products as well as the securities mentioned above, you will take the Series 7 plus the Series 63.

What Are the Basic Facts About the SIE Exam?

- The Exam is 75 questions
- All questions are multiple choice
- Candidates are allowed 105 minutes to complete the exam
- The passing score is 70% *or some other number TBD*
- The cost of the exam is $*110 or some other amount TBD*
- Exam results are good for four years from the date of passing the test
- Passing the exam does <u>not</u> qualify the individual to work within the industry by itself!
- To become licensed to work as an agent the individual must also:
    - Secure employment at a broker-dealer
    - Pass the appropriate top-off exam
    - Pass the state-securities-law exam, the Series 63

o Register through FINRA with a U4 submitted by the broker-dealer

What Are the Prerequisites?

There are no prerequisites for the Securities Industry Essentials (SIE) Exam. Historically, there were no prerequisites for the Series 6 or Series 7 Exam. Now, the SIE is the prerequisite for both tests.

While a college degree may be required by a broker-dealer advertising for a position or as a general hiring policy, it is not a regulatory requirement. To take the SIE, the Series 6, or the Series 7, the candidate is not required to have a college degree.

What Information Is Covered on the SIE?

As its name suggests, the Securities Industry Essentials (SIE) Exam covers the essential information related to the securities industry. While this information was covered in both the Series 6 and Series 7 exams, FINRA has decided to separate the essential information covered in the new Securities Industry Essentials (SIE) Exam from the more detailed and job-specific information covered in the top-off exams taken after the individual has been hired and sponsored by a member broker-dealer.

As FINRA explained when introducing the exam to the industry, "the SIE assesses basic product knowledge; the structure and function of the securities industry markets, regulatory agencies and their functions; and regulated and prohibited practices."

The same FINRA notice explains that the four main topic areas of the exam are as follows:

The first topic area, "Knowledge of Capital Markets," focuses on topics such as types of markets and offerings, broker-dealers and depositories, and economic cycles. The second, "Understanding Products and Their Risks," covers securities products at a high level as well as associated investment risks. The third, "Understanding Trading, Customer Accounts and Prohibited Activities," focuses on accounts, orders, settlement and prohibited activities. The final section, "Overview of the Regulatory Framework," encompasses topics such as SROs, registration requirements and specified conduct rules.

How Is This Exam Manual Organized?

This book follows the Securities Industry Essentials (SIE) Exam Outline provided by FINRA. There are four sections of the FINRA outline, which is why this book, also, has four chapters.

Chapter 1 covers primary offerings of securities, such as IPOs or initial public offerings. Types of broker-dealer businesses and their basic financial and regulatory requirements are explored. Finally, we look in some detail at basic economic factors affecting securities investments, including inflation, interest rates, and the business cycle.

The largest chapter, Chapter 2, is called "Understanding Products and Their Risks." Here, we explore insurance and securities products in detail, following with a detailed examination of investment risks related to various investment approaches.

Chapter 3 looks at customer accounts, trading securities, and FINRA regulations of agents.

The last chapter, Chapter 4, focuses on the regulation of the securities industry. Here, we explore federal securities legislation as well as FINRA in detail.

After each chapter, you will take a chapter review exercise, and then a chapter review quiz. At the end of the four chapters, you will find two full-length practice exams, 75 questions each. A detailed glossary follows the practice exams. Finally, an index of frequently used terms is found at the end of the manual.

How Should I Approach Exam Questions?

Some exam questions will be straight forward. Many, however, will be challenging based on the way they are presented. No matter what the structure of the question, the best way to avoid the trap is to read the question carefully. Make sure you didn't skip a word or insert a word.

Now, look at the four answer choices. Your job is to eliminate three of them. And, you can do it in any order.

What you don't want to do is rush through the question looking for familiar phrases and grabbing the first answer that looks decent.

That is a trap. Some questions present a false pattern and try to exploit it. Some questions are extra-wordy. Some use negative words—except, least likely, avoid—to confuse the test taker. And, all candidates have strengths and weaknesses, making some topics harder than others even when the questions are basic.

Don't expect to know the answer just from reading the question. The answer is always one of the four choices given. Again, your job is to eliminate the other three answers based on what you've learned through the book, training videos, and/or practice questions.

Where Can I Get More Information, Including How to Sign Up for the Exam?

FINRA provides information on the SIE and other license exams at http://www.finra.org/industry/qualification-exams.

At the time of this writing, Prometric is the sole provider of testing services for FINRA. The Prometric website is at https://www.prometric.com/en-us/Pages/home.aspx.

CHAPTER 1: Knowledge of Capital Markets

Public companies raise money by issuing **stocks** and **bonds** to investors, who can trade the **securities** with other investors on the **secondary market**. Examples of public companies include Starbucks, Facebook, and McDonald's.

Private companies, on the other hand, are often owned by just one family or a small group of founders and investors. Their securities do not trade on a secondary market. Examples of private companies include The Chicago White Sox, Five Guys, and Koch Brothers.

Accessing the public markets provides a large amount of capital for the issuer. But, going forward, a public company must provide full disclosure of material facts to their investors, the securities regulators, and the public.

That is why many companies stay private. It is easier to run a business without having to disclose all material information, or worrying about liability to investors for failure to properly disclose something that leads to losses on their stocks or bonds.

If a private company goes public, their first offering of common stock is an **initial public offering** or **IPO**. In an IPO, a company sells a percentage of ownership to investors, using the proceeds to expand or accomplish other stated goals.

When the issuer receives the proceeds of the offer, that is a **primary** offering or the **primary market**. If early shareholders sell their shares to the public, we call that a **secondary offering**. Many IPOs involve both the issuing company and the early investors selling shares to the public for the first time. This is known as a **combined offering**.

Facebook's IPO was a combined offering. According to the final prospectus, the company received approximately $6.7 billion while the early investors received just over $9 billion. Investors paid $38 for the IPO shares, which, as of this writing, trade for $178.30 on the secondary market.

Many IPO investments, however, do not work out for investors. Buying common stock is always risky. Buying an IPO is especially so.

Market Structure

Securities are issued to investors on the primary market to raise capital for the issuer. Securities are, then, traded among investors on the secondary market. Typically, the media starts talking about an IPO only when it starts trading. When you see the CEO and others ring the opening bell, this marks the day the IPO shares begin to trade among investors on the secondary market.

This section, on the other hand, is concerned with what happens before that first opening bell is rung.

To complete a securities offering, under the **Securities Act of 1933**, an issuer first registers with the **Securities and Exchange Commission**. The **SEC** is part of the federal government, with the Chairman appointed by the President of the United States.

The SEC wants to see what the issuers will tell their potential investors in the **prospectus,** which is part of the **registration statement**. They require the issuers to provide the material or relevant facts on the company: history, competitors, products and services, risks of investing in the company, financials, board of directors, officers, etc. And, they require it to be written clearly. Only if investors understand the risks and rewards of an investment do they have a chance of determining a good opportunity from a bad one.

The SEC and other securities regulators do not protect investors from making bad choices. Their concern is that the issuer provides enough pertinent information so investors can decide on investing or taking a pass. If information is misstated or omitted from the offering documents, investors are defrauded. The SEC and state securities regulators are both out to protect investors from fraudulent offers of securities.

The issuer hires **underwriters**, also called **investment bankers**, to help them offer securities. The underwriters help the issuer file a registration statement with the SEC. Now, the **cooling-off period**, which lasts a minimum of 20 days, begins. During this period, no advertising is allowed, and, while indications of interest are taken, no final sales are made until the SEC finally clears the issue.

A registered representative must deliver a preliminary prospectus to anyone giving an indication of interest. This disclosure document contains all material information except the release date and the final public offering price. As amendments are filed to this preliminary prospectus, or "red herring," a range of likely prices for the stock are typically listed.

The SEC reviews the registration statement (part of which becomes the prospectus) for clarity and to make sure that at least the boiler plate disclosures have been made. If a section looks incomplete or unclear, they'll make the issuer/underwriters rewrite it.

But the SEC cannot and does not determine the information is accurate or complete. They don't know the issuer's history, and the financial statements the issuer provides—who knows if they're accurate? Since the SEC cannot and does not verify information, the issuer and the underwriters hold a **due diligence meeting** during the cooling-off period, a final meeting or series of meetings to make sure they provided the SEC and the public with accurate and full disclosure.

The issuer can publish one type of advertising during the cooling-off period, called a **tombstone**. A tombstone lays out the basic facts: the issuer, the type of security, number of shares, amount to be raised, and then the names of the underwriters.

August 18, 1993

2,875,000 Shares
Common Stock

2,875,000 Shares to be offered to the public. The Company engages in the business of selling microcomputer products and providing associated technical services, training and repair to a defined market segment.

RandomAccess™

NASDAQ/NMS Symbol (RNDM)

Price $4.00 per Share

CHATFIELD DEAN & CO.

MEMBER: NASD, SIPC

Foster Jeffries & Co., Inc. • Walford and Company, Inc.

If the three underwriters sold all 2.875 million shares for $4 each, the issuer, RandomAccess, probably received about $10 million, with the three broker-dealers keeping the rest. A tombstone is not an offer to sell the securities. As the disclaimer states, "The offer is made only by the Prospectus."

Even though the SEC requires issuers to register their securities offerings, they don't approve or disapprove of the offering or pass judgment on any aspect of the prospectus. They don't guarantee accuracy or adequacy of the information provided by the issuer and its underwriters. And there must be a prominent legend such as:

> Neither the Securities and Exchange Commission nor any state securities commission has approved or disapproved of these securities or passed upon the adequacy or accuracy of this prospectus. Any representation to the contrary is a criminal offense.

If the issue of stock is authorized for listing on **NYSE**, **NASDAQ**, or other major exchanges, the issuer and underwriters only register with the SEC, since the securities are **federal covered securities**. But, if the issue will not trade on those exchanges, the stock also must be registered with the states where it will be offered and sold.

➤ *Investment Banking*

An investment banking firm negotiates the terms of the underwriting deal with the company planning to go public and then acts as the **managing underwriter** of a group of underwriters collectively known as the underwriting **syndicate**.

The managing underwriter spells out the basic terms of the underwriting and issues a letter of intent to the issuing corporation in which the risks to and obligations of each side are spelled out. The underwriter relies on a market-out clause, which explains that certain unforeseen events will allow the underwriter to back out of the deal. If the company's drug making facilities are shut down by the FDA due to contamination, for example, the underwriter can back out of the underwriting engagement.

For municipal securities and for some corporate securities offerings, a potential managing underwriter submits a bid or responds to an RFP (request for proposals). This is known as a **competitive bid** as opposed to a **negotiated underwriting**. In a competitive bid, the syndicate who can raise the money at the lowest cost to the issuer wins. In a negotiated underwriting, the managing underwriter negotiates the terms of the deal with the issuer, and then forms a syndicate of underwriters.

Even though firms like Morgan Stanley and Goldman Sachs are fiercely competitive, they also routinely work with each other when underwriting securities. Sometimes Goldman Sachs is the managing underwriter; other times Goldman Sachs is just one of many underwriters in the syndicate. Depends which firm brought the deal to the table.

The syndicate often gives an issuer a **firm commitment**. This means the underwriters bear the risk of any unsold securities and make up the difference by buying them for their own accounts. That's a last resort, though. The whole point of doing the underwriting is to sell all the securities as fast as possible at the highest price possible.

Underwriters act as agents for the issuer when they engage in a **best-efforts, all-or-none**, or **mini-max** underwriting. Here, if the minimum amount is not raised, the underwriters are off the hook. In a best-efforts underwriting, the issuer will accept what the underwriters raise. In the other types, money is returned to investors if the minimum amount is not raised during the offering period. Broker-dealers involved in either type of **contingency offering** (all-or-none, mini-max) must place customer payments in an escrow account so that if the offering is canceled, investors receive their money plus their pro rata share of any interest payments. If the underwriter were to place such payments into its own account, this would be a violation of FINRA rules.

The firms in the syndicate usually handle different amounts of an offering, and their liability for any unsold shares is spelled out in an agreement among the underwriters. Not surprisingly, the agreement among underwriters is called the **agreement among underwriters,** sometimes referred to as the **syndicate letter.**

Syndicate members in a firm commitment have their firm's capital at risk, meaning they act in a **principal** capacity. The syndicate manager, therefore, often lines up other broker-dealers to help sell the offering. This group of sellers is referred to as the **selling group**. The selling group acts in an **agency** capacity for the syndicate, trying to sell shares but bearing no financial risk for the ones they can't. They have customers who might want to invest—the syndicate is happy to share part of the compensation with these firms.

So, in a firm commitment underwriting the syndicate members have capital at risk, but selling group members never do in any type of underwriting.

Securities regulators are concerned with protecting investors. Investors can be defrauded when an issuer pulls most of the value out of the company and gives it to the underwriters either in the form of cash or generous warrants to buy shares at fractions-of-a-penny. Why would an issuer want to do that? Maybe they don't want to pay for the services with money and would rather just take it out of the value of the investors' shares by letting the warrants dilute their equity.

Or, maybe the issuer owns a percentage of one of the underwriters. Moving money from this company over to that one would be a neat trick for the issuer, so why not just pay top dollar for the underwriting both in terms of fees and underwriter options/warrants? Promoters are people who founded the company or have a big ownership interest in it. If the offering doesn't pass the smell test in terms of underwriter or promoter compensation, the regulators will shut it down through legal action.

For a good example of underwriter compensation, we can pull up the prospectus for Facebook's IPO. When we do, we see that the shares were sold to investors at a POP of $38, with the spread to the underwriters at about 42 cents per share.

FINRA insists the terms of the offering among the various underwriters be spelled out clearly:

> *"Selling syndicate agreements or selling group agreements shall set forth the price at which the securities are to be sold to the public or the formula by which such price can be ascertained, and shall state clearly to whom and under what circumstances concessions, if any, may be allowed."*

Specific Types of Offerings

In a **registered secondary** offering the key word is *secondary*. As with all secondary or non-issuer transactions, the proceeds are not going to the issuer. Rather, they are going to, for example, a former CEO or board member who is now offering his or her restricted shares to the public. The restricted shares were not registered; now they are being registered and offered to investors on the secondary market. Remember that if the issuing corporation does an additional offer of stock, it is not a secondary offering. Rather, it is a "subsequent primary distribution."

When the issuer gets the proceeds, the word is "primary," not "secondary."

A specific type of firm commitment is called a **standby underwriting**. While a broker-dealer cannot buy IPO shares for its own account just because it wants to, they can act as a standby purchaser for the issuer, buying any shares the public doesn't. Usually, when we see the phrase "standby" on the exam, we associate it with an additional offering of stock, which inherently involves a **rights offering**. Shareholders are owners of a certain percent of a company's profits; therefore, if new shares are sold to other people, the % owned by existing shareholders would be decreased or "diluted" if they didn't get first right of refusal on a certain number of shares. That's why issuers performing an additional offering of stock typically do a rights offering that provides existing shareholders the right to buy their % of the new shares. To ensure that all rights are used/subscribed to, a standby underwriter may be engaged to agree to buy any rights that shareholders don't use and exercise them to buy the rest of the shares being offered.

Some offerings of securities are registered now but will be sold gradually at the current market price. That means if you buy in the first round, you might end up paying more, or less, than the investors who buy shares at the then-current "market price." What if there is no "market" for the shares being offered in an at the market offering? Then, the SEC has a real problem with broker-dealers or their associated persons telling investors they're buying the security "at the market."

If the stock doesn't trade on an exchange, the broker-dealer may not tell the customer the security is being offered to (or purchased from) the customer at the so-called "market price." That would be a "manipulative, deceptive, or other fraudulent device or contrivance," according to the SEC. If the firm is the only firm willing to make a **bid / offer** on the stock, that, by definition, means there is no actual market for the security.

An issuer might want to register a certain number of securities now but sell them gradually or on demand over the next few years. If so, the issuer can use a **shelf registration.** For example, if they want to borrow money by issuing bonds, they might want to get them registered now but wait and hope that interest rates will drop over the next few years, at which point they can issue the bonds and borrow the money at more attractive rates in the future, with the offering already on-deck and ready to go. Or, if the company has a dividend reinvestment program (DRIP) in place, or must continuously issue shares when executives and key employees exercise stock options, they are likely to use a shelf registration.

The term "when-issued" is an abbreviation for the longer form of securities that are traded "when, as, and if issued." As the name implies, when-issued refers to a transaction made conditionally, because a security has not yet been issued—only authorized. U.S. Treasury securities—sold at auctions—new issues of stocks and bonds, and stocks that are offered continuously or over time are all examples of when-issued securities.

Stabilization

Normally, anyone caught trying to artificially move the price of a security on the secondary market is subject to regulatory problems, civil liability to other traders, and sometimes even criminal penalties. If a few big traders of some small-company stock get together and come up with a plan to enter large buy orders at certain times throughout the day to boost the price, they are engaging in market manipulation.

On the other hand, right after a new offer of securities, the lead underwriter can prop up the price of the stock on the secondary market to some extent through **stabilization.** If the public offering price or POP is $10, but the stock starts trading on NASDAQ or NYSE for only $9.50, the managing/lead underwriter can place bids to buy the stock to provide a floor price for the investors nice enough to buy the IPO. Now, the bid can't be higher than the POP of $10, and it also can't be higher than the highest independent bid for the stock. That means the bid had better be bona fide and cannot come from a subsidiary of the managing underwriter's firm, for example. If another market maker is quoting $9.50, the managing underwriter can bid $9.50, but not $9.51. And, should the price rise to the public offering price again, no bids above the POP could be placed.

These quotes are known to change by the second or fractions of seconds, but each time the managing/lead underwriter places a bid to buy the stock on the secondary market, they must keep it no higher than the highest current bid for the stock.

Since this is an unusual situation, stabilizing bids must be identified as stabilizing bids on the NASDAQ trading system. Before the managing underwriter enters any stabilizing bids, the firm must first submit a request to NASDAQ MarketWatch to enter one-sided stabilizing bids. It is typically the managing underwriter who enters stabilizing bids, but whether it's that firm or another syndicate member, remember that only one firm can be placing stabilizing bids.

What if there is no independent market maker for the stock? Then, no stabilizing bids can be placed. The syndicate also must disclose any plans for stabilization in a legend (box of text) in the offering document that refers to disclosures in the "plan of distribution" section of the prospectus regarding stabilization activities.

Exempt Securities

The Securities Act of 1933 is a piece of federal legislation, so it's not surprising the federal government is not required to follow it. That's right, government securities are exempt from this act. T-Bills, T-Notes, T-Bonds, STRIPS, and TIPS are not required to be registered.

States, counties, and cities—those who issue municipal securities—also got an exemption from the registration process under the Securities Act of 1933. The federal government generally does not exert that much control over any State or local government, and municipal governments are not as likely to go bankrupt as corporations. So, if a school board puts out an issue of municipal securities based on fraudulent financial statements, the SEC could go after them in federal court. But, these municipal securities issuers do not file registration statements with the SEC and wait for the SEC to tell them it's okay to proceed.

Charitable/fraternal/religious/benevolent organization securities are exempt. So are bank securities, which are already regulated by bank regulators (FDIC, FRB, and Comptroller of the Currency). Securities issued by Small Business Investment Companies (SBICs) are also exempt, since they are only offered and sold to institutions and other sophisticated investors who don't require so much protection.

Short-term debt securities that mature in 270 days or less—commercial paper, bankers' acceptances, other promissory notes—are also exempt from this registration process. If a corporation had to get through the registration process just to borrow money for a few days, weeks, or months, interest rates would likely have moved before the deal could be completed. On the other hand, if they want to borrow money for several years by issuing bonds or sell ownership stakes, the regulators feel maybe they ought to slow down and reveal material facts to investors.

We will look at all securities mentioned above later in the textbook.

So, commercial paper, T-Notes, and municipal bonds are **exempt securities**. They are good to go without any paperwork being filed with the SEC. There are also transactions that qualify for exemptions, called **exempt transactions**.

Unlike an exempt security, an exempt transaction must be claimed by the issuer with some paperwork to back up what they did or are about to do. Under **Regulation A**, for example, an issuer can sell up to $5,000,000 worth of securities in a year without having to jump through all the usual hoops. Rather than filing a standard registration statement, the issuer files an **offering circular**, a much more scaled-down document.

The SEC oversees interstate commerce, meaning commerce among many states. Therefore, if the issuer wants to sell only to residents of one state, the SEC doesn't get involved. There is already a state securities regulator who can deal with this one. Therefore, intra-state offerings are exempt if they match this statement, "Any security which is a part of an issue offered and sold only to persons resident within a single State or Territory, where the issuer of such security is a person resident and doing business within or, if a corporation, incorporated by and doing business within, such State or Territory."

These offerings are registered with the securities regulator of that state or territory rather than the federal government. The state where the offering takes place is where the issuer is located and doing business. The issuer doesn't just pick a state at random in which to offer the securities.

These intra-state offerings are performed under an exemption to the Securities Act of 1933 called Rule 147. As the rule states, the offering is not required to be registered with the SEC provided "That the issuer be a resident of and doing business within the state or territory in which all offers and sales are made; and that no part of the issue be offered or sold to non-residents within the period of time specified in the rule." So, if the issuer's business is in the state, 80% of its gross revenue is derived there, 80% of its assets are located there, and 80% of the net proceeds will be used in that state, a Rule 147 exemption can be claimed to avoid registration with the SEC. But, as the second requirement clarified, the buyers can't sell the security to a non-resident for a time specified by the rule—which is nine months.

To be an eligible investor, the individual must be a resident of the state, or a partnership, LLC, corporation, trust or other entity that has its principal office within the state. And, if an entity is formed to acquire part of the offering, it would only be eligible if all beneficial owners of the organization are residents of the state or territory (e.g. Puerto Rico).

The SEC is out to protect the average investor from fast-talking stock operators. But, the SEC doesn't provide as much protection to sophisticated investors such as mutual funds, pension funds, or high-net-worth individuals. If anybody tries to scam these investors, they'll be in just as much trouble as if they scammed an average investor, but the SEC doesn't put up as much protection for the big, institutional investors, who can usually watch out for themselves. Therefore, if the issuer wants to avoid the registration process under the Act of 1933, they can limit the offer and sale of the securities primarily to these accredited investors. Accredited investors include institutions such as:

- banks
- broker-dealers
- insurance companies
- investment companies
- small business investment companies (Venture Capital)
- government retirement plans
- company retirement plans of a certain minimum size

An accredited investor also includes an executive officer, director, or general partner of the issuer. If Amazon wants to sell shares of Amazon to Jeff Bezos and the members of the board, how much protection do these investors need from the company they run?

Accredited investors also include individuals or married couples with at least $1 million net worth excluding the value of their primary residence. If not relying on net worth, an accredited investor can qualify based on income. Individuals earning at least $200,000 a year in the most recent two years and married couples earning at least $300,000—with a reasonable expectation of making at least that much this year—are also accredited investors.

Exemptions relate to registration requirements. Whether an offer is registered, it is subject to anti-fraud regulations. As **Regulation D** announces from the start, "Regulation D relates to transactions exempted from the registration requirements of section 5 of the Securities Act of 1933. Such transactions are not exempt from the antifraud, civil liability, or other provisions of the federal securities laws. Issuers are reminded of their obligation to provide such further material information, if any, as may be necessary to make the information required under Regulation D, in light of the circumstances under which it is furnished, not misleading."

Under Regulation D an issuer finds various offerings that can be completed without the usual registration requirements having to be met. Let's look at the best-known exempt transactions, performed under either Rule 505 or 506.

A **Reg D/private placement** transaction is exempt based on the issuer offering to an unlimited number of accredited investors but only to a maximum of 35 **non-accredited purchasers**. Under Rule 505 the issuer can only offer and sell up to $5 million in a 12-month period. The issuer must inform all investors that they will receive "restricted securities" that cannot be sold until after a 6-month minimum holding period, which we discuss in just a few paragraphs. Also, there can be no general solicitation or advertising in connection with this private placement offering.

Even though the issuer isn't filing a registration statement with the SEC, it still must provide information to the investors. As the rule states, "Rule 505 allows companies to decide what information to give to accredited investors, so long as it does not violate the antifraud prohibitions of the federal securities laws. But companies must give non-accredited investors disclosure documents that generally are equivalent to those used in registered offerings. If a company provides information to accredited investors, it must make this information available to non-accredited investors as well. The company must also be available to answer questions by prospective purchasers."

And, even though there is no registration statement required, when the offering is completed, issuers must file a Form D that discloses the basic facts of the offering. For example, by looking up their Form D, we see that Five Guys sold $10 million of stock through a private placement in which they tried to raise $15 million. Beyond that, we see little information, only that Five Guys takes in somewhere between $25 million and $100 million in revenue. If Five Guys does an IPO someday, then we will have access to all pertinent information on the issuer.

You can see the Form D at:
http://www.sec.gov/Archives/edgar/data/1467164/000146716409000001/xslFormDX01/primary_doc.xml

If the issuer doesn't want limits placed on the amount of money raised, they utilize Rule 506 instead. Then, they decide if they want to solicit investors and advertise the offering to prospects or not. Under one type of Rule 506 offering the issuer will offer and sell to up to 35 non-accredited purchasers, but unlike under Rule 505 the issuer must reasonably believe the non-accredited purchasers are either sophisticated or are relying on an independent (from the issuer) purchaser representative who can explain the risks and rewards of the deal. Because the issuer will use non-accredited purchasers here, no solicitation or advertising is allowed.

If the issuer wants to be able to solicit investors, they must limit them to accredited investors only. This is the other type of exempt transaction under Rule 506.

No matter which of these exemptions is used, the issuer must file a Form D - Notice of Exempt Offering of Securities. And, investors receive "restricted shares" subject to mandatory minimum holding periods. The securities offered and sold through a private placement are not required to be registered, but FINRA requires member firms to file a copy of the **private placement memorandum (PPM)** with their Firm Gateway. The PPM must be filed no later than 15 calendar days after the first sale is made. Or, if no PPM is going to be used with the offering, that fact must be reported to FINRA.

Crowdfunding

Even though we just looked at concerns for non-accredited purchasers in Reg D private placements, anyone can invest in a "crowdfunding" securities offering. Because of the risks involved with this type of investing, however, investors are limited in how much they can invest during any 12-month period.

The limitation depends on net worth and annual income. If either the investor's annual income or net worth is less than $100,000, then during any 12-month period, he can invest up to the greater of either $2,000 or 5% of the lesser of his annual income or net worth.

If both his annual income and net worth are equal to or more than $100,000, then during any 12-month period, an investor can commit up to 10% of annual income or net worth, whichever is less, but not to exceed $100,000.

As when determining who is and is not an accredited investor, the value of the investor's primary residence is not included in the net worth calculation. In addition, any mortgage or other loan on a primary residence does not count as a liability up to the fair market value of the home.

Companies may not offer crowdfunding investments to investors directly. Rather, they must use a broker-dealer or funding portal registered with the SEC and a member of the Financial Industry Regulatory Authority (FINRA).

Investors open an account with the crowdfunding intermediary to make an investment, and all written communications relating to the crowdfunding investment will be electronic.

Before an investor can make a crowdfunding investment the broker-dealer or funding portal operating the crowdfunding platform must ensure that he reviews educational materials about this type of investing. In addition, the investor must positively affirm that he understands he can lose the investment, and that he can bear such a financial loss.

Investors also must demonstrate they understand the risks of crowdfunded investing. The sharing of views by the crowd is considered by some to be an integral part of crowdfunding. Broker-dealers and funding portals, through their crowdfunding platforms, are required to have communication channels transparent to the public. For example, on an online forum—relating to each investment opportunity.

In these channels, the crowd of investors can weigh in on the pros and cons of an opportunity and ask the company questions. All persons representing the company must identify themselves.

Investors have up to 48 hours prior to the end of the offer period to change their mind and cancel their investment commitment for any reason. Once the offering period is within 48 hours of ending it is too late to pull out. However, if the company makes a material change to the offering terms or other information disclosed to investors, investors are given five business days to reconfirm the investment commitment.

Investors are limited in their ability to resell their investment for the first year and may need to hold for an indefinite period. Unlike investing in companies listed on a stock exchange where investors can quickly and easily trade securities on a market, crowdfunding is similar to holding a direct participation program interest. To sell the investment an interested buyer must be located.

Depositories and Clearing Facilities

If a customer buys 500 shares of SBUX, his broker-dealer finds a market maker who wants to sell 500 shares right now at their offer price. Such trades settle "T + 2" or two business days from the trade date. But, what does that part—the next two business days—involve, if the trade is already completed?

When he buys those 500 shares of SBUX, let's say at $30 a share, his account will show the 500 shares among his positions and will debit the $15,000 plus a commission for the purchase. But, those are just numbers on a screen at this point. Until the transaction is cleared and settled, nothing is completed. The firms that clear transactions in securities are known as **clearing agencies** or **clearing facilities.**

There are two types of clearing agencies: clearing corporations and depository. Clearing corporations include: The National Securities Clearing Corporation, the Fixed Income Clearing Corporation, and the Options Clearing Corporation (OCC). The only depository is the Depository Trust Company or DTC.

The SEC explains that, "Clearing Agencies are self-regulatory organizations that are required to register with the Commission. There are two types of clearing agencies -- clearing corporations and depositories. Clearing corporations compare member transactions (or report to members the results of exchange comparison operations), clear those trades and prepare instructions for automated settlement of those trades, and often act as intermediaries in making those settlements. Depositories hold securities certificates in bulk form for their participants and maintain ownership records of the securities on their own books. Physical securities are maintained in vaults, and ownership records are maintained on the books of the depository. Clearing corporations generally instruct depositories to make securities deliveries that result from settlement of securities transactions. In addition, depositories receive instructions from participants to move securities from one participant's account to another participant's account, either for free or in exchange for a payment of money."

Types of Broker-Dealer Businesses

An **introducing broker-dealer** has a relationship with customers in which it makes recommendations to customers on how and what to trade, but lets another firm handle the execution of the trades. A firm that executes transactions for an introducing broker-dealer is sometimes called an **executing broker-dealer**. The introducing and executing broker-dealers split commissions/fees according to a written agreement.

An introducing broker-dealer more typically contracts with a **carrying broker-dealer.** The carrying broker-dealer acts as the introducing broker-dealer's back office, handling customer assets and clearing transactions through a clearing broker-dealer. FINRA requires the firms to execute a contract between the carrying firm and the introducing firm stipulating the terms of the agreement for the carrying firm to hold customer assets and execute trades on behalf of the introducing firm.

Or, an introducing broker-dealer may work with a **clearing** or **self-clearing broker-dealer** directly. The clearing broker-dealer also performs back-office functions for the introducing broker-dealer. As the name implies, they are members of the clearing agencies and clear trades for themselves and other firms.

A clearing member firm is a broker-dealer that also provides many functions of a retail bank. They hold customer assets, and receive dividends, interest payments, and deposits from customers. One of the main sources of revenue and profit for such firms is the interest they earn on customer cash versus the small rates paid to customers.

As you can imagine, clearing members have stricter financial requirements than broker-dealers who avoid handling customer assets.

We looked at clearing facilities/agencies, including the National Securities Clearing Corporation, and the related Depository Trust Company. Clearing member firms are members of a clearing agency as well as various exchanges and other SROs. If a broker-dealer is not a clearing member, it must have an arrangement with a clearing member firm to clear and settle its trades. An introducing broker-dealer typically pays a clearing member a fee per-trade. Also, if the clearing member extends any margin loans to customers, the introducing broker-dealer pays interest on such loans.

The term **prime brokerage** refers to bundled services that clearing firms offer to active traders, such as hedge funds. Hedge funds require more leverage than a retail customer and the ability to borrow securities for short sales. A clearing prime broker, a full-service broker-dealer, provides such specialized services for highly capitalized, actively traded accounts.

Regulatory Requirements of Broker-Dealers

FINRA-member broker-dealers must have **principals**, also known as supervisors. For most firms, one of these principals must be registered as a Series 27 - Financial and Operations Principal (FINOP). A "FINOP" principal can supervise the following activities:

- Back office operations
- Preparation and maintenance of a member firm's books and records
- Compliance with financial responsibility rules that apply to self-clearing broker-dealers and market makers

A principal with a Series 27 registration is responsible for filing regular FOCUS (Financial and Operational Combined Uniform Single) reports. FOCUS reports show items including amounts the firm owes to customers and other parties, as well as amounts owed to the firm. Securities borrowed for short sales, and securities that were failed to receive are also indicated. Also, the current values of securities owned by the firm are listed.

The SEC establishes broker-dealer net capital requirements under the Securities Exchange Act of 1934 and the rules issued under the Act. Whether a firm has a customer who is slow to pay when buying or slow to deliver when selling, the firm's own capital may be required to settle the transaction. Member firms who underwrite securities frequently perform firm commitment underwritings in which they promise to buy shares that investors do not subscribe to. Not to mention that broker-dealers are businesses that have all the typical general operating expenses that other professional service firms do.

FINRA-member broker-dealers are required to provide, on request, information about its financial condition to its customers. As the rules state:

(a) A member shall make available to inspection by any bona fide regular customer, upon request, the information relative to such member's financial condition as disclosed in its most recent balance sheet prepared either in accordance with such member's usual practice or as required by any state or federal securities laws, or any rule or regulation thereunder.

(b) As used in paragraph (a) of this Rule, the term "customer" means any person who, in the regular course of such member's business, has cash or securities in the possession of such member.

Broker-dealers becoming insolvent can have a significant negative impact on the markets, so the SEC requires broker-dealers to constantly monitor and report their financial condition. What's critically important here is the liquid net worth of the firm. Like any business, broker-dealers have assets that can be readily sold and those that can't. Therefore, when calculating their net capital, member firms exclude their illiquid assets. These assets that are not easily sold for their full value are also called non-allowable assets for purposes of calculating net capital. Illiquid or "non-allowable" assets include equity in real estate, exchange memberships, furniture and fixtures, and intangible assets such as goodwill or pre-paid expenses. Notice that while these assets have value, the value is either too hard to determine or would involve selling, say, $5,000 worth of office furniture for a few hundred dollars.

The firm also owns securities. While securities do have a discernible market value, that value is often volatile. Some securities trade so infrequently that determining any market value can be difficult. So, if the regulators don't want broker-dealers counting intangible assets, it's not surprising they also don't want member firms counting their securities at 100% of today's market value. Rather, the typical reduction in value—called taking a haircut—for common stock is 15%. If the stock trades in a limited trading market, the haircut/reduction in value is 40%. And, if the security has no ready market, the regulators require broker-dealers to treat them as worthless—a 100% haircut is taken.

The regulators even require an extra haircut if a security would make up too much of a firm's net capital, called an undue concentration. If a non-exempt security's value is more than 10% of the firm's tentative net capital, the firm must take an additional haircut at the same rate by which the position exceeds the 10% threshold on the security's value.

And, if a customer has a **fail to deliver** after selling stock, the firm must set up a fail to deliver account on its books in the amount of the sales proceeds for the transaction. Believe it or not, at this point the position is still an allowable asset. However, the longer the fail-to-deliver drags on, the bigger the required haircut. On the fifth business day following settlement the fail-to-deliver must be aged for purposes of computing net capital. The position would now be **marked to the market** with a 15% haircut taken on that. Even though the asset has been aged, it is still an allowable asset. It just needs to get itself an extra-short haircut to be counted in the firm's net capital.

Aggregate Indebtedness, Alternative Standard

The net capital of a firm is based on its aggregate indebtedness, which the SEC defines as, "the total money liabilities of a broker or dealer arising in connection with any transaction whatsoever." Aggregate Indebtedness includes "money borrowed, money payable against securities loaned and securities 'failed to receive,' the market value of securities borrowed to the extent to which no equivalent value is paid or credited, customers' and non-customers' free credit balances, and credit balances in customers' and non-customers' accounts having short positions in securities."

Firms using the aggregate indebtedness standard must not allow their aggregate indebtedness to exceed 1500 percent of their net capital if they are an established firm, or 800 percent of net capital for the first 12 months after commencing business as a broker or dealer. Firms electing to use the alternative standard for computing net capital must notify their designated examining authority (FINRA, or the exchange) of their intention to use the alternative standard. These firms must not allow their net capital to drop below the greater of $250,000 or two percent of "aggregate debt items." Notice that the aggregate indebtedness standard involves comparing indebtedness to net capital, while the alternative standard goes the other way—net capital is compared to the firm's indebtedness. Point is, however the firm measures it, their net capital is extremely important to FINRA, the SEC, and the markets overall.

The SEC defines a *free credit balance* as:

> "Liabilities of a broker or dealer to customers which are subject to immediate cash payment to customers on demand, whether resulting from sales of securities, dividends, interest, deposits, or otherwise."

Why is a customer's "free credit balance" a form of indebtedness to the firm? Because that cash has been put to work by the firm and is owed to the customer upon demand. In other words, it's just like at a bank, where the money in someone's savings account has been put to work by the bank and is owed to the customer upon demand. In fact, that's why they call them "demand deposit accounts" at the bank.

Broker-dealers must follow stringent requirements when investing a customer's unused cash. As SEC rules require, **sweep programs** must be explained clearly to brokerage customers. Investors can leave their un-invested cash in their brokerage accounts. Or, they can have the cash swept into a money market mutual fund, which receives SIPC protection. Or, they can choose to have it swept into a bank account, where it receives FDIC insurance. The latter is called a "bank sweep program," for obvious reasons.

Some broker-dealers have the cash swept into multiple bank accounts. That way, rather than stopping at $250,000 of protection per-customer, these sweep programs provide up to $500,000 in protection. Whatever the customer chooses, it is his responsibility to monitor his cash position to be sure it does not exceed either FDIC or SIPC coverage.

Broker-dealers earn interest on bank sweep accounts, much more than they credit to the customers. In fact, many well-known firms earn hundreds of millions of dollars each year just on the spread between what they earn and what they pay on un-invested customer cash.

If that seems unfair, there is a simple solution for customers—put the cash back into stocks, bonds, mutual funds, etc. The broker-dealer makes money either way: the interest on the unused cash, or the commissions on the trades.

Net Capital Computations

To run a net capital computation a member firm starts by figuring its **net worth**. Net worth is all assets minus all liabilities. Then, because many firms are capitalized by taking out subordinated loans, if the subordinated loan has been approved by the regulators the firm then adds it to their net worth. At this point they have their total available capital.

Of course, we aren't going to let them count everything, or at full value. Therefore, the firm would then reduce that "total available capital" by subtracting out the illiquid or non-allowable assets we looked at. Remember, if the asset is not something sellable for a fair or certain price, it is non-allowable. After subtracting the non-allowable assets such as equity in real estate or prepaid expenses the firm has arrived at their tentative net capital.

And the formula is:

Net Worth

+ <u>Subordinated Debt</u>

Total available capital

- <u>Non-allowable assets</u>

Tentative net capital

Now, the firm must apply the various "haircuts" we looked at. Finally, fails to deliver are aged, at which point the firm's net capital has been computed. And, the formula would look like this:

Net Worth

+ <u>Subordinated Debt</u>

Total available capital

- <u>Non-allowable assets</u>

Tentative net capital

- <u>Haircuts</u>

Net Capital

Minimum Net Capital Requirements

So, that's how net capital is computed. How much net capital is a firm required to have? That depends on its activities. We discussed carrying and clearing firms who accept funds and securities from customers. The minimum net capital for these firms is $250,000.

The minimum net capital for introducing firms is either $5,000 or $50,000, depending on their activities. An introducing firm that neither receives customer assets directly or indirectly nor holds customer assets can operate with just $5,000 of net capital. An introducing broker or dealer who introduces transactions and accounts to a carrying member firm and who receives but does not hold customer assets can operate with a minimum net capital of $50,000. Also, although such a firm could participate in a syndicate performing a firm commitment underwriting, they could not enter into a commitment to purchase shares themselves on a principal basis.

Firms who engage in the sale of redeemable shares of registered investment companies (open-end funds, UITs), including interests in separate accounts (variable annuities, variable life insurance) can operate with minimum net capital of $25,000. These brokers or dealers "must promptly transmit all funds and promptly deliver all securities received in connection with [their] activities as a broker or dealer, and may not otherwise hold funds or securities for, or owe money or securities to, customers."

So, we see a pattern. If the member is completely responsible for customer assets, its minimum net capital is $250,000. The less responsible the firm is for customer assets, the lower their minimum net capital requirement. With an open-end mutual fund, shareholder records are maintained by the transfer agent, so if the member firm does not hold customer assets or owe them money/securities, their required net capital is not extremely high. And, of course, the lowest minimum net capital requirement of just $5,000 makes sense if the firm is just signing up customers but letting a carrying firm handle all the customers' assets.

Member firms who act as dealers must maintain minimum net capital of $100,000. A dealer is essentially a firm trading their own account as a principal. SEC rules define a firm as a "dealer" if it either writes options not trading on a registered national securities exchange like the CBOE or engages in more than 10 transactions in any calendar year for its own account.

So, a "dealer" could be so determined based on a small number of transactions on a principal basis (for its own account). A market maker, on the other hand, publishes BID and OFFER prices and engages in many transactions in securities all through the trading session. Market makers provide the markets with liquidity and, not surprisingly, their minimum net capital requirement is much higher than firms merely introducing accounts or helping customers buy and sell mutual funds.

A market maker's net capital requirement is also based on the number of securities in which it makes a market. For stocks trading above $5, the requirement is $2,500 for each stock. For stocks trading at $5 or below, the requirement is $1,000.

A "market maker" for purposes of these rules is defined as "a dealer who regularly publishes bona fide, competitive bid and offer quotations in a recognized interdealer quotation system; or (ii) furnishes bona fide competitive bid and offer quotations on request; and, (iii) is ready, willing and able to effect transactions in reasonable quantities at his quoted prices with other brokers or dealers."

The fact that certain activities lead to higher and lower net capital requirements would seem more important to the exam than the precise amount of net capital required. Still, we encourage you to learn everything we mention in this textbook, since knowledge is like money—it's better to have it and not need it than the other way around.

FINRA reserves the right to increase a firm's required net capital to protect investors. As the rules state, "FINRA may, with respect to a carrying or clearing member or all carrying or clearing members, prescribe greater net capital or net worth requirements than those otherwise applicable, including more stringent treatment of items in computing net capital or net worth, or require such member to restore or increase its net capital or net worth."

The big idea about net capital is if a firm is not meeting its minimum requirement, to protect investors and the securities markets overall, several restrictions apply. Unless FINRA says otherwise, such a firm is required to suspend all business operations during any period in which it is not meeting its requirements.

And, unless FINRA permits it, no equity capital may be withdrawn from the owners and investors of the firm within one year of contributing it. Carrying or clearing members not meeting their minimum net capital requirement "shall not, without the prior written approval of FINRA, withdraw capital, pay a dividend or effect a similar distribution that would reduce such member's equity, or make any unsecured advance or loan to a stockholder, partner, sole proprietor, employee or affiliate, where such withdrawals, payments, reductions, advances or loans in the aggregate, in any 35 rolling calendar day period, on a net basis, exceeds 10% of its excess net capital."

Carrying or clearing members also are not allowed to expand their business operations if their net capital is deficient for 15 consecutive business days. Expanding a member's business would include hiring registered representatives, initiating market making activities in new securities, or opening branch offices, among other things. If their net capital gets too low, carrying or clearing firms are not only prevented from expanding their business but also told to reduce their business activities by FINRA until their net capital is back in line. The rules here define a "business reduction" as "reducing or eliminating parts of a member's business to reduce the amount of capital required," which includes:

- closing one or more branch offices
- collecting unsecured or partially secured loans, advances, or other receivables
- accepting no new customer accounts
- restricting the payment of salaries or other sums to partners, officers, directors, shareholders, or associated persons of the member
- accepting only unsolicited customer orders
- reducing the size or modifying the composition of its inventory and reducing or ceasing market making

Factors That Affect the Securities Markets

Part of what makes investing in stocks and bonds so difficult is the fact that even if investors pick solid companies, their investments are still subject to inflation, interest rates, yield curves, credit spreads, currency valuations, the business cycle, fiscal policy, and monetary policy.

Inflation, Deflation

Putting cash in a coffee can might seem safe, but as prices overall rise, that cash loses **purchasing power**. Even when we deposit money in an FDIC-insured bank, we usually find the low rates of interest the bank pays do not keep pace with **inflation**. It might look as if we are earning more dollars, but because of inflation those dollars can't buy as much as they used to. We used to be able to afford a dozen eggs. Now because of inflation we can only afford ten and a half.

Inflation relates to supply and demand. When the demand for goods and services exceeds their supply, prices system-wide rise or inflate. Since many workers in the American economy have no ability to raise their own paychecks, inflation is a problem. At first, maybe consumers have more money for gasoline by cutting back on snack chips. Maybe they can pay the power bill if the whole family agrees to brown-bag their lunch. While it's nice to see American families pull together, we don't like to see the snack chip company or the local restaurants lose revenue, as those companies represent hundreds or thousands of working families, as well.

Sometimes economists worry about the opposite scenario, **deflation**. Deflation occurs when the supply of goods and services is greater than demand. While inflation can make things too expensive for consumers to buy, deflation can make things ever cheaper. With deflation at work, profit margins at businesses will be squeezed, as the companies pay last month's prices for raw materials and then struggle to sell their finished goods at next month's cheaper prices.

That's assuming they can sell anything to anyone. Would you rush out to buy something today if you knew it would be cheaper tomorrow? Wouldn't we all be tempted to put off our purchases indefinitely, waiting for the prices of cell phones, clothing, and automobiles to drop in our favor? That would lead to lay-offs. And then those workers would have less money to spend and less confidence in their ability to buy on credit. About two-thirds of the American economy is driven by consumer spending, so if consumers aren't spending, that's a problem.

We'll look at the **Federal Reserve Board** and its **Federal Open Market Committee (FOMC)** in detail up ahead. For now, we'll point out that by moving their interest rate targets up or down, the Federal Reserve Board and its FOMC try to achieve maximum employment, stable prices and stable economic growth. The Fed raises interest rates to fight inflation. To stimulate a sagging economy, the Fed lowers interest rates.

Typically, inflation and economic expansion go together, as do deflation and economic stagnation. However, as the U.S. saw in the late 1970s, sometimes the overall economy suffers high inflation even as the economy shrinks and workers experience high unemployment rates. This rare situation is known as **stagflation**, a blend of the words "stagnation" and "inflation."

Inflation is measured by the **CPI**, or "**Consumer Price Index**." The CPI tracks the prices consumers are paying for the basic things consumers buy (groceries, movie tickets, milk, blue jeans, gasoline, etc.) and tracks the increases or decreases in those prices. Sometimes economists exclude certain items which are volatile-- food and energy--to track what's called **core inflation**. Why? A one-time weather event such as a hurricane could drastically disrupt production of food and oil, sending prices upward, but that one-time event would not necessarily indicate that prices are rising throughout all areas of the economy.

Investors adjust the returns on their investments by the CPI to calculate their **inflation-adjusted** or **real rate of return.** If an investor receives 4% interest on her bond when the CPI is 2%, her inflation-adjusted return is just 2%. Take the rate of return and then subtract out the CPI to calculate real or inflation-adjusted return. If an investor receives just 1% when the CPI is 2%, his return would be -1% in terms of inflation-adjusted return. He is, in other words, losing purchasing power.

From the Bureau of Labor Statistic's website, we see that:

The CPI represents all goods and services purchased for consumption by the reference population. BLS has classified all expenditure items into more than 200 categories, arranged into eight major groups. Major groups and examples of categories in each are as follows:

FOOD AND BEVERAGES (breakfast cereal, milk, coffee, chicken, wine, full service meals, snacks)

HOUSING (rent of primary residence, owners' equivalent rent, fuel oil, bedroom furniture)

APPAREL (men's shirts and sweaters, women's dresses, jewelry)

TRANSPORTATION (new vehicles, airline fares, gasoline, motor vehicle insurance)

MEDICAL CARE (prescription drugs and medical supplies, physicians' services, eyeglasses and eye care, hospital services)

RECREATION (televisions, toys, pets and pet products, sports equipment, admissions);

EDUCATION AND COMMUNICATION (college tuition, postage, telephone services, computer software and accessories);

OTHER GOODS AND SERVICES (tobacco and smoking products, haircuts and other personal services, funeral expenses).

Economists also monitor the **PPI, or Producer Price Index**. This is a family of indices showing the prices received by producers at various stages of the production cycle: commodity level, intermediate demand, and final demand. If the CPI and PPI are revealing inflation, the Fed's Federal Open Market Committee (FOMC) will raise interest rates to let some air out of the economy. If prices start to collapse we can end up with deflation, so "the Fed" will pump some air back into the economy by lowering interest rates.

Okay. So, what are interest rates?

Interest Rates

If an entrepreneur needs $50,000 to start a bakery, chances are she has to borrow the money. The $50,000 she borrows is the **principal** amount of the loan. The extra money she pays to borrow the principal over time is the **interest**. When there's a lot of money to be lent out, lenders drop their interest rates. When money is tight, however, lenders charge higher rates. One way corporations borrow money is by selling bonds to investors, who act as lenders. How much should the corporate borrower pay the buyers of the bonds?

How about zero? Zero percent financing sounds tempting to a borrower. Unfortunately, the buyers of debt securities demand compensation. They're the lenders of the money, and they demand the best interest rate they can receive in return for lending their capital. So, bond issuers pay investors only what they have to pay them. Interest rates, then, are the result of constant spoken and unspoken negotiations going on between providers of capital and those who would like to borrow it.

The exam may mention any of the following interest rates:

- **Discount rate:** the rate banks pay when borrowing from the Federal Reserve.
- **Fed funds rate:** the rate banks charge each other for overnight loans in excess of $1 million. Considered the most volatile rate, subject to daily change.
- **Broker call loan rate:** the rate broker-dealers pay when borrowing on behalf of their margin customers.

- **Prime rate:** the rate that the most creditworthy corporate customers pay when borrowing through unsecured loans.
- **LIBOR:** stands for London InterBank Offered Rate, a benchmark rate that many large international banks charge each other for short-term loans.

The **London Interbank Market** is where large international banks go to get short-term loans at the most competitive rates possible. The rate mentioned above, LIBOR, is fixed daily by the British Banker's Association and represents an average of the world's most creditworthy banks' interbank deposit rates for large loans with maturities between overnight and one year. LIBOR is the most frequently used benchmark for short-term interest rates. Creditworthy borrowers might be able to borrow at "LIBOR plus five basis points," while shaky borrowers would have to pay a much higher premium to LIBOR.

Yield Curves

The longer a bondholder's money is at risk, the more yield he demands. If your bond matures in 2038 while another investor's bond matures in 2030, isn't your money at risk for 8 more years? That's why your bond would be offered at a higher yield. If the other investor buys a bond yielding 3.65%, yours might be offered at 3.89%. The extra .24% is your reward for taking on extra risk.

In the world of fixed-income securities it is generally accepted that short-term = bonds with up to three-year maturities, intermediate-term = bonds with four to ten-year maturities, and long-term = bonds with maturities > 10 years.

A **yield curve** displays the yields offered by debt securities of similar credit quality across various terms to maturity. Typically, the longer the maturity on the bond, the higher the yield demanded by investors. This situation is known as a **normal yield curve**, where intermediate-term bonds yield more than short-term bonds, and then long-term bonds yield more than both short-term and intermediate-term bonds, as well.

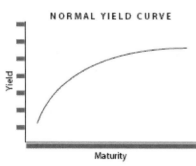

A normal yield curve implies that economic conditions are stable. For the majority of its history the yield curve for U.S. Treasuries has been in this state. Notice that though yields are higher, they also flatten out here rather than forming a steep slope. On the other hand, the test could mention a "steep yield curve" in which the curve buckles inward because the yields on longer maturities are so much higher than those on shorter maturities. This often happens before the economy goes into a rapid expansion.

As we'll see, the expansion phase of the business cycle often comes with higher interest rates and inflation, so fixed-income investors demand significantly higher yields on long-term bonds suddenly, causing a steep yield curve. We've seen that if the "Fed" sees inflation up ahead, they will raise interest rates. A steep yield curve suggests that this has already been factored into the bond market.

If we see the same yields among T-Bills, T-Notes, and T-Bonds, we are looking at a **flat yield curve**. The yield curve typically flattens when investor expectations for inflation are so low that they are not demanding higher yields to hold long-term debt securities. This typically occurs at the end of a Fed tightening cycle. At that point the Fed raises short-term interest rates until they are in line with intermediate- and long-term rates, and temporarily, with investors expecting no immediate threat from inflation, the yields are about the same across the board. A flat yield curve is thought to signal an economic slowdown.

So, when the economy expands, the Federal Reserve Board typically goes into a series of interest-rate tightening. Towards the end of this cycle, the yield curve can often flatten, which usually signals the party is over for the economy, at least for a while.

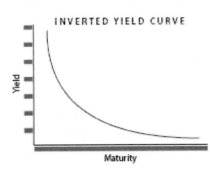

An **inverted yield curve** often follows a period of high interest rates. When bond investors feel that interest rates have peaked, they hurry to lock in the high interest rates for the longest time. In a rush of activity, they sell off their short-term bonds to buy long-term bonds at the best interest rate they're likely to see for a while. If the crowd is selling short-term bonds, the price drops [and the yield increases]. And if they're buying long-term bonds, the price increases [and the yield drops]. That causes the yield curve to invert, which is thought to be one of the surest signs that the economy is about to contract. The situation also signals lower inflation up ahead, possibly deflation.

Credit Spreads

A yield curve displays yields across different maturities. On the other hand, a yield or **credit spread** considers yields between different credit qualities. A credit spread shows the difference in yields between high-rated and low-rated bonds, or between Treasury and junk bonds. If investors demand a much greater yield on low-rated bonds than on high-rated bonds, that's a negative indicator for the economy. If investors don't demand a much higher yield on the low-rated bonds, that means they are confident about issuers' ability to repay, which is a positive indicator. So, when the yield spread narrows, that is good news, while, on the other hand, when the yield spread widens, there could be trouble up ahead.

If the 10-year U.S. Treasury Note currently yields 3%, while 10-year junk bonds yield 8%, the spread or "risk premium" is 5 percentage points. Investors are demanding a "risk premium" of 5 extra percentage points (500 basis points) of yield to buy the riskier bonds. If the T-Note is yielding 2% while high-yield bonds yield 5%, the credit spread has narrowed to just three percentage points, implying more confidence on the part of bond investors.

Global and Geopolitical Factors

As recently as the early 1970s the value of the U.S. dollar was tied to a specific weight of gold. When a country ties its currency either to a commodity such as gold, or to another currency, they are using a **fixed exchange rate** system.

Like most world currencies, the U.S. Dollar's value is today determined by a free-market, supply-and-demand system known as a **floating-rate currency** system. How does a dollar compare to the yen, or the Euro in terms of its **exchange rate**? That is a question whose answer can change every day of the week, depending on many factors. Primarily, the exchange rate between the dollar and another currency is determined by the supply and demand for the currencies and the amounts held in foreign reserves. Is the U.S. suddenly the place to invest? If so, the value of the dollar will rise, and vice versa.

A while ago the Swiss central bank stopped using a fixed exchange rate system that kept the Swiss Franc from rising above 1.20 Euro. This sudden move from a fixed to a floating-rate system shocked currency and securities markets. Why?

Imports and exports are directly affected by the relative values of currencies. If the companies that export from Switzerland to other European nations face buyers whose currency is weak, they will not be able to sell to them. Similarly, the strength of the American dollar relative to foreign currencies affects our imports and exports. As our dollar strengthens, our exports become less attractive to consumers in other countries, whose weak currency can't buy our expensive goods.

When our dollar *weakens*, our exports become *more* attractive because suddenly their strong currencies can buy our relatively cheap products and services. Likewise, a strong dollar makes foreign travel less expensive for Americans, whereas a weak dollar makes foreign travel more expensive. It's just a way of asking how much of their stuff our dollar can buy.

The **balance of trade** number tracks money in and money out of the economy for imports and exports. If we export more to a country than we import from it, we have a balance of trade surplus with that nation. If we import more from a country than we export to it, we have a balance of trade deficit with that nation. The exam could refer to the difference between a country's exports and imports as their current account. Therefore, if a country imports more than it exports, it runs a current account deficit and a current account surplus when it exports more than it imports.

Also note that under "exports" and "imports" we include goods and services. So, whether the U.S. is manufacturing and exporting finished goods, we do export many services in terms of legal, accounting, investment banking, and professional consulting, etc.

The strength of the dollar and trade deficits constantly work towards an equilibrium. If a weak dollar increases foreign demand for American-made goods, that increased demand for American-made goods will also increase the demand for dollars, making them stronger. And then it will be harder to export to foreign buyers. On the other hand, if a strong dollar hurts exports, the lack of foreign demand for American-made goods will also eventually drive down the value of the dollar, which should eventually increase the attractiveness of our exports again.

Interest rates also factor into the value of our currency. When interest rates in the United States are much higher than interest rates abroad, the demand for U.S. assets will increase the demand for the dollars needed to buy them (e.g., bank accounts, stocks, bonds, and real estate), and increase the value of the dollar compared to foreign currencies. On the other hand, if interest rates in the United States are lower than interest rates abroad, the demand for foreign assets will likely strengthen and the demand for U.S. assets will likely weaken. This will cause the demand for foreign currencies to strengthen, leading to a depreciation of the dollar compared to foreign currencies.

So, if we had a trade deficit with the European Union, would a strong dollar or a weak dollar help to bring us back to a surplus? Well, if we were already importing more from the EU than we were exporting, we would want to make our exports more attractive to the Europeans and our imports from the EU less attractive to Americans, which would happen as the dollar weakens. The dollar weakening is another way of saying the other currency is strengthening, remember.

The **balance of payments** statistic tracks all money coming in versus going out of the economy. So, it counts both imports vs. exports as well as investments and other financial transactions. If more money is coming in than going out, we have a surplus. If more money is going out than coming in, we have a deficit. If a test question says that foreigners are paying off loans to American banks, this could lead to a balance of payments surplus for the U.S., for example.

The value of the dollar compared to another currency also comes into play when an investor buys an **ADR**. We look at ADRs in Chapter 2. For now, just know that American investors can buy shares of Toyota or Nissan, for example, as ADRs (**American Depository Receipts**), priced in American dollars. This way, we don't have to figure out how much we just paid for a stock priced at 176.453 yen. However, the relative value of the dollar to the yen comes into play, especially when it comes time to pay dividends. When the underlying stock pays the dividend in the foreign currency, the foreign currency received by the bank is converted to U.S. dollars. If the U.S. dollar is strong, the foreign currency purchases or converts to fewer U.S. dollars for the holder of the ADR. As a result, the dividend received by the holder of the ADR is lower. So, a weak dollar would be beneficial to the holder of an ADR, since the dividend paid would convert to more U.S. dollars.

Investing in an ADR involves currency exchange risk, but it also involves buying stock in a company. The success of the company's operations and financing affect the ADR investor, who often receives dividends from the issuer. On the other hand, some speculators trade the foreign currencies themselves. The foreign exchange market (abbreviated Forex) allows speculators to benefit from fluctuations between various currencies.

Trading currencies, however, is a high-risk strategy. As Fidelity's website explains, "Currency prices are highly volatile. Price movements for currencies are influenced by, among other things: changing supply-demand relationships; trade, fiscal, monetary, exchange control programs and policies of governments; United States and foreign political and economic events and policies; changes in national and international interest rates and inflation; currency devaluation; and sentiment of the marketplace. None of these factors can be controlled by you or any individual advisor and no assurance can be given that you will not incur losses from such events."

The site explains that there are 16 currencies that can be traded, with trades settling in any of these local currencies:

- Australian dollar (AUD)
- British pound (GBP)
- Canadian dollar (CAD)
- Danish krone (DKK)
- Euro (EUR)
- Hong Kong dollar (HKD)
- Japanese yen (JPY)
- Mexican peso (MXN)
- New Zealand dollar (NZD)

- Norwegian krone (NOK)
- Polish zloty (PLN)
- Singapore dollar (SGD)
- South African rand (ZAR)
- Swedish krona (SEK)
- Swiss franc (CHF)
- U.S. dollar (USD)

There may also be at least one ADR issued by companies in most of those nations above. If so, an American buying the ADR would *also* be exposed to currency fluctuations. But as the Swiss food giant Nestle explains, the currency fluctuation angle should not be overstated: The ADR share prices carry foreign currency risk depending on the movement of the US dollar against the Swiss franc. Most of the ADRs trade in line with the underlying security. The spread is in general small, reflecting the cost of foreign exchange conversion and other execution costs. If the currency of the underlying stock rises against the US dollar, the ADR price is expected to rise (and vice versa). That's from http://www.nestle.com/investors/faqs/adrs-faqs#exchange, btw, an excellent run-down on ADRs.

The standard of safety in the securities markets is provided by government debt issued by the United States Treasury in the form of T-Bills, T-Notes, and T-Bonds, etc. Not only do investors receive their interest from these debt securities, but also getting paid at maturity is never a concern. Another name for the debt of a national government is **sovereign debt**. Common abbreviations for such debt include U.S. Treasuries, U.K. Gilts, German Bunds, and French Oats.

Not all sovereign debt is stable. That's why investors must check credit ratings as they do when investing in corporate bonds. Sovereign debt is generally a riskier investment when it comes from a developing country, and a safer investment when it comes from a developed country. The stability of the government is a key factor in determining the credit risk. Nations with high rates of inflation or unpredictable currency exchange rates offer higher yields to investors and carry higher risk, as well.

When a nation or an entire region of the global economy suddenly has trouble servicing its sovereign debt, panic can hit the fixed-income, currency, and stock markets around the world. Lenders—the owners of the bonds—can't seize the assets of a government, so the only way out of the mess is for the government to secure financing and/or renegotiate the terms of the outstanding debt. For example, in the spring of 2010 several nations in the European Union (e.g., Greece, Turkey, and Portugal) suddenly appeared unable to meet their debt obligations. This, of course, sent the yields on their sovereign debt sky-high, as investors sold off the bonds in a panic. The European Union, along with the European Central Bank and the International Monetary Fund, had to intervene by offering a rescue package worth 750 billion euro to keep the economies of those nations afloat.

If an issuer of sovereign debt is experiencing strife of any kind, it may become less willing and able to meet its debt obligations. Sometimes issuing countries restructure their debt, which is usually bad news for bondholders. Restructured debt typically leaves bondholders with lower interest and principal payments. Sometimes maturity dates are extended, forcing investors to wait longer for their return of principal.

When a government has trouble meeting its debt obligations, it often devalues its currency. As we saw, a devalued currency can help increase a nation's exports; however, in these situations the currency's value tends to fall so far that citizens are unable to buy basic goods, and international confidence in the nation's economy tends to drop. Soon, stocks and bonds issued by companies in that nation falter on the secondary market, and international investors pull out of the nation or region entirely.

Economic Indicators

People often talk about the economy in terms of whether it is good or bad. But, how do we measure something as big and complex as the American economy? One way is by tracking **Gross Domestic Product (GDP)**. As the name implies, Gross Domestic Product measures the total output of a nation's economy. It is an estimate of the total value of all goods and services produced and purchased over a three-month period. If the GDP number comes in at 3%, that means the economy grew at an annual rate of 3% over the financial quarter. If GDP is −2%, the economy is shrinking at an annual rate of −2%. The GDP numbers that are factored for inflation are called "real GDP."

The Federal Reserve Board monitors many **economic indicators** to determine whether inflation is threatening the economy, or whether the Fed needs to provide stimulus to a sagging economy. The following **employment indicators** reveal how many people are working and how much compensation they're receiving. If people are not working, that signals an economic slowdown, and the Fed might lend a hand by lowering interest rates. If too many people are working, that signals inflation, and the Fed might cool things down by raising interest rates.

- Average Weekly New Claims for Unemployment Insurance: if people are showing up for unemployment insurance at a higher rate, that is negative. If the number of new claims drops, that means economic activity is picking up—positive.
- Unemployment Rate (Non-farm Payroll): also called "payroll employment." Includes full-time and part-time workers, whether they are permanent or temporary employees. Tracks how many people are working in the private sector. Released monthly. Called "non-farm" because it does not measure seasonal agricultural jobs.
- Employment Cost Index (ECI): measures the growth of wages and benefits (compensation). Quarterly figure.

A **leading indicator** shows up before something happens and is used to predict. A **coincident indicator** tells us where we are now, and a **lagging indicator** gives us data about where we have just been, confirming a trend.

Leading (predict changes in the economy):

- the average weekly hours worked by manufacturing workers
- the average number of initial applications for unemployment insurance
- the amount of manufacturers' new orders for consumer goods and materials
- the speed of delivery of new merchandise to vendors from suppliers
- the amount of new orders for capital goods (equipment used to make products) unrelated to defense
- the amount of new building permits for residential buildings

- the S&P 500 stock index
- the inflation-adjusted monetary supply (M2)
- the spread between long and short interest rates
- consumer confidence
- bond yields

Coincident (current state of the economy):

- the number of employees on non-agricultural payrolls
- industrial production
- manufacturing and trade sales
- personal income levels

Lagging (confirm trends, do not predict):

- the value of outstanding commercial and industrial loans
- the change in the Consumer Price Index for services from the previous month
- the change in labor cost per unit of labor output
- inventories
- the ratio of consumer credit outstanding to personal income
- the average prime rate charged by banks
- length/duration of unemployment

The following table shows what the main indicators tend to reveal to an economist. For example, if the S&P 500 is up, that means the economy could be headed for an expansion, and when the S&P 500 is down, the economy could be headed for a contraction. The "Fed" typically intervenes to smooth out the rough patches in the economy, so if they see inflationary signals, they start raising interest rates. If they see deflationary signals, they provide economic stimulus by lowering interest rates.

INFLATIONARY/EXPANDING	DEFLATIONARY/CONTRACTING
S&P 500 Up	S&P 500 Down
Building Permits Up	Building Permits Down
# of Manufacturing Workers Up	# of Manufacturing Workers Down
Unemployment Claims Down	Unemployment Claims Up
Consumer Confidence Up	Consumer Confidence Down
Manufacturers' New Orders Up	Manufacturers' New Orders Down
Capital Goods Spending Up	Capital Goods Spending Down

INFLATIONARY/EXPANDING	DEFLATIONARY/CONTRACTING
Personal Income Up	Personal Income Down
Manufacturing & Trade Sales Up	Manufacturing & Trade Sales Down
Payroll Employment Up	Payroll Employment Down
Inventory Levels Down	Inventory Levels Up
Duration of Unemployment Down	Duration of Unemployment Up

GDP

People often talk about the economy in terms of whether it is good or bad. But, how do we measure something as big and complex as the American economy? One way is by tracking **Gross Domestic Product (GDP)**. As the name implies, Gross Domestic Product measures the total output of a nation's economy. It's an estimate of the total value of all goods and services produced and purchased over a three-month period. If the GDP number comes in at 3%, that means the economy grew at an annual rate of 3% over the financial quarter. If GDP is −2%, the economy is shrinking at an annual rate of −2%. The GDP numbers that are factored for inflation are called "real GDP."

Business Cycle

Gross Domestic Product (GDP) for the U.S. measures the value of goods and services produced and provided by workers stationed in the United States over a financial quarter. If GDP is increasing, the economy is growing. If GDP is declining, so is the economy.

The American economy is subject to the **business cycle** or the boom-and-bust cycle. The four phases of the business cycle are: **expansion, peak, contraction,** and **trough**. The period between the peak and the trough is called either a **recession** or a **depression**, depending on the severity. A depression is more prolonged and severe than the more frequently occurring recession. One definition of a recession is two consecutive quarters of inflation-adjusted GDP decline.

But, that is more likely a definition used by a journalist than an economist. As the former head of the San Francisco Federal Reserve Bank explains, "Economists use monthly business cycle peaks and troughs designated by the National Bureau of Economic Research (NBER) to define periods of expansion and contractions. The NBER website lists the peaks and troughs in economic activity starting with the December 1854 trough. The website also defines a recession as:

> a significant decline in economic activity spread across the
> economy, lasting more than a few months, normally visible in real

GDP, real income, employment, industrial production, and wholesale-retail sales. A recession begins just after the economy reaches a peak of activity and ends as the economy reaches its trough. Between trough and peak, the economy is in an expansion. Expansion is the normal state of the economy; most recessions are brief and they have been rare in recent decades.

While there is no standard definition of a depression, economists generally consider a depression to be a more severe and prolonged version of a recession. For example, the Great Depression involved two severe economic downturns. The first lasted from August 1929 all the way through February 1933. After an expansion lasting 21 months, the economy went into a depression again, this time lasting from May 1937 all the way to June 1938.

Stocks of companies operating in certain industries are more dependent on this business cycle than others. These **cyclical** stocks tend to perform well during an expansion but poorly during a contraction. **Cyclical industries** involve expensive purchases and include: heavy equipment, steel, automobiles, durable goods such as refrigerators and dishwashers, travel, and aerospace. Large purchases are what consumers and businesses cut back on first when the economy hits a rough patch. During a robust economy, consumers begin purchasing new cars and refrigerators once again.

Other industries can survive a contraction more easily and are, therefore, called **defensive** or non-cyclical. These industries include: food, clothing, pharmaceuticals, healthcare, alcohol and tobacco. Food is a defensive industry, but the test could say "restaurants."

That's not what we mean. We mean supermarkets and food supply companies. Restaurants get clobbered in a recession, as they are one of the first items consumers reduce or eliminate from their budgets. Similarly, clothing is a defensive industry, but we don't mean designer suits, which people cut back on in a recession. We mean the basics, like underwear, socks, gloves, and T-shirts.

If the industry space does better during a recession, it is considered **counter-cyclical**. Counter-cyclical stocks are negatively correlated to the business cycle. During a contraction, they thrive. During an expansion, they struggle. There are not many types of business models that improve when consumers have less money to spend, but during a period of high unemployment employment placement agencies typically see an increase in revenue.

Similarly, education and training companies who prepare people for careers in automotive, electronics, or nursing, etc. are also countercyclical. When people lose a job, they tend to find other careers that they are willing to pay to enter.

While countercyclical stocks do well during a contraction, they also suffer during expansions. And expansions typically last longer. If unemployment is low, the two types of companies mentioned would see their revenue decrease.

Although we usually associate the term **interest-rate sensitive** with bonds and preferred stocks, there are also common stocks whose market prices tend to drop when interest rates rise. Companies who pay a generous and relatively fixed dividend tend to experience a decline in market value if interest rates rise. Also, companies who issue a lot of long-term bonds may see their stock price drop when interest rates rise. That's because their cost of borrowing will likely increase in the future and hurt their profits. As we'll see, common stock is all about the expectation of future profits, so companies who do a lot of borrowing get hurt when interest rates increase.

On the other hand, some companies do better when interest rates rise. For example, banks, insurance companies, and certain broker-dealers often earn higher profits when interest rates increase, especially if the yield curve is steep. Broker-dealers make much of their profits by holding customer cash and earning interest on it until the customer buys stock or requests a withdrawal. The steeper the yield curve, the better the profits, as it is for banks and insurance companies.

So, the same economic climate produces winners and losers. During a recession, car makers and high-end retailers may suffer, but Wal-Mart and Priceline might report higher profits as Americans suddenly become cost-conscious. When interest rates rise, utility companies and heavy equipment makers might get hurt while, on the other hand, banks, insurers, payroll and certain broker-dealers might report better results.

If convinced a recession is coming an investor should purchase defensive stocks. People will, after all, keep buying razor blades, groceries, medicine, and liquor regardless of the current economic climate. If an expansion is expected, an investor should purchase cyclical stocks, like automobile and trucking or railroad companies.

How does the investor know when the recessions and recoveries are about to appear? He doesn't, but the stock market is always about speculation.

Also, we keep mentioning the more commonly used GDP, but the exam may ask about **GNP (Gross National Product),** too. Gross National Product for the U.S. counts the production of U.S. workers stationed here as well as working overseas for American companies. It does not count the production of, say, Japanese citizens working at a Toyota or Mitsubishi plant in Mississippi. Gross Domestic Product counts what is produced domestically, by both U.S. workers and foreigners working here in the United States.

So, GNP tells us how much American workers are producing wherever they're stationed, while GDP tells us what is produced here in America, whoever is doing that work.

Monetary and Fiscal Policies

Economic policy makers use **monetary** and **fiscal policies** to influence the economy. Monetary policies are enacted by the Federal Reserve Board and its Federal Open Market Committee. Monetary policies involve setting targets for short-term interest rates to either fight inflation or stimulate a sagging economy.

The Federal Reserve Board (The Fed) requires that its member banks keep a certain percentage of their customer deposits in reserve. This is called the **reserve requirement**. If the Fed raises the reserve requirement, banks have less money to lend out to people trying to buy homes and start businesses. So, if the economy is overheating, the Federal Reserve Board could raise the reserve requirement to cool things down, and if the economy is sluggish, they could lower the requirement to make more money available to fuel the economy.

However, of the three main tools of monetary policy changing the reserve requirement is the most drastic measure and, therefore, the tool used least often by the Federal Reserve. The exam could refer to a **multiplier effect** as the reason the tool is used less often than the others. In a nutshell that means that if banks can lend out maybe $10 for every $1 they have on reserve, when the Federal Reserve Board changes the amount required to be deposited in reserve by just a little bit, the effects are multiplied throughout the financial system. The multiplier effect is calculated by taking total bank deposits divided by the reserve requirement.

The Fed's Federal Open Market Committee (FOMC) can also use **open market operations** and either buy or sell U.S. Treasury securities on the secondary market. If they want to cool things down by raising interest rates, they sell Treasuries on the open market to depress their price and, thereby, increase their yield. If they want to fuel a sluggish economy by lowering interest rates, they buy Treasury securities, thereby driving up their price, which is the same thing as pushing down their yield.

Yields and rates are the same thing. It is the price of debt securities that moves in an inverse relationship to rates/yields. We will look at interest rates and bond prices in more detail up ahead.

When people say the FOMC is raising short-term interest rates by 25 basis points, they're talking about the **discount rate,** which is the rate the Federal Reserve Board charges banks that borrow directly from the FRB. If banks have to pay more to borrow, they will in turn charge their customers more to borrow from them. So, if the Fed wants to raise interest rates, they just raise the discount rate and let the banking system take it from there.

The Federal Reserve Board does not set tax policy—they enact monetary policy. And, typically, they only influence short-term interest rates, although if circumstances require it, they can also influence longer-term rates reflected by Treasury Notes and Treasury Bonds, discussed more in a later chapter.

As we'll also see, the Securities Exchange Act of 1934 covers many aspects of the securities industry. This legislation gave the Federal Reserve Board the power to establish margin requirements under Regulation T and Regulation U. These regulations stipulate how much credit can be extended by broker-dealers and banks in connection with customer margin accounts. So, as with the other tools above, the Federal Reserve Board can make credit more available or less available through margin requirements, depending on the direction of their current monetary policy.

You can think of the Federal Reserve Board/FOMC as a sort of pit crew trying to perform tune-ups on an economy that never pulls over for a pit stop. If the economy starts going too fast, they let some air out of the tires by raising the reserve requirement, raising the discount rate, and selling Treasury securities. If the economy starts to slow down, they pump some air into the tires by lowering the reserve requirement, lowering the discount rate, and buying Treasuries.

Inflation is most likely to occur during the phase of the business cycle called the "peak," a time associated with the phrase "irrational exuberance," during which too many investors and entrepreneurs are convinced that things will keep improving forever. To fight inflation the Fed slows things down by raising interest rates. Deflation is found during the contraction. To fight deflation the Fed pumps air back into the economy by lowering interest rates.

There are many ways the exam can refer to the same thing here, too. If the Federal Reserve is fighting inflation, this could be referred to as "tight credit" or a "tight money policy." If the "Fed" is pumping inflation back into the economy, the exam could call this "loose credit" or a "loose-money policy."

Fiscal policy is what the President and Congress do: tax and spend. **Keynesian** economists recommend that fiscal policy be used to increase aggregate (overall) demand for goods and services. To stimulate the economy, just cut taxes and increase government spending. Reduced taxes leave more money for Americans to spend and invest, fueling the economy. If the government is spending more on interstate highway construction, this means a lot more workers are going to be hired for construction crews. Or maybe the federal government orders military transport vehicles from a unit of GM. If so, GM will order a lot more parts from suppliers and hire more workers, who would make and spend more money to push the economy along.

On the other hand, if we need to cool things down, followers of Keynesian economics suggest that the federal government increase taxes and cut spending. Higher taxes leave less money for Americans to spend and invest, and decreased spending puts less government money into companies, who, in turn, spend less money on supplies, equipment, and salaries.

Financial Statements

Many successful American businesses are privately owned. Five Guys and Toys 'R' Us, for example, are well-known companies, but we would have to estimate their revenue, expenses and profits since private companies do not report their financial results to the public. By comparison, if we want to know the revenue and net income after tax for Starbucks or Microsoft, we can go to the SEC's **EDGAR** site and pull up the company's most recent quarterly or annual reports.

It's not that Five Guys and Toys 'R' Us do not have income statements, balance sheets, and statements of cash flows. They do not publish their **financial statements**. Starbucks, Microsoft, and McDonald's, on the other hand, are reporting companies who must disclose all relevant information to the investing public, even to those who will never invest in their stock.

An issuer of securities can only pay the interest on their bonds if they have enough revenue to cover it. The preferred stockholders will only get paid if the profits are dependable, and the common stock will rise over the long term only if the profits at the company rise. The financial statements released by public companies disclose the company's revenue, expenses, and profits, as well as their financial condition and their cash flows.

Each statement tells a different story about the same company.

Income Statement

The company's revenue and net income are disclosed on the **income statement**. We'll look at another financial statement called the **balance sheet** up ahead. For now, let's point out the difference between the two statements, put out by the same company. The balance sheet is a snapshot of the company's financial strength at the time the report is run. The report could change weekly, even daily. The income statement, on the other hand, shows the results of the company's operations over previous financial quarters and fiscal years. Once that report is run, it never changes.

A public company had to register its securities offering with the SEC under the **Securities Act of 1933** when it went public. That same company is then a reporting company required to file quarterly, annual, and other reports with the **SEC** under the **Securities Exchange Act of 1934,** as well as making these reports available to their stock and bondholders.

This allows those who invested in these public companies to see the financial condition (balance sheet) of their company and whether the sales and profits are increasing, decreasing, or flattening (income statement). Because the issuer uploads the information to the SEC's EDGAR website, anyone with curiosity can see the details of the issuer's operations, not just current investors.

An income statement can also be referred to as a "statement of earnings" or "statement of operations," while the balance sheet is often referred to as the "statement of financial condition." Whatever we call it, although the reports are primarily for shareholders, this information is available to anyone who wants to see it.

That includes the company's competitors, which is a reason many companies stay private. For example, if Five Guys is in secret talks to acquire another fast food chain, they would rather keep that quiet as opposed to letting McDonald's see their plans and maybe try to out-bid them. On the other hand, if McDonald's is planning to open a certain number of restaurants in Africa next year, they would have to let the investment world know about it either on their next scheduled filing or by releasing an 8K.

If you go to your favorite financial website or search for a company's "10-K" or "annual shareholder report," you can see the financial statements for companies such as Microsoft, Oracle, and Starbucks. For now, though, let's start small.

Let's say there is an 11-year-old in your neighborhood, who launched a lemonade stand for the summer. Her name is Shelly.

Each glass of lemonade sells for $1, and the dollars Shelly receives through this summer are called **sales** or **revenue**. She sells 10,000 glasses of lemonade, so the revenue is exactly $10,000 over the summer. Revenue is the top line of the income statement.

In some businesses there are returns, refunds, and discounts. Retailers, for example, often report their **net revenue** or **net operating revenue**. This is their revenue after all the returns, refunds, and discounts have been accounted for.

The lemonade stand had no discounting or returns, so the revenue is what it is. However, $10,000 in revenue is not the same thing as $10,000 of profit. The lemonade Shelly sold was produced by a combination of the following ingredients: purified water, fresh lemons, lemon juice, sugar, and ice. Those are the goods used to make the product sold, which is why the money spent on them is called the **cost of goods sold** or **cost of revenue**. Shelly also has to serve the product in recyclable cups, which cost $1,000, on top of the $2,000 paid for the ingredients.

So, now the $10,000 in revenue is down to $7,000 after subtracting the $3,000 for "cost of goods sold."

Like any business, the lemonade stand has operating expenses to cover. Operating expenses are the expenses not directly associated with the production of the company's products: office rent, administrative salaries, office supplies, entertainment costs, travel costs, etc. While Shelly worked the stand herself most of the time, she also hired your sister to come up with some marketing plans. Her $500 of compensation represents an operating expense.

There are other operating expenses, including advertising. Advertising expense was $500 over the summer.

Operating expenses are often referred to as "SG&A" for **"selling, general, and administrative"** expenses. At a manufacturing company, the labor of the workers on the production floor would generally be part of cost of goods sold, since that labor goes directly into the cost of the finished product. The compensation to the so-called "white-collar workers" out in the cozy offices is part of "selling, general, and administrative" expenses.

If the lemonade stand hires baristas to serve the lemonade, their labor is part of cost of goods sold, while the compensation for her sister's marketing work is an operating expense, not directly related to producing and serving the product.

Shelly also paid the boy next door to build you a stand for $200, and that is a different type of expense. She plans to be in business for the next five years, and she will use that stand each summer. So, she subtracts 1/5 of that $200 on the income statement each year. Instead of subtracting $200 all at once, she only subtracts $40 to depreciate this vital piece of equipment. Even though the business spent the money all up front, next year it will also subtract $40 as a **depreciation** expense on the income statement. The accountants will do that five times until they have depreciated the cost of the stand to zero.

To depreciate an asset involves spreading its cost over its estimated useful life. A manufacturing company would not expense a $10 million piece of equipment the way they would expense the paper and toner used in the office. The latter are consumed and expensed all at once, while the equipment is slowly written down on the income statement to spread the cost over its estimated useful life.

Tangible assets are depreciated, while intangible assets are written down using **amortization**. If a company is manufacturing a drug under a patent with a limited life, they amortize the patent over time, as they would depreciate a plastic injection molding machine over several years. In either case, an asset's cost is being spread over its estimated useful life by taking a series of charges on the income statement through these non-cash expenses called either depreciation or amortization.

There are other assets subject to depreciation at the lemonade stand. Shelly had to buy several large coolers, a couple of blenders, a money drawer, a calculator, and a copy of QuickBooks™. These fixed assets all work out to $300, which are depreciated over three years, subtracting another $100 this year.

We have accounted for cost of goods sold, operating expenses, and depreciation.

Now, there are **interest** payments and **taxes** to account for before arriving at the company's **net income** or **net loss** for the reporting period. Shelly's mom had to spot her some credit to buy her first batch of ingredients and, unfortunately, she charges her interest on the loan. On the plus side, Shelly gets to deduct that interest before figuring taxable income, just as homeowners deduct the interest paid on their mortgages. So, she subtracts the $20 of interest, and the taxable income is $5,840. Taxes work out to $40, and after paying those, the lemonade stand shows a **net profit**, or **net income after tax**, of $5,800.

Let's review the lemonade stand's results of operations over the summer:

Sales/Revenue	$10,000
Cost of Goods Sold	– $3,000
Operating Expenses	– $1,000
Depreciation, Amortization	– $140
OPERATING INCOME	$5,860
Interest Expense	– $20
PRE-TAX INCOME	$5,840
Taxes	– $40
NET INCOME after tax	$5,800

Statement of Cash Flows

Some subtractions on the income statement do not involve an outlay of cash. Depreciation and amortization spread an asset's historical cost over an estimated useful life, but no cash is being spent when we record the expense on the income statement.

Therefore, since there's a difference between an accounting entry called "depreciation" and actual cash being spent, analysts ignore intangible expenses like that when focusing on **cash flow**, which is how much cash is being generated (or consumed) by a company. One way to estimate cash flow is to take the net income from the income statement and then add back two non-cash charges: depreciation and amortization.

The lemonade stand does not have a lot of depreciation and amortization going on, but companies that invest in expensive factories, warehouses, and equipment can show quite different figures for net income on the one hand and cash flow from operations on the other. When they add back the depreciation that reduced their net income, their cash flow is a much higher amount.

In the issuer's 10-K, we also find a separate **statement of cash flows** that shows how much cash has been provided or used by the business over the reporting period. Net income and the cash generated by the business over the period are often quite different numbers. The accrual method of accounting is most widely used, and it involves the company booking revenue/sales before any cash has been exchanged. The statement of cash flows eliminates this sort of distortion, as well as intangible expenses like depreciation/amortization. A good fundamental analyst knows that some companies have been known to book "profits" when they are not generating enough cash to stay afloat.

The statement of cash flows is separated into three distinct ways in which a company can generate (or exhaust) cash: cash flows from operating activities, cash flows from investing activities, and cash flows from financing activities. **Cash flows from operating activities** are what that phrase sounds like: the company provided or exhausted this much cash through their core operations. For example, Starbucks generates most of its cash by operating thousands of successful coffee shops, but it can also generate cash through investing activities and through financing activities.

Cash flow from operations shows us the net income from the income statement, adds back depreciation/amortization, and then records the changes in working capital (from the balance sheet). After dealing with the change in the line items under current assets and current liabilities (working capital), the company can then calculate and report the net cash provided/used by operating activities.

Cash flow from investing activities indicates how much cash was used or generated, usually from investing in capital equipment, and to some extent buying and selling securities, e.g. U.S. Treasuries. Capital equipment ("capex") can be thought of as all the hard, tangible infrastructure that brick-and-mortar companies have to invest in to operate, stay afloat and maybe make a profit (buying a printing press, remodeling existing stores, building new stores, etc.). If a company is like MSFT or ORCL, they might go on a business buying binge, which is reflected in their cash used for acquisitions. Big increases in this number could indicate that the company is making strategic acquisitions of former competitors, or it could mean that they're generating too much of their returns by buying up smaller fish as opposed to operating successfully.

Cash flow from financing activities is the cash provided/used through any activity involving the shareholders (owners) or bondholders (creditors) of the company. If stock is issued, cash is generated, while if the company engages in share buyback programs, cash is used. If a company issues bonds, cash is generated, while when it finally redeems or calls those bonds, cash is used up.

Also, when the company pays dividends to shareholders, or interest payments to creditors, this is cash that is used by the company. Young, growing companies often issue stock to finance their operations. That may be fine, but new stock issues dilute the value of the existing shareholders' equity. More mature companies, with plenty of cash, often buy back their shares to make each existing share more valuable. Either way, we could track these activities under this section of the statement of cash flows.

The terms "cash flows from investing activities" and "cash flows from financing activities" could be potentially confusing. Remember that if a company buys Government securities or shares of a public company on the open market, we would see that under "cash flows from investing activities." And, if the company invests in a printing press, that is under cash flows from investing activities, too.

Cash flow from financing activities includes the cash generated by issuing stocks or bonds and the cash used buying back stock and/or retiring bonds.

Balance Sheet

When applying for a loan, the lender wants to know two important things: how much money does the borrower make, and what kind of collateral does he have? The borrower could submit a statement of cash flow showing all sources of income minus expenses. But the lender would also like to see what kind of **assets** he is holding minus his **liabilities.**

The basic formula for the balance sheet is expressed as:

$$\text{Assets} = \text{Liabilities} + \text{Stockholders' Equity}$$

or

$$\text{Assets} - \text{Liabilities} = \text{Stockholders' Equity}$$

Assets represent what a company owns. Liabilities represent what a company owes. We take what a company owns, subtract what it owes, and that is the **net worth** of the company. Another name for net worth is **stockholders' equity**

Assets

Assets are divided into three types. The first type is **current assets**. Current assets represent cash and anything that could be converted to cash in the short-term: **cash & equivalents**, **accounts receivable**, and **inventory**. Cash is cash, and it's a good thing. "Equivalents" are money market instruments earning some interest, which is also a good thing. If they mature in the near term, commercial paper, bankers' acceptances, repurchase agreements, and T-Bills are considered "cash equivalents" here on the balance sheet.

From her profits at the lemonade stand, Shelly wisely deposited $560 into a savings account at the end of the summer. File that under "cash." Accounts receivable is what customers owe the company. Shelly was nice enough to sell lemonade on credit to two of her friends over the summer, and they ran up a tab of $40 between them. She intends to collect on those sales in the near-term, so we list that payment as an asset.

Inventory is the stuff the company makes and plans to sell. When temperatures dropped suddenly in late August, Shelly was left holding a large quantity of lemons, sugar, etc. She made as much lemonade as possible and turned it into popsicles. Next season, she intends to sell that inventory for $40, making the inventory a current asset.

The second type of assets, **fixed assets,** include office buildings, factories, equipment, furniture, etc. This is the stuff a company uses as opposed to putting directly into its finished products. Fixed assets could all be converted into cash, but this stuff was not purchased to be sold; it was purchased to generate revenue: printing presses, industrial control systems, fleet of delivery vans, etc. A large corporation lists the value of the real estate, as well as the value of the assembly line equipment, as well as the furniture and even the artwork hanging on the walls of the visitor lobby, under fixed assets.

Then there are **intangible assets**. Intangible assets include patents, trademarks, and **goodwill**. When a company acquires another company, they usually pay more than just the value of the fixed assets. They're paying for the brand-identity, the customer base, etc. So, that excess paid above the hard, tangible value of assets you can touch and see is called "goodwill."

Then, we would add all three types of assets and call the sum your **total assets**.

Liabilities

On the other side of the equation we find liabilities, which represent what a company owes. Anything that must be paid in the short term is a **current liability**. **Accounts payable**, **accrued wages**, and **accrued taxes** all represent bills the company must pay currently, which is why they're called current liabilities. Your mom picked up a few batches of ingredients over the summer and put them on her credit card. Just as soon as she remembers doing so, Shelly intends to pay her mother back the $60, listed under accounts payable. And, she owes her sister $100, which is listed under accrued wages.

The principal amount of a loan or a bond that must be paid more than a year out is a **long-term liability**. Shelly owes her mother $240 in principal, which is why it is listed under long-term liabilities. Add the current and the long-term liabilities together and we have **total liabilities** of $400.

Stockholders' Equity/Net Worth

Stockholders' Equity is sometimes called Shareholders' Equity or "net worth." Whatever we call it, equity equals ownership, and the stockholders own a percentage of the company. What is that ownership worth at the time the balance sheet is printed? That is stockholders' equity.

Companies place the total par value of their preferred stock under this heading. Common stock is assigned a par value of, say, $1, so if a company has 1,000,000 shares of common stock, they would list the par value as $1,000,000 and place it under stockholders' equity.

If investors bought the stock in the IPO at $11, that represents a surplus of $10 above the par value, so the company would list **paid-in surplus** of $10,000,000, as well. And then any earnings that have been retained are listed as **retained earnings**.

Footnotes

In a company's quarterly and annual shareholder reports the financial statements are accompanied by **footnotes** that help clarify the numbers. For example, what does the company mean by "equivalents" in its "cash and equivalents" line item—debt securities with six months to maturity? Three months? When does a company recognize "revenue"? Is it when the company ships pies to a distributor, or only when someone has paid for the product? Also, unusual revenue events or charges need to be explained so that investors do not get the wrong idea about their long-term impact.

Whenever the numbers in a financial statement require further clarification, the footnotes section is used to provide it. A 10-K or **annual shareholder report,** for example, presents the consolidated financial statements and then follows up with "notes to consolidated financial statements" that help clarify all the numbers presented from the balance sheet, income statement, and statement of cash flow.

Chapter 1 Review Exercises

DIRECTIONS: underline the word or phrase that completes each statement

1. Securities are issued on the (primary/secondary) market.

2. Securities are traded on the (primary/secondary) market.

3. The (Securities Act of 1933/Securities Exchange Act of 1934) covers broad aspects of the securities markets.

4. The (Securities Act of 1933/Securities Exchange Act of 1934) applies exclusively to the primary market.

5. When a public company completes an offer of common stock several years after the IPO, this is known as (a secondary offering/an additional primary distribution).

6. The cooling-off period for an offer of securities is a (minimum of/maximum of) 20 days.

7. When an issuer files exclusively with the State securities department where it operates, the exemption claimed under the Securities Act of 1933 is referred to as (Regulation D/Rule 147).

8. The issuer will accept what the underwriters raise in a (best efforts/mini-max) underwriting.

9. In a firm commitment underwriting, syndicate members act as (principal/agent) for the issuer.

10. The issuer is required to file notice with the SEC when (offering exempt securities/completing an exempt transaction).

11. In a private placement offered under Regulation D, a (minimum of/maximum of) 35 non-accredited purchases can purchase shares.

12. Of these two, the type of broker-dealer whose minimum net capital is $100,000 is a (clearing member/dealer).

13. When calculating its net capital, a broker-dealer takes its tentative net capital and subtracts (haircuts/non-allowable assets).

14. Carrying or clearing members are not allowed to expand their business operations if their net capital is deficient for (15/30) consecutive business days.

15. Deflation is thought to occur when (supply exceeds demand/demand exceeds supply).

16. Fiscal policy is enacted by (Congress/Federal Reserve Board).

17. Monetary policy is enacted by (Congress/Federal Reserve Board).

18. Core inflation excludes (food & energy/clothing & inessentials).

19. If yields for short-term, intermediate-term, and long-term Treasuries are the same, the yield curve is said to be (flat/inverted).

20. An American holding an ADR in a Japanese company benefits when the US Dollar, relative to the Yen, (strengthens/weakens).

21. Japanese nationals working temporarily at a Toyota plant in Alabama are counted towards (GDP/GNP) for the United States.

22. Japanese nationals working temporarily at a Toyota plant in Alabama are counted towards (GDP/GNP) for Japan.

23. Durable goods such as refrigerators and dishwashers represent a (cyclical/defensive) industry.

24. The FOMC is expected to sell US Treasuries on the secondary market when pursuing a (loose/tight) monetary policy.

25. To stimulate the American economy, Congress could (increase/decrease) spending.

Answers

1. Securities are issued on the (<u>primary</u>/secondary) market.
2. Securities are traded on the (primary/<u>secondary</u>) market.
3. The (Securities Act of 1933/<u>Securities Exchange Act of 1934</u>) covers broad aspects of the securities markets.
4. The (<u>Securities Act of 1933</u>/Securities Exchange Act of 1934) applies exclusively to the primary market.
5. When a public company completes an offer of common stock several years after the IPO, this is known as (a secondary offering/<u>an additional primary distribution</u>).
6. The cooling-off period for an offer of securities is a (<u>minimum of</u>/maximum of) 20 days.
7. When an issuer files exclusively with the State securities department where it operates, the exemption claimed under the Securities Act of 1933 is referred to as (Regulation D/<u>Rule 147</u>).
8. The issuer will accept what the underwriters raise in a (<u>best efforts</u>/mini-max) underwriting.
9. In a firm commitment underwriting, syndicate members act as (<u>principal</u>/agent) for the issuer.
10. The issuer is required to file notice with the SEC when (offering exempt securities/<u>completing an exempt transaction</u>).
11. In a private placement offered under Regulation D, a (minimum of/<u>maximum of</u>) 35 non-accredited purchases can purchase shares.
12. Of these two, the type of broker-dealer whose minimum net capital is $100,000 is a (clearing member/<u>dealer</u>).
13. When calculating its net capital, a broker-dealer takes its tentative net capital and subtracts (<u>haircuts</u>/non-allowable assets).
14. Carrying or clearing members are not allowed to expand their business operations if their net capital is deficient for (<u>15</u>/30) consccutive business days.
15. Deflation is thought to occur when (<u>supply exceeds demand</u>/demand exceeds supply).
16. Fiscal policy is enacted by (<u>Congress</u>/Federal Reserve Board).
17. Monetary policy is enacted by (Congress/<u>Federal Reserve Board</u>).
18. Core inflation excludes (<u>food & energy</u>/clothing & inessentials).
19. If yields for short-term, intermediate-term, and long-term Treasuries are the same, the yield curve is said to be (<u>flat</u>/inverted).
20. An American holding an ADR in a Japanese company benefits when the US Dollar, relative to the Yen, (strengthens/<u>weakens</u>).
21. Japanese nationals working temporarily at a Toyota plant in Alabama are counted towards (<u>GDP</u>/GNP) for the United States.
22. Japanese nationals working temporarily at a Toyota plant in Alabama are counted towards (GDP/<u>GNP</u>) for Japan.
23. Durable goods such as refrigerators and dishwashers represent a (<u>cyclical</u>/defensive) industry.
24. The FOMC is expected to sell US Treasuries on the secondary market when pursuing a (loose/<u>tight</u>) monetary policy.
25. To stimulate the American economy, Congress could (<u>increase</u>/decrease) spending.

Chapter 1 Review Quiz

1. Which of the following terms is associated with the secondary—rather than the primary—market?
   A. Investment banker
   B. Tombstone advertisement
   C. Market maker
   D. Public Offering Price (POP)

2. In an IPO, often both the issuing company and the early investors offer shares to the public for the first time. This is known as which of the following?
   A. Flipping
   B. A combined offering
   C. Stabilization
   D. A mini-max offering

3. A true statement of the cooling-off period imposed under the Securities Act of 1933 is:
   A. Binding sales to retail investors are taken during this period.
   B. 20 days is the maximum duration of this period.
   C. No final sales are made until the SEC grants the issuer a release date.
   D. A registered representative must deliver a preliminary prospectus upon request for any investor giving an indication of interest.

4. When the Securities and Exchange Commission establishes the effective or release date for an offer of securities, investors can accurately conclude which of the following?
   A. The securities are listed for trading on either the NYSE or NASDAQ.
   B. The SEC has neither approved nor disapproved of the securities offering.
   C. If they are debt securities, the issue is of investment grade.
   D. The disclosure document has been deemed accurate and complete.

5. In which of the following types of underwriting engagements does the syndicate act as a principal by taking on the obligation to pay for any unsold securities?
   A. Standby
   B. All-or-None
   C. Best Efforts
   D. Mini-Max

6. Securities exempt from the Securities Act of 1933's registration requirements include which of the following?
   A. A municipal bond issued by a U.S. State
   B. A municipal bond issued by a County or City of the United States
   C. A bond issued by a charitable or fraternal organization
   D. All choices listed

7. An offering of which of the following securities is required to be registered under the Securities Act of 1933?
A. A T-Bond
B. Commercial paper maturing in 91 days
C. A stock authorized for listing on NASDAQ
D. Securities issued by Small Business Investment Companies

8. Which of the following is not required to be registered with the SEC?
A. An initial public offer authorized for listing on the NYSE
B. A Rule 147 transaction offered exclusively in the issuer's State to investors in that State
C. An additional offer of common stock by an issuer trading on NASDAQ
D. An additional offer of common stock by a bank holding company

9. In a private placement effected through Regulation D, which of the following is accurate?
A. The maximum number of accredited investors is 35.
B. The minimum number of non-accredited purchasers is 35.
C. No solicitation is allowed.
D. An accredited investor includes a married couple with $1 million of liquid assets.

10. When an issuer completes a private placement, they are required to do which of the following?
A. File a Form D - Notice of Exempt Offering of Securities
B. File the Private Placement Memorandum (PPM) no later than 15 calendar days after the first sale is made
C. If no PPM is to be used, file a report to FINRA of this fact
D. All choices listed

11. To which of the following do member broker-dealers remit payment for securities purchases?
A. National Securities Clearing Corporation
B. Depository Trust Company
C. Options Clearing Corporation
D. Fixed Income Clearing Corporation

12. Which of the following holds customer assets, receives deposits of cash and securities, and processes withdrawals of cash and securities?
A. Introducing Broker-Dealer
B. Clearing Broker-Dealer
C. Executing Broker-Dealer
D. Investment Banker

13. A principal registered as a "FINOP" can supervise which of the following activities?
A. Back office operations
B. Preparation and maintenance of a member firm's books and records
C. Compliance with financial responsibility rules
D. All choices given

14. Which of the following accurately describes a broker-dealer's responsibility to customers concerning financial condition?
A. Institutional—but not retail—investors receive the broker-dealer's audited balance sheet at least quarterly.
B. Customers—defined as investors with either cash or securities under the firm's possession and control—are entitled to a copy of the broker-dealer's most recent balance sheet upon request.
C. All broker-dealers, regardless of their activities, must provide a copy of their most recent balance sheet to any customer upon request.
D. Broker-dealers typically file balance sheets with FINRA, who, then, freely provides copies to customers and any member of the public, for a nominal fee.

15. Liabilities of a broker or dealer to customers which are subject to immediate cash payment to customers on demand, whether resulting from sales of securities, dividends, interest, deposits, or otherwise are defined by FINRA as which of the following?
A. Free credit balance
B. Margin balance
C. Liquid assets
D. Fixed assets

16. For an introducing broker-dealer, the required minimum net capital is which of the following, depending on their activities?
A. $100,000; $200,000
B. $50,000; $100,000
C. $25,000; $75,000
D. $5,000; $50,000

17. For a clearing broker-dealer, what is the minimum required net capital?
A. $100,000
B. $150,000
C. $200,000
D. $250,000

18. Member firms who act as securities "dealers" must maintain minimum net capital of
A. $50,000
B. $100,000
C. $150,000
D. $250,000

19. Which of the following must maintain a minimum net capital of $25,000?
A. Introducing broker-dealers
B. Executing broker-dealers
C. Firms who maintain custody of customer securities or cash (carrying and clearing members)
D. Firms who engage in the sale of redeemable shares of registered investment companies

20. Inflation is thought to result under which of the following scenarios?
A. Supply of goods and services exceeds demand
B. Demand for goods and services exceeds supply
C. The Federal Reserve Board sells Treasury securities on the open market
D. All choices listed

21. A graph showing the yields of debt securities of similar credit quality across various maturities is known as which of the following?
A. A yield spread
B. A yield curve
C. A bond ladder
D. A scatter graph

22. When a nation ties its currency to a fixed weight of gold, we refer to this monetary system as which of the following?
A. Fixed exchange rate
B. Floating-Rate
C. Keynesian exchange rate
D. Inverted exchange rate

23. Which of the following industry spaces is most likely "counter-cyclical" in nature?
A. Restaurants and hotels
B. Healthcare and pharmaceuticals
C. Employment placement services
D. Food service

24. Which of the following actions taken by the "Fed" would tend to stimulate a sluggish economy?
A. Selling Treasury securities on the secondary market
B. Relaxing the reserve requirement
C. Increasing the discount rate
D. Increase Regulation T requirements

25. Which of the following fiscal policy initiatives tend to stimulate a sluggish economy?
A. Reducing spending
B. Increasing marginal tax rates
C. Increasing spending
D. All choices listed

Answers

1. C
2. B
3. C
4. B
5. A
6. D
7. C
8. B
9. D
10. D
11. B
12. B
13. D
14. C
15. A
16. D
17. D
18. B
19. D
20. B
21. B
22. A
23. C
24. B
25. C

CHAPTER 2: Understanding Products and Their Risks

Types of Securities

Insurance-Based Products

Before putting their money at risk, most investors first build a layer of protection. Step one is usually to establish an emergency fund at the local bank. Step two is to talk to their insurance agent.

To protect their family against a sudden loss of income the agent may discuss disability, long-term care, and life insurance. To protect against running out of income in retirement, the agent may discuss annuities.

Annuities

An **annuity** is an investment sold by an insurance company that either promises a minimum rate of return to the investor or allows the investor to allocate payments to various funds that invest in the stock and bond markets. These products offer regular payments for the rest of the annuitant's life, but owners of annuities can instead take money out as lump sums or random withdrawals on the back end. Annuities are part of the retirement plans of many individuals, and they can either be part of the safe-money piece or can provide exposure to the stock and bond markets.

The three main types of annuities are fixed, indexed, and variable.

Fixed annuities

A **fixed annuity** promises a minimum rate of return to the investor in exchange for one big payment into the contract or several periodic **purchase payments**. The purchase payments are allocated to the insurance company's **general account,** so the rate of return is "guaranteed." But, that just means it's backed by the claims-paying ability of the insurance company's general account. So before turning over your money to an insurance company, expecting them to pay it back to you slowly, you might want to check their **A.M. Best** rating and their history of paying claims.

In a fixed annuity, the insurance/annuity company bears all the investment risk. This product is suitable for someone who wants a safe investment, something that promises to make dependable payments for the rest of his life, no matter how long he ends up living. The fixed annuity offers peace of mind if not a high rate of return.

Indexed Annuities

A special type of fixed annuity is the **equity-indexed annuity** or just **indexed annuity.** With this product, the investor receives a guaranteed minimum rate of return when the stock market has a bad year. But, he/she receives a higher rate of return when an index—usually the S&P 500—has a good year. Do they receive the full upside, as if they owned an S&P 500 index fund? No, and that must be made clear by the sales representative. The contract is also not credited with the dividends associated with the S&P 500, and those dividends can easily be worth 2 or 3% of the index's total return for the year.

Equity indexed annuities have a **participation rate**. A participation rate of 70% means the contract gets credited with 70% of the increase in the S&P 500. If the index goes up 10%, the contract makes 7% . . . unless that amount is higher than the annual **cap.**

Yes, these contracts also have a cap placed on the maximum increase for any year, regardless of what the stock market does. So, with a participation rate of 70% and a cap of 6%, what happens if the S&P goes up 20%? Although 70% of that is 14%, if you're capped at 6%, then 6% is all the contract value will rise that year. As you can see, indexed annuities are really about the downside protection, which is why a securities license is not required to sell fixed annuities, equity-indexed or otherwise.

Variable Annuities

Inflation is measured by the **Consumer Price Index**. Investors adjust the returns on their investments by the CPI to calculate their **inflation-adjusted** or **real rate of return.** If an investor receives 4% interest on her bond when the CPI is 2%, her inflation-adjusted return is just 2%. Take the rate of return and then subtract out the CPI to calculate real or inflation-adjusted return. If an investor receives just 1% when the CPI is 2%, his return would be -1% in terms of inflation-adjusted return. He is, in other words, losing purchasing power.

Unlike a fixed annuity, a **variable annuity** doesn't promise a rate of return. That's why it is called a "variable" annuity—the return varies. In exchange for bearing the risks in the stock and bond markets, the variable annuitant gets the opportunity to do much better than he would have in a fixed annuity, protecting his purchasing power from the ravages of inflation.

Could he do worse? Yes, but if he wants a guarantee, he buys a fixed annuity where the insurance company guarantees a certain rate of return. Now he lives with purchasing power risk, because if the annuity promises 2%, that's not going to be sufficient with inflation rising at 4%. If he wants to protect his purchasing power by investing in the stock market, he buys a variable annuity, but now he takes on all the risks involved with that.

Variable annuities use mutual fund-type accounts as their investment options, called **subaccounts.** In a deferred annuity, the annuitant defers taxation until he takes the money out, which is usually at retirement. The money grows much faster when it's not being taxed for 10, 20, maybe even 30 years, but every dance reaches the point where we must pay the fiddler. It's been a fun dance, for sure, but the reality is we will pay ordinary income tax rates on the earnings we have been shielding from the IRS all these years—when we decide to get our own hands on the money.

Features of Annuities

An annuity comes with a mortality guarantee, which means once it goes into the pay-out phase, the annuitant will receive monthly payments for as long as he is alive (a mortal). The fixed annuity states what the check will be worth at a minimum, while the variable annuity—well, it varies. In the variable annuity, the annuitant will receive a check each month, but it could be meager if the markets aren't doing well.

A fixed annuity is an insurance product providing peace of mind and tax deferral. A variable annuity is a mutual fund investment that grows tax-deferred and offers some peace of mind. But, whether it's fixed or variable, the insurance company offers a **death benefit** that promises to pay a beneficiary at least the amount of money invested by the annuitant during his life—period. In a regular old mutual fund investment, we could put in $80,000 and when we die the investment could be worth $30,000, which is all our heirs would inherit. In a variable annuity, the death benefit would pay out the $80,000.

And, if the value of the investment was more than the $80,000 cost basis, the heirs would receive the $90,000 or whatever the account was worth. Note that in the variable annuity, this death benefit is only in effect while the annuitant is deferring any payments from the contract. As we'll see, once we flip the switch to receive payments in a variable annuity, well, anything can happen.

Insurance companies sell peace of mind. Both the mortality guarantee and the death benefit help a lot of investors sleep better. For maximum peace of mind, individuals should buy a fixed or indexed annuity. For some peace of mind and the chance to invest in the stock and bond markets, individuals should consider a variable annuity.

A variable annuity offers the investment choices from a family of mutual funds (growth, value, high-yield bonds, etc.), the tax deferral from an IRA or 401(k) plan, plus a death benefit similar to a life insurance policy. A fixed annuity—or indexed annuity—offers the tax deferral, the death benefit, and a dependable stream of minimum payments, even if the annuitant lives to 100.

Purchasing Annuities

The categories of fixed, indexed, and variable annuities refer to the way payments are calculated on the way out. In terms of buying annuities the two major types are immediate and deferred. These terms refer to how soon the contract holder wants to begin receiving payments—now, or later? These are retirement plans, so we do need to be 59½ to avoid penalties. Therefore, some customers might want or need to wait 20 or 30 years before receiving payments. If so, they purchase a deferred annuity.

The tax deferral is nice, but if the individual is already, say, 68, she may want to retire now and start receiving payments immediately. As you can probably guess, we call that an immediate annuity. While there are immediate variable annuities, it is more common to buy the fixed immediate annuity. Why? The whole point of buying an immediate annuity is to know that—no matter what happens to social security and your 401(k) account—there is a solid insurance company contractually obligated to make a payment of at least X amount for as long as you live. An immediate variable annuity would work out well only if the investments did—while there is some minimal payment guaranteed, it is meager.

An immediate fixed annuity does not offer a high rate of return, but it does provide peace of mind to investors in retirement. Many financial planners would suggest at least some of their customers' retirement money be in a fixed immediate annuity—maybe just enough to provide a monthly payment covering monthly expenses. Figuring withdrawal rates from retirement accounts is tricky, so having a payment of X amount from a solid insurance company could smooth out the bumps.

Customers can buy annuities either with one big payment or several smaller payments. The first method is called "single premium" or "single payment." The second method is called "periodic payment." If an investor has a large amount of money, she can put it in an annuity, where it can grow tax-deferred. If she's putting in a big single purchase payment, she can choose either to wait (defer) or to begin receiving annuity payments immediately. If she's at least 59 ½ years old, she can begin the pay-out phase immediately. That's called a single-payment immediate annuity. Maybe she's only 42, though, and wants to let the money grow another 20 years before taking it out. That's called a single-payment deferred annuity (SPDA).

Many investors put money into the annuity during the accumulation phase (pay-in) gradually, over time. That's called "periodic payment," and if they aren't done paying in yet, you can bet the insurance company isn't going to start paying out. So, if you're talking about a "periodic payment" plan, the only way to do it is through a periodic deferred annuity. There is no such thing as a "Periodic Immediate Annuity".

To review, then, there are three methods of purchasing annuities:

- Single-Payment Deferred Annuity
- Periodic-Payment Deferred Annuity
- Single-Payment Immediate Annuity

Again, variable annuities use subaccounts as the investment vehicles in the plan. But, annuities add both features and extra expenses for the investor on top of all the investment-related expenses. Tax deferral is nice. So are the death benefit and the annuity payment that goes on as long as the individual lives. But, that stuff also adds maybe 1.0–1.5% per year in expenses to the investor.

Variable annuities come with a **free-look period**, which is generally a minimum of 10 business days. If the consumer decides he or she doesn't want to keep the product, he or she can cancel without losing any premiums or surrender charges to the company. For fixed annuities, consumers have the same free look period their state requires of insurance policies.

Receiving Payments (Settlement Options)

Some investors make periodic purchase payments into the contract while others make just one big purchase payment. Either way, when the individual gets ready to annuitize the contract, he tells the insurance company which payout option he's choosing. And, he is not able to change this decision—he makes the decision and that's that.

If the individual throws the switch to receive payments and chooses life only or straight life he'll typically receive the largest monthly payout. Why? Because the insurance company sets those payments and the insurance company knows better than he does when he's going to die. Not the exact day or the exact method, of course, but they can estimate it with amazing precision. Since the insurance/annuity company is only required to make payments for as long as he lives, the payments are typically the largest for a "life only" or "straight life" annuity settlement option. How does the individual win? By living longer than the actuarial tables predict.

If this option seems too risky, the individual can choose a "unit refund life annuity." This way he is guaranteed a certain number of payments even if he does get hit by the proverbial bus. If he dies before receiving them, his beneficiary receives the balance of payments.

So, does the annuitant have family or a charity she wants to be sure receives the balance of her payments? If not, why not go with the life only/straight life option—tell the insurance company to pay her as much as possible for as long as she lives.

If she does have family, friends, or a charity she'd like to name as a beneficiary, she can choose a **period certain** settlement option. In that case, the insurance company must do what the name implies—make payments for a certain period. To either her or the named beneficiaries. For older investors, this option typically leads to a lower monthly payment, since the insurance company will now be on the hook for several years even if the annuitant conveniently expires. If it's a 20-year period certain payout, the payments are made to the beneficiary for the rest of that period, even if the annuitant dies after the first month or two.

The annuitant could also choose life with period certain, and now we'd have an either-or scenario with the insurance company. With this option, the company will make payments for the greater of his life or a certain period, such as 20 years. If he dies after 2 years, the company makes payments to his beneficiary for the rest of the term. And if he lives longer than 20 years, they just keep on making payments until he finally expires.

Finally, the joint with last survivor option typically provides the smallest monthly check because the company is obligated to make payments for as long as either the annuitant or the survivors are alive. The contract can be set up to pay the annuitant while he's alive and then pay the beneficiaries until the last beneficiary expires. Or, it can start paying the annuitant and the beneficiary until both have finally, you know.

Covering two persons' mortality risks (the risk they'll live a long time) is an expensive proposition to the insurance company, so these monthly checks are typically smaller than either period certain or life-only settlement options.

Variable Annuities: Accumulation and Annuity Units

There are only two phases of an annuity, the accumulation period and the annuity period. An individual making periodic payments into the contract, or one who made one big purchase payment and is now deferring the payout phase, is in the accumulation phase, holding **accumulation units**. When he throws the switch to start receiving payments, the insurance company converts those accumulation units to **annuity units**.

In a fixed annuity, the annuitant knows the minimum monthly payment he can expect. A variable annuity, on the other hand, pays out the fluctuating value of those annuity units. And, although the value of annuity units fluctuates in a variable annuity during the payout phase, the number of those annuity units is fixed. To calculate the first payment for a variable annuity, the insurance company uses the following:

- Age of the annuitant
- Account value
- Gender
- Settlement option

Health is not a factor—there are no medical exams required when determining the payout. This is also why an annuity cannot suddenly be turned into a life insurance policy, even though it can work in the other direction, as we'll discuss elsewhere.

AIR and Annuity Units

As we said, once the number of annuity units has been determined, the number of annuity units is fixed. So, for example, maybe every month he'll be paid the value of 100 annuity units.

Trouble is, he has no idea how big that monthly check is going to be, since no one knows what 100 **annuity units** will be worth month-to-month, just like nobody knows what mutual fund shares will be worth month-to-month.

So, how much is an annuity unit worth? All depends on the investment performance of the separate account compared to the expectations of its performance.

Seriously. If the separate account returns are better than the assumed rate, the units increase in value. If the account returns are exactly as expected, the unit value stays the same. And if the account returns are lower than expected, the unit value drops from the month before. It's all based on the **Assumed Interest Rate (AIR)** the annuitant and annuity company agree to use.

If the **AIR** is 5%, that means the separate account investments are expected to grow each month at an annualized rate of 5%. If the account gets a 6% annualized rate of return one month, the individual's check gets bigger. If the account gets the anticipated 5% return next month, that's the same as AIR and the check will stay the same. And if the account gets only a 4% return the following month, the check will go down.

The Separate vs. General Account

An insurance company is one of the finest business models ever conceived. See, no one person can take the risk of dying at age 32 and leaving the family with an unpaid mortgage, a stack of bills, and a sudden loss of income, not to mention the maybe $15,000 it takes just for a funeral. But, an insurance company can take the risk that a certain number of individuals will die prematurely by insuring a large number of and then using the laws of probability over large numbers that tell them how many individuals will die each year with only a small margin of error.

Once they've taken the insurance premiums that individuals pay, they then invest what's left after covering expenses and invest it wisely in the real estate, fixed-income, and stock markets. They have just as much data on these markets, so they can use the laws of probability again to figure out that if they take this much risk here, they can count on earning this much return over here within only a small margin of error.

And, most insurance companies are conservative investors. That's what allows them to crunch numbers and know with reasonable certainty they will never have to pay so many death benefits in one year that their investments are totally wiped out. This conservative investment account that guarantees the payout on whole life, term life, and fixed annuities is called the **general account**. In other words, the general account is for the insurance company's investments. Typically, it is comprised mostly of investment-grade corporate bonds.

Many insurance companies also create an account that is separate from the general account, called the **separate account**. It's really a mutual fund family that offers tax deferral, but we don't call it a mutual fund, even though it's also covered by and registered under the same Investment Company Act of 1940. The Investment Company Act of 1940 defines a separate account like so:

> "Separate account" means an account established and maintained by an insurance company pursuant to the laws of any State or territory of the United States, or of Canada or any province thereof, under which income, gains and losses, whether or not realized, from assets allocated to such account, are, in accordance with the applicable contract, credited to or charged against such account without regard to other income, gains, or losses of the insurance company.

When the **purchase payments** are invested in the general account, they are guaranteed a certain rate of return. When the purchase payments are invested in the separate account, welcome to the stock and bond markets, where anything can happen.

Types and Characteristics of Cash and Cash Equivalents

Bank deposits and fixed annuities are safe-money investments. **Money market securities** are also safe

investments that hold a steady value over the short-term. They are not always guaranteed, but the risk taken on most money market securities is extremely low. The exam may refer to money market securities as "cash equivalents" because, basically, they are just as good as cash. Better actually, because unlike cash hidden in a coffee can, money market instruments earn interest.

It's not a high rate of interest, but at least we are putting our cash to work and not risking it in the stock market, where anything can happen, or the bond market, where interest rates could rise and depress the value of our holdings.

The problem with investing too much in cash equivalents is that we miss the big opportunities that arise when stocks or bonds experience bull markets.

T-Bills

T-Bills are short-term obligations of the United States Treasury, which means they are as safe as the money in your pocket. But, unlike the money you carry around, T-Bills earn interest. Guaranteed interest.

That's right, the interest and principal are guaranteed, and the U.S. Treasury has never defaulted. So, if you don't need to withdraw a certain amount for several months or longer, you can buy the 3-month or 6-month T-Bill and usually earn higher yields than you'd earn in a savings account. There are no fees to buy T-Bills if you buy them directly through www.treasurydirect.gov.

Bank CDs usually yield about the same as T-Bills, but the bank's FDIC insurance stops at $250,000 per account. T-Bills, on the other hand, are guaranteed no matter how large the denomination. Any given Monday T-Bills are available by auction through the website mentioned above from as small as $100 par value to as large as $5 million. No matter how big the bill, it's guaranteed by the U.S. Treasury, the folks to whom we pay our federal income taxes.

Bankers' Acceptances

A **bankers' acceptance** is a short-term credit investment created by a non-financial company and guaranteed by a bank as to payment. "BAs" are traded at discounts to face value in the secondary market. These instruments are commonly used in international transactions, and the exam might associate them with importing and exporting. As with a T-Bill, bankers' acceptances are so short-term it would make no sense to send interest checks to the buyer. Instead, these short-term debt securities are purchased at a discount from their face value. The difference between what we pay and what we receive is the interest income.

The BA or bankers' acceptance is backed both by a bank's full faith and credit and the goods being purchased by the importer.

Commercial Paper

Commercial paper is typically used by companies as a source of working capital, receivables financing, and other short-term financing needs. To build major items such as an $800 million factory, a company generally issues long-term bonds (funded debt), and pays the lenders back slowly. But if Microsoft needs a mere $50 million for a few months, they would probably prefer to borrow it short-term at the lowest possible interest rate.

If so, they issue **commercial paper** with a $50 million face amount, selling it to a **money market mutual fund** for, say, $49.8 million. Again, the difference between the discounted price and the face amount represents the interest earned by the investor. Commercial paper is generally issued only by corporations with high credit ratings from S&P, Moody's, or Fitch.

Commercial paper could be described as an unsecured promissory note, as opposed to the BA we just examined, which provides collateral to the lender. Some large corporations issue their commercial paper directly to investors, which may be mutual funds, pension funds, etc. The industry calls this "directly placed commercial paper." When corporations use commercial paper dealers to sell to the investor, the industry refers to this as "dealer-placed commercial paper."

Tax-Exempt Municipal Notes

We'll look at municipal securities in a moment, but for now just know that cities, counties, and school districts can borrow money long-term by issuing bonds, and they can borrow short-term by issuing anticipation notes. For example, property taxes are collected twice a year. If the city wants some of that money now, they can issue a **tax anticipation note**, or TAN. If it's backed by revenues—from sewer and water services, for example—it's a **revenue anticipation note**, or RAN. If the note is backed by both taxes and revenues, they call it a **tax and revenue anticipation note**, or TRAN. Through a **bond anticipation note** or BAN the issuer borrows money now and backs it with part of the money they're going to borrow when they issue more bonds.

The interest paid on these municipal notes is lower than the nominal rates paid on a corporation's commercial paper, but that's okay—the interest paid is also tax-exempt at the federal level. So, if an investor or an institution is looking for safety, liquidity, and dependable, tax-exempt interest over the short-term, they purchase these anticipation notes directly or through a tax-exempt money market mutual fund.

Certificates of Deposit (CD)

To earn a higher interest rate than what their bank offers on savings or checking accounts, many bank customers put relatively large amounts into **certificates of deposit** or **CDs**. These are long-term deposits that pay higher rates of interest if the depositor agrees to leave the funds untouched during a certain time frame. CDs are typically offered in terms of three or six months, and for as long as one, two, three or five years. Those are typical terms, but savers can find certificates of deposit with terms as short as seven days or as long as 10 years. Obviously, the bank would have to entice someone with a higher rate to get him to agree to leave a large deposit untouched for 10 years. And, a saver, on the other hand, could not expect a high rate of return when locking up funds for a mere seven days. Investors agree not to withdraw funds until the CD matures, which is why CDs usually offer higher yields than a regular savings account. As with any fixed-income investment, rates typically increase with the length of deposit terms.

Deposits in bank CDs are backed by the Federal Deposit Insurance Corporation for up to $250,000 per depositor and ownership category, per insured bank. Bank CDs are insured by the FDIC just like other bank deposits, so this is about as safe as "safe money" gets. As you might imagine, the yields on these government-insured deposits are also modest. Then again, for the liquid part of one's portfolio, bank CDs are often appropriate.

The drawbacks include the fact they are long-term deposits, not as liquid as a savings account or a money market mutual fund. If the individual wants her money out now to cover a roof replacement, she will be penalized and probably lose all or most of the interest she was going to make. Bank CDs are not bonds to be traded on the secondary market. CDs don't do much to protect purchasing power, either, but they are great at maintaining an investor's needs for liquidity and capital preservation. The rates offered on certificates of deposit can change every week.

A $250,000 investment is equally safe in a T-Bill or a bank CD. Above that amount, the T-Bill is safer. And, either way, T-Bills are securities that can be bought and sold any day the securities markets are open, while CDs, on the other hand, are commitments to keep money on deposit for a specified length of time.

Negotiable/Jumbo CDS

Some investors step outside the realm of FDIC insurance and purchase **jumbo** or **negotiable CDs**. The denominations here are often several millions of dollars. Therefore, jumbo CDs are usually not insured by the FDIC but are, rather, backed by the issuing bank. That makes their yields higher. Pulling out of a bank CD usually leads to a forfeiture of interest. On the other hand, with CDs investors have a negotiable security they can sell to someone else. That makes the security liquid, but not immune to investment loss.

Insurance-based products provide financial protection. Investments in money market securities provide a rainy-day fund that earns interest and can be tapped in an emergency without having to sell at a loss. To earn higher rates of return, investors purchase longer-term **debt securities**.

Businesses borrow money short-term by issuing money market securities. To borrow from investors long-term, companies issue fixed-income securities that are usually called **bonds.** Businesses sell stock to some investors and bonds to others, forming their **capital structure**. Equity investors are owners; bond investors are loaners. Loaners are creditors who must be paid their interest and principal on time but don't get a vote in corporate management decisions. Owners don't have to be paid anything, but their potential reward is much bigger than those who buy the company's bonds.

For the issuing company, there are advantages and disadvantages to both types of financing. Equity financing gives the business breathing room since there are no interest payments to meet. But, equity investors take a share of profits, have a voice in corporate matters, and never go away. Debt financing adds the burden of interest payments that could force the company into bankruptcy. However, if the company meets the interest and principal payments, the bondholders are paid off, never making a claim on the company's profits.

Corporate bonds are debt securities representing loans from investors to a corporation. Investors buy the bonds on the primary market, and the corporation pays them interest on the loan until the principal amount is returned with the last interest payment at the end of the term. The bonds are liquid, meaning the lenders can sell the bonds on the secondary market if they need to convert to cash. But, when they sell the bonds, investors could receive less (or more) than they paid for them. That is what separates long-term bonds from bank deposits. Even if both T-bonds and bank CDs are guaranteed by the US Government, the T-bond is a security whose market value is subject to fluctuation.

That is also why the yields are typically much higher, as we saw when looking at the yield curve.

A corporation issuing bonds is using **leverage.** A company with a leveraged capital structure has financed operations by issuing debt securities or taking out long-term bank loans.

A bond has a specific value known as the **par value** or **principal** amount. Since it's printed on the face of the certificate, it is also called the **face amount** of the bond. Bonds usually have a par value of $1,000 and, occasionally, $5,000. This is the amount an investor will receive with the last interest payment from the issuer. Up to that point, the investor has only been receiving interest payments against the money he loaned to the corporation by purchasing their bond certificates.

The bond certificate has "$1,000" or whatever the par value is printed on the face, along with the interest rate the issuer will pay every year. This interest rate could be referred to as the **coupon rate** or **nominal yield**. Whatever it's called, the income that a bondholder receives is a fixed, stated amount. If they buy a 5% bond, investors receive 5% of the par value ($1,000) every year, which is $50 per year per bond. In other words, if he owns $1,000,000 par value of a bond with a 5% nominal yield, the bondholder's interest income is $50,000 a year. Typically, that would be received as two semiannual payments of $25,000.

If an issuer issues bonds that all mature on the same date in the future, we call this a **term maturity**. On the other hand, if the bonds are issued all at once but then mature gradually over time, we call this a **serial maturity**. Municipal bonds are often issued as serial maturities. In this case, the municipality floats, say, a $50,000,000 issue in which a portion of the bonds will mature each year over, say, 20 years. The longer out the maturity, the higher the yield offered to those investors, and the lower the yield offered on the bonds coming due in just a year or two.

In a **balloon maturity,** some of the bonds issued come due in the near-term, while most of the principal is paid off all at once, usually at the final maturity date.

Corporate Bonds

In a notice to investors, the SEC explains that, "Companies use the proceeds from bond sales for a wide variety of purposes, including buying new equipment, investing in research and development, buying back their own stock, paying shareholder dividends, refinancing debt, and financing mergers and acquisitions."

A default on a municipal bond is a rare thing, but corporations can end up unable to pay the interest on their bonds—or return the principal at maturity—and thereby go into default. To protect bondholders from this, Congress passed the Trust Indenture Act of 1939. Under this act if a corporation wants to sell $5,000,000 or more worth of bonds that mature in longer than one year, they must do it under a contract or indenture with a trustee, who will enforce the terms of the indenture to the benefit of the bondholders. In other words, if the issuer defaults, the trustee can move to forcibly sell off the assets of the company, so bondholders can recover some of their money. The trustee is typically a large bank.

A corporate bond pays a fixed rate of interest to the investor, and that bond interest must be paid, unlike a dividend on stock that is paid only if the board of directors declares it from profits. We'll see that a bondholder doesn't suffer as much price volatility as a stock investor. But, unlike the owner of common stock, bondholders don't vote on corporate matters. The only time bondholders get to vote is if the corporation goes into bankruptcy. Creditors are offered various scenarios by the corporation, and the bondholders vote on the terms. In other words, the only time bondholders get to vote is when they wish they didn't.

Since bankruptcy is a concern, corporations often secure bonds by pledging assets like airplanes, government securities, or real estate. These bonds secured by collateral are called **secured bonds**. The issuer of a secured bond pledges title of the assets to the trustee, who might end up selling them if the issuer gets behind on its interest payments. Investors who buy bonds attached to specific collateral are secured creditors, the most likely creditors to get paid should the company become insolvent.

Unsecured bonds are like personal loans from the local bank. Secured bonds are like the mortgage loans homeowners take out from the local bank.

In fact, if the collateral used is real estate, we call the secured corporate bond a **mortgage bond**. Just as a mortgage lender sometimes must foreclose/seize the home, the owners of mortgage bonds could seize the real estate backing the loan should the issuer get behind on their payments.

If the collateral is securities, we call it a **collateral trust certificate**. And if the collateral is equipment, such as airplanes or railroad cars, we call it an **equipment trust certificate**. Since secured bonds are usually the safest bonds issued by the company, they offer the lowest coupon payment, too.

Most corporate bonds are backed by a promise known as the "full faith and credit" of the issuer. That's why we might want to see what S&P and Moody's say about an issuer's full faith and credit. If the credit is AAA, we won't be offered a large coupon payment. But if the issuer is rated right at the cut-off point of BBB (Baa for Moody's), then we demand a higher interest rate in exchange for buying bonds from an issuer just one notch above junk status. Regardless of the rating, if we buy a bond backed by the full faith and credit of an issuer, we are buying a **debenture**.

Debenture holders are general creditors with claims below those of the secured bondholders. In a bankruptcy, debenture holders must compete with other unsecured creditors of the company, e.g., suppliers with unpaid invoices. Therefore, debentures pay a higher yield than secured bonds, since they carry more risk.

Some bonds are guaranteed bonds, which means a party other than the issuer has promised to pay interest, principal, or both if the issuer of the bonds cannot. Often a parent company will guarantee the bonds issued by one of its smaller subsidiaries to improve the credit rating. A "guaranteed bond" does not imply the investor is guaranteed against loss. Outside of bank products backed by the FDIC, investors should never expect to be guaranteed against all investment risk. Being guaranteed against default is as good as it gets.

Subordinated debentures have a claim below debentures. Since these bonds have more credit/default risk, they pay a higher yield than debentures and secured bonds.

Beneath all creditors, stockholders make their claims on the company's assets. Preferred stockholders get preference, and common stock is always last in line. Common stock represents the lowest claim on a company's assets, which is why it is called the most "junior" security issued by a company.

Sinking Fund

Bonds pay interest-only until the end of the term. Since the issuing corporation must return the principal value of the bond at some point, they usually establish what's known as a **sinking fund**. With this sinking fund established, the company would be able to return the principal or complete a "call." Having this money set aside can only help the rating by S&P and Moody's, too.

Some bonds—especially municipal bonds—are escrowed to maturity, which means the funds needed to retire the bond issue are already parked in a safe, interest-bearing account holding Treasury securities. Having the debt service covered by a verifiable escrow account tends to make such bond ratings AAA and easy to sell on the secondary market.

U.S. Government Securities

The rate of default on high-yield corporate bonds has ranged in recent years from about 1% to 13%. On the other hand, the rate of default on U.S. Treasury securities has remained at zero, going all the way back to when Alexander Hamilton first issued them in the late 1700s during the first Washington Administration. If you buy a bill, note, or bond issued by the United States Treasury, you eliminate default risk. You're going to get your interest and principal for sure. You just aren't going to get rich in the process. In fact, you usually need to be rich already to get excited about U.S. Government debt.

These fixed-income securities are for capital preservation. Working people need to save up for retirement through common stock or equity mutual funds. The less daring will save up by investing through corporate bonds or bond mutual funds. But if one already has millions of dollars, the goal might become preserving that capital as opposed to risking it trying to get bigger returns. If you sell your company for $10 million, for example, you might put $2 million into T-Bonds. If they yield 5%, that's $100,000 in interest income going forward, after all, with no risk to the principal.

U.S. Treasury securities are virtually free of default risk. They carry most of the other risks corporate bondholders face, but default risk is eliminated. Therefore, if an investor compares the yield on, say, a 10-year Treasury Note to the yield on a 10-year corporate bond, the higher yield offered on the corporate bond indicates the market's perceived default risk. If the Treasury Note yields 3.0% while the 10-year corporate bond yields 4.5%, the **risk premium** demanded by investors is that difference of 1.5%. To take on default risk, investors require 1.5 percentage points more in return.

Agency Bonds

Agency bonds or **agency issues** are debt securities issued by either Government Sponsored Enterprises (GSEs) or Federal Government agencies which may issue or guarantee these bonds. GSEs are usually federally-chartered but privately-owned corporations such as FNMA (Federal National Mortgage Association) and FHLMC (Federal Home Loan Mortgage Corporation). Government agencies include the Small Business Administration, GNMA (Government National Mortgage Association), and the FHA (Federal Housing Authority). A key difference here is that securities issued by GSEs are not direct obligations of the US Government, while those issued or guaranteed by GNMA (Ginnie Mae), the SBA, and the FHA are guaranteed against default just like T-Bills, T-Notes, and T-Bonds.

Agency securities tend to promote a public purpose. For example, FNMA and FHLMC purchase mortgages from lenders, which encourages lenders to make more loans and increase home ownership. Similarly, the Federal Farm Credit Banks provide assistance to the agricultural sector, while the Small Business Administration provides assistance to small businesses.

Fannie Mae (FNMA) and Freddie Mac (FHLMC) are public companies with common stock, unlike GNMA. While the US Government has provided financial assistance to these entities, it has not guaranteed their debt securities or preferred stock issues, let alone their common stock. So, while investing in Ginnie Mae involves no credit or default risk, this is not the case with Fannie and Freddie.

A minimum investment of $25,000 is required for GNMA mortgage-backed securities. Investors receive monthly interest and principal payments from a pool of mortgages. When will the mortgages in the pool be paid off? That is an uncertainty. If interest rates drop, the mortgages will be repaid sooner than expected, which we call prepayment risk. If interest rates go the other way, it will take longer than expected for the homeowners to pay off the mortgages, which we call extension risk.

GNMA, FNMA, and FHLMC mortgage-backed securities all carry this risk, which we mentioned earlier.

GNMA is backed by the full faith and credit of the US Government. Still, the yields are typically higher than what one would receive on a Treasury security of a similar term due to prepayment and extension risk. Interest rates on mortgage securities from FNMA and FHLMC are also higher than on Treasury and higher than corporate bonds to reflect the compensation for the uncertainty of their maturity as well as their higher credit risk. While FNMA and FHLMC buy mortgages and issue mortgage-backed securities, GNMA adds her guaranty to mortgage-backed securities that have already been issued. FNMA and FHLMC do guarantee payment to investors, but, again, neither is the federal government, and both charge fees to provide the guarantee.

Municipal Securities

Across the street from our former office used to sit an old brick industrial building that was supposed to be turned into a major condominium and townhouse development back before the bottom fell out of the real estate market. Unfortunately, the developers borrowed $15 million but pre-sold only one condominium, sending the property into foreclosure.

So, the park district, whose land sits next to the foreclosed property, wanted to tear down the outdated structure for their operations. The park district needed $6 million to acquire and develop the property and, therefore, raised that amount by issuing **municipal bonds**. In a recent election, a majority of Forest Parkers voted to allow the park district to raise property taxes slightly to create the funds needed to pay off a $6 million bond issue to be used to better the community.

The bonds pay investors tax-exempt interest at the federal level. Illinois residents also escape state income tax on the bond interest.

For us, all it took to see the connection between this municipal securities section and the so-called "real world" was to walk 15 steps to the front window and see that the building pictured below has now been torn down and carted away brick-by-brick, all because a municipal taxing authority borrowed money by issuing bonds.

There are two main types of municipal bonds: **general obligation** and **revenue**. General obligation bonds are safer than revenue bonds because they are backed by the municipality's ability to collect and raise taxes from various sources. However, some states are considered safer issuers than others, and the same goes for counties, school districts, port authorities, etc. Revenue bonds are only as safe as the revenue source tied to the bonds.

To make the bonds more marketable and keep interest payments as low as possible, many municipal bonds come with a **credit enhancement** from an insurance company who insures against default. If interest rates rise, bond prices drop. That is not what is covered here. The insurance policies cover interest and principal payments, not market or interest rate risk. Examples of municipal bond insurance (or assurance) companies include AMBAC and MBIA.

Because some municipal bonds are insured and some are not, bond ratings agencies including Moody's and S&P typically indicate whether a rating is "pure" or "insured." A "pure" rating is based on the credit quality of the issuer only, while an "insured" rating implies the credit quality is based on the insurance policy backing the bonds against default.

General Obligation Bonds

The phrase **general obligation** means the municipality is legally obligated to pay the debt service on the bonds issued. GOs are backed by the full faith and credit of the municipality. Where does a municipality get the money they'll need to pay off the bonds? If necessary, they'll dip into all the sources of general revenue available to a city or state or park district, like sales taxes, income taxes, parking fees, property taxes, fishing licenses, marriage licenses, whatever. And, if they must, they'll even raise taxes to pay the debt service on a general obligation bond.

General obligation bonds are backed by the full taxing power of the issuer, and that's why GOs require **voter approval**. As we said, Forest Parkers first had to approve a $6 million bond issue before the park district could do the borrowing and back up the loan with their increased property taxes.

States get most of their revenue from sales and income taxes, while local governments rely on property taxes. Since local governments (cities, park districts, school districts) get much of their revenue from property taxes, a GO bond is associated with property taxes, called **ad valorem**. That phrase means the property tax rises or falls "as to value" of the property.

A municipality might assess property at 50% of its market value. So, a home with a market value of $400,000 would have an **assessed value** of only half that, or $200,000. A homeowner takes the assessed value of his home and multiplies it by a rate known as the **millage rate** to find his tax bill. If the millage rate is "9 mills," we multiply the assessed value of $200,000 by .009 to get a tax bill of $1,800. That $1,800 goes to support many different overlapping municipalities, for example: water district, park district, school district, library & museum district, village government, and county government.

Some municipalities limit the number of mills that can be levied against property. If so, they might end up issuing **limited tax bonds**, which means there are limits on the taxes that can be used to pay the debt service. Maybe property tax rates can only go so high to pay the debt service on a GO, or maybe only certain taxes can be used but not others. School districts are often limited as to how high property taxes can go to support their bonds, while other governmental units have no such limits. So, if you see limited tax bonds, associate the term with GOs.

Whenever the issuer's full faith and credit backs the bonds, we refer to the bonds as "general obligations." There is a peculiar type of municipal bond backed by that full faith and credit but also by the revenues generated at the facility being built with the bond proceeds. These bonds are called **double-barreled bonds.**

For example, a hospital is something all residents of a municipality benefit from, which is why the county or state might put its full faith and credit behind the bond issue. However, hospitals also generate revenues, which can be used to pay debt service. In this case, the issuer has two sources of revenue to pay debt service, which is why we call it a double-barreled bond. Anything backed by the issuer's full faith and credit as well as revenues is called a double-barreled bond. Since the full faith and credit of the issuer backs the issue, we consider this a GO.

Revenue Bonds

Rather than putting the full faith and credit of the issuer behind it, a revenue bond identifies a specific source of revenue, and only that revenue can be used to pay the interest and principal on the bonds. Have you ever driven on a toll way or paid a toll to cross a bridge? What did you drop in the basket? A **user fee.** That money you put in the toll basket helped to pay the debt service on the revenue bond issued to build the toll way or toll bridge. If money problems arise, the issuer won't raise property taxes. They'll raise the user fees.

You don't like the higher tolls? Use the freeway. But, homeowners aren't affected one way or another since their property taxes cannot be used to pay off revenue bonds. Facilities that could generate enough revenue to pay off the bonds include airports, convention centers, golf courses, and sports stadiums. The stadium where the New York Mets play their home games was built with the proceeds of a revenue bond. As an article in Bloomberg explains, "The Mets sold $613 million municipal bonds in 2006 backed by payments in lieu of property taxes, lease revenue and installment payments to finance the construction of Citi Field. The team also issued $82.3 million of insured debt in 2009, the year the 42,000-seat ballpark opened in Queens."

Unfortunately, the revenues a few years ago were significantly lower than what the consultants predicted. That caused the bonds' rating to drop. The next year, however, with attendance up 20%, the revenues improved just enough to boost the credit rating to one notch above junk. What about future seasons? Turns out, predicting the credit rating for the bonds is about as reliable as predicting where the Mets will place in their division each year.

General obligation bond ratings are based on the credit score of the issuer. On the other hand, revenue bonds are only as strong as the revenues generated by the project being built. When the revenues are tied to the success and popularity of a baseball team, it is not surprising the credit rating could be upgraded and downgraded many times before maturity.

Since we don't have property tax on the table, the municipal government doesn't need voter approval to issue a revenue bond. So, we don't associate "voter approval" with a revenue bond. That is for general obligation bonds only.

There are other ways a municipality could identify specific sources of revenue for a bond issue. For example, if the residents of a county wanted their roads paved, the county could add a special tax on gasoline throughout the county and let motorists pay for the new roads each time they fill up their tanks. This **special tax** is used to pay the debt service on the revenue bonds, which are issued to raise the money required to pave the roads. That's an example of a **special tax bond**, a type of revenue bond. Any tax not a property or sales tax is considered a special tax, including special taxes on business licenses, excise taxes, and taxes on gasoline, tobacco, hotel/motel, bottled water, and alcohol. The exam might even refer to these as "sin taxes."

There are also **special assessment bonds**. Say a wealthy subdivision in your community experiences problems with their sidewalks. The concrete is chipped, threatening the property values of the homes in the exclusive subdivision. The residents want the municipality to fix the sidewalks. The municipality says, okay, if you pay a special assessment on your property, since you're the only ones who'll benefit from this improvement. That special assessment will be the revenue used to pay the debt service on a special assessment bond, which is issued to raise the money to fix the sidewalks.

See how it works? They identify a future source of revenue, like tolls, ticket sales, or special taxes on gasoline. Then, since they need all that money right now, they issue debt securities against this new source of revenue they're creating. They take the proceeds from selling the debt securities and get the project built. Then those revenues they identified come in, and they use them to pay the interest and, eventually, the principal due to investors who bought the bonds.

Cities like Chicago and New York have public housing projects, which are under HUD, a unit of the federal government. Municipalities issue **PHA (Public Housing Authority)** or **NHA (New Housing Authority) bonds** to raise money for housing projects. The debt service is backed by the rental payments, which are in turn backed by contributions from Uncle Sam. PHAs and NHAs are considered the safest revenue bond because of this guaranteed contribution from the federal government. Sometimes they are referred to as "Section 8" bonds because something needs at least three names in this business.

Industrial Development Revenue bonds are used to build or acquire facilities that a municipal government will then lease to a corporation. These **IDRs** carry the same credit rating as the corporation occupying the facility. The issuing municipality does not back the debt service in any way. Again, the debt service will be paid only from lease payments made by a corporation, so it's the corporation that backs the debt service. As you know, corporations have been known to go belly-up occasionally. If they're the ones backing up the debt service, you can imagine what happens when they themselves no longer have any assets behind them.

And if it happens, the issuer won't be there to bail out the bondholders. While revenue bonds are only serviced by specific sources of revenue, a **moral obligation bond** provides for the possibility of the issuer going to the legislature and convincing them to honor the "moral obligation" to pay off the debt service. This is a moral obligation, not a legal one, and it would take legislative action to get the money authorized.

Callable Bonds

A bond has a maturity date that represents the date the issuer will pay the last interest check and the principal. At that point, it's all over—the debt has been paid in full, just like when you pay off your car, student loan, house, etc. This can be referred to as "maturity" or **redemption**. As we saw earlier, many bonds are repurchased by the issuer at a set price if interest rates drop. So, a bond might not make it to the maturity date due to an early redemption or "call." Either way, the debt would have been retired by the issuer.

Municipal bonds are frequently callable by the issuer. Refunding a current issue of bonds allows municipalities to finance their debt at lower rates going forward. Or, there could be a covenant in the bond indenture for the current issue that is burdensome, motivating the issuer to start over. An optional redemption gives the issuer the option to refinance/refund their debt as of a certain date at a stated price, or over a series of prices and associated call dates. Some bonds are issued with mandatory call provisions requiring the issuer to call a certain amount of the issue based on a schedule or on having enough money to do so in the sinking fund.

When issuers redeem callable bonds before the stated maturity date, they may call the entire issue or just part of it. For obvious reasons, the call provisions can, therefore, be referred to as in-whole redemptions or partial redemptions. The refunding is sometimes done through a direct exchange by bondholders of the existing bonds for the new issue. Usually, though, the issuer sells new bonds to pay off the existing issue.

When **refunding** an issue of bonds, issuers either perform a **current refunding** or an **advance refunding**. If the issuer uses the proceeds of the "refunding bonds" to promptly call (within 90 days) the "prior issue," we refer to this as a current refunding. On the other hand, when the issuer places some of the proceeds of the refunding issue in an escrow account to cover the debt service on the outstanding issue, we refer to this as an advance refunding. Because an escrow account is, literally, money in the bank, the prior issue whose debt service is now covered by the escrow deposit is not required to be included on the issuer's debt statement. Do we just take the issuer's word the U.S. Treasury securities held in the escrow account are sufficient to cover the debt service on the prior issue?

No. Rather, an independent CPA issues a "verification report" verifying the yield on the escrow deposit will be sufficient to pay off the outstanding or refunded issue of bonds. Because of the certainty surrounding a refunded issue of bonds, these bonds are typically rated AAA and are among the safest of all municipal bonds on the market. Because of their inherent safety, refunded bonds are also liquid.

The typical advance refunding is performed by placing proceeds from the sale of the refunding issue in an escrow account holding Treasury securities, with only the escrow account used to cover the debt service on the prior issue of bonds. In a "crossover refunding" the promised revenue stream backing the prior issue continues to be used to meet debt service until the bonds are called with proceeds from the escrow account.

Paying off a debt is sometimes referred to as a debt being "defeased." Therefore, the exam could refer to the refunding bonds as being issued to defease the prior issue of outstanding bonds.

Refunding bonds are not tax-exempt. Municipalities, in other words, can borrow money on the cheap for infrastructure, but if they could issue tax-exempt refunding issues, some governmental entities would do nothing but issue refunding bonds in a never-ending attempt to maximize their budgets.

Methods Used to Determine the Value of Fixed-Income Securities

Investors purchase U.S. Treasury securities to eliminate credit risk. But, here's the catch: U.S. Treasury securities are just as exposed to interest rate and reinvestment risk as are corporate and municipal bonds.

That is because bonds are issued with a fixed interest rate. If the bond is an 8% bond, it will always be an 8% bond, and it will always pay 8% of the par value every year no matter who owns it at the time or how much she paid for it. For purposes of illustration, the par value is $1,000. 8% of $1,000 is $80 per year to the bondholder in interest income, split into two payments of $40. With $1,000,000 in 8% bonds, the investor receives $80,000 a year in interest income, in semiannual payments of $40,000.

Bonds are fixed-income securities. If it's a 5% bond, it pays $50 a year per $1,000 of par value. If it's a 13% bond, it pays $130 a year.

So, if a bond pays a nominal yield of 8%, it will always pay 8%. Therefore, whenever interest rates change, they change the bond's market price. Investors are not required to sell the bonds, but if they do, they could realize a loss. And, if they hold their positions, they will see the market values of their positions have dropped when they check their monthly account statements.

It's true if the bondholder always holds to maturity, he gets the par value back. It's also true that investors are human beings who run into financial emergencies. That's why bonds do not work as well as money market mutual funds or bank CDs for emergency funds. Because of interest rate risk, long-term bonds need to be held long-term. Even U.S. Treasury Bonds can lead to large losses if liquidated after interest rates rise.

Earlier, we said bonds are loans that the lenders can liquidate. Here's the catch: no one knows what their market prices will be in the future. When rates on new bonds rise, the secondary market prices of existing bonds drop. That's interest rate risk.

The good news is when interest rates drop, bond prices on the secondary market rise.

Yields and Rates are the same thing. Bond Prices move in the other direction, which is called an **inverse relationship**.

Discount Bonds

Par value is what is returned to the bondholder at maturity and what the coupon rate is multiplied against. But, bonds are not bank deposits. Rather, they are securities trading on a secondary market. Among other factors, a bond's market price fluctuates in response to changes in interest rates. If a bondholder has a bond that pays a nominal yield of 8%, what is the bond worth when interest rates in general climb to 10%?

Not as much. If you had something that paid you 8%, when you knew you could be receiving more like 10%, how would you feel about the bond?

Not too good. But, when interest rates fall to 6%, suddenly that 8% bond looks good, right? It's all relative.

Current Yield

When we take a bond's market price into consideration, we're looking at **current yield**. Current yield (CY) takes the annual interest paid by the bond and divides it by what an investor would have to pay for the bond.

Current Yield = Annual Interest divided by Market Price

So, let's say after an investor buys an 8% bond, interest rates rise, knocking down the market price to just $800. What is the current yield if that happens?

$80/$800 gives us a current yield of 10%.

Did the bond's market price just drop, or did its current yield rise? Those are two ways of saying the same thing.

Yield answers the question, "How much do I get every year compared to what I pay to get it?" If interest rates rise to 10%, suddenly this bond that pays only 8% isn't worth as much. The only motivation for buying this 8% bond is if an investor could get it at a **discount**. And, if she can get the $80 that the bond pays in annual interest for just $800, isn't she getting 10% on her money? That's why we say her current yield is 10%, higher than the nominal yield that never, ever changes.

Rates and yields up, price down. Rates are what new bonds pay. Yields are what existing bonds offer, after we factor in their market price.

A **discount bond** is a bond trading below par value. When you see a current yield higher than the coupon rate of the bond, you're looking at a discount bond. An 8% bond with a 10% current yield, for example, must be a discount bond. An 8% bond with a 6% current yield would *not* be a discount bond. As we'll see in a minute, it would, in fact, be a "premium bond."

Yield to Maturity

Yield to maturity (YTM) is the return an investor gets if she holds the bond to maturity. It is sometimes called basis and represents the only yield that really matters to an investor. It factors in all the coupon payments and the difference between the market price paid for the bond and the par value received at maturity. At maturity, an investor receives the par value, which is $1,000. If the investor puts down only $800 to buy the bond and receives $1,000 when the bond matures, doesn't she receive more at maturity than she paid?

She does, and that's why her yield to maturity is even higher than her current yield. She gets all the coupon payments, plus an extra $200 when the bond matures. If you see a yield-to-maturity higher than the coupon rate or the current yield, you're looking at a discount bond. For example, a bond with a 4% nominal yield trading at a 5.50 basis or yield to maturity is a discount bond.

Yield to Call

Like homeowners, sometimes issuers get tired of making interest payments that seem too high. That's why many bonds are issued as callable, meaning after a certain period the issuer can buy the bonds back from investors at a stated price. A bond that matures in 10 or 20 years is often callable in just 5 years. If a bond is trading at a discount, rates have risen. Therefore, it is unlikely such a bond would be called. But, if it were called, the investor would make his gain faster than if he had to wait until maturity. That's why **yield to call** (YTC) is the highest of all for a discount bond.

Premium Bonds

So, that is what happens when interest rates rise. What happens when interest rates fall? Bond prices rise. If you owned this 8% bond and saw that interest rates had just fallen to 6%, how would you feel about your bond?

Pretty good. After all, it pays 2% more than new debt is paying. Do you want to sell it? Not really. But you might sell it if investors were willing to pay you a **premium**.

Current Yield

Bond investors push the price of the bond up as interest rates go down. Maybe your bond is worth $1,200 on the secondary market now. Dividing our $80 of annual interest by the $1,200 another investor would have to pay for the bond gives us a current yield of just 6.7%. That's lower than the coupon rate.

So, wait, did the price of this bond just rise, or did its current yield drop?

Exactly right!

When you see a coupon of 8% and current yield of 6.7% (or anything lower than that 8% printed on the bond), you're looking at a **premium bond**. A discount bond trades below the par value, while a premium bond trades above the par value.

The nominal yield of the bond doesn't change. Therefore, the only way to push a yield lower than the nominal yield stated on the bond is to have an investor pay more than par for the bond. Similarly, the only way to push the yield higher than the nominal yield stated on the bond is to have an investor pay less than par for the bond.

Yield to Maturity

If you sell your bond, you obviously don't care about the next investor's yield. But, when this investor's bond matures, how much does she get back from the issuer? Only $1,000. So, she put down $1,200 and will only get back $1,000 at maturity. Her Yield to Maturity (YTM) goes down below both the nominal and current yields.

Yield to Call

Remember when we decided a person who buys a bond at a discount wants the bond to return the principal amount sooner rather than later? Well, if you pay more than the par value for a bond, you're going to lose money when the bond returns your principal, no matter when that happens. So, if you're going to lose money, you want to lose it slowly to increase your yield. That's why a person who purchases a bond at a premium will have a lower yield to call than yield to maturity. He's going to lose money in either case, so he'd prefer to lose it over 10 or 20 years (maturity) rather than just 5 years (call).

So, yield to call is the lowest yield for a bond purchased at a premium. And, if there are successive call dates, the earliest call date will produce the worst or lowest yield to the investor.

Disclosing Yield on Customer Confirmations

When a customer purchases a bond, the broker-dealer sends her a **trade confirmation** no later than the settlement date. And, on this trade confirmation the firm must disclose either the YTM or the YTC. Should they disclose the best possible yield or the worst possible yield?

Always prepare the customer for the worst or most conservative yield, so there are no bad surprises, right? Okay, for a discount bond, which yield is lower, YTM or YTC? YTM. That's what the firm would disclose to a customer who purchases a bond at a discount.

For a premium bond, which yield is lower?

Yield to Call. So, that's what the firm would disclose to a customer who purchases a bond at a premium. The exam might call this calculation "yield to worst," by the way or even "YTW." The worst yield the investor can receive is the one based on the earliest call date.

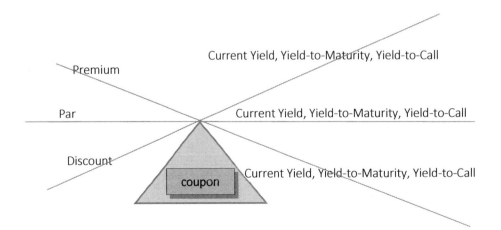

As important as it is to inform customers that even a safe investment in U.S. Treasuries could lead to a large loss of principal, we also don't want to overstate this relationship of interest rates to bond prices. When rates rise, bond prices drop. However, bondholders will reinvest their semiannual interest payments at higher rates, too. So, it's not all bad.

And, even though bond prices rise when rates drop, bondholders reinvest their fixed interest payments at lower rates/yields.

The price swings we just looked at have nothing to do with credit quality. Rather, they are related to the term to maturity. The longer the term to maturity, the more volatile the bond's market price. Within the world of bonds, the longer the term, the riskier the investment.

Credit Ratings

So, bond prices rise and fall based on interest rate movements. And, their market prices also depend on their perceived credit risk. Nothing worse than lending a corporation money and then finding out they are not going to pay you back. This is known as a "default," and it's the worst thing that can happen to a bond investment.

How likely is it that a bond will go into default? Isn't going to happen on a United States Treasury security. It might happen on some municipal securities. But when you get into the category of corporate bonds, you see it happens more than you'd like.

Luckily, Moody's, S&P, and Fitch all assign bond ratings designed to help investors gauge the likelihood of default. The highest quality issuers have AAA/Aaa (S&P/Moody's) ratings. The **investment grade** issues go from AAA/Aaa down to BBB/Baa. And below that, we're looking at high-yield or junk bonds.

Standard & Poor's (& Fitch)	Moody's
AAA	Aaa
AA	Aa
A	A
BBB	Baa
BELOW THIS IS JUNK, NON-INVESTMENT GRADE, HIGH-YIELD, SPECULATIVE	
BB	Ba
B	B
C	Caa

There is also a "D" rating indicating the bond is already in default. Only the savviest and most aggressive bond traders would trade a bond rated that low.

Credit quality is the highest on the AAA/Aaa-rated bonds. As credit quality drops, you take on more default risk, so you expect to be compensated for the added risk through a higher yield. High yield and low quality go hand in hand, just as low yield and high quality do. How does a bond become "high yield" or "junk"? That means a new issue of low-rated bonds offers high coupon rates to get an investor interested in lending the money, and existing bonds trade at lower and lower prices as people get nervous about a possible default. As the price drops, the yield increases.

When S&P, Moody's, or Fitch downgrade an issuer's credit rating, the market price of those bonds drops, increasing their yield. We saw that with the bonds that financed the ballpark used by the New York Mets.

Types and Characteristics of Equity Securities

Some investors seek income. They loan a corporation $100,000 and receive $4,000 a year in interest payments for 10 years. That 4% yield is nice, but at the end of the term, the investor will only receive $100,000, which will have lost purchasing power over 10 years due to inflation.

Other investors give up that steady income to reach for the risky and uncertain growth offered by the stock market. Rather than lending money to a corporation, these equity investors buy **common stock** in the company. This way, if the company becomes more valuable, so do the shares of common stock the investor holds. As we saw earlier, Facebook (FB) went public at $38 but is currently worth close to four times that amount. Bond investors do not quadruple their money. That's because they receive no upside, no share of profits.

Common Stock

Common stock, on the other hand, is all about the profits a company makes. Unlike with bonds, common stock does not give the investor a stated rate of return. If shareholders receive 64 cents per-share of common stock as a dividend this year, they might or might not receive that much next year. A famous toy maker just cut its dividend in half as it tries to turn itself around. And, many companies never pay dividends.

Both the income produced by common stock and the market value of the stock itself are unpredictable. Therefore, common stock investors should only invest the money they could afford to lose.

Bond interest is a fixed expense to the issuer paid to the bondholder. Profits at most companies are unpredictable and, therefore, so are the dividends and the market price of the issuer's common stock.

Rights and Privileges

Common stockholders are owners of the corporation and vote at all annual and special meetings. The owner of common stock has the right to vote for any major issue that could affect his status as a proportional owner of the corporation. Things like stock splits, board of director elections, mergers, and changes of business objectives all require shareholder approval.

Owners of common stock typically have the right to vote on:

- Members of the board of directors
- Proposals affecting material aspects of the business

- Ratifying the auditors
- Mergers & Acquisitions
- Stock Splits
- Liquidation of the company

One thing shareholders never vote on is whether a dividend is paid and, if so, how much. The board of directors decides if a dividend is to be declared from profits and, if so, how much the payment per-share will be. Dividends benefit the shareholder now, while the profits that are reinvested back into the business should eventually help to increase the value of the stock, benefiting the shareholder in the long run.

At the annual shareholder meeting votes are cast per-share, not per-shareholder. Therefore, a mutual fund holding 45 million shares of Wells Fargo (WFC) has a lot more votes than a retail investor holding 300 shares at the Wells Fargo annual meeting. In fact, the retail investor's vote is almost meaningless compared to what the mutual fund decides to do with their 45 million votes.

Either way, all shares get to be voted. If a shareholder owns 100 shares of common stock, he has 100 votes to cast in corporate elections. Let's say there are three seats up for election on the Board of Directors. There are two ways the votes could be cast. Under **statutory voting**, he can only cast the number of shares he owns for any one seat. So, he could cast up to 100 votes for any one seat, representing a total of 300 votes for three seats. Under statutory voting abstaining on any of the seats up for election provides no benefit to the shareholder.

Under **cumulative voting**, however, he could take those 300 votes and split them any way he wanted among the three candidates. He could even abstain on the other seats up for election and cast all 300 votes for one candidate. That's why cumulative voting gives a benefit to the small/minority shareholders. If they can get a candidate on the slate who will look out for the small shareholders, the minority shareholders can cast all their votes for that one candidate and shake things up.

Beyond voting, common stockholders have the right to inspect the corporation's financials through quarterly (10-Q) and annual (10-K) reports. Public companies must file these reports with the SEC, but even a shareholder in a private company has this same right. Shareholders may also see the list of stockholders and the minutes of shareholder meetings.

Common stockholders have a **pre-emptive right** to maintain their percentage of ownership. This means if the company wants to raise money in the future by selling more common stock, existing shareholders must get a chance to buy their percentage of the upcoming issue. If not, their ownership would be diluted. Investors buying the stock on the secondary market up to a certain date also receive rights to buy more shares from the additional offering. Rights offerings avoid dilution of equity by giving owners a chance to maintain their percentage of ownership, if they choose to.

Should a corporation claim bankruptcy protection and have to be liquidated, common stockholders get in line for their piece of the proceeds. Unfortunately, they are last in line. They are behind all the creditors, including bondholders, and behind preferred stockholders.

But, at least they are in line, and if there are any residuals left, they get to make their claim on those assets, known as a **residual claim** on assets or "residual rights." Common stock is the most "junior" security, since all other securities represent senior claims on the company's assets.

Shareholders have **limited liability**, which means they are shielded from the debts of the company and lawsuits filed against it. Unlike a sole proprietor whose business is going sour, shareholders of a corporation would not be sued by creditors. This is true whether the company is public or private.

Common stock owners have a claim on earnings and dividends. As owners, they have a share of the profits or net income of the company. Some of the profits are reinvested into the business, which tends to make the share price rise. Some of the profits might be paid to shareholders as dividends.

Dividends

Not all shareholders are looking for dividends. An investment in Berkshire Hathaway today, for example, would be made without the issuer stating any plans to pay dividends, ever. The only type of investor interested in this stock, then, is a growth investor.

But, there are growth & income investors and equity-income investors for whom dividends are important. Dividends are a share of profits paid out to shareholders if the Board of Directors for the corporation votes to declare them. The day the Board declares the dividend is known as the **declaration date**. The board decides when they'll pay the dividend, too, and we call that the **payable date**. The board also sets the deadline for being an owner of stock if you want this dividend, and we call that the **record date** because an investor must be the owner of record as of that date to receive the dividend.

Now, since an investor must be the owner of record as of the record date to receive the dividend, there will come a day when it's too late for investors to buy the stock and get the dividend.

Why? Because stock transactions don't "settle" until the second business day following the **trade date**, which means you might put in your purchase order to buy 1,000 shares of ABC on a Monday, but you aren't the official owner until that transaction settles on Wednesday. Your broker-dealer must send payment to their clearing agency, and the seller must deliver the 1,000 shares before the transaction has settled. This process takes two business days for common stock and is known as **regular way settlement**, or "T + 2," where the "T" stands for Trade Date. Assuming there are no holidays, a trade taking place on Monday settles on Wednesday, while a trade on Thursday settles on Monday.

So, if an investor must be the owner of record on the record date, and it takes two business days for the buyer to become the new owner, wouldn't she have to buy the stock at least two business days prior to the record date? Yes.

On the other hand, if she buys it just one business day before the record date, her trade won't settle in time. We call that day the **ex-date** or **ex-dividend date**. Starting on that day investors who buy the stock will not receive the dividend. On the ex-date, it's too late. Why? Because the trades won't settle in time, and the purchasers won't be the owners of record with the transfer agent as of the record date. If the trade takes place on or after the ex-date, the seller is entitled to the dividend. If the trade takes place before the ex-date, the buyer is entitled to the dividend.

The regulators set the ex-date, as a function of regular way or T + 2 settlement. The ex-date is one business day before the record date.

Investors don't qualify for the dividend starting with the ex-dividend date; therefore, the amount of the dividend is taken out of the stock price when trading opens. If the dividend to be paid is 70 cents, and the stock is set to open at $20, it would open at $19.30 on the ex-date.

Let's look at how the process looks from a press release:

```
Equity Office declares first quarter common dividend

Mar 16, 2005-- Equity Office Properties Trust (EOP), a publicly
held office building owner and manager, has announced that its
Board of Trustees has declared a first quarter cash dividend in
the amount of $.50 per common share. The dividend will be paid on
Friday 15 April 2005, to common shareholders of record at the
close of business on Thursday 31 March 2005.
```

March 16th is the Declaration Date. The Payable Date is April 15th. The Record Date is Thursday, March 31st. The article doesn't mention the Ex-Date (because that's established by the exchange regulators), but we can figure it must be Wednesday, March 30th. If you bought the stock on Wednesday, your trade wouldn't settle until Friday, April 1st, which means the seller's name would be on the list of shareholders at the close of business on Thursday, March 31st.

A dividend can be paid in the following ways:

- Cash
- Stock
- Shares of a subsidiary
- Product

ADRs

Americans who own shares of Toyota or Nissan own **American Depositary Receipts (ADRs)**. ADRs allow American investors to diversify their portfolio with foreign investments that trade in the U.S. financial system and U.S. currency while giving foreign companies easier access to U.S. capital markets. The ADR investor buys an American Depositary Receipt that represents a certain number of American Depositary Shares of a foreign corporation's stock. The shares are held in a U.S. bank in the foreign country, which issues a receipt to the investor in America. The custodian bank provides services including registration, compliance, dividend payments, communications, and recordkeeping. These fees are typically deducted from the gross dividends received by the ADR holders.

Or, if the issuer does not pay dividends, broker-dealers and banks cover the custody fees charged by depositary banks and then pass the charges on to their customers. ADRs file a registration statement called an F-6 which discloses information on the structure of the ADR including fees that may be charged to the ADR holders. Some ADRs grant voting rights to the investor; some do not.

If dividends are declared, they are declared in the foreign currency and must be converted to dollars. That is why ADR owners are subject to currency risk. Also, if the stock is worth a certain number of yen on the Japanese markets, that won't work out to as many U.S. dollars when our dollar is strong, although it works out to more American dollars when our dollar is weak.

As the SEC explains in an investor bulletin, "Today, there are more than 2,000 ADRs available representing shares of companies located in more than 70 countries."

There are currently three levels of ADR trading, ranging from the more speculative issues trading over-the-counter to those, like Toyota, trading on the NYSE or NASDAQ. Level 1 ADRs trade over-the-counter. Level 2 ADRs trade on exchanges. Level 3 ADRs are part of a public offering that then trades on the NYSE or NASDAQ. In other words, some ADRs merely establish a trading presence in the U.S. while Level 3 ADRs also raise capital for the foreign issuer.

Subscription or Stock Rights

As we mentioned, one of the rights common stockholders enjoy is the right to maintain their proportionate ownership in the corporation. We call this a pre-emptive right because the existing shareholders get to say yes or no to their proportion of the new shares before the new shareholders get to buy them. Otherwise, if you owned 5% of the company, you'd end up owning less than 5% of it after they sold the new shares to everyone but you, called dilution of equity.

For each share owned, an investor receives what's known as a subscription right. It works like a coupon, allowing the current shareholders to purchase the stock below the market price. If a stock is trading at $20, maybe the existing shareholders can take two rights plus $18 to buy a new share. Those rights act as coupons that give the current shareholders two dollars off the market price. So, the investors can use the rights, sell them, or let them expire.

Preferred Stock

Income investors who want to buy stock would more likely buy **preferred stock** than common.

Preferred stock receives preferential treatment over common stock if the company must be forcibly liquidated to pay creditors through a bankruptcy proceeding, and it always receives dividends before owners of common stock can be paid. Some investors refer to a preferred stock position in a private company as "first money out," because if there are distributions of profits, preferred stock gets theirs first.

And, unlike common stock, the preferred stock dividend is a stated percentage of par value. The par value for a preferred stock is assumed to be $100, though a test question would most likely tell you what the par value is if it's required to answer the question. Whatever it is, the stated dividend is a percentage of the par value of the preferred stock. Six percent preferred stock would pay 6% of $100 per-share, or $6 per-share per year.

We hope.

Dividends must be declared by the Board of Directors—or, not declared. Preferred stockholders aren't creditors. They're just owners whose main concern is to receive dividends. If the board doesn't declare a dividend, do you know how much an owner of a 6% **straight preferred stock** would receive?

Nothing. However, if the investor owned **cumulative preferred stock**, the company would have to make up the missed dividend in future years before it could pay dividends to common stockholders. If the company missed the six dollars this year and wanted to pay a dividend to common shareholders next year, cumulative preferred stockholders would have to get their $12 first. Most preferred stock has this cumulative feature, and partial or skipped dividends are a rarity.

If an investor wants the chance to earn more than the stated 6%, he should buy **participating preferred stock**. With this feature, if the issuer increases the dividend paid to common stockholders, they will also raise the dividend paid to participating preferred stockholders. A test question might say that participating preferred stock pays a dividend that is "fixed as to the minimum but not as to the maximum," while straight or cumulative preferred stock pays dividends that are "fixed both as to the minimum and the maximum."

Adjustable-rate preferred stock pays a rate of return tied to another rate, typically a U.S. Treasury security—T-Bill or T-Note, for example. If T-Bill rates rise, so does the rate paid on the adjustable-rate preferred stock, and vice versa. Because the rate adjusts, the price remains stable.

As with bonds, corporate issuers often get tired of paying preferred stockholders a high dividend rate when new investors would accept a lower rate of interest. While most types of preferred stock go on for "perpetuity," **callable preferred stock** may be retired early at the issuer's discretion. If an investor had purchased 5.5% preferred stock a few years ago and then interest rates went down so new investors would accept, say, 3%, the issuer would likely issue 3% preferred stock to new investors and use some of the proceeds to retire the existing issue.

When investors bought the callable preferred stock, the call price and the first possible date were named. So, if rates go down at that point, the issuer might buy back the callable preferred stock, forcing shareholders to reinvest at lower rates. Because it can be retired early, callable preferred stock tends to pay the highest dividend rate of all types of preferred stock.

Preferred stock does not derive its value from the market price of the issuer's common stock. We saw that common stock receives a share of the company's increased profits. Preferred stock, on the other hand, is a fixed-income security. So, a 5% preferred stock—whether straight, cumulative, or callable—would not be expected to rise even if the market price of the issuer's common stock were to double or triple. That means if some investors owned FB preferred stock, neither the income received nor the market price of their investment has changed, while, meantime, the value of the common stock has gone up by a factor of 4X.

As always, there is an exception. But, there is only one type of preferred stock with a market price tied to the market price of the issuer's common stock. This type is known as **convertible preferred stock**. Unlike all other types of preferred stock, convertible preferred stock is not just a fixed-income security. This type lets an investor exchange one share of preferred stock for a certain number of the issuer's common shares.

For all other types of preferred stock, the price has nothing to do with the price of the company's common stock, or even their increased profits. The exception there is convertible preferred stock, but all other types of preferred stock are purely fixed-income securities with market prices tied to credit quality and interest rates.

Unlike a bond, preferred stock generally does not have a **maturity date**, and unlike common stock, usually does not give the owner voting rights. Two specific cases where preferred stock does get to vote are: 1) the corporation defaults on the dividend payment a certain number of times and 2) the corporation wants to issue preferred stock of equal or senior status.

To review how common and preferred stock relate to each other, let's note the similarities and differences between the two.

SIMILARITIES	DIFFERENCES
dividends must be declared by the board of directors to be paid	preferred stock is a fixed-income security paying a stated rate of return
both are equity securities	preferred stock has a higher claim on dividends and on assets in a bankruptcy
	common stock has voting rights and pre-emptive rights

Types and Characteristics of Pooled Investments

In the securities industry, there are many ways to refer to the same thing. What some call a "pooled investment vehicle" others refer to as a "packaged product" or a "mutual fund." Whatever we call these investments, a **pooled investment** vehicle pools the capital of many investors together, with that capital then managed by a professional. Rather than investing directly in a company, investors buy investment products that come with various features.

The best-known pooled investment vehicle is the mutual fund. While some investors buy shares of SBUX, many prefer to own shares of a mutual fund that devotes a percent of the portfolio to SBUX and other large-cap stocks. Similarly, rather than putting $100,000 into one issuer's bonds, many investors prefer the diversification and professional management offered by a bond fund.

Investment Companies

A mutual fund is an investment portfolio managed by an investment adviser. Investors buy shares of the portfolio. The adviser uses the money from investors to invest in stocks and bonds. When an investor sends in money, the portfolio gets bigger, but it also gets cut into more slices to accommodate the investment into the fund. The only way for the slices to get bigger is for the portfolio to become more valuable. The portfolio value rises when securities in the fund increase in market value and when they pay income to the portfolio.

That is the same way it happens in any securities account. When the market values of the securities in the account drop, the account value is down for the day unless income is received that outweighs the drop. For example, if an account was worth $100,000 when the markets opened and then just $98,817 when the markets closed, the investor is down for the day. . . unless he happened to receive dividends and interest of more than that decline of $1,183.

There are two main advantages of owning stocks and bonds through mutual funds as opposed to owning them directly. The first is the professional portfolio management. The second is diversification. If an investor has $400 to invest, he can't take a meaningful position in any company's stock, and even if he tried, he would end up owning just one company's stock. Common stock can drop in a hurry, so we never put all our money in just one or two issues. Diversification protects against this risk, and mutual funds own stocks and bonds from many different issuers, usually in different market sectors. So, even a small investment is diversified, while a common stock investor with a small amount would risk everything on just one issuer.

Advantages of Mutual Funds

Advantages of investing through mutual funds vs. buying stocks and bonds directly include:

- Investment decisions made by a professional portfolio manager
- Ease of diversification
- Ability to liquidate a portion of the investment without losing diversification
- Simplified tax information
- Simplified record keeping
- Automatic reinvestments of capital gains and income distributions at **net asset value**
- Safekeeping of portfolio securities
- Ease of account inquiry

The first point is probably the main reason people buy mutual funds—they have no knowledge of stocks, bonds, taxation, etc., and they have even less interest in learning. Let a professional portfolio manager—often an entire team of portfolio managers—decide what to buy and when to buy or sell it. As we mentioned, it's tough to have your own diversified portfolio in individual stocks and bonds because a few hundred or thousand dollars will only buy a few shares of stock or a few bonds issued by just a few companies.

On the other hand, a mutual fund would usually hold stock in, say, 100 or more companies, and their bond portfolios are also diversified. Therefore, even with the smallest amount of money accepted by the fund, the investor is diversified. This is called the "undivided interest concept," which means that $50 from a small investor owns a piece of all the securities in the portfolio, just as $1 million from a larger investor does.

Another bullet said, "Ability to liquidate a portion of the investment without losing diversification." That means if an investor owns 100 shares of IBM, MSFT, and GM, what is he going to do when he needs $5,000 to cover an emergency? If he sells a few shares of each, he'll pay three separate commissions. If he sells 100 shares of any one stock, his diversification is reduced. With a mutual fund, investors redeem a certain number of shares and remain just as diversified as they were before the sale. And, they can usually redeem shares without paying fees.

Mutual funds can diversify their holdings by:

- Industries

- Types of investment instruments
- Variety of securities issuers
- Geographic areas

If it's a stock fund, it is typically a growth fund, a value fund, an income fund, or some combination thereof. No matter what the objective, the fund usually buys stocks from issuers across many different industries. In a mutual fund prospectus, there is typically a pie chart that shows what percentage of assets is devoted to an industry group. Maybe it's 3% in telecommunications, 10% retail, and 1.7% healthcare, etc. That way if it's a bad year for telecommunications or retail, the fund won't get hurt like a small investor who owns shares of only one telecom company and one retail company.

A bond fund can be diversified among investment interests. That means they buy debentures, secured bonds, convertible bonds, zero coupons, mortgage-backed securities, and even a few money market instruments to be on the safe side.

Even if the fund did not spread their investments across many different industries, they would purchase securities from a variety of issuers. If they focus on the retail sector, they can buy stock in a variety of companies—Walmart, Target, Sears, Nordstrom, Home Depot, etc. And, since any geographic area could be hit by an economic slump, a tropical storm, or both, most funds spread their holdings among different geographic areas.

The Investment Company Act of 1940 defines a **diversified company** as:

```
"Diversified company" means a management company which meets the
following requirements: At least 75 per centum of the value of its
total assets is represented by cash and cash items (including
receivables), Government securities, securities of other
investment companies, and other securities for the purposes of
this calculation limited in respect of any one issuer to an amount
not greater in value than 5 per centum of the value of the total
assets of such management company and to not more than 10 per
centum of the outstanding voting securities of such issuer.
```

So, how does the "Act of 1940" then define a **non-diversified company**?

```
"Non-diversified company" means any management company other than
a diversified company.
```

If the fund wants to promote itself as being diversified, it must meet the definition above. For 75% of the fund's assets, no more than 5% of its assets are in any one company, and it doesn't own more than 10% of any company's outstanding shares.

If it doesn't want to abide by the definition, it must refer to itself as a "non-diversified fund." The term "management company" includes both open-end and closed-end funds. From there, each could be either diversified or non-diversified, leaving us with the following four types of management company:

- Diversified Open-End Fund
- Non-Diversified Open-End Fund
- Diversified Closed-End Fund
- Non-Diversified Closed-End Fund

Because closed-end funds use leverage, the most aggressive type above is the non-diversified closed-end fund.

Types of Funds

There are many types of open- and closed-end funds. Let's start with the most aggressive type, equity.

Equity

The primary focus of **equity funds** is to invest in common stock. Within equity funds, we find different objectives. **Growth funds** invest in companies likely to grow their profits faster than competitors and/or the overall stock market. These stocks usually trade at high p/e and price-to-book ratios.

Value funds, on the other hand, seek companies trading for less than the portfolio managers determine they're truly worth. These funds buy stock in established companies currently out of favor with investors. Since the share price is depressed, value stocks tend to have high dividend yields. Value funds are considered more conservative than growth funds.

What if he can't make up his mind between a growth fund and a value fund? There are funds that blend both styles of investing, and the industry calls these **blend funds**. In other words, no matter how creative the portfolio managers might get, they end up being either a growth fund, a value fund, or a blend of both styles.

If an investor's objective is to receive income from equities, an **equity income fund** may be suitable. These funds buy stocks that provide dependable dividend income. Receiving dividends tends to reduce the volatility of an investment, so equity income funds are lower risk than growth funds. They may also invest in debt securities to keep the yield consistent.

What if the investor can't decide between a mutual fund family's growth funds and its income funds? Chances are, he will choose their "growth and income fund." A growth and income fund buys stocks in companies expected to grow their profits and in companies that pay dependable, respectable dividends. Since we've added the income component, growth and income funds have lower volatility than growth funds. Many allocate a percentage to fixed-income to assure a regular source of dividend distributions to the shareholders.

So, from highest to lowest volatility, we have growth, then growth & income, and then equity income funds.

Bond (Fixed-Income)

Stock is not for everyone. Even if an investor owns equity mutual funds, chances are he will put a percentage of his money into bond funds, as well. If the investor is not in a high tax bracket, we'll recommend taxable bond funds—corporate and U.S. Government bonds.

The investor's time horizon determines if she should purchase short-term, intermediate-term, or long-term bond funds. Her risk tolerance determines if she needs the safety of U.S. Treasury funds or is willing to reach for higher returns with high-yield funds. If the investor is in a taxable account and wants to earn interest exempt from federal income tax, her agent might put her into a tax-exempt bond fund, which purchases municipal bonds. If the investor is in a high-tax state such as Maryland, Virginia, or California, she might want the "Tax-Exempt Fund of Maryland," Virginia, or California. Now, the dividends she receives will be exempt from both federal and state income taxes.

Whichever tax-exempt fund she chooses, the next question is, "How much of a yield does she want, and how much risk can she withstand?" Her answers determine how long the average maturity of the fund, and whether to focus on high-yield or investment-grade bond funds.

Money Market

An investor's need for liquidity determines how much to place in **money market mutual funds**. There are both taxable and tax-exempt money market mutual funds. The **tax-exempt money market funds** buy short-term obligations of states, counties, cities, school districts, etc. They pay low rates of interest, but since it's tax-free, investors in high marginal tax brackets come out ahead.

The benefit of the money market mutual fund is its stable value. The money investors put here can be turned right back into the same amount of money without worrying, unlike the money in a bond or stock fund. Investors earn low returns but can often write checks against these accounts, which are treated like a sale of so-many shares times $1 each.

Another use for these funds is as a vehicle in which to sweep a brokerage customer's cash after a deposit, dividend, interest payment, or sale occurs. Money market mutual funds are a holding place for cash that is not ready to be either invested long-term or spent by the customer.

As the SEC explains, "Money market funds pay dividends that reflect prevailing short-term interest rates, are redeemable on demand, and, unlike other investment companies, seek to maintain a stable NAV, typically $1.00. This combination of principal stability, liquidity and payment of short-term yields has made money market funds popular cash management vehicles for both retail and institutional investors."

Some of these funds keep at least 99.5% of their portfolio in Treasury securities and are called government money market funds. The funds that hold municipal securities are tax-exempt money market funds. Those holding corporate debt securities are known as prime money market funds. These three types can be for retail or institutional investors.

Because of the financial crisis of 2008 the SEC wants to prevent future runs on money market funds during extraordinary situations. The problem is if funds artificially maintain an NAV of $1 when their portfolio may suddenly not be worth that amount, there is a first-mover advantage for investors to hurry up and pull out. To prevent this the SEC now requires institutional prime and tax-exempt money market mutual funds to value their NAV at the actual market value of the securities--called floating the NAV. This way, there is a natural disincentive to run for the exits and end up receiving only, say, 97 cents on the dollar.

Also, except for government money market funds, both retail and institutional prime and tax-exempt funds can impose both liquidity fees of up to 2% to discourage redemptions and even a temporary halt to redemptions if the situation is dire. If the board of directors for the fund decides the redemption gate is in the best interest of the shareholders, they can impose it for up to 10 business days. No more than one 10-day gate or halt could be imposed, however, in any 90-day period.

As with all funds, investors pay operating expenses in exchange for the benefits provided by the investment product. Money market funds do not charge sales charges, but typically impose a 12b-1 fee of .25% as well as management fees and transfer agent fees, etc.

So, while money market mutual funds are a safe and liquid investment, their liquidity is not as automatic and across the board as it once was, especially outside of government money market funds.

Specialty Funds

Specialty/specialized funds focus their approach to investing. Some funds specialize in an industry, some in geographic regions, some in writing covered calls, etc. Investors can buy the Latin America, the Europe, or the Pacific Rim fund. They would then hope those regions don't go into an economic slump or suffer a natural disaster. When the fund concentrates heavily in an industry or geographic region, it takes on more volatility.

Most equity funds hold stocks in many different industries. On the other hand, there are **sector funds** that do exactly as their name implies—focus on industry sectors. If we buy a "growth fund," so far, we have no idea which industries the "growth companies" compete in. On the other hand, if we buy the Communications Fund, the Financial Services Fund, or the Healthcare Fund, we know which industry space the companies operate in. Concentrating in just one sector is the definition of aggressive investing. Investment results are unpredictable year by year. So, make sure the investor has a long holding period and high risk tolerance before recommending sector funds in a test question.

There are **asset allocation** funds for conservative investors. Rather than maintaining one's own mix of, say, 20% large cap value, 20% small cap growth, 40% high-yield bond, and 20% short-term Treasuries and constantly having to rebalance, investors can invest in an asset allocation fund that matches their goals. A similar type of fund is called a **balanced fund.** Here, the portfolio is always balanced between stocks and bonds and generally diversified among types of each. There is not a set percentage for us to know here. Rather, the fund's prospectus would explain the parameters established by the board of directors.

A popular way to invest these days is through **age-based portfolios** or **lifecycle funds.** These funds shift the allocation from mostly-equity to mostly-fixed-income gradually as the investor gets closer and closer to his goal of retirement. Another name for these investments is **target funds.** If she plans to retire in or around 2050, for example, the individual would invest in the Target 2050 fund offered by a mutual fund family. The investments would be diversified, and that mix would become more conservative as we get closer and closer to the year 2050.

529 Savings Plans typically offer an age-based portfolio that is much more aggressive for kids 0-6 years old than those who are now 18 and in need of the funds. For example, the allocation for the youngsters might be 90% equity/10% fixed-income, while those 18 years old would be in a portfolio closer to 70% fixed-income/20% money market/10% equity.

Both international and **global funds** appeal to investors who want to participate in markets not  confined to the U.S. The difference between the two is that an **international fund** invests in companies located anywhere but the U.S., while a global fund would invest in companies located and doing business anywhere in the world, including the U.S. When investors move away from the U.S., they take on more political risk as well as currency exchange risk. For developed markets like Japan and Singapore, the political risk would be lower than in emerging markets such as Brazil and China. Both types of markets, however, would present currency exchange risk to U.S. investors.

Precious metals funds allow investors to speculate on the price of gold, silver, and copper, etc. by purchasing a portfolio usually of mining companies who extract these metals. Since a mine's costs are fixed, it only makes sense to open them for production when the price of what you're mining goes high enough to make it worth your while. Therefore, these funds typically hold stock in mining companies as opposed to holding precious metals themselves.

What if the investor does not believe portfolio managers are likely to beat an index such as the S&P 500 with their active management over the long-term? He can buy an **index fund** that tracks an index as opposed to a fund trying to trade individual stocks. An index is an artificially grouped basket of stocks. Why are there 30 stocks in the Dow Jones Industrial Average, and why are the 30 stocks that are in there in there?

Because the company who put the index together says so. Same for the S&P 500. S&P decided these 500 stocks make up an index, so there you have it. Investors buy index funds because there are no sales charges and low expenses. Since there's virtually no trading going on, the **management fees** should be—and typically are— low. So, for a no-brainer, low-cost option, investors can put their money into an index and expect to do about as well as that index.

Well-known indexes include the Dow Jones Industrial Average. The "Dow" is price-weighted, which means the stock price itself determines how much weighting the stock receives within the index. If a stock trades at $100, for example, its weighting is much higher than a stock trading at $11 per-share. The S&P 500, like most indexes, is market-cap-weighted. The share price of MSFT doesn't matter, but the fact that all their outstanding shares are worth, say, $200 billion means MSFT could be weighted 20 times more heavily than other stocks within the index. Because the S&P 500 contains such a large percentage of the major stocks trading on the secondary market, its movement is considered to represent the movement of the overall stock market. We mentioned this when looking at beta, which measures how much one stock moves compared to the overall market, as measured by the S&P 500.

Neither the Dow nor the S&P 500 cares whether the stock trades on the NYSE or NASDAQ. It's the size of the company and the market cap that matter here. And, all 30 stocks within the Dow Jones Industrial Average would also be included with the 500 stocks in the S&P 500.

The most famous "Dow" is the **Dow Jones Industrial Average** (DJIA). But, there is also the Dow Jones Transportation Average and the Dow Jones Utility Average. Together, these three make up the Dow Composite, which provides what the publishers of the indices call a "blue-chip microcosm of the U.S. stock market."

Another well-known market-cap-weighted index is the **NASDAQ 100.** This index represents the 100 largest non-financial company stocks, all trading on NASDAQ. Stocks such as Facebook, Google, Microsoft, and Amazon are found here.

A well-known small cap index is the **Russell 2,000.** There are also bond indices for bond investors who want to pay low management fees and engage in passive investing.

Open-end index funds are for long-term investors. If an investor wants to do as well as one of the indices above, this is where he goes. But, because it is an open-end fund, the shares must be redeemed, with everyone who redeems that day receiving the same NAV next calculated by the fund. In a few pages, we'll see that Exchange-Traded Funds (ETFs) are another low-cost way to match the performance of an index, only these shares are traded throughout the day just as shares of MSFT or IBM are traded throughout the day. For a small investment of money, the open-end index funds are more cost-effective because the ETFs charge commissions. An investment of $100 into an ETF would be a bad move, even if the commission were just $9. That is like a self-imposed 9% front-end load! But, for investments of several thousands of dollars, the ETF is at least as cost-effective as its open-end cousin.

Open-End Funds

Sales Charges vs. Expenses

Mutual funds are investment products, and it costs money to market these products to investors. To cover the costs of advertising and compensating sales people some open-end mutual funds charge **sales charges.** Unlike the ongoing operating expenses we'll look at, a sales charge is a one-time deduction taken out of an investor's investment into the fund.

Sales charges cover distribution expenses: printing and mailing sales literature, advertising the fund through magazines, radio, TV, and the internet, compensating sales people, etc.

If a mutual fund charges a maximum sales charge of 5.5%, that means when the investor cuts her check, 5.5% of it goes to the distributor and the broker-dealer who sold her the fund. Only the other 94.5% goes into the mutual fund for investment purposes.

So, if the **net asset value (NAV)** is $9.45 but the **public offering price (POP)** is $10.00, the extra 55 cents is the sales charge. How big is that sales charge? It is exactly 5.5% of the investor's $10 check. The sales charge as a percentage equals:

$$\text{(POP minus NAV) divided by the POP}$$

If we plug our numbers into that formula, we see that $10 minus $9.45 is 55 cents. 55 cents divided by the POP of $10 equals 5.5%. Another way to refer to POP is the gross amount invested. NAV can also be referred to as the net amount invested, what is left after the front-end sales charge is deducted.

The fund is made up of perhaps 500 different stocks and bonds, all trading throughout the day. At the end of each day the markets are open the fund recalculates the net asset value or NAV. Mutual funds use **forward pricing**, which means when a customer puts in a purchase or redemption order at 10 AM, she won't know how many shares she'll buy or how many dollars she'll receive yet. Only when the NAV is next calculated are purchase and redemption orders processed.

If a mutual fund company were to allow certain large investors to see what the NAV is at about 4 p.m. Eastern and then receive the previous day's NAV, this is a violation known as late trading. As the SEC website explains, "Late trading refers to the practice of placing orders to buy or redeem mutual fund shares after the time as of which a mutual fund has calculated its net asset value (NAV), usually as of the close of trading at 4:00 p.m. Eastern Time, but receiving the price based on the prior NAV already determined as of that day. Late trading violates the federal securities laws concerning the price at which mutual fund shares must be bought or redeemed and defrauds innocent investors in those mutual funds by giving to the late trader an advantage not available to other investors. In , the late trader obtains an advantage – at the expense of the other shareholders of the mutual fund – when he learns of market moving information and is able to purchase or redeem mutual fund shares at prices set before the market moving information was released."

The NAV is the value of one share of the portfolio. The assets of the portfolio equal the value of the securities plus any cash they've generated, minus any liabilities. Where did the liabilities come from? The fund might borrow to handle redemptions because they don't always want to sell stocks and bonds to pay investors who are redeeming.

If the fund has $10,000,000 in assets and $550,000 in liabilities, the net assets of the fund are $9,450,000. If there are 1 million shares, the NAV per-share is $9.45. Investors will receive $9.45 per-share if they redeem their A-shares today, but they'll pay a POP higher than that if they're buying. Buyers of the B-shares will pay $9.45, but those redeeming/selling their shares will receive $9.45 per-share minus whatever percentage they leave behind to the contingent deferred sales charge.

A-, B- and C-shares

An open-end mutual fund that adds sales charges can take the sales charge from investors either when they buy or when they sell their shares of the fund. A-shares charge a **front-end load** when the investor acquires them. B-shares charge a **back-end load** when the investor sells them. For a B-share, the investor pays the NAV, but will leave a percentage behind when she sells. The percentage usually starts to decline in the second year, and after several years (6 to 8), the back-end load goes away completely. At that point, the B-shares are converted to A-shares.

B-shares are associated with **contingent deferred sales charges**. As the name implies, the sales charge is deferred until the investor sells, and the amount of the load is contingent upon when the investor sells. If the NAV is $10, the investor receives the $10, minus the percentage the fund keeps on the back end. So, if she sells 100 shares and there is a 2% back-end sales charge, she gets $1,000 minus $20, or $980 out the door.

Since the back-end or deferred sales charge eventually goes away, as long as the investor isn't going to sell her shares for, say, seven years, she should purchase B-shares, right?

Well, not exactly. While sales charges cover distribution costs, such costs are also covered by a **12b-1 fee**. Yes, a 12b-1 fee also covers distribution costs. You've heard of **no-load funds**, but you may not have gotten the whole story. A no-load fund can charge a 12b-1 fee, as long as it doesn't exceed .25% of the fund's assets. Every quarter, when they take money out to cover expenses, these no-load funds can also take an amount not to exceed 25 basis points—one-quarter of 1%.

But, while 12b-1 fees are associated with no-load funds, loaded funds also charge 12b-1 fees.

So, again, should the investor buy the A-share or the B-share? The choice has to do with the 12b-1 fee. The A-shares for the growth fund might charge a load as high as 5.5% on the front end, but the 12b-1 fee will often be .25%, while the B-shares will charge a 12b-1 fee of, say, 1.00%.

That complicates things. While the person who bought the B-shares is waiting for that contingent deferred sales charge schedule to hit zero, he's paying an extra .75% every year in expenses in this example. .75% times seven years is an extra 5.25%.

And, this 12b-1 fee is a percentage. As an investor's assets are growing over time, that .75% is also taking more money from him, even if it's a flat percentage.

As we'll soon see, 5.5% would probably be the maximum sales charge on the A-shares. If the investor puts in more money, she can reduce the sales charge to 3 or even 2%, which is why long-term investors with a large amount of money should almost always buy the A-shares. In fact, investors with $1 million or more will find that funds with sales charges waive those charges for investments of that size. Does that hurt the salesperson? No, the agent wants and earns most of the 12b-1 fee. The bigger the account value, the higher that fee.

Then, there are also C-shares, which usually don't charge an upfront load but do carry a 1% 12b-1 fee. The level 1% 12b-1 fee is the reason these are referred to as **"level load."** The level load shares are intended for shorter-term investments only.

So, which type of share should an investor buy? As a general guideline:

- Long-term investor with $50,000+ to invest – A-shares
- Long-term investor with small amount to invest – B-shares
- Short-term investor with up to $500,000 to invest – C-shares

The difference in expenses between A-shares on one hand and B- and C-shares on the other has to do with the 12b-1 fee. However, the 12b-1 fee is just one expense. The fund also charges a management fee to cover the cost of the investment adviser serving as portfolio manager. That fee is the same for all investors across the board and must be a separate line item. Management fees are not covered by any other charge. Rather, they must be clearly disclosed.

Other expenses cover transfer agent, custodial, legal and accounting services involved with running the fund. To see what the dollar amounts are investors can check the **statement of additional information** or **SAI**. For example, according to the SAI for the American Balanced Fund, the investment adviser received $189 million managing the portfolio the previous year. The transfer agent, by comparison, received $74 million.

When we add the management fee, the 12b-1 fee, and the "other expenses" fee, we have the total operating expenses for the fund. Divide the total expenses by the assets of the fund, and we arrive at the fund's **expense ratio**. The expense ratio shows the administrative efficiency of the fund.

Both loaded and no-load open-end funds charge the following expenses, which are deducted from the fund's assets going forward:

- Management (investment advisory) fees
- Distribution fees
- Administrative service fees
- Transfer agent service fees
- Custodian fees
- Auditing and legal fees
- Shareholder reporting fees
- Registration statement and prospectus filing fees

Again, not all open-end funds have sales charges, but all open-end funds deduct operating expenses from portfolio income. Shareholders don't get a bill for the operating expenses, but whatever the fund takes out represents money that could have been paid to the shareholders in the form of dividends.

An open-end fund could be managed by an investment adviser, who then uses an outside distributor, transfer agent, etc. Management fees might be enough to interest the adviser to keep the fund open. At American Funds, on the other hand, the distributor, transfer agent, and investment adviser are all the same company. With over 50 different mutual funds all taking in fees from portfolio income it is not surprising this company has grown since 1931 to be one of the biggest players in the industry.

Reducing the Sales Charge

Although A-shares charge a front-end load, investors can reduce that sales charge by employing various methods laid out in the prospectus.

Breakpoints

Breakpoints are quantity discounts. If the investor invests $1,000, he pays a higher sales charge than if he invests $100,000. For mutual funds, investors are rewarded with breakpoints. Let's say the L&H Fund had the following sales charge schedule:

INVESTMENT	SALES CHARGE

INVESTMENT	SALES CHARGE
<$50,000	5.5%
$50,000 – $99,999	5.0%
$100,000 – $149,999	4.0%
$150,000 – $199,999	3.0%

That means an investor who buys $100,000 worth of the fund will pay a much lower sales charge than an investor who invests $20,000. In other words, less of her money will be deducted from her check when she invests. A breakpoint means at this point the fund will give the shareholder this break. A lower sales charge means an investor's money ends up buying more shares. For mutual funds, we don't pick the number of shares we want; we send in a certain amount of money and see how many shares our money buys us. With a lower sales charge, our money will buy more shares. Fractional shares are common. For example, $1,000 would buy 12.5 shares if the POP were $80.

Breakpoints are available to individuals, husbands & wives, parents & minor child in a custodial account, corporations, partnerships, etc. So, if the mom puts in $30,000 and also puts in $20,000 for her minor child's UGMA account, that's a $50,000 investment in terms of achieving a breakpoint. The child cannot be an adult; he must be a minor. Corporations and other businesses qualify for breakpoints. About the only people who don't qualify for breakpoints are investment clubs.

A securities agent can never encourage an investor to invest a lower amount of money to keep him from obtaining a lower sales charge offered at the next breakpoint. That's called **breakpoint selling** and is a violation of FINRA rules. Likewise, if an agent fails to point out to an investor that a few more dollars invested would qualify for a breakpoint, that's just as bad as actively encouraging him to stay below the next breakpoint.

If a front-end-loaded fund has a breakpoint at $50,000, the registered representative should inform any investor who has even close to $50,000 to invest about that breakpoint. If the customer in the question has, say, $46,000, the agent must inform him about the breakpoint available for just $4,000 more.

Letter of Intent
What if the investor didn't have the $100,000 needed to qualify for that breakpoint? He could write a **letter of intent** explaining to the mutual fund his intention to invest $100,000 in the fund over the next 13 months. Now, as he sends in new money, say, $5,000 at a time, the fund applies the lower 4% sales charge, as if he'd already invested the full amount. The lower sales charge means he ends up buying more shares, right?

So, guess what the fund does? It holds those extra shares in a safe place, just in case he fails to invest that $100,000 he intended to. If he doesn't live up to his letter of intent, no big deal. He just doesn't get those extra shares. In other words, the higher sales charge applies to the money invested.

Also, that letter of intent could be backdated up to 90 calendar days to cover a previous purchase. If an investor bought $3,000 of the L & H fund on March 10, he might decide in early June that he should write a letter of intent to invest $50,000 over 13 months. He could backdate the letter to March 10 to include the previous investment and would then have 13 months from that date to invest the remaining $47,000.

If a test question says one of your customers wants to invest today in a mutual fund with a front-end sales charge and is anticipating a large year-end bonus, make sure to inform the customer about the letter of intent (LOI) feature. That way he can approximate how much he'll be able to invest over the next 13 months and pay the lowest possible sales charge percentage.

Rights of Accumulation

If an investor's shares appreciate up to a breakpoint, the investor will receive a lower sales charge on additional purchases. In other words, when an investor is trying to reach a breakpoint, new money and account accumulation are counted the same way. So, if an investor's shares have appreciated to, say, $42,000 and the investor wanted to invest another $9,000, the entire purchase would qualify for the breakpoint that starts at $50,000. In other words, the $42,000 of value plus an additional $9,000 would take the investor past the $50,000 needed to qualify for the 5% sales charge.

This is known as **rights of accumulation**. It has nothing to do with a letter of intent. If you write a letter of intent to invest $100,000, you'll need to invest $100,000 of new dollars into the fund to get the breakpoint you're intending to get.

Rights of accumulation means you could save money on future purchases, based on the value of your account.

Combination Privilege

Most funds are part of a "family" of funds. Many of these fund families let investors combine a purchase in their Income Fund with, say, their Index or Growth Fund to figure a breakpoint. They call this a **combination privilege**. So, if the individual invests $20,000 in the Income Fund and $30,000 in the Growth Fund, that's considered a $50,000 investment in the family of funds, and that's the number they'd use to figure the breakpoint.

Conversion/Exchange Privilege

The fund might also offer a **conversion/exchange privilege**. This privilege allows investors to sell shares of, say, the L & H Growth Fund to buy shares of the L & H Income Fund at the NAV, rather than the higher POP. However, while buying the new shares on a net asset value basis is nice for the investor, the IRS considers the sale a taxable event. That means a capital gain or loss is realized on the date of the sale. An answer choice that mentions "deferring taxation until the new shares are sold," might sound logical but is also incorrect.

Structure and Operation

The following parties do not work for free. Who pays their expenses? The shareholders of the fund do, ultimately, as the following parties are paid through the deduction of operating expenses against the assets of the fund. The higher the expenses, the lower the dividend distributions to the shareholders of the fund, and vice versa.

Board of Directors

A mutual fund has a **board of directors** that oversees operations and policies of the fund or family of funds. The board's responsibilities include:

- establish investment policy
- select and oversee the investment adviser, transfer agent, custodian
- establish dividends and capital gains policy
- approve 12b-1 plans

As with a public company, the shareholders of the fund elect and re-elect the board members. Shareholders also vote their shares to approve the investment adviser's contract and 12b-1 fees. Independent board members have no other connection to the mutual fund sponsor or investment adviser, while the other board members either currently or recently had such a connection.

Investment Adviser

Each fund has an **investment adviser**, whose job is to manage the fund portfolio according to its stated objectives. For example, Capital Research and Management Company is the investment adviser for the American Funds. The board of directors sets the policies for investing, but it is Capital Research and Management making each purchase and sale for the portfolio.

Shareholders and the board vote to hire and retain investment advisers, who are paid a percentage of the fund's net assets. That's why they try so hard. The more valuable the fund, the more they get paid. Their fee is typically the largest expense to a mutual fund. Investment advisers must advise the fund (select the investments) in keeping with federal securities and tax law. They must also base their investment decisions on careful research of economic/financial trends.

Custodian

The fund also keeps its securities and cash under the control of a **custodian**. Keeping track of all the dividends received from common and preferred stock held in the portfolio, interest payments from the bonds and money market instruments owned by the fund, purchases and sales, etc., is a big job, and the custodian performs it. The custodian is responsible for the payable/receivable functions involved when the portfolio buys and sells securities. That means they release the money and receive the securities purchased, and they accept the money and deliver the securities sold by the portfolio manager. When a security in the portfolio pays a dividend, the custodian receives it.

Transfer Agent

The **transfer agent** is the party that issues new shares to buyers and cancels shares that sellers redeem. Most of these shares are electronic files (book entry), but it takes a lot of work to issue and redeem them. While the custodian receives dividends and interest payments from the portfolio securities, it is the transfer agent that distributes income to the investors in the fund. The transfer agent acts as a customer service rep for the fund and often sends out those semi-annual and annual reports that investors must receive. Investors can purchase and redeem shares directly with the transfer agent. The transfer agent also handles name changes when, for example, mutual fund shares are re-titled in the name of the estate for a now deceased investor.

So, if it concerns portfolio securities, that's the custodian. If it concerns shareholders of the fund, that's the transfer agent.

Distributor

Funds are sponsored by broker-dealers acting as underwriters, who bear the costs of distributing the fund up front and are then compensated by the sales charge that they either earn themselves or split with the broker-dealers who make the sales. Underwriters/distributors also prepare sales literature for the fund, since they're the ones who will be selling the shares, either directly to the public or through a network of broker-dealers. If a fund acts as its own distributor, it usually covers the distribution costs through a 12b-1 fee, as we mentioned. The fund can call itself "no load" if the 12b-1 fee does not exceed .25% of net assets. To call itself "100% no-load" the fund could have neither a sales charge nor a 12b-1 fee.

These are the methods of distribution for mutual fund shares:

- Fund/to underwriter/to dealer/to investor
- Fund/to underwriter/to investor
- Fund/to investor (no-load funds)

Closed-End Funds

The third type of investment company defined by the Investment Company Act of 1940 is the **management company**, under which we find both open-end funds and closed-end funds. So far, we've been talking mostly about the open-end funds. Let's say a few words on the closed-end variety at this point.

The main difference between the two is that open-end fund companies continually issue and redeem shares. When an agent finds an investor for an open-end fund, the fund issues new shares to the investor, which is why he had to sell them with a prospectus. Open-end funds don't do an IPO and then force shareholders to trade the fixed number of shares back and forth. Rather, they issue new shares every time someone wants to buy them, and they let shareholders sell back the shares when they are ready to redeem them.

On the other hand, closed-end funds issue shares just as any public company such as Facebook or Starbucks does. They do an initial offering, at which point there is a fixed number of outstanding shares. What if a shareholder wants to sell his closed-end fund this afternoon? He trades it the same way he trades any other share of stock. How much will he receive? Whatever a buyer is willing to pay. These things usually trade at a discount to their NAV, or at a premium. It just depends on the supply and demand for the shares, and since this is such a small part of the secondary market, the pricing is less than efficient.

And, since closed-end shares trade the same way GE or MSFT shares trade, investors can both purchase them on margin and sell them short. As we discuss elsewhere, "selling short" involves borrowing shares from a broker-dealer and selling them, with the obligation to buy them back and replace them later. If the price falls, you buy low after you already sold high. If the price rises, you're in trouble.

Another difference between open- and closed-end funds is that an investor would purchase, say, 100 shares of the closed-end fund and pay whatever that costs. For an open-end fund, he would cut a check for, say, $1,000, and see how many shares he ends up with next time they figure the NAV. In almost all cases, he will receive "full and fractional shares" with an open-end fund, which means that $100 would turn into 12.5 shares if the POP were $8.00. That little "point-5" of a share is the fractional share. For a closed-end fund, he would either buy 12 shares or 13 shares, not 12.5

Open-end funds only issue common stock to investors. Closed-end funds, on the other hand, issue preferred shares and use other forms of leverage, usually through bank borrowings or issuing auction rate preferred shares. These funds attempt to earn higher returns through such leverage, but the use of leverage also increases risk.

The investment objectives between an open-end and a closed-end fund could be the same. There are closed-end corporate bond funds, tax-exempt bond funds, aggressive growth funds, etc. Nuveen Investments (www.nuveen.com) is the largest issuer of closed-end municipal bond funds. Why would an investor want those versus the open-end variety? Well, what happens to yield when the price of the bond drops—it goes up, right? So, if he can buy someone's closed-end bond fund at a discount, he just goosed his yield a little bit. What about when he wants to sell his shares someday? Nobody knows.

The expenses for closed-end funds include:

- Management fees
- Interest expense on borrowings
- Shareholder servicing
- Custodial fees
- Trustee fees
- Professional fees
- Shareholder reporting expenses
- Stock exchange listing fees
- Investor relations expenses

Open-end funds would not have stock exchange listing fees, as their shares do not trade among investors on the secondary market.

Although it's true closed-end funds have a fixed number of shares, investors in the fund can reinvest their distributions into more shares. And, there are rights offerings for closed-end funds if the board of directors decides to do an additional offering of shares. The difference is with open-end funds new investors can buy shares created on-the-fly by the open-end investment company.

Unit Investment Trusts (UITs)

Management companies are one type of registered investment company. **Unit Investment Trusts** are another. The Investment Company Act of 1940 defines a Unit Investment Trust (UIT) as:

```
an investment company which (A) is organized under a trust
indenture, contract of custodianship or agency, or similar
instrument, (B) does not have a board of directors, and (C) issues
```

```
only redeemable securities, each of which represents an undivided
interest in a unit of specified securities; but does not include a
voting trust.
```

The main differences between management companies and UITs include the fact that UITs do not trade their portfolio, do not therefore have an investment adviser, and do not have a board of directors. A UIT is a "supervised, unmanaged investment company," because while the portfolio is supervised by a trustee, the securities in it are not traded by an investment adviser the way most management companies would actively manage their assets. Running the trust does involve fees for bookkeeping, trustee fees, administrative fees, etc., but—again—no management fees are charged. When the shares are purchased an upfront sales charge is often added, or a deferred sales charge is imposed when the unit holder redeems.

Like a closed-end fund, a finite number of shares are offered to investors on the primary market. But, unlike, a closed-end fund, unit investment trust interests are redeemable as opposed to having to be traded at prices based on supply and demand. Also, unlike both open- and closed-end funds, unit investment trusts have a termination date, which means they have a limited duration. On the termination date, everything is liquidated, unit holders are paid out, and that's that.

Face-Amount Certificates

The Investment Company Act of 1940 defines a **face-amount certificate** company as:

```
an investment company which is engaged or proposes to engage in
the business of issuing face-amount certificates of the
installment type, or which has been engaged in such business and
has any such certificate outstanding
```

Think of a face-amount certificate as a debt security in which the certificate is purchased at a discount and redeemed at a future date for the higher face amount. Or, if presented early, the investor will receive the "surrendered value" at that point in time.

ETFs

As its name implies, an **ETF** or **exchange-traded fund** is a fund that trades on an exchange, as opposed to being redeemed or sold back to the issuer.

An ETF is typically an index fund, so if an investor wants to do as well as an index, she can track that index by purchasing an exchange-traded fund (ETF). To track the S&P 500, she can buy the "Spider," which is so named because it is an "SPDR" or "Standard & Poor's Depository Receipt." Of course, we already saw she could do that with an S&P 500 open-end index fund. But, that is an open-end fund that must be redeemed. No matter what time of day, if we put in a redemption order, we all receive the same NAV at the next calculated price. So, if the S&P 500 drops 80 points in the morning and rises 150 points by mid-afternoon, there is no way for us to buy low and then sell high. ETFs facilitate "intra-day trading," which means you can buy and sell these things as many times as you want throughout the day.

Unlike the open-end versions, these ETFs can be bought on margin and can be sold short by investors who are "bearish" on the overall market or an index. If an investor is bearish on technology stocks overall, the answer might be for him to sell the QQQ short, as it represents the NASDAQ 100, the 100 hundred largest non-financial company stocks trading on NASDAQ. If he's right, he'll profit as those stocks drop in price. Or, an investor mostly in large cap stocks could hedge his risk by selling shares of the Dow ETF (Diamonds) short. This way if the index rises, his stocks make money, and if the index drops his short sale makes money.

So, are the ETFs cheaper than the open-end index fund versions?

Depends how you do it. For a small amount of money, the open-end mutual fund is a great option. For larger amounts of money, though, the ETF is typically cheaper, as the flat commission paid becomes a smaller and smaller percentage of the amount invested. In other words, if the commission is $10 either way, a purchase of $300 is a bad idea, while a purchase of $30,000 would make that $10 insignificant.

As with the open-end index funds, ETFs offer diversification. For a rather small amount of money, an investor can own a little piece of, say, 500 different stocks with the SPDR, or 100 stocks with the QQQ. It is also easy to implement asset allocation strategies with ETFs. An investor can find ETFs that track all kinds of different indexes (small cap, value, growth, blue chip, long-term bonds, etc.). If an investor wanted to be 80% long-term bonds and 20% small-cap stock, that goal could be achieved with just two low-cost ETFs. This point is not necessarily a comparison to the open-end index funds, which would offer the same advantage. Rather, it is a comparison to purchasing individual bonds or small cap stocks. To spread the risk among many bonds and small cap stocks, an investor would have to spend large sums of money. With an ETF (as with the open-end index funds) diversification can be achieved immediately with a much smaller investment.

An ETF such as the SPDR (SPY) or Mid-Cap SPDR (MDY) is appropriate for most investors with a time horizon and risk tolerance suitable for stock (equity) investing in general.

REITs

Investing in real estate has many advantages and disadvantages. The advantages are that property values often appreciate and that real estate provides diversification to a securities portfolio, since usually real estate and the stock market are not correlated. The disadvantages include the fact that real estate takes a lot of capital, and it isn't liquid. It often takes months or even years to get a property sold, or sold for a decent price. So, the lack of liquidity keeps many investors from buying real estate, especially commercial real estate (shopping malls, skyscrapers, factories, etc.).

This is where publicly traded **REITs** come in. **A Real Estate Investment Trust** (REIT) is a company that owns a portfolio of properties and sells units/shares to investors. Investors can buy into REITs that own apartment buildings, office buildings, shopping centers, hotels, convention centers, self-storage units, timber—you name it. This way they can participate in real estate without having to be wealthy, and they can sell their shares as easily as selling shares of other publicly traded stock.

The type of REIT just described is called an **Equity REIT**. A different type of REIT provides financing for real estate projects as opposed to just buying up and managing properties. These are called **Mortgage REITs,** and they provide financing as well as buy up mortgages and mortgage-backed securities. Some REITs do a little of both, and are called, fittingly, **Hybrid REITs.**

Private Funds

Investment company products are open to retail investors. Publicly traded REITs are also open to retail investors, who do not have to sign net worth and risk acknowledgment statements the way they do for privately held REITs and the real estate limited partnerships we'll look at in a few pages. Private funds—including hedge funds, venture capital funds, and private equity funds—are also open only to sophisticated investors due to their risky investment strategies and relative lack of liquidity.

Hedge Funds

In general, **hedge funds** are only open to institutions and to individuals called **accredited investors**. An accredited investor has over $1 million in liquid net worth or makes > $200,000 per year. If it's a married couple, the assets held jointly count toward that $1 million figure, or the annual income needs to be > $300,000. The equity in the investor's primary residence is not counted toward the net worth minimum—we're talking about $1 million of net worth that could be invested.

Why does the investor need to meet net worth or income requirements? Because these hedge funds often use high-risk trading strategies including short selling, currency bets, and high levels of leverage, etc. If you're an average Joe and JoAnne, it wouldn't make sense to let you risk all of your investment capital on such high-risk investing. On the other hand, if you're a wealthy individual or an institution, chances are your hedge fund investment is just a percentage of the capital you invest. So, if you lose $1 million, chances are you have several more million where that came from.

A typical arrangement for a hedge fund is to have a limited number of investors form a private investment partnership. The fund typically charges 2% of assets as a management fee and extracts the first 20% of all capital gains. Then, they start thinking about their investors (we hope). Once you buy, there's a good chance you will not be able to sell your investment for at least one year. Rather than trying to beat an index such as the DJIA, hedge funds generally go for "absolute positive investment performance"—usually 8% or so—regardless of what the overall market is doing. In other words, hedge funds are designed to profit in *any* market environment, while index funds only work when the overall market—or the section of it represented by the index—is having a good year.

Now, although a **non-accredited purchaser** cannot invest directly in a hedge fund, there are mutual funds called **funds of hedge funds**, which she can invest in. As the name implies, these mutual funds would have investments in several different hedge funds. In most cases, the investor would not be able to redeem her investment, since hedge funds are illiquid. Also, these investments would involve high expenses, since there would be the usual expenses of the mutual fund, on top of the high expenses of the hedge funds the mutual fund invests in.

Private Equity

Like a hedge fund, a **private equity fund** is structured as a limited partnership and is open only to sophisticated investors, as it is not liquid and generally takes on much greater risk than an open- or closed-end fund. As the name implies, private equity groups invest in securities not publicly traded. They often approach a company like Frank & Emma's Fruit Pies and cut a deal to buy all the common stock plus maybe a premium. After they appoint some better managers and board members, improve the profits at the acquired company, and get some good media buzz, maybe they then approach investment bankers to do an IPO so the owners can cash in as investors clamor for the stock. Private equity funds are typically set up for a period of time, maybe 10 years. After that, investors receive their money back from the general partner who set up the fund, plus—we hope—a profit.

The use of leverage is associated with private equity groups, whose acquisitions are often referred to as leveraged buyouts.

Venture Capital

Unlike private equity investors, **venture capital** firms typically focus on providing investments to early-stage companies, and rather than using leverage, VC firms typically use cash. Also, while private equity funds typically buy a company outright, venture capital funds typically make smaller investments in several companies in exchange for a minority stake.

 While private equity firms usually buy more mature companies, venture capitalists invest in earlier-stage companies. Because most companies will fail, venture capital funds invest smaller amounts in dozens of companies. The "VC" firms who invested early in companies such as Oracle, Microsoft, and Facebook realized mind boggling returns when those companies then offered shares to the public.

Uncovering the next grand-slam is the goal of a venture capitalist. Unfortunately, it's hard to see the future before it arrives.

Private equity investors buy a company they expect to make more efficient and profitable, with—they hope— little risk of failure over the near-term. These investors plan to install new management and run the company for a while themselves. Venture capital investors, on the other hand, know most of their investments will be losers; therefore, the returns are made on the handful of performers that survive and thrive. VC funds provide investment capital with a much more hands-off approach to running the companies in which they invest.

A private equity firm would purchase a company like the makers of Hostess snack cakes, fix it up, and then sell it. A venture capital firm would provide financing to an up-and-coming gluten-free snack cake maker who just did their first $1 million in revenue. And a hedge fund is more of a heavily traded portfolio of securities than a fund providing private investment capital to companies at various stages of their development.

Since mutual fund portfolios are open to retail investors, they can't focus on high-risk investment strategies. But, when the investors are all wealthy individuals and institutions, the regulators can relax a bit. Regulators, remember, provide necessary protection to investors, and sophisticated investors don't need so much protection to keep the playing field level. That's why such sophisticated investors can invest in the private funds we just looked at—private equity, venture capital, and hedge funds.

These investors can also invest in **direct participation programs**.

A C-corporation is taxed as a business entity, with the owners then getting taxed on any dividend income they distribute to themselves from the business's profits. C-corporations, in other words, lead to the double taxation of dividends for the owners.

On the other hand, in a direct participation program (**DPP**) the owners of the business take a share of the business entity's net income or net loss on their own personal income taxes. The partnership itself is not taxed. Rather, the partners are taxed on their share of the net income or net loss that flows through the business directly to them. Partnerships—like LLCs and S-corporations—are associated with **flow through** of net income/net loss to the owners.

Types of Programs

There are partnerships organized to perform all kinds of business, from movie making to sports teams, from construction projects to law firms. Broker-dealers often raise capital for their investment banking customers looking to form natural resource or real estate ventures through DPP offerings.

Oil & gas programs could involve exploring for natural resources, developing proven reserves, or buying an income/production program. **Exploratory programs** for oil and gas are the riskiest programs with the highest return potential as well. The act of exploring for oil is sometimes called "wildcatting," which provides a hint of the risk/reward nature.

Exploration generates **intangible drilling costs** or **IDCs.** As opposed to capitalized costs sunk into the

oil rig and other equipment, intangible drilling costs are the costs/expenses that leave nothing to be recovered. IDCs include labor costs and the expense of the geological survey indicating there is—or should be—oil or natural gas down below. The IDCs in these programs are so high in the first few years that this type of program typically provides the most tax shelter to the investor, especially in the early years. Beyond IDCs, drilling programs take depreciation expenses on any equipment owned, which also may provide tax shelter to the LPs.

Sometimes DPPs drill for oil or gas in an area where these natural resources are already being extracted, with engineering studies confirming the existence of oil or natural gas below the ground. Such programs are called **developmental programs**. They're less risky than exploratory programs, but with a lower return potential.

Some call these "step-out" programs, as if someone is starting at the existing well and stepping out so many paces before constructing another one. These programs also provide tax shelter through the intangible drilling costs we just looked at. And, there is depreciation on the expensive equipment if the partnership owns that equipment as opposed to leasing it.

The safest natural resources programs buy existing production and are called **income programs**. These investments provide immediate cash flow and are, therefore, the safest programs with the lowest potential reward. The main tax advantage offered from these programs comes in the form of **depletion**. When oil or natural gas is sold, the partnership takes a charge against their revenue. If the business entity owns the drilling equipment, depreciation may also provide tax shelter to the LPs.

In real estate, which is riskier, buying raw land or buying an apartment complex already filled with renters? **Raw land** is purely speculative and is, therefore, the riskiest type of real estate DPP. You buy parcels of land betting an airport or industrial park will be built in the next few years. If you're right, the land appreciates in value. If not, it doesn't. And, you receive no income or tax benefits on raw land as you sit waiting for its value to go up. There is nothing to deplete, and land does not depreciate the way apartment buildings and oil rigs do.

New construction programs are aggressive programs, but once the projects are completed the townhouses or condominiums can be sold for capital gains. So, they're safer than raw land and probably provide a lower reward potential. They also involve more costs, of course, as someone has to finance all that construction. For a construction program lasting several years, the LPs are likely to receive a share of net loss at the beginning, as the partnership sinks capital into building a townhouse community on the front end, hoping to sell enough units on the back end to turn a profit.

Existing properties DPPs are similar to income programs for oil. Here, the business is already up and running, with immediate cash flow. Investors can examine the financial statements and know what they're getting into, as opposed to an investment in raw land. Therefore, existing property DPPs offer lower risk and lower reward to investors. The tax shelter comes through depreciation of the buildings themselves as well as any maintenance equipment owned by the partnership.

Another common type of limited partnership is the **equipment leasing program**. These partnerships typically lease equipment that other companies do not want to own. For example, computers, transportation equipment, oil drilling and construction equipment, etc., might not be cost-effective for the users to own; therefore, it makes more sense to lease such equipment from an equipment leasing program. Tax benefits for equipment leasing would come largely through depreciation of the equipment.

Surprisingly, there is no requirement a "DPP" must be formed as a limited partnership. Here is how FINRA defines the term "direct participation program":

> *...a program which provides for flow-through tax consequences regardless of the structure of the legal entity or vehicle for distribution including, but not limited to, oil and gas programs, real estate programs, agricultural programs, cattle programs, condominium securities, Subchapter S corporate offerings and all other programs of a similar nature, regardless of the industry represented by the program, or any combination thereof.*

GPs and LPs

The owners who provide most of the capital to the business are the **limited partners (LPs)**. They are called "limited partners" because their liability is limited to their investment. If they invest $100,000, then $100,000 is all they can lose as passive investors in the partnership. Creditors can't come after the LPs for their personal assets if the business goes bankrupt. Lawsuits of all types could be filed against the partnership, but, again, the LPs would not have their personal assets at risk in such cases.

To maintain their limited liability status the limited partners need to stay out of day-to-day management of the business. Day-to-day management is left solely to the **general partner (GP)**. As manager, the GP can also be compensated for these managerial efforts through a salary. While the LPs provide most of the capital, the GP (general partner) must have at least a 1% financial interest in the partnership as well. The GP is granted the authority to acquire and sell property on behalf of the business and sign any documents on behalf of the business required to carry out its management. The GP must keep accurate books and records and must provide annual financial statements to the LPs. Typically, the GP can also admit new limited partners at his discretion.

Unlike an LP, the general partner has unlimited liability. That is why the GP is often a corporation, providing the individual controlling the business protection for his or her personal assets. The general partner is also a fiduciary to the limited partners. That means the GP must maintain a duty of loyalty and good faith to the investors trusting him to manage the business using their invested capital.

The GP's fiduciary responsibility to the limited partners means he must put the interests of the partnership ahead of his own interests or the interests of other businesses in which he is involved. The GP can't compete with the partnership through some other business venture and, therefore, can't charge some bogus "no compete" payment—since they can't compete in the first place. When the GP sells a building, piece of equipment, or the business itself, he/they must refrain from receiving economic gain at the expense of the limited partners. As with an investment adviser, if there are any conflicts of interest involved, these must be fully disclosed to the LPs.

On the other hand, the LPs have no such duty to refrain from owning businesses that compete with the partnership.

The GP could provide a loan to the business, but as a fiduciary to the LPs, he would have to disclose any conflicts of interest he might have. For example, if he's lending money to the partnership through a savings & loan institution that he controls or owns shares in, this potential conflict of interest that could end up clouding his judgment must be disclosed. On the one hand, he wants to help the business. On the other hand, he likes to help his own lending institution. That is an example of a conflict of interest an honest GP will consider and disclose to the LPs rather than waiting for them to sue for breach of fiduciary duty.

Limited partners stay out of day-to-day management decisions, but because of **partnership democracy** they do get to vote on major issues like suing the GP or dissolving the partnership. Why would they sue the GP? Maybe the oil & gas program turns out to be a scam in which the sponsor is using partners' money to fund other businesses or a high-rolling lifestyle.

If the exam asks if LPs can make loans to the partnership, the answer is yes. In other words, some of the capital LPs provide to the partnership can be through debt securities paying a reasonable rate of interest. If you're in business for yourself, you may have fronted some cash to your business and then had the business pay you a rate of interest on the "promissory note." Same idea here. Some partnerships might have investors providing capital in exchange for debt securities that later to convert to equity in the business. There are many ways to structure the financing of a DPP.

Documents

The General Partner is responsible for filing the **certificate of limited partnership** with the state where the entity is organized. This is a public document that provides only the most basic information, including the name and address of the partnership, the name and addresses of all the general partners as well as the registered agent who would accept any "service of process" should a lawsuit arise against the business. The GP signs and files this document with the state where the business is organized.

The **partnership agreement** is signed by all partners and is the foundation for the partnership. In this agreement, we would find the following information:

- business purpose of the partnership
- effective date and term of operation (if termination date or event is stated)
- required capital commitments now and in future for GP and LP
- name and address of GP
- principal place of business for the partnership
- powers and limitations of the GP's authority
- allocation of profits and losses
- distributions of cash
- transfer of interests
- withdrawal, removal of a partner

Corporations are presumed to go on for perpetuity. A partnership is also assumed to live on indefinitely unless the partnership agreement establishes a date or triggering event for dissolution of the entity. For example, a new construction program may dissolve when the last townhouse has been sold. Or, if the GP dies, the business may dissolve according to the stipulations in the agreement.

Structured Products

As opposed to buying common stock or bonds issued by, say, GE, structured products are created and sold by financial intermediaries with terms mutually agreed upon by both parties.

We have looked at both bonds and ETFs in earlier sections. An **ETN (Exchange Traded Note)** has characteristics of both a bond and an ETF. An ETN is a type of unsecured debt security issued by a financial institution, e.g., Barclays Capital. This type of debt security differs from other types of bonds and notes because ETN returns are based upon the performance of an underlying benchmark minus fees. The benchmark could be a market index, a foreign currency, or commodities. No coupon payments are distributed during the investor's holding period and no principal protections exist. The issuer is borrowing the investor's money for a certain time frame, paying it all back (we hope) with interest at maturity, with the rate of interest dependent on the performance of the benchmark.

At maturity, the issuer pays the investor a sum of money based on the performance of the benchmark, investor fees, and the calculation explained in the prospectus for the ETN. During the holding period, the value of the ETN fluctuates primarily based on two factors: the performance of the benchmark and the creditworthiness of the issuer. As with any bond, if the issuer's creditworthiness drops, so does the value of the security. ETNs can be traded on the secondary market, but, as with anything that can be traded on the secondary market, the price received could be less than what the investor paid. And, ETNs are generally not as liquid as stocks, bonds, and money market securities. The test might say ETNs are subject to market risk, credit risk, and liquidity risk.

While ETFs invest in securities that allow them to track the underlying benchmark, ETNs do not own what they are tracking.

OTC options are exotic options traded on the over-the-counter market, where participants can choose the characteristics of the options traded (offers flexibility).

HOLDRs are a financial product created by Merrill Lynch and traded daily on the American Stock Exchange that allows investors to buy and sell a basket of stocks in a sector, industry or other classification in a single transaction. The abbreviation stands for Holding Company Depository Receipt. There are currently 17 different HOLDRs currently trading on AMEX.

HOLDRs are often confused or lumped in with ETFs. As Think Advisor explains, "Essentially, a HOLDR is a static basket of stocks selected from an industry. As a result, HOLDRs do not track an underlying index like ETFs, and represent a rather narrow slice of an industry. Not only are HOLDRs completely unmanaged, their components almost never change. Furthermore, if a company is acquired and removed from a HOLDR, its stock is not replaced. This can result in even more concentration and added risk. In contrast, indexes that ETFs invest in can change and rebalance with some regularity, and generally contain more components. Such is the case with Barclay's 'iShares' and Vanguard's ETFs called 'VIPERs' (Vanguard Index Participation Equity Receipts), which collectively track Standard & Poor's and MSCI indexes." (http://www.thinkadvisor.com/2005/08/18/holdrs-vs-etfs-what-investors-should-know.

The term **leverage** sometimes refers to borrowed money but more generally refers to an investment promising higher returns on a percentage basis due to increased exposure to risk. For example, in a margin account the investor takes on the risk of borrowing money at a rate of interest, hoping to receive twice the returns he would have made on a percentage basis by being twice as exposed to the risks of the marketplace. With call options speculators can make much larger percentage gains than on the underlying stock and do so by putting down just a percentage of the stock's market price. On the other hand, options can lead to quick and painful losses when the speculator is on the wrong side of the market.

A leveraged ETF uses derivatives to increase the fund's exposure to the underlying index. Some funds are "2X," or exposed to the index in a way that will double the gains or losses. In other words, they are designed to go up or down 10% if the S&P 500 or other index goes up or down just 5%. Some funds are even "3X," designed to triple the exposure to the index and, therefore, triple the gains (or losses) to investors.

Leveraged funds are only for the short-term. In fact, the exposure is re-set each trading day and designed to capture the 2 or 3X returns for just that one day. The products are really designed for institutional and other sophisticated investors due to their complexity and amplified exposure to stock, bond, or commodities markets.

ETF shares can be sold short, as the shares trade throughout the day alongside shares of any public company you care to name. This allows investors to hedge their market risk by betting against the overall market with a percentage of their portfolio. If a trader thinks the S&P 500 will drop today, he can sell an ETF tracking the index short. If he's right, he'll make some money with that speculation, which will offset whatever he loses on his stock portfolio.

Inverse ETFs are designed to bet against an index, and most such funds do so at a 2 or 3X multiplier by using derivatives. This means a leveraged inverse ETF is designed to move in the opposite direction of the index by a factor of 2 or 3. A 2X leveraged inverse fund is designed to, for example, rise 10% if the index drops 5%. Another name for a leveraged inverse fund is an "ultra-short fund."

As tricky as an inverse and leveraged ETF might be, we would have to nominate the **viatical** or **life settlement** as the most alternative of all alternative investments. The investment vehicle is created when someone with a life insurance policy wants to receive most of the benefit right now while he's alive. If the policy has a $1 million death benefit, the viatical settlement would involve the buy-side purchasing the policy for more than its cash surrender value but at a discount to the $1 million death benefit. The third-party buyer then becomes the owner of the policy, paying any premiums due. Then, when the insured dies, the investor collects the full death benefit of $1 million.

But, wouldn't that imply that the sooner the insured dies the higher the investor's yield, and vice versa? Indeed. As we said—an extremely alternative approach to investing. A viatical settlement meets the definition of a security according to the state securities regulators. However, it is not liquid. If you purchase a viatical settlement, you may have to keep paying premiums, and you will only receive payment when the insured dies because there is no secondary market for these alternative investments. Unlike a bond investment, there is no annual return offered, and the actual return the investor receives is unpredictable since no one—except those relying on foul play—can accurately predict when someone is going to die.

The advantage is that this sort of investment would provide diversification to the investor. And, since death benefits are not taxable, the gain made upon payout is tax-free.

Mortgages are pooled and sold to investors through Ginnie Mae and Fannie Mae securities. Life settlements are sometimes pooled into "death bonds." Here, investors buy shares of a diversified pool of life insurance policies. As with an individual life settlement, the investors will profit based on how long premiums must be paid on the policies versus how soon the death benefits in the pool are paid out to investors.

Types and Characteristics of Derivative Securities

Derivative securities are contracts that derive their value from some other thing, known as the underlying instrument. Derivatives include warrants, options, futures, and forwards. The underlying instruments whose value drives the derivatives' value could be common stock or stock indexes, interest rates, or agricultural commodities such as corn and soy beans.

A **warrant** gives the holder the right to buy the issuer's common stock for a set price regardless of how high the stock price rises on the secondary market. There are no dividends attached to a warrant. If an investor owns a warrant, all he owns is the opportunity to purchase a company's stock at a pre-determined price. If a warrant lets him buy XYZ for $30 per-share as of some future date, he will benefit if the stock price rises above $30 by that date.

When issued, the exercise price stated on the warrant is above the current market price of the stock. It usually takes a long time for a stock's price to go above the price stated on the warrant, assuming that ever happens at all. But, they're good for a long time, typically somewhere between two and ten years.

Warrants are often included in a bond offering. As we saw earlier, corporations pay interest to borrow money through bonds. If they include warrants, they can "sweeten the deal" and offer investors a lower interest payment. Why would one investor take 4% when his buddy gets 6% on his bond? Doesn't the buddy make $60 a year, while the other investor only makes $40 per $1,000? Yes. But if the company's common stock rises, the buddy will be making $60 a year, while the other investor could make a profit on the common stock.

Warrants are issued by the company itself. Equity options, on the other hand, are created by options exchanges and are based on the price of various public company stocks. So, MSFT might issue warrants to certain investors, but a MSFT call or put option is not issued by Microsoft. It is issued by the options exchanges, with Microsoft's permission but not their participation.

Options

A guy steps into a tavern. He sits down at the last open stool and slaps a stack of twenties on the bar, just loud enough to get the bartender's attention. The bartender looks up from the pitcher of pale ale she's pouring.

"Just a second," she says, afraid to take her eyes off the thick head of foam forming at the top.

"No hurry," the guy says, although it's clear he's not in the mood to wait.

Bartender finally comes up and takes his order. Bourbon and Pepsi. Not Coke—Coke's for losers. He wants *Pepsi* with his bourbon, okay?

The bartender shrugs and mutters something as she mixes his drink.

Three guys sitting to his right take the bait.

"You don't like Coke, huh, buddy?" says the dark-haired guy in the wrinkled white shirt.

"Nope," the guy says. "Don't like the drink, don't like the stock."

"What, you're a trader?" the blond guy with big shoulders says, wiping foam from his mustache.

"Just a guy who says Coke is headed where it belongs—in the toilet."

The three friends laugh and mutter among themselves for a while, not quite within earshot of the big guy badmouthing Coca-Cola.

"That's a bold statement," the dark-haired guy says. "My dad drove a route for Coke twenty years by the way."

"Good for him," the guy says. "Used to be a decent company—that's history, though. I say Coke is a dog, and I'll bet anybody at this bar it won't go above twenty-five bucks a share the rest of the year."

He says the last part loud enough to get everyone's attention. Even the jukebox seems to quiet down at this point.

"Oh yeah?" someone shouts from a corner booth. "I'll take that bet."

"Me, too!" someone yells from over by the pool tables.

Pretty soon the guy has over a dozen happy hour customers standing in line to bet that Coca-Cola common stock will, without a doubt, rise above $25 a share at some point between today (March 1) and the rest of the year.

The guy breaks out a stack of cocktail napkins and on each one he writes the following:

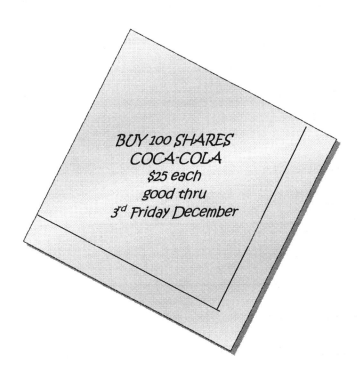

BUY 100 SHARES
COCA-COLA
$25 each
good thru
3rd Friday December

Anyone who thinks Coca-Cola common stock will rise above $25 a share has to pay $300. Guy ends up collecting $300 from 15 different customers, walking out with $4,500 in premiums.

What's his risk as he steps onto the rainy sidewalk outside?

Unlimited. See, no matter how high Coca-Cola common stock goes between today and the 3rd Friday of December, this guy would have to sell it to any holder of the cocktail napkin for $25 a share. Theoretically, his risk is unlimited, since there's no limit to how much he'd have to pay to get the stock.

What if the stock never makes it above $25 in the next 9 months? That's his best possible outcome. If it never makes it above $25, no one will ever call him to buy the stock for $25. In short, he'll walk away with the $4,500 in premiums, laughing at all the suckers at the bar who bet the wrong way.

What the guy sold at the bar was a Coca-Cola Dec 25 call @3. As the writer of that option, he granted any buyer willing to pay $300 the right to buy 100 shares of Coca-Cola common stock for $25 per-share anytime between today and the end of the contract. When would the person holding that option want to use or exercise it?

Only if Coca-Cola were worth more than $25 a share. In fact, since they each paid $3 a share for this right, Coca-Cola will have to rise above $28—their breakeven point—before it ever becomes worth the trouble of exercising the call.

Either way, the guy who wrote the calls gets the $4,500 in premiums. If Coke never makes it above $25, he'll never have to lift a finger. Just smile as the calls expire on the third Friday of December. We said derivatives are a zero-sum game. If an option expires, the seller realizes his maximum gain, while the buyer realizes his maximum loss. In this case, the buyers would lose a total of $4,500, and the seller would make/keep that amount.

Think of a call option as a bet between a buyer and a seller. The buyer says the price of something is going up. The seller disagrees. Rather than argue about it, they buy and sell call options.

The buyer pays the seller a **premium**. Because he pays some money, he gets the right to buy 100 shares of a stock for a set price within a stated time frame. If the buyer has the right to buy the stock, the seller has the obligation to sell the stock to the buyer at the already agreed upon price, if the buyer chooses to exercise that right.

Buyers have rights. Sellers have obligations.

The buyer pays a premium, and he receives the right to buy the underlying stock at a stated price. That price is known as the **strike price** or **exercise price**.

Calls

A "MSFT Aug 70" **call** gives the call buyer the right to buy MSFT common stock for $70 at any time up to the **expiration date** in August. If the stock goes up to $90 before expiration, the owner of the call could buy the stock for $70. If MSFT went up to $190, the call owner could buy it at the strike price of $70. So, you can probably see why call buyers make money when the underlying stock goes up in value.

Call buyers are betting the stock's market price will go above the strike price. That's why they're called "bulls." Bull = up. If you hold an Aug 70 call, that means you're "bullish" on the stock and would like to see the underlying stock go above 70. How far above?

As far as possible. The higher it goes, the more valuable your call becomes. Wouldn't you love to buy a stock priced at $190 for only $70?

That's what call buyers are hoping to do.

So, for a call, compare the strike price to the stock's market price. Whenever the underlying stock trades above the strike price of the call, the call is **in-the-money**. A MSFT Aug 70 call is in-the-money as soon as MSFT begins to trade above $70 a share. If MSFT were trading at $80 a share, the Aug 70 call is in-the-money by exactly $10.

Notice how we are not referring to a buyer or seller when we say a call is in-the-money. One problem with buying options is you might end up paying, say, $5 a share and even though the call does go in-the-money by $3 a share, you lose that difference. We'll talk about buyers' gains and losses in a minute. For now, understand that any time the market price is higher than the strike price, the call is in-the-money. Period.

The Premium

Option **premiums** represent the probability that a buyer could win. If the premium is cheap, it's a long shot. If the premium is expensive, things are probably already working in favor of the buyer with time left for things to get even better.

For example, if MSFT common stock now trades for $28 a share, the right to buy it next month for $40 is all but worthless, while the right to buy it for $30 has some chance of working out for the buyer and would, therefore, trade at a higher premium. The right to buy the stock for $30 through next month is also not worth as much as the right to buy it for $30 through the next three or four months, right? The premiums would show this is exactly right. For call options, the premiums rise as the strike prices drop, and as time goes out.

If today were St. Patrick's Day, a MSFT Mar 20 call is worth more than a MSFT Mar 25 call, but a MSFT May 20 call is worth more than both. Why? The right to buy MSFT for $20 is worth more than the right to pay $25, and the right to do so for two extra months is worth even more.

Exercise, Trade, Expire

Sometimes options are opened and closed; sometimes they are exercised; and sometimes they expire worthless. If the call goes in-the-money, the investor could choose to exercise it. That means he buys stock at the strike price and sells it immediately at the current market price.

The investor could also close his position by selling it. If he bought to open, he sells the option to close. If he sold to open, he buys the option back to close.

And, finally, the option could expire worthless. When that happens, the buyer loses all he paid, while the seller makes his maximum gain.

Puts

SELL!

100 Shares IXR @40

Thru 3rd Friday October

If we clipped the following coupon from the newspaper, what would it allow us to do?

That coupon represents an IXR Oct 40 put. As the holder/owner/buyer of this put we have the right to sell IXR stock for $40.

What if IXR is only worth $2?

Great! We get to sell the stock for $40 at any time before the end of trading on Friday, October 20, even if it's worth only two bucks on the open market. In fact, even if it's worth zero, we can sell it for the $40 strike price.

That's how a put works. A put buyer gets the right to sell IXR at the strike price before the contract expires. No matter how low IXR goes, the holder of an Oct 40 put has the right to sell 100 shares of IXR for $40 each before the end of trading on the third Friday of October.

Who buys puts? Investors who think a stock is about to drop in price. Bears.

Strange as it seems, as the stock price drops below the strike price, the value of the put goes up.

Think of it like this—if a stock is now at $20, wouldn't you like to sell it to someone for $40? If you were ready to exercise the put, you could buy the stock for $20, then immediately sell it to the put writer for $40. That would involve exercising the put. As we saw with calls, though, options investors don't always exercise their options, but, rather, close the positions for their intrinsic value. If they take in more than they spend, they end up with a profit. If they spend more than they take in, they don't.

For puts, intrinsic value is the amount of money a put's strike price is above the market price, which is another way of saying the market price has fallen below the strike price. An October 40 put has how much intrinsic value when the underlying stock trades at $20?

$20. Wouldn't you love to sell something worth only $20 for $40?

Talk about putting it to someone! The owner of a put profits when he can sell higher than the market price. He needs the stock price to go down, below the strike price. That's when he profits, when the stock is losing value.

If we buy stock, we are betting that its price is going up. If it goes down, we lose. If we sell a stock short, we are betting that the price is going down. If it goes up, we lose.

Maybe the problem with both strategies, then, is that the investor is betting all one way. What he could do, instead, is hedge his bet.

To **hedge** a stock position means to "bet the other way, too." The term "hedge" is based on the way people grow hedges to establish the boundaries around their property. In this case, the property is stock—with a hedge, the owner can establish the boundaries in terms of what he's willing to lose.

Let's say a stock in an investor's portfolio looks like it is about to drop. What should we tell him to do? Sell the stock? Yes, but that is a drastic measure, especially when it is also possible that the stock will rally, and we would hate to miss out if it did.

So, instead of taking a drastic measure, maybe the investor could buy an option that names a selling price for the stock. Which option gives an investor the right to sell stock at a particular price?

A put. So, if he thought one of his stocks might drop sharply, the investor could buy a put, giving him the right to sell the stock at the put's strike price, regardless of how low it goes.

It's like a homeowner's insurance policy. If you own a home, you buy insurance against fire. Doesn't mean you hope your house burns down, but, if it does burn down, you will be glad you paid the premium for the policy.

Buying puts against stock you own is a form of insurance. Insuring your downside, you might say.

A question might look like this:

Jimmy Joe purchases 100 shares of QSTX for $50 a share. Mr. Joe is bullish on QSTX for the long-term but is nervous about a possible downturn. To hedge his risk and get the best protection, which of the following strategies would you recommend?
A. sell a call
B. buy a call
C. sell a put
D. buy a put

If an investor buys stock, he is bullish, or betting the price will go up. To hedge, he'd have to take a bearish position, betting that the stock might go down. There are two "bearish" positions he can take to bet the other way or "hedge." He could sell a call, but if the test wanted you to recommend that strategy, the question would have said something about "increasing income" or "increasing yield."

And this one doesn't. This one gives you the key phrase:

> "...and get the best protection..."

Whenever you see the word "protection," remember that the investor has to BUY an option. If an investor is long stock, he would buy a put for protection.

So, Mr. Jimmy Joe paid for protection in the question. If he has a put, he has the right to sell his stock for a minimum price rather than seeing how far the price drops on the secondary market. On the other hand, the question might have looked like this:

Barbara Bean purchases 100 shares of QSTX for $50 a share. Barbara is bullish on QSTX for the long-term but is afraid it may trade sideways in the short-term. To hedge her risk and increase income, which of the following strategies would you recommend?
A. sell a call
B. buy a call
C. sell a put
D. buy a put

As we saw, we do not increase our income by buying a put. When we buy something, money comes out of our wallet. In this case, Barbara Bean must sell an option. What is the only bearish option she could sell?

A call. Call sellers are bearish. Or, bearish-neutral. If the stock goes "sideways," the call will expire in Barbara's favor.

Since Barbara already owns the stock, this would be a **covered call**. Let's say she bought the stock at $50, then writes a Sep 60 call at $3. If the stock goes up more than she expected, what would happen? This investor would be forced to honor her obligation to sell the stock at the strike price of $60. But, she only paid $50 for the stock, so she profits. And, she took in $3 for writing the call. So, she made $13, which represents her maximum gain.

Her maximum loss is much larger than the investor who bought the put in the preceding question. In this case the investor has not purchased a sale price for her stock. All she did was take in a premium of $3. That is the extent of her downside insurance. She paid $50 for the stock and took in $3 for the call. So, when the stock falls to $47 she has "broken even."

After that what's to prevent her from losing everything from that point down to zero? Nothing. So, $47-per-share is her maximum loss. This illustrates why buying puts is for protection of a long position, while selling covered calls is just a way to generate premiums if the investor feels the stock is likely to trade in a narrow range for the duration of the call options.

Since they sell something they eventually must buy back, short sellers hope the stock's price goes down. If an investor sells a stock short for $50, he hopes it will drop to maybe $1 or $2 a share. If the stock goes up instead, what is his risk?

Unlimited loss. Remember, he still has to buy this stock back, and he does not want to buy it back for more than he first sold it. Which option gives an investor the right to buy stock at the strike price?

Calls. So, if this investor wants protection, he buys a call. As with an insurance policy, he does not want to use the call, but it names the maximum price he must pay to repurchase the stock he sold short.

A test question could look like this:

An investor sells short 100 shares of ABC at $50. In order to protect against an increase in price, which of the following strategies would you recommend?

A. buy a put
B. sell a put
C. sell a call
D. buy a call

The answer is "D," buy a call. Again the word "protection" means the investor has to buy an option. If he is concerned about his purchase price, he buys a call, which gives him the right to purchase stock at a strike price. Maybe he's willing to risk having to repurchase the stock at $55 but not a penny higher. Therefore, he buys a Sep 55 call for $2. Using our T-chart, where would we plug in the numbers? If he sells the stock at $50, that's a credit to his account, so let's place $50 in the credit column. He paid $2 for the call, so that's "2" in the debit column.

Okay, where does this investor break even, then? $48. 50 in the credit column, 2 in the debit column, so 48 would make things even.

And if you prefer to analyze the position, start with step one—look at the stock position. He shorted the stock at $50, which means he wants it to go down. If he paid $2 for the option, doesn't the stock have to work his way by exactly $2 before he breaks even?

It does. So when the stock goes down to $48, this investor breaks even. Is there anything to prevent him from making everything from that point down to zero? No. So $48 is his maximum gain, too. Breakeven down to zero.

What about his maximum loss? Well, let's say disaster strikes. The stock skyrockets to $120 a share. Does he have to buy it back at that price in order to "cover his short"? No. At what price could he buy back the stock?

The strike price of $55. That was the protection he bought. And, if he exercised his call, his T-chart would show that $50 came in when he sold short, while $57 came out (when he bought the stock at $55 after buying the call at $2). That's a loss, but it's only a loss of $7, which isn't too bad considering how risky it is to sell a security short.

So if a short seller needs protection, he buys a call. It's the same thing as long stock–long a put, only upside down.

Now, let's look at the mirror image of the covered call. Say this same short seller wanted to hedge his bet while also increasing income. If he starts out bearish, he hedges with a bullish position. To increase income, he'll have to sell a position. Only bullish position he can sell is a put. So, he ends up short the stock and also short a put. In other words, he sells the stock short and also sells a put on that underlying stock. If the stock gets put to him, presumably he'll use those shares to cover his short stock position.

If he shorts the stock at $50 and sells a Jun 40 put @ 3, where would he break even? Well, short sellers want to see the stock go down. However, since he took in $3, he can let his stock position work against him by $3. This investor breaks even at $53.

Right? That's what selling an option does for a hedger; it offsets the potential loss by the amount of premium collected. And, your T-chart tells you that $50 came in when he sold the stock short, plus $3 that came in for selling the put. So, 53 is the breakeven point.

What's the most he can lose? Well, how high could the stock rise? Unlimited. Does he have the right to buy the stock back at a set price? No. So, his maximum loss is unlimited.

Like the covered call writer, he has also capped his "upside" or his maximum gain. His upside is down, remember. When the stock goes down to zero, does he get to buy it back at zero?

Not after writing that put option. The investor who bought the Jun 40 put is going to make him buy the stock for $40. Now the investor realizes his maximum gain. Sold the stock at $50, bought it back at $40. That's a gain of $10. He also took in $3 for writing the put. So, his maximum gain is $13. Stock price vs. Strike price + Premium.

Futures

The buyer of an options contract has the right to do something. On the other hand, a **futures contract** is a binding agreement between two parties that obligates the two sides to buy and sell something for a set price, with delivery occurring at a specified future date. In the world of commodities including corn, orange juice, and crude oil there is today's cash price—known as the spot price. And then, there is the futures price specifying what the commodity can be bought or sold for as of some future delivery date. Will the price of corn, orange juice or crude oil rise above or fall below that futures price by next December? That is why they open the markets for trading every day.

A grain farmer typically does not wait to harvest 1,000 acres of corn and soybeans in the fall and then see how much the cash or spot price might be at that point. With futures contracts the farmer can sell some corn and soybean futures to buyers who want to lock in a purchase price now for delivery, say, next November. The farmer, this way, can lock in a minimum price he'll receive for some of his corn and beans in case crop prices drop by the time he harvests them. And the buyers who need his corn and beans can lock in a maximum purchase price on what they need to buy in the near future.

Those who use futures to lock in purchase or sale prices related to their businesses are called hedgers. Those who use futures to bet on the near-term price movement of a commodity are called speculators. Common commodities traded include, corn, soybeans, crude oil, live cattle, sugar, and cocoa, to name just a few.

If a farmer is producing corn, and a cereal maker needs to buy corn, the farmer can sell some of his crop even before it's harvested, while the cereal maker can lock in a maximum price for corn set for delivery as of a certain month. In this case, the farmer producing the commodity is short, while the cereal producer is long in the futures contract.

Long positions profit when the price of the commodity rises, while short positions profit when the price of the commodity drops, just as they do with options and common stock. What the two sides are doing, then, is identifying their risk and betting that way. The cereal producer is hurt if the price of the commodities they need rises. Therefore, they bet that way and profit if their risk materializes. The farmer can't take the chance that all his grain will be sold at depressed prices in the future; therefore, he sells some contracts now representing what could end up being the highest price for delivery the market sees for years. In other words, he'll be glad he sold the corn at $12 a bushel back then if it ends up being worth only $3.50 on the spot market by the time it's harvested.

Futures contracts are standardized by the exchange where they trade. That means the quantity, the quality, and the delivery are all standard terms so the prices of the commodities traded mean the same thing to everyone in the market. For example, the quality specifications of each type of crude oil traded are standardized so "light sweet crude" is the same no matter who produces it. As of this writing, the standard terms of coffee futures involve 37,500 pounds of coffee per contract with expiration months in March, May, July, September, and December. Corn futures contracts cover 5,000 bushels each, expressed as a price per-bushel with a minimum "tick size" of ¼ of 1 cent per bushel.

Most options contracts that are near- or in-the-money are closed out before expiration because the buyer of a call option that goes in the money, for example, doesn't want to come up with the cash to buy the stock at the strike price any more than the seller wants to go buy the stock and deliver it.

With futures, all buyers and sellers need to reverse/offset their contracts before expiration to avoid making or accepting delivery of grain, live cattle, or light sweet crude, etc. With futures both sides are obligated to perform the contract if they're holding at expiration. Of course, speculators and hedgers go through brokers, who remind their customers with open long or short positions to close them out before expiration, just as my broker-dealer does for everyone trading options. Even if a retail investor forgot to liquidate a contract to buy 400,000 pounds of live hogs, he would not see a semi-truck pull up to his front door the next day. Rather, he would receive a receipt good for 400,000 pounds of live hogs. Even the hedgers typically liquidate their futures contracts rather than taking delivery of corn, soybeans, etc.

These days the underlying instrument for futures contracts is not just the raw materials/commodities used to produce other products. Stock indexes, interest rates, currencies, and other financially based instruments are used to create financial futures. For example, rather than trading S&P 500 index options, a speculator could trade the S&P 500 futures contracts, e.g., the E-Mini S&P and the E-Mini NASDAQ-100. Or, he could speculate on interest rate movements or foreign currency values. There are even contracts for emissions credits, weather, and bandwith available.

As with all derivatives, futures are a "zero-sum game," meaning if one side makes $30,000 it's because the other side lost $30,000. The contracts are also sometimes called "wasting assets," along with options. That is somewhat different from common stock, where one investor can earn dividends over time and sell the stock to someone else, who might end up doing the same before passing it on to another investor. Also, futures give traders leverage, putting them at risk without having to put down much of their own money initially.

Options, on the other hand, are paid in full. If you buy 3 ORCL Oct 40 calls @2, you must pay the full $600 upfront (3 times the $200 represented by the "@2").

Not so with futures. A futures contract is not something you buy or sell, really. Rather, both sides agree to the daily margin settlement that will occur as the price of the commodity moves day by day. The futures exchange requires both parties to put up an initial amount of cash, called either margin or a good faith deposit—usually between 5 and 15% of the contract value. Then, since the futures price will change daily, the difference in the strike price and the daily futures price is settled daily also.

On the other hand, if you buy those ORCL Oct 40 calls for $2 a share, you don't lose anything right now if they start trading for, say, $1 a share. I mean, it stinks, but until the contract expires, it's just a "paper loss" when you're trading options. However, with futures the exchange will pull money out of one party's margin account and put it into the other's so that each party has the appropriate daily loss or profit. If the margin account goes below a certain value, a margin call is made and the account owner must deposit more margin to keep the game going. This process of recalculating values daily is known as marking to market, just as it's called in a margin account for stocks and bonds.

When you buy an option, you can only lose what you pay. For example, no matter how far ORCL drops, you can only lose the $2-per-share premium. With a long futures position, however, you would continue to lose as the price of the commodity continues to drop.

As with options, the buyer would only pay the contract price—and the seller receive it—upon delivery. But, as with options, most futures contracts do not lead to delivery. Futures traders offset (reverse) their trades before settlement to avoid having to provide or accept delivery of the actual commodity itself. Maybe 1% of all contracts lead to delivery of the underlying commodity.

Forwards

A **forward** is like a futures contract in that it is a derivative that specifies a price for something for delivery at a specified future date. However, a forward is not traded on an exchange. Also, forward contracts are not standardized the way options and futures contracts are standardized by the exchanges on which they trade. On the options and futures exchanges, we find clearinghouses, which act as a buffer between every buyer and seller. I mean—how do you know for sure the other side can deliver 100,000 shares of ORCL or a million barrels of light sweet crude? You don't, but luckily the options and futures exchanges have all the buyers and sellers going through clearinghouses, which guarantee the performance of every contract, period.

So, forwards are side deals between two parties. How do you know the other side is good for the contract if there's no exchange enforcing margin requirements, settlement dates, and guaranteeing all contracts are good?

That's the counterparty risk that forwards present to both sides of the contract. On a regulated exchange, options and futures traders do not have to worry about the financial strength of the other side of the contract. The advantage of trading in forwards is the flexibility they allow both sides of the contract—the expiration date, the size of the contract, the terms of the contract, etc., are up to the two parties as opposed to the standardized contracts available on the commodity futures and options exchanges. Some companies have a specific need for a type of derivative that may not be offered on the options or futures exchanges. In that case, they may want to structure a private derivative contract with another party called a "forward."

INVESTMENT VEHICE	FEATURES	RISKS	TAX IMPLICATIONS	LOW/MED/HIGH RISK
Common stock	Claim on earnings/dividends Voting rights Pre-emptive rights Unlimited gain	Market Business Legislative	Dividends taxable Capital gains taxable	High
Preferred stock	Fixed-Income No voting rights No pre-emptive rights	Interest-rate risk Credit risk Reinvestment risk	Dividends taxable Capital gains taxable	Low-Med
ADRs	Common stock in foreign companies Purchased in US $s Traded on American markets	All risks of common stock PLUS, currency exchange risk	Dividends taxable Capital gains taxable Foreign Gov't could tax Investor receives credit for US taxes	High
REITs	Stock in operating real estate portfolio High dividend yields	All risks of common stock	Dividends are ordinary (not qualified) Capital gains taxable	High
Corporate Bonds	A loan to a corporation Receive interest-only, principal with	Interest rate Credit	Interest taxable as ordinary income all three levels Capital gains	Med

INVESTMENT VEHICE	FEATURES	RISKS	TAX IMPLICATIONS	LOW/MED/HIGH RISK
	last payment	Reinvestment Call Inflation	taxable	
Municipal Bonds	A loan to a state, city, school district, park district, etc. Tax-exempt interest	Interest rate Credit Reinvestment Call Inflation Legislative	Interest exempt at federal and (maybe) state level Capital gains taxable	Low-Med
Treasuries	A loan to the US Government Guaranteed interest, principal	No credit risk All *other* risks to bondholders	Interest taxable at federal level Capital gains taxable all levels	Low
Zero Coupons	Bought at discount, mature at par No reinvestment risk	Interest Rate Credit Inflation Liquidity	Tax on annual accretion	Depends on issuer
Money Market Securities	Short-term debt securities High liquidity	Purchasing Power Risk/Inflation Risk	Taxable all levels (unless T-Bills or Muni)	Low
Options	Derivatives based on stock, indexes,	Capital risk	Gains/losses generally short-	High

INVESTMENT VEHICE	FEATURES	RISKS	TAX IMPLICATIONS	LOW/MED/HIGH RISK
	currencies, etc.		term	
Non-qualified Variable Annuities	Insurance-and-Securities Product No limits on income or contributions	Risks to stock and bond investors, depending on subaccount choices	Tax-deferred earnings Earnings taxed as ordinary income No RMDs	Med-High depending on subaccount allocations
Fixed Annuities	Insurance Product No limits on income or contributions No RMDs	Purchasing Power Risk	Tax-deferred earnings Earnings taxed as ordinary income No RMDs	Low—obligation of insurance company
DPPs/Limited Partnerships	Tax Shelter Illiquid investments Net worth requirements	Depends on program Legislative risk (tax code) Liquidity	Tax Shelter if investor has passive income	High
Unit Investment Trusts	Portfolio of preferred stock or bonds Non-managed Redeemable	Interest rate Credit Reinvestment Call Inflation	Distributions taxed as bond interest or preferred stock dividends	Medium-High
Exchange Traded Funds (typically)	Trade-able Non-Managed	Depends on index	Tax-efficient	Depends on index

INVESTMENT VEHICE	FEATURES	RISKS	TAX IMPLICATIONS	LOW/MED/HIGH RISK
	Purchased on Margin Sold Short Low Expenses			
High-Yield/Junk Bonds	Credit quality of issuer in doubt High yields Capital Appreciation	All risks to bondholders Increased credit risk and volatility	Depends on issuer: corporate or municipal	Medium
Warrants	Right to buy issuer's stock at set price long-term Often attached to bond or preferred stock offering	Same risks as to holder of common stock Liquidity risk Time	Price-per-share added to cost basis when exercised to buy stock	High

Types of Risk

Saving money and investing money are not the same thing. In a savings account, the only risk is that your money will lose purchasing power. When you invest, on the other hand, you take the risk that you could lose your money. This is called **capital risk**. If you buy U.S. Treasury Bonds, you eliminate capital risk, but if you buy corporate bonds or common stock, you face the risk of losing some or all your invested capital. Investing in common stock presents significantly more capital risk than investing in corporate bonds, which is why the potential reward is also higher on common stock.

The prospectus for a growth fund typically declares that its investment goal is "growth of capital," and then goes on to say that "dividend income, if any, will be incidental to this goal." In other words, the fund invests in growth stocks, but some companies expected to grow will also pay dividends, and this fund does not mind cashing their checks. It's just that the dividends have nothing to do with the fund's reasons for investing in the stock. It's the growth or capital appreciation they're after.

The next section is called "important risks," such as:

```
Stock market risk, or the risk that the price of securities held
by the Fund will fall due to various conditions or circumstances
which may be unpredictable.
```

Market Risk

Market risk is a type of **systematic risk,** which means it affects securities across the board, as opposed to an **unsystematic risk,** which affects only particular stocks or bonds or industry sectors. Market risk is the risk that an investment will lose value due to an overall market decline. As the prospectus says, the circumstances may be unpredictable. For example, no one can predict the next war or credit crisis, but when events like that take place, they can have a devastating effect on the overall market.

Whether they panic because of war, weather, or whatever, the fact is when investors panic, stock prices plummet. We might think of stock market risk as the fact that even though the company might be doing well, the stock investment in that company could drop because the overall stock market panics.

Unfortunately, diversification does not help. If the overall market is going down, it doesn't matter how many different stocks we own; they're all going down. That's why we would have to bet against the overall market to protect against market risk. The S&P 500 index is generally used to represent the overall market; therefore, investors use options, futures, and Exchange-Traded Funds to bet that the overall market will drop.

Beta is a risk measurement of how volatile an individual stock is compared to the overall market. If MSFT has a beta of .8, it goes up and down only 80% as much as the overall market as measured by the S&P 500. If the S&P 500 rises 10%, MSFT goes up only 8%, and when the S&P 500 drops 10%, MSFT drops only 8%. If SBUX has a beta of 1.3, it is 30% more volatile than the overall market—or 1.3 times as volatile. If the S&P drops 4%, SBUX drops 5.2%, and so on.

A stock with a beta of 1 is in line with the overall market in terms of volatility. A stock with a beta of less than 1 is less volatile than the overall stock market. But, stocks in general are volatile, so that investment could scare off many investors.

Natural Event Risk

Natural event risk refers to the fact that a tsunami, earthquake, or hurricane could have a devastating effect on a country's economy, and possibly the economy of an entire area such as Europe or Southeast Asia.

Unfortunately, natural event risk does not fit neatly in the systematic or unsystematic risk category. While a tsunami would have a negative impact on markets overall, there are many weather-related events that hit certain sectors or issuers only, making it an unsystematic risk. For example, food and energy producers are affected by weather events that might not impact other industries. A Florida frost impacts orange juice, unlike a tsunami, which impacts entire regions of the globe.

And, there are some industries that do better after natural disasters such as a flood or hurricane: mold remediation, construction, disaster recovery, etc.

Interest Rate Risk

Interest rate risk is the risk that rates will rise, pushing down the market prices of bonds. The longer the term on the bond, the more volatile its price, too. When rates go up, all bond prices fall, but the long-term bonds suffer the most. And, when rates go down, all bond prices rise, but the long-term bonds go up the most.

So, a 30-year government bond has no default risk, but carries more interest rate risk than a 10-year corporate bond. The reason we see short-term and intermediate-term bond funds is because many investors want to reduce interest rate risk. Maybe they have a shorter time horizon and will need this money in just a few years—they can't risk a big drop in market value due to a sudden rise in interest rates. They will probably sacrifice the higher yield offered by a long-term bond fund, but they will sleep better knowing that rising rates won't be as devastating to short-term bonds.

In a bond fund prospectus, we see that the important risks include:

```
Risk that the value of the securities the Fund holds will fall as
a result of changes in interest rates.
```

Interest rate risk. Rates up, price down—and it's more severe the longer the term to maturity.

Purchasing Power Risk

Purchasing power risk is sometimes called **inflation risk** and even constant dollar risk. If inflation erodes the purchasing power of money, an investor's fixed return can't buy what it used to. Fixed-income investments carry purchasing power or inflation risk, which is why investors often try to beat inflation by investing in common stock. The ride might be a wild one in the stock market, but the reward is that we should be able to grow faster than the rate of inflation, whereas a fixed-income payment is fixed. Retirees living solely on fixed incomes are more susceptible to inflation or purchasing power risk than people in the workforce, since salaries tend to rise with inflation. The longer the retiree has to live on a fixed income, the more susceptible she is to inflation risk.

Unfortunately, common stock is often too volatile for investors with shorter time horizons and high needs for liquidity. The solution is often to put the majority of a retiree's money into short-term bonds and money market instruments with a small percentage in large-cap stock, equity income, or growth & income funds. That way, the dependable income from the short-term debt securities will cover the living expenses, while the smaller piece devoted to conservative stock investments will likely provide some protection of purchasing power. Not to mention that blue chip stocks almost by definition pay dividends, and dividends tend to increase over time. So, putting a reasonable percentage of a retiree's money into blue chip stocks is not necessarily risky, as might have been thought in the past.

Call Risk

A bond fund prospectus typically warns of **call risk**, or "the risk that a bond might be called during a period of declining interest rates." Most municipal and corporate bonds are **callable**, meaning that when interest rates drop, corporate and municipal bond issuers will borrow new money at today's lower rate and use it to pay off the current bondholders much sooner than they expected.

The problems for the current bondholders are that, first, the bond price stops rising in the secondary market once everyone knows the exact call price to be received. And, second, what do they do with the money they just received from the issuer? Reinvest it, right? And, where are interest rates now? Down—so they probably take the proceeds from a 9% bond and turn it into a 6% payment going forward. That means on a million dollars of principal they used to get $90,000 per year; now they can look forward to just $60,000 in interest income. Couldn't we protect ourselves by buying non-callable bonds? Sure, but they'll offer lower rates than what they pay on callable bonds. As they say, there is no free lunch.

Prepayment and Extension Risk

Prepayment risk is the form of call risk that comes with owning a mortgage-backed security. A homeowner with a mortgage will typically take advantage of a sudden drop in interest rates by refinancing. Therefore, if an investor holds **mortgage-backed securities** like those issued or guaranteed by GNMA, FNMA, or FHLMC (Ginnie, Fannie, Freddie), that investor will take a hit if interest rates drop suddenly and all the principal is returned sooner than expected. This is called **prepayment risk.**

When the investor receives the principal sooner than expected, she typically ends up reinvesting it into similar mortgage-backed securities and receiving a lower rate of interest going forward, while the homeowners in the pool of mortgages, on the other hand, are enjoying paying lower interest rates going forward.

On the other hand, if interest rates rise, homeowners will take longer than expected to pay off the mortgages. This scenario is called **extension risk.** Notice that most debt securities have stated maturities, while an investment in most mortgage-backed securities comes with an estimate only. Sort of like bonds without maturity dates.

Since GNMA (Ginnie Mae) securities are guaranteed by the U.S. Treasury, their main risk is prepayment—or extension—risk. An investment in FNMA or FHLMC securities have that plus credit/default risk.

Reinvestment Risk

If bond investors don't spend the interest payments to meet living expenses, they reinvest them into new bonds. What kind of yields will debt securities offer when they reinvest the coupon payments? No one knows, which is why it's a risk, called **reinvestment risk**. It's frustrating to take a 6% interest payment and reinvest it at 3%, but it does happen. To avoid reinvestment risk, some investors buy a debt security that pays nothing to reinvest along the way: zero coupons, i.e., Treasury STRIPS. A zero-coupon bond returns a higher principal amount to the investor rather than paying any regular interest over the term to maturity.

Even though bond investing is less risky than stock investing, notice how bondholders can get hurt many ways. If it's a corporate bond, they could end up with a default. Whether it's a corporate, municipal, or a U.S. Treasury bond, when rates go up, the price of the bond drops. If rates go down, callable bonds are called, and the party's over, and with non-callable bonds they must reinvest the interest checks every six months at a lower rate going forward. And, even if none of the above happens, inflation could inch its way up, making the coupon payments less valuable.

Political Risk

Political risk is part of the package with investments into **emerging markets**. An emerging market is a country or region where the financial markets are immature and unpredictable. They're not fully developed, a little awkward, a bit volatile, basically like teenagers—bright future, but some days you really aren't sure if they're going to make it. If you own stocks and bonds in companies operating and trading in undeveloped economies, what happens if the Chinese government gets tired of capitalism and seizes the companies whose shares you used to own? Total loss. Or maybe the transition from communism to "capitalism" doesn't go so well, and suddenly the whole country is shut down with riots in the streets and government tanks rolling in. When this type of thing happens, emerging market investments are affected.

Investing in emerging markets is high-risk, but it also protects U.S. investors against a down year for the domestic stock market. Even if the S&P 500 drops, companies in Brazil or China may do well and take their related stock markets up with them.

Currency Exchange Risk

Since most countries use a different currency from the American dollar, **currency exchange risk** is also part of the package when investing in foreign markets, emerging or otherwise. The value of the American dollar relative to foreign currencies, then, is a risk to both international and emerging markets investors. So, even if it's a **developed market**, such as Japan, if we are investing internationally into Japanese stocks, the value of the yen versus the dollar presents foreign exchange or currency risk. If we are investing in China, we have that risk, plus the political risk of investing in companies operating in an immature capitalist system likely to suffer many setbacks before all the kinks are worked out.

Unsystematic Risk

While diversification does not reduce systematic risk, it does reduce the unsystematic risks we will look at next. Un-systematic risk relates to an issuer or industry space, as opposed to the overall market. The risk that regulators will increase regulations on the automobile industry is not system-wide, affecting only a few issuers and industries. Diversifying a portfolio reduces these more specific risks by spreading them out among stocks of different issuers operating in different industry sectors.

Or, a municipal bond investor might diversify her holdings geographically to avoid the risk that an area of the country could be hit by a weather event or an economic slump. Although municipal bond investors generally seek safety, they can also enhance their yield by purchasing some lower-rated municipal bonds with some percentage of the account assets. After all, even conservative bond funds frequently put 20% or so in so-called "junk" bonds issued by corporations or municipalities.

Municipal bonds come in many flavors, also, so investors might purchase bonds used for many different purposes—some general obligation and some revenue—to avoid being too dependent on just toll roads, for example, or airport revenues. While an individual bond investor could use a registered representative to put together a diversified portfolio, more likely the registered representative would find a mutual fund portfolio already designed to achieve what the investor is looking for.

Buying stock in any company presents **business risk**. Business risk includes the risk of competition, a labor strike, the release of inferior products, and the risk of **obsolescence**, which is the risk that a company's offerings suddenly become a thing of the past, or obsolete. Shareholders in companies producing telegraph equipment, typewriters, and 8-track players all felt the sting of obsolescence risk. Nowadays, investing in a newspaper carries more risk of obsolescence than investing in a company that manufactures underwear. The risk of poor management, of better competitors, or of products becoming obsolete are all part of business risk.

In other words, the stock we own is only as solid as the businesses who issued it. So, we also need to diversify the portfolio so that it's not all subject to the same type of business risk. Airlines, retailers, and financial services companies, for example, would face different business risks. And, this shows how inherently risky stock investing is. Investors can get hurt by the individual companies they invest in, as well as the fact that the stock market overall can drop in value, whether the individual companies do well or not.

Legislative or Regulatory Risk

Legislative or **regulatory risk** means that if industry regulations or the tax code changes, certain securities could be negatively affected. If the federal government announced that all car makers must get 35 mpg for their large SUVs and pickup trucks by the following year, this would probably depress the value of certain stocks and bonds issued by companies including Ford and GM. Or, what if an investor bought a portfolio of tax-exempt municipal bonds, and then Congress decided to eliminate the exemption for municipal bond interest? Most likely, investors would dump their municipal bonds, forcing the market prices down.

Different industries are subject to different regulatory risks, so diversification can protect the investor from legislative risk somewhat. For this reason, mutual funds focusing on just one industry sector are riskier than the typical fund that is broadly diversified.

And, not all industries are harmed by increased regulations. For example, when legislation such as Dodd-Frank and the American Healthcare Affordability Act is passed, the need for consultants who can guide companies through the changes increases. When the tax code becomes more complex, CPAs and other tax-planning or tax-law professionals typically have more work to do, possibly at higher rates.

Credit/Default Risk

Credit risk is the risk that the issuer of a bond will be unable to pay interest or return principal to the bondholders. U.S. Treasury securities have little or no default risk, but some municipal securities and most corporate bonds carry default/credit risk to some degree. Even if the issuer never misses a payment, if S&P and Moody's downgrade their credit score, the market value of the bonds would also drop.

The terms credit risk and default risk are typically used interchangeably.

Liquidity Risk

Liquidity is the ability to quickly turn an investment into cash without having to sell at a loss. Government securities are more liquid than municipal securities, and listed stocks more liquid than those trading in the non-Nasdaq OTC market. So, thinly traded securities have **liquidity risk** compared to securities with more active secondary markets. Insurance companies invest their net premiums in liquid, investment-grade bonds because they often have to liquidate their portfolio to pay claims after, say, a hurricane or flood. If they had to find buyers for illiquid junk bonds or real estate holdings, they would likely end up selling at unfavorable prices.

Opportunity Cost

If we pass up an investment opportunity to make 5%, our **opportunity cost** is 5%, and we need to do better than 5% with the opportunity we choose instead. If we could have made 5% and end up making 7% with another investment, we made 2% better than your opportunity cost.

INVESTMENT RISK	SIGNIFICANCE	NOTES	
Systematic	Affect the overall market	"Non-diversifiable"	Diversification won't help; investor must "hedge"
Un-systematic	Affect stocks only	Diversifiable	Buy many stocks in many industries
Market	Markets panic due to war, weather events, etc.	Measured by Beta	Hedge with options, futures, ETFs, etc.
Business	How strong is the issuer?	Competition, obsolescence	Diversify your holdings
Political	Emerging markets, e.g., China, Vietnam	Unstable political-economic systems	Don't confuse with "legislative risk"
Legislative/ Regulatory	Changes to laws/regulations	Tax code changes EPA requirements, OSHA mandates	Could have negative effect on stock or bond price
Currency	Value of dollar	ADRs, international and global investing	Weak dollar makes ADR more valuable
Interest Rate	Rates up/Market price down	Long-term bonds most susceptible, measured by "duration"	Preferred stock is rate-sensitive, too
Credit, Default	Issuer could fail	Downgrade in credit rating lowers value of bond	Low bond values = high-yield
Purchasing Power	Inflation erodes buying	Fixed-income presents	Live and die by the CPI

INVESTMENT RISK	SIGNIFICANCE	NOTES	
	power	purchasing power risk	
Reinvestment Risk	Investing at varying rates of interest	If rates down, investor goes forward at lower rate	Zero-coupons avoid this risk
Liquidity Risk	Trying to sell when there are few or no buyers	Esoteric securities, partnerships, hedge fund investments are illiquid	Thinly traded stocks less liquid
Opportunity Cost	What you give up to invest elsewhere	If you give up a 5% T-Bond investment, 5% is your opportunity cost	Try to do better than 5%

Chapter 2 Review Exercises

DIRECTIONS: underline the word or phrase that completes each statement

1. Purchase payments are invested in the (general/separate) account within an equity indexed annuity.

2. Purchase payments are invested in the (general/separate) account within a variable annuity.

3. The percentage of the underlying index's increase credited each year to the equity indexed annuity contract is known as the (participation rate/annual cap).

4. Individuals concerned about protecting purchasing power typically choose to invest in (variable/equity indexed) annuities.

5. An individual purchases a non-qualified variable annuity with a single payment of $50,000. Five years later, with the contract worth just $41,000, the individual dies. Therefore, his beneficiary will receive ($41,000/$50,000).

6. Typically, the largest monthly check is received when the annuitant chooses the settlement option known as (life with period certain/straight life).

7. Of these two money market securities, (commercial paper/bankers' acceptances) are backed by collateral.

8. Of these two money market securities, (commercial paper/negotiable CDs) is/are issued at a discount to face value.

9. Assuming both mature in 10 years, the same issuing corporation's (debentures/subordinated debentures) would offer a higher nominal yield to investors.

10. Newly-issued (Treasury Notes/Treasury Bonds) mature in 30 years.

11. Generally, (general obligation/revenue) bonds offer higher nominal yields to investors.

12. Another name for a "self-supporting" municipal bond is a (general obligation/revenue) bond.

13. Owners of ABC common stock have the right to vote before the ABC Board of Directors declares a (stock split/cash dividend).

14. Large shareholders of a corporation prefer that the method of voting used at the annual and special meetings is the (cumulative/statutory) method.

15. To prevent dilution of shareholder equity, companies issue (rights/warrants) to owners of their common stock.

16. On the ex-dividend date, the market price for the common stock (rises/decreases) by the amount of the cash dividend to be paid.

17. An American investor holding an ADR position benefits when the American dollar (strengthens/weakens) relative to the currency used in the issuer's home country.

18. The only type of preferred stock that pays higher dividends when dividends are raised for the common stock is (participating/adjustable) preferred stock.

19. The only type of preferred stock whose market price is tied to the market price of the issuer's common stock is (participating/convertible) preferred stock.

20. A management company that adheres to the limits imposed by the 75/5/10 rule is known as a (diversified/non-diversified) fund.

21. A (growth/value) fund is typically associated with higher dividend yields.

22. An (international/global) fund invests in companies located anywhere but the U.S., while an (international/global) fund would invest in companies located and doing business anywhere in the world, including the U.S.

23. Precious metals mutual funds tend to invest in (bullion/shares of mining companies).

24. All open-end funds impose (sales charges/operating expense fees), but not all open-end funds impose (sales charges/operating expense fees).

25. To see the dollar amount paid by a mutual fund to the investment adviser of the fund, investors should consult the (prospectus/Statement of Additional Information).

26. The ABC Equity Income Fund holds a substantial position in XYZ common stock. When XYZ pays a dividend, the (custodian/transfer agent) for the ABC Equity Income Fund receives the funds.

27. When the ABC Equity Income Fund distributes a dividend to shareholders, it is the (custodian/transfer agent) who disburses funds to the shareholders.

28. The use of leverage is common among (closed-end/open-end) funds.

29. An investment company associated with no investment adviser and board of directors is a/an (Unit Investment Trust/closed-end management company).

30. Of these two investment vehicles, (Exchange Traded Funds/money market mutual funds) typically have lower operating expenses.

31. (Venture capital/private equity) funds typically invest in early-stage companies, while (venture capital/private equity) funds typically invest in established companies.

32. Although many direct participation programs provide tax shelter to the limited partners, (raw land/oil exploration) programs do not.

33. A warrant, often issued in conjunction with a bond offering, is a (short-term/long-term) derivative allowing the holder to buy common stock at a stated price that is (above/below) the stock's market price at the time of issuance.

34. An example of a bullish options investor is one who (buys calls/sells calls), while an example of a bearish investor is one who (buys puts/sells puts).

35. The seller of a put option is neutral and (bearish/bullish), while the seller of a call option is neutral and (bearish/bullish).

36. An example of a systematic risk is (business/market) risk.

37. An example of an unsystematic risk is (legislative/inflation) risk.

38. The risk that government regulations will have a negative effect on an issuer's stock is known as (legislative/political) risk.

39. Interest rate risk is the risk that after purchasing a bond, interest rates in general will (rise/fall), while call and reinvestment risk involve interest rates in general (rising/falling).

40. The main risk of buying a T-bond and holding to maturity is (interest rate/purchasing power) risk.

Answers

1. Purchase payments are invested in the (<u>general</u>/separate) account within an equity indexed annuity.
2. Purchase payments are invested in the (general/<u>separate</u>) account within a variable annuity.
3. The percentage of the underlying index's increase credited each year to the equity indexed annuity contract is known as the (<u>participation rate</u>/annual cap).
4. Individuals concerned about protecting purchasing power typically choose to invest in (<u>variable</u>/equity indexed) annuities.
5. An individual purchases a non-qualified variable annuity with a single payment of $50,000. Five years later, with the contract worth just $41,000, the individual dies. Therefore, his beneficiary will receive ($41,000/<u>$50,000</u>).
6. Typically, the largest monthly check is received when the annuitant chooses the settlement option known as (life with period certain/<u>straight life</u>).
7. Of these two money market securities, (commercial paper/<u>bankers' acceptances</u>) are backed by collateral.
8. Of these two money market securities, (<u>commercial paper</u>/negotiable CDs) is/are issued at a discount to face value.
9. Assuming both mature in 10 years, the same issuing corporation's (debentures/<u>subordinated debentures</u>) would offer a higher nominal yield to investors.
10. Newly-issued (Treasury Notes/<u>Treasury Bonds</u>) mature in 30 years.
11. Generally, (general obligation/<u>revenue</u>) bonds offer higher nominal yields to investors.
12. Another name for a "self-supporting" municipal bond is a (general obligation/<u>revenue</u>) bond.
13. Owners of ABC common stock have the right to vote before the ABC Board of Directors declares a (<u>stock split</u>/cash dividend).
14. Large shareholders of a corporation prefer that the method of voting used at the annual and special meetings is the (cumulative/<u>statutory</u>) method.
15. To prevent dilution of shareholder equity, companies issue (<u>rights</u>/warrants) to owners of their common stock.
16. On the ex-dividend date, the market price for the common stock (rises/<u>decreases</u>) by the amount of the cash dividend to be paid.
17. An American investor holding an ADR position benefits when the American dollar (strengthens/<u>weakens</u>) relative to the currency used in the issuer's home country.
18. The only type of preferred stock that pays higher dividends when dividends are raised for the common stock is (<u>participating</u>/adjustable) preferred stock.
19. The only type of preferred stock whose market price is tied to the market price of the issuer's common stock is (participating/<u>convertible</u>) preferred stock.
20. A management company that adheres to the limits imposed by the 75/5/10 rule is known as a (<u>diversified</u>/non-diversified) fund.
21. A (growth/<u>value</u>) fund is typically associated with higher dividend yields.
22. An (<u>international</u>/global) fund invests in companies located anywhere but the U.S., while an (international/<u>global</u>) fund would invest in companies located and doing business anywhere in the world, including the U.S.
23. Precious metals mutual funds tend to invest in (bullion/<u>shares of mining companies</u>).

24. All open-end funds impose (sales charges/<u>operating expense fees</u>), but not all open-end funds impose (<u>sales charges</u>/operating expense fees).

25. To see the dollar amount paid by a mutual fund to the investment adviser of the fund, investors should consult the (prospectus/<u>Statement of Additional Information</u>).

26. The ABC Equity Income Fund holds a substantial position in XYZ common stock. When XYZ pays a dividend, the (<u>custodian</u>/transfer agent) for the ABC Equity Income Fund receives the funds.

27. When the ABC Equity Income Fund distributes a dividend to shareholders, it is the (custodian/<u>transfer agent</u>) who disburses funds to the shareholders.

28. The use of leverage is common among (<u>closed-end</u>/open-end) funds.

29. An investment company associated with no investment adviser and board of directors is a/an (<u>Unit Investment Trust</u>/closed-end management company).

30. Of these two investment vehicles, (<u>Exchange Traded Funds</u>/money market mutual funds) typically have lower operating expenses.

31. (<u>Venture capital</u>/private equity) funds typically invest in early-stage companies, while (venture capital/private equity) funds typically invest in established companies.

32. Although many direct participation programs provide tax shelter to the limited partners, (<u>raw land</u>/oil exploration) programs do not.

33. A warrant, often issued in conjunction with a bond offering, is a (short-term/<u>long-term</u>) derivative allowing the holder to buy common stock at a stated price that is (<u>above</u>/below) the stock's market price at the time of issuance.

34. An example of a bullish options investor is one who (<u>buys calls</u>/sells calls), while an example of a bearish investor is one who (<u>buys puts</u>/sells puts).

35. The seller of a put option is neutral and (bearish/<u>bullish</u>), while the seller of a call option is neutral and (<u>bearish</u>/bullish).

36. An example of a systematic risk is (business/<u>market</u>) risk.

37. An example of an unsystematic risk is (<u>legislative</u>/inflation) risk.

38. The risk that government regulations will have a negative effect on an issuer's stock is known as (<u>legislative</u>/political) risk.

39. Interest rate risk is the risk that after purchasing a bond, interest rates in general will (<u>rise</u>/fall), while call and reinvestment risk involve interest rates in general (rising/<u>falling</u>).

40. The main risk of buying a T-bond and holding to maturity is (interest rate/<u>purchasing power</u>) risk.

1. XYZ 4% preferred stock ($100 par value) is convertible @25. Currently, XYZ common trades at $28 per share; therefore, the parity of XYZ preferred stock is:
   A. $100
   B. $112
   C. $33
   D. $53

2. What is true of a bond with an 8% coupon trading at a 10% Yield to Maturity?
   A. The price of the bond went up.
   B. It is trading at a discount.
   C. Interest rates have fallen.
   D. The bond is trading at a premium.

3. Which of the following bonds is trading at a premium?
   A. 8% coupon, 9.10 yield to maturity
   B. 8% coupon, 9.50 yield to maturity
   C. 8% coupon, 7.70 yield to maturity
   D. 8% coupon, 8.00 yield to maturity

4. An investor buys an ABC Apr 85 call @3.25. With ABC trading @89.50, he exercises the call and immediately sells the stock for a
   A. loss of $125
   B. gain of $125
   C. loss of $50
   D. gain of $450

5. Which of the following bond ratings implies the highest yield?
   A. Aa
   B. Baa
   C. BBB
   D. Ba

6. All the following are true of corporate zero-coupon bonds EXCEPT:
   A. Interest is received at maturity.
   B. Interest is taxed annually.
   C. The bonds pay no interest.
   D. The bonds are less sensitive to changes in interest rates than coupon bonds.

7. An IBM Mar 75 put @3 has how much time value with IBM @74?

A. $1
B. $2
C. 0
D. $3

8. Which of the following projects funded by municipal bonds is least likely to require voter approval?

A. building a public middle school
B. constructing a turnpike
C. building a prison
D. building a public high school

9. All the following might lower the credit rating on a GO bond except

A. Unemployment rates are rising
B. Population has decreased
C. Unemployment rates are falling
D. Lack of economic diversity

10. A general obligation bond pays a 7% coupon. A comparable corporate bond pays a 9.5% coupon. Therefore

A. A customer in the 15% tax bracket should buy the municipal security.
B. A customer in the 30% tax bracket should buy the municipal security.
C. A customer in the 30% tax bracket should buy the corporate bond.
D. Both customers should purchase the municipal security.

11. How much intrinsic value does a MSFT Jan 90 call have with MSFT common stock trading at $85?

A. $5
B. $90
C. $85
D. Zero

12. IBM is trading at $93. Which of the following options would, therefore, trade for the highest premium?

A. IBM Aug 90 call
B. IBM Oct 90 call
C. IBM Aug 95 put
D. IBM Nov 100 put

13. Which of the following statements is accurate?

A. Variable annuities offer more downside protection than equity-indexed annuities
B. Equity-indexed annuities offer more downside protection than variable annuities
C. Both equity-indexed and variable annuities are "securities"
D. Equity-indexed annuities offer more upside potential than variable annuities

14. Non-systematic risks are reduced through

A. diversification
B. buy and hold strategies
C. hedging strategies
D. covered call writing

15. A 20-year zero-coupon Treasury bond is most susceptible to which of the following?

A. credit risk
B. reinvestment risk
C. call risk
D. purchasing power risk

16. Whether for an open-end or closed-end fund, the management fee is charged to cover the services of the

A. Board of directors
B. Investment adviser
C. Transfer agent
D. Distributor/sponsor

17. Which of the following risks is "non-diversifiable"?

A. Business risk
B. Legislative risk
C. Liquidity risk
D. Interest rate risk

18. Which of the following risks is most important to explain to an investor in a money market mutual fund?

A. Default
B. Interest rate
C. Purchasing power
D. Liquidity

19. A mutual fund investor purchasing A-shares should know that all the following can reduce the sales charge % EXCEPT:

A. Aggregating purchases across various accounts, e.g. IRA, Roth IRA, etc.
B. Aggregating purchases made by a husband and wife.
C. Reinvesting all dividends and capital gains promptly.
D. Appreciation of the account value.

20. Policies and restrictions for a mutual fund portfolio include issues such as what % may be allocated toward high-yield debt securities or common stock not trading on American exchanges or included in the S&P 500. Such investment policy is developed by which of the following?

A. Board of directors
B. Investment adviser
C. Custodian
D. Shareholders by a majority vote

21. Cash value is guaranteed by the claims-paying ability of the insurance company for which of the following policy types?

A. Term life
B. Whole life
C. Variable life
D. All choices listed

22. The greatest threat to an investor holding common stock is

A. Its par value is arbitrarily determined
B. Cash dividends never have to be declared or paid
C. The market value could drop significantly
D. Preferred stock receives preference in liquidation

23. A bond with a 4% nominal yield paying interest semiannually matures in 9 years. At maturity, an investor holding $100,000 par value would receive which of the following amounts?

A. $100,000
B. $102,000
C. $104,000
D. $120,000

24. Ian McSheehan is convinced ABC common stock will drop sharply in the near-term. To profit from this assertion while taking on the least risk, you would recommend that Ian

A. Purchase ABC call options
B. Purchase ABC put options
C. Sell ABC call options
D. Sell ABC put options

25. The FIRST thing to make clear to a prospect to whom a registered representative is recommending a direct participation program is that

A. Such programs provide tax advantages
B. Such programs lack liquidity
C. Such programs offer higher returns than fixed-income products
D. Such programs tend to open investors up to influential investors

Answers

1. B
2. B
3. C
4. B
5. D
6. D
7. B
8. B
9. C
10. B
11. D
12. D
13. B
14. A
15. D
16. B
17. D
18. C
19. C
20. A
21. B
22. C
23. B
24. B
25. B

Trading, Settlement and Corporate Actions

Trading Orders and Strategies

Most retail investors buy stock, hoping its value will increase. An investor who buys 500 shares of SBUX establishes a **long** position. A long stock position is called a **bullish** position, meaning the investor expects the market price to rise.

Not many investors know they can also bet against a stock. To profit from a stock losing market value, they establish a **short** stock position within a margin account. If the investor believes SBUX will drop, he is **bearish** on the stock. The broker-dealer borrows 500 shares and sells them in the customer's account. This is known as a short sale or "selling short." These short sales occur only in margin accounts, never in cash accounts.

Within a margin account, the customer entering a short sale makes a cash deposit of 50% of the market value. When he is ready to purchase the stock, and return it to the broker-dealer, his order is entered as a buy-to-cover. If the stock's price has dropped since he sold it short, the investor profits. If not, he loses.

Because a sale order could be a short sale or the liquidation of a long position, sell orders are marked as either "long" or "short."

For options, the buyer of a call is bullish on the underlying security, while the buyer of a put is bearish. The seller of a call is both bearish and neutral on the underlying security, while the seller of a put is both bullish and neutral.

When selling call options, the writer either holds the underlying shares, or he doesn't. If he does, the calls are covered. If not, he is writing naked calls.

Writing naked calls and selling stock short are both bearish positions that present unlimited risk to the investor. Therefore, customers are only allowed to engage in such transactions if the broker-dealer determines they understand and can handle the risk.

1st Market, NYSE

Fifteen years ago, distinguishing the NYSE/1st Market from the OTC/2nd Market was getting complicated but not too bad. The NYSE was an exchange that used open outcry like all **auction markets** did at the time.

But, your industry changes fast. Even though the NYSE is still an auction market and is still an exchange, most of the trading is done electronically. And, electronic trading is what we used to safely associate with the "OTC/2nd market," which we will discuss next.

Securities trading on the NYSE, and on NASDAQ, are listed securities. The term should not be associated with securities trading over-the-counter but not on NASDAQ, e.g., the Over-the-Counter Bulletin Board.

Unlike non-NASDAQ OTC securities, issuers who want to list their securities for trading on NYSE must meet and maintain the exchange's rigid listing criteria. If a company lists its security on the NYSE (or NASDAQ), it will be monitored by the exchange, and if they do not meet all obligations under exchange and SEC rules, the security will suddenly not be trading, which is not a distraction any company needs.

Companies also list their debt securities on the NYSE. To meet the requirements, the issue must have a principal value of at least $5 million. If the bond is convertible, it can only be listed if the underlying common stock is subject to real-time last sale reports in the US, and the par value must be $10 million or larger. Even if the issue of debt securities meets those minimum sizes and requirements, the NYSE will only list the issue if it meets one of several criteria that basically require that the issuer have its stock listed on the NYSE, or that an issuer with stock listed on the exchange is either a majority owner or in common control with the other issuer, or that any NYSE-listed issuer has guaranteed the issue. There is also a criterion based on the credit rating of the issue being at least "B", which, as you probably remember or know, is a junk rating.

As the website for NYSE Bonds indicates:

> "NYSE Bonds operates the largest centralized corporate bond market in the U.S., providing an opportunity for participants to trade bonds in a fair, open environment. On NYSE Bonds, firm and executable orders entered by members or sponsored participants are displayed on the order book, and executed on a strict price/time priority."

There are also specific NYSE requirements for special securities, including Real Estate Investment Trusts (REITs), closed-end investment companies, non-US companies, etc.

Participants

The NYSE now uses both a manual auction and an electronic trading model. That means that even though most trading is done electronically, the exchange also uses the live auction process at the open, at the close, and during any time of extreme volatility or price imbalances between would-be buyers and sellers. The firms in charge of running those manual auctions used to be called "specialists" but are now known as Designated Market Makers or DMMs. The firms are called "DMM Units," while the individuals performing the function of "DMM" are the "DMMs."

As the excellent video at www.nyse.com explains, DMMs are like commercial airline pilots—they must be there for the take-off and the landing, and they must step in whenever there is turbulence. During the rest of the flight, they merely participate in the process, watching over things. As of this writing, DMM Units include the following firms: Knight Capital Group, Goldman Sachs, Barclays, and J. Streicher & Co.

Like other market participants, DMMs also trade electronically throughout the day using computerized mathematical formulae designed to determine buying and selling opportunities called trading algorithms. Like the specialists before them, Designated Market Makers are given the responsibility to maintain a fair and orderly market in a security. Their job is to provide liquidity, especially during times of market volatility. To prevent panic, they step in ready to buy or sell securities for their own account to keep the flow of trading moving. They also must quote at the National Best Bid or Offer (NBBO) a required percentage of the time. The NBBO is what it sounds like—the best prices for the security nationwide.

A DMM does not participate in every trade in the security. They are simply the individual overseeing trading in that stock and living up to the DMM's many obligations. When they trade, they can act in either a principal or an agency capacity.

The term "DMM" is used loosely. The firm is the "DMM Unit," while the individual associated with the firm who sits down on the exchange floor is known as the "DMM" or "Designated Market Maker" in a particular exchange-listed security like GM, GE, or IBM.

Other NYSE participants include floor brokers and off-floor supplemental liquidity providers (SLPs). Floor brokers execute trades on the exchange floor on behalf of their clients, who include banks and broker-dealers. They earn a commission for filling orders, so the more orders they can fill, the more money they can make. Floor brokers are physically present on the trading floor and are active participants during opening and closing auctions, as well as throughout the trading day. They also can enter orders electronically, usually through hand-held devices.

Supplemental Liquidity Providers (SLPs) provide supplemental liquidity to the market by complying with requirements to buy or sell at times of volatility or price imbalances. They are off-floor electronic participants required to maintain a bid or an offer at the NBBO 10% of the trading day for the security they are assigned and, in return, receive rebates/liquidity fees from the exchange. So, the DMMs and the SLPs are the only participants who are required to trade on the NYSE. But, while the Supplemental Liquidity Providers are required to bid or offer for the security, the Designated Market Maker must do both, maintaining a two-sided quote in the security.

Why all the concern for liquidity? A lack of liquidity can lead to a panic or take a mild panic and turn it into a full-blown crisis. The better the balance of orders and the ease of execution, the better the markets function. The regulators hold this truth to be self-evident. As NYSE explains at their website, "Supplemental Liquidity Providers (SLPs) are electronic, high volume members incented to add liquidity on the NYSE and NYSE MKT. All their trading is proprietary, which means it is done for their own account as opposed to just filling orders for others. All NYSE and NYSE MKT stocks are eligible, but not all have SLPs. Supplemental Liquidity Providers are primarily found in more liquid stocks with greater than 1 million shares of average daily volume."

During the live auctions at the open and close floor brokers are gathered around a group of computers called a trading post. The trading post is just a spot on the floor surrounded by video display terminals and telecommunications equipment. The DMM is positioned at the trading "post" for a particular security and may be surrounded by one or two floor brokers or maybe a whole crowd if something big is happening with the company's stock. For its long and storied history, the NYSE held live, open-outcry double auctions on their listed securities. These days most trading is done electronically, usually through high-tech devices running sophisticated mathematical models. Still, no matter how hi-tech the trading gets these days, it is interesting that during times of extreme volatility, the NYSE functions more efficiently when everyone moves away from the computers and starts interacting with each other face-to-face and in real-time.

The NYSE also states on their website: Electronic Market Makers and Brokers are active participants who participate electronically in all NYSE and NYSE MKT stocks. They include the same market makers found on other fully electronic exchanges.

Orders

There is still a live-auction process used at the NYSE, but orders are usually routed electronically these days to the NYSE's Display Book, which is an electronic system that automatically fills market orders and holds limit orders showing where investors are willing to buy and sell a security and at what number of units. As the NYSE explains on their website:

```
"The NYSE OpenBook Real-Time product provides a real-time view —
aggregated and refreshed every second — of the New York Stock Exchange's
limit-order book for all NYSE-traded issues. NYSE OpenBook Real-Time
lets traders see aggregate limit-order volume at every bid and offer
price, thus responding to customer demand for depth-of-market data and
raising the NYSE market to an even greater level of transparency."
```

Think of the display book as an electronic system to track open orders and act as an order management and execution medium. Executed transactions are also reported to the Consolidated Tape, which we'll look at.

So, that's the electronic display book. The live-auction process, on the other hand, takes place around the trading pit for a particular issue at the opening and closing of the trading session and also during times of extreme volatility or price imbalances between buyers and sellers. The humans participating in this process are known as the trading crowd.

Records

NYSE rules require members to preserve for at least three years (two years readily accessible) a record of "every order received by such member or member organization, either orally or in writing, which record must include the name and amount of the security, the terms of the order, the time when it was so received and the time at which a report of execution was received." If an order is cancelled, a record of that must be kept including the time of the cancellation.

Before entering any order, a trade ticket must be filled out and must indicate the account for which the order is being executed. Accounts, as we'll see in a later chapter, can be held by an individual, a husband-and-wife, a mother-for-the-benefit-of-her-daughter, etc. How the account is named and/or designated is a very big deal, and the account name or designation cannot be changed unless authorized in writing by the account holder and a principal of the broker-dealer. A record of the essential facts used by the person authorizing the change must also be kept for three years (two years readily accessible). This means if a cash account becomes a margin account, the designation has changed, and records must be kept showing that the customer was aware of the change and authorized it, as did a principal at the firm. Or, if the account holder gets married or divorced and changes her name, this is also a very big deal, like virtually everything else in your industry.

2nd Market, OTC

The NYSE is an auction market, sometimes referred to as the "first market." The OTC (Over-the-Counter) market, on the other hand, is a **negotiated market**, and sometimes referred to as the **second market**.

NASDAQ

NASDAQ (NASDAQ) stands for the **National Association of Securities Dealers Automated Quotation** system. What is a "securities dealer"? We're talking about broker-dealers who execute transactions in securities for customers, including well-known firms such as TD Ameritrade, Morgan-Stanley, Merrill Lynch, Charles Schwab, and E-Trade. As you may know from working at a broker-dealer yourself, many precise records are involved with executing a buy or sell order for securities, and the process is highly regulated by FINRA, the SEC, and the state securities regulators. When billions of dollars are moving back and forth between investors every day, the potential for fraud or costly mistakes is huge.

The NASDAQ system has three levels of access. Level 1 is for registered representatives and individual investors, and it shows the highest bid and lowest offer price for a security, as well as last sale and volume information. The highest bid and lowest offer is the **inside market** representing the best prices buyers and sellers can trade at immediately.

If a customer wanted to see what each market maker was quoting, he would need Level 2 access, which shows the two-sided quote, with size, for each market maker in the security. It also shows last-sale and volume information updated in real time. NASDAQ Level 2 is a subscription service for pension funds, mutual funds, and other large institutional investors.

NASDAQ Level 3, unlike the first two levels, is not just a display system. Level 3 is for market makers inputting and updating their quotes on the security in real time. It displays all information the other levels see, and allows a firm's trading desk to update their quotes for the securities in which they make a market.

Securities

The OTC securities that meet the requirements of NASDAQ trade on the **NASDAQ Global Select, NASDAQ Global** or **NASDAQ Capital** markets. Requirements for listing on the NASDAQ Global market are stringent, and the requirements for initial and maintained listing on the NASDAQ Global Select market are, according to the NASDAQ website, "the highest standards of any stock market in the world."

To help smaller companies raise capital, the NASDAQ Capital Market exists and has lower listing requirements designed to help less proven companies raise capital from aggressive investors while still maintaining reasonably high listing standards. By "standards" for listing we mean companies that want to list on the Global or Global Select tiers must meet high standards of financial strength and liquidity for their stock, and companies listing on those or even just the NASDAQ Capital Market must maintain high corporate governance standards.

The requirements for initial listing are higher than for continued listing. For example, the national best bid on the stock must be at least $4 to list initially, but the company doesn't get threatened with a de-listing unless the bid falls below $1. NASDAQ explains this approach ensures companies are as strong as possible before their stock starts trading on an exchange, especially the top two tiers (Global, Global Select).

A company can get their stock onto the NASDAQ Capital Market without showing a profit at all or by showing net income/profits of just $750,000 if using one of the other standards for financial strength. Then again, if the net income is only $750,000, the company would still have to have— among other things—1 million publicly held shares, 300 round lot shareholders, and at least three broker-dealers acting as market makers for the stock.

We mentioned that companies trading on the NYSE can have their securities de-listed. Similarly, NASDAQ explains:

> NASDAQ is entrusted with the authority to preserve and strengthen the quality of and public confidence in its market. NASDAQ stands for integrity and ethical business practices to enhance investor confidence, thereby contributing to the financial health of the economy and supporting the capital formation process. NASDAQ Companies, from new public Companies to Companies of international stature, are publicly recognized as sharing these important objectives. NASDAQ, therefore, in addition to applying the enumerated criteria set forth in the Rule 5000 Series, has broad discretionary authority over the initial and continued listing of securities in NASDAQ to maintain the quality of and public confidence in its market, to prevent fraudulent and manipulative acts and practices, to promote just and equitable principles of trade, and to protect investors and the public interest. NASDAQ may use such discretion to deny initial listing, apply additional or more stringent criteria for the initial or continued listing of particular securities, or suspend or delist particular securities based on any event, condition, or circumstance that exists or occurs that makes initial or continued listing of the securities on NASDAQ inadvisable or unwarranted in the opinion of NASDAQ, even though the securities meet all enumerated criteria for initial or continued listing on NASDAQ.

So, NASDAQ mentions the authority of the Listing Qualifications Department to use its discretionary authority to deny or terminate the listing of a security. They then explain how this works in one of their many interpretative materials (IMs). A common reason a company's security gets de-listed from NASDAQ is that one of the officers or directors turns out to be a bad actor. The "IM" mentions that these individuals are usually officers, directors, substantial shareholders, or consultants. The explanation then continues with: Based on this review, NASDAQ may determine that the regulatory history rises to the level of a public interest concern, but may also consider whether remedial measures proposed by the Company, if taken, would allay that concern. Examples of such remedial measures could include any or all the following, as appropriate:

- the individual's resignation from officer and director positions, and/or other employment with the Company
- divestiture of stock holdings
- terminations of contractual arrangements between the Company and the individual
- the establishment of a voting trust surrounding the individual's shares in the issuer

NASDAQ explains they are willing to discuss with companies, on a case-by-case basis, what type of remedial measures can be taken to put out the fire. Or, if they conclude the public interest concern is so serious nothing can remediate it, staff can deny an initial or continued listing on NASDAQ. If that happens, the issuer of the security can seek a review of this decision by a panel of people independent of NASDAQ. The panel may end up accepting, rejecting, or modifying NASDAQ's decision to deny or de-list the company's security.

It isn't just bad behavior that can lead to a de-listing. If the issuer files for bankruptcy protection, or if their auditing accountants issue a disclaimer opinion or refuse to certify the financial statements contained in filings such as the annual 10-K report, the stock can be de-listed. Remember that stocks trading on NASDAQ are issued by companies with solid financials and current reporting, so if the issuer is facing bankruptcy or their accountants won't certify its financial statements, it makes sense that NASDAQ would start to show this issuer the exit to protect investors.

Market Makers

To enter quotes through the NASDAQ system, broker-dealers who want to act as market makers must get access to the system and get their registration accepted by NASDAQ. They also must meet certain requirements:

- Execution of all applicable agreements with NASDAQ
- Membership in—or an arrangement with a participant of—a clearing agency registered with the SEC
- Compliance with all NASDAQ and SEC rules concerning the system
- Maintenance of the physical security of the equipment located on the premises of the NASDAQ Market Maker, NASDAQ ECN or Order Entry Firm to prevent the improper use or access to NASDAQ systems
- Acceptance and settlement of each NASDAQ trade identified as belonging to the participant
- Input of accurate information into the System, including, but not limited to, whether the member acted in a principal, agent, or riskless principal capacity

The Market Maker Registration Form is short and sweet, as you can see at http://www.NASDAQtrader.com/content/AdministrationSupport/AgreementsTrading/marketmakerregistration.pdf. If you click that link, you'll see that NASDAQ is asking for basic information: full name of member and CRD (Central Registration Depository) number, MPID (if adding securities to existing market making activities), clearing arrangement and NSCC account #, and list of stock symbols to be quoted. As NASDAQ explains at http://www.NASDAQtrader.com/Trader.aspx?id=MarketMakerProcess, the process of becoming a NASDAQ market maker involves these steps:

- Complete the Market Maker Registration Form (PDF) and fax it to NASDAQ Subscriber Services. If new services are required, also complete the NASDAQ Port Request Form (PDF) or the NASDAQ Front-End Access Form (PDF).
- Have your clearing agency call the National Securities Clearing Corporation (NSCC) to ensure a clearing arrangement.
- Contact the local FINRA District Office to express an interest in becoming a NASDAQ market maker. The District Office will write to you requesting information.
- Compile all information, and send it to the local FINRA District Office for review. (If all information is completed properly, the District Office will interview you and determine if you are qualified to be a NASDAQ market maker.)
- The FINRA District Office will forward an approval form to NASDAQ's Subscriber Services department. (If your firm is not a FINRA member, the approval will be made by The NASDAQ Stock Market LLC.)
- A NASDAQ Subscriber Services representative will notify you if you are permitted to make markets and will activate all your services.

If the firm is going through this process, they must be sure they are ready to start making markets. NASDAQ rules state the firm's status as a market maker in that security would automatically terminate if the market maker failed to enter a quote on it within 5 business days after their registration became effective.

When a market maker becomes registered with NASDAQ, NASDAQ assigns an MPID (Market Participant Identifier). I see this morning that the following market makers have been assigned the following MPIDs:

FIRM	MPID
Blackrock Capital Markets, LLC	BRCM
Bear, Stearns & Co., Inc.	BEAR
Mesirow Financial, Inc.	MESF
Morgan Stanley	MSPW
MetLife Securities Inc.	MSII

Muriel Siebert & Co., Inc.	SBRT

So, if this is the first time a firm has acted as a NASDAQ market maker, an MPID would have to be assigned. For existing market makers adding stocks to their market making activities, the MPID would already have been assigned. Many market makers, including some in the chart above, have several MPIDs, so the first MPID issued by NASDAQ to the market maker is called the Primary MPID. Market makers with multiple trading centers would then request Supplemental MPIDs from NASDAQ.

NASDAQ rules state that if a market maker ceases to live up to its obligations relating to the primary MPID in any security, it will not be able to use any of the supplemental MPIDs to trade in that security, either. Quotes entered by the other trading centers using the Supplemental MPIDs are referred to as "attributable quotes/orders."

Whether it's the Primary MPID or one of the Supplemental MPID trading centers, the name of the system into which quotes are entered is currently known as the "NASDAQ Quotation Montage." All quotes entered by NASDAQ market makers, ECNs, and NASDAQ order entry firms are firm quotes and are immediately executable. We will see later in the chapter that some systems allow market participants to merely indicate interest in maybe buying or selling securities (nominal or subject quotes), but that is not the case with NASDAQ.

All quotes are firm; all orders ready to go. As NASDAQ rules state:

> *For each security in which a member is registered as a NASDAQ Market Maker, the member shall be willing to buy and sell such security for its own account on a continuous basis and shall enter and maintain a two-sided quotation ("Principal Quote"), which is attributed to the market maker by a special market participant identifier ("MPID") and is displayed in the NASDAQ Market Center at all times, subject to the procedures for excused withdrawal.*

The quotes are not just firm, but must be for a minimum size—one normal unit of trading.

Market makers provide liquidity to the markets. If the market maker wants to withdraw temporarily for a legitimate reason, they request an excused withdrawal from FINRA. Why would a market maker want to do that? Maybe the security trades in a volatile market and the one experienced trader the firm has is suddenly unavailable. Or, there could be an equipment malfunction, or maybe they lost their clearing agreement. Or, if they somehow come into possession of material, inside information, they must excuse themselves from making a market, no matter how tempting it would be to just keep on trading.

Reasons that a market maker may not use to request an excused withdrawal include: a sudden influx of orders, sudden price changes, or a news release. In other words, if you sign up as a market maker, don't complain about volatility. It's your job to deal with it, keeping the markets functioning as smoothly as possible.

If, on the other hand, a market maker wants to terminate its activities on NASDAQ, it simply withdraws its quotes from the system, which gives FINRA the heads up that the firm is terminating its registration for that security. If the firm wants to jump back into making a market in that security, the firm must wait at least 20 business days before registering once again. And, if a market maker fails to follow the rules and obligations of FINRA, they can be suspended or even terminated as a market maker.

An excused withdrawal indicates the market maker wants to take a break from trading activities entirely. But, if the firm wants to remain in the system, they can agree to fill orders at another member's quotations being disseminated through the NASDAQ system.

Getting registered to act as a market maker takes much more effort than adding securities to the list of stocks in which the firm trades. In fact, for a newly authorized security, a registered market maker's registration for that security is effective immediately if the request was made within five business days (after) of the security's inclusion in the system. Even if the request is made more than five business days after the security starts trading on NASDAQ, the registration would be effective on the next business day.

Normal business hours for the NASDAQ system are from 9:30 AM – 4:00 PM Eastern, and market makers are required to be open for business during those times. Firms can voluntarily trade either before or after the normal trading session. The early session runs from 7:00 AM to 9:30 AM Eastern, and the late session from 4:00 PM to 8:00 PM. Trading that occurs before or after normal business hours carries certain risks, which is why firms must provide their customers with an extended hours trading risk disclosure before allowing them to trade outside the "regular trading hours" of 9:30 AM – 4:00 PM. Such risks pointed out to customers include:

- Lower liquidity
- Higher volatility
- Risk of news announcements (which are usually made after normal trading hours)

Order-Entry Firms

Market makers buy and sell securities for their own account. Order-entry firms enter orders into the NASDAQ system. They do not buy and sell for their own account the way a market making firm does. As the SEC explains, "Order entry firms route orders to the NASDAQ Market Center for execution against displayed orders and quotations, and for display under the anonymous SIZE MPID. Order entry firms may not display trading interest under an attributable MPID."

So, some broker-dealers make markets. Some broker-dealers merely enter orders to buy and sell NASDAQ stocks on behalf of their customers, routing such orders to the market maker with the best quote for the security.

Order-entry firms use the NASDAQ subscription service called ACES (Advanced Computerized Execution System) to quickly route their orders to their preferred market makers' internal trading systems for execution. The order-entry firm sends the order through the ACES system from its NASDAQ terminal. The system sends a confirmation back to the order-entry firm once the trade has been executed by the market maker.

There is no maximum size for orders entered through the system, and it is used for NASDAQ stocks trading on any of the three tiers (Global Select, Global, Capital Market). The ACES system also provides automatic ACT reporting, a reporting system explored in more detail up ahead.

Non-NASDAQ OTC

Companies such as Oracle, Cisco, Microsoft, and Google are NASDAQ OTC stocks.

Non-NASDAQ OTC stocks include companies many have never heard of:

Auburn Bancorp, Inc.	ABBB
Applied Enrgetics Preferred	AERGP
Dakota Gold Corporation	DAKO
Global Stevia Corp	GSTV
China Ginseng Holdings	CSNG

The above companies' stocks trade through the Over-the-Counter Bulletin Board (OTCBB), where there are over 3,300 securities trading by way of more than 200 market makers. The **OTCBB (Over-the-Counter Bulletin Board)** is a trading system that is both over-the-counter and Non-NASDAQ. As FINRA points out: any reference to the OTC Bulletin Board should never include the word "listed" and should not be associated with "NASDAQ®."

FINRA explains:

Exchanges (such as NASDAQ and the NYSE) have specific quantitative and qualitative listing and maintenance standards, which are stringently monitored and enforced. Companies listed on an exchange have reporting obligations to the market, and an on-going regulatory relationship exists between the market and its listed companies. OTC quotation services (OTCBB, OTC Markets) facilitate quotation of unlisted securities. As such, any regulatory relationship between an OTC quotation service and the issuers may be relatively limited or non-existent.

A stock such as MSFT or IBM must meet the listing and maintenance standards of the NASDAQ or NYSE, "which are stringently monitored and enforced" by those exchanges. On the other hand, the OTCBB and OTC Markets only facilitate quotations for those who want to trade in securities that trade over-the-counter but not on NASDAQ.

NASDAQ defines the Over the Counter Bulletin Board (OTCBB) as:

> *An electronic quotation medium for subscribing members to reflect market making interest in OTCBB-eligible securities. Subscribing market makers can utilize the Service to enter, update, and display their proprietary quotations in individual securities on a real-time basis.*

Regardless of how much or how little the OTCBB monitors the issuers whose securities trade there, FINRA monitors and regulates the broker-dealers who trade securities through the system as market makers. In other words, the issuer known as China Ginseng Holdings do not have to meet rigid criteria to have its stock trade through the OTCBB system; however, the broker-dealers making markets in that stock are regulated by FINRA, the SEC, etc.

Many investors think the OTCBB is all about matching their orders with other buyers or sellers. No, in the OTCBB market, a market maker sets the market price. He buys from a seller and then decides how much to charge a buyer.

Securities eligible to trade through the OTCBB system meet the following criteria:

- security is <u>not</u> listed on a national securities exchange in the US, *and*
- issuer is subject to SEC reporting requirements and is current in filing those reports *or* the issuer is a banking institution/bank holding company not subject to SEC reporting and is current in its filings with its appropriate banking/financial regulator

If the issuer is not current in its SEC regulatory filings, the modifier *E* will appear next to the stock symbol, e.g., ABCDE. At that point, the issuer has 30 days to get right with the regulators at the SEC (or 60 days if it reports to a banking regulator-only). If not, the issuer's securities will be removed from the OTCBB until they get their regulatory filings in order.

Does that mean the securities can no longer trade anywhere? No, as we'll see, there are areas of the OTC Markets where such outcast securities are welcomed. The OTCBB is the part of the Non-NASDAQ OTC where issuers are current in their filings with the SEC. The OTC Markets/Pink Quote, on the other hand, is the part of the Non-NASDAQ OTC market where issuers may or may not be current in their SEC filings.

Either way, this is the Non-NASDAQ Over-the-Counter market, meaning the issuers do not have to meet stringent requirements in terms of financial strength and are not monitored and regulated by an exchange. The Non-NASDAQ part of the Over-the-Counter market also isn't subject to the rigorous oversight of trading that insists on transparency and best execution and that sort of thing.

OTC-eligible securities include domestic equities not trading on a national exchange in the US, ADRs not trading on a national exchange in the US that are registered with the SEC and current in their reporting, stocks undergoing the de-listing process from NYSE, NYSE Amex, or NASDAQ, and direct participation programs not listed on a national exchange that are current in their reports. As the FINRA rule relating to the OTCBB system indicates:

Notwithstanding the foregoing paragraphs, a member shall not be permitted to quote a security if:

- *the issuer of the security has failed to file a complete required annual or quarterly report by the due date for such report three times in the prior two-year period*
- *the security has been removed from the OTCBB due to the issuer's failure to satisfy [the requirements] above, two times in the prior two-year period.*

In other words, if the issuer is not going to report on time to the SEC, it is not going to be quoted long through the OTCBB.

A security removed from the OTCBB system might start trading through the **OTC Markets Group**. There are three different tiers for this electronic trading facility. As their website indicates, "Due to the wide range of OTC companies, OTC Markets Group developed the OTC Market Tiers to help bring increased clarity, transparency and disclosure to the OTC Market. Securities are assigned a Market Tier based on their reporting method (SEC Reporting, Alternative Reporting Standard) and disclosure category – Current, Limited or No Information." From the highest to lowest tier, we have the:

- OTCQX - best OTC companies with the highest financial standards and superior information availability
- OTCQB - current in their reporting with a U.S. regulator. There are no financial or qualitative standards to be in this tier
- OTC Pink - includes shell or development stage companies with little or no operations as well as companies without audited financials and as such should be considered extremely speculative by investors.

Not long ago non-NASDAQ securities were traded so infrequently there was a "three-quote rule" or "contact rule" that required broker-dealers to get three estimates before filling a customer order. Now that the electronic trading systems above are available, the requirement to get quotes from different market makers is waived if there are at least two priced quotations displayed in the OTCBB or OTC Pink marketplace

Third Market

Securities listed on the New York Stock Exchange trade on the exchange and on various other facilities. OTC market makers have been able to make markets in NYSE-listed securities for quite some time now, and we call this the **third market**. If the exam asks on which market we would find shares of GE or IBM trading "over-the-counter," the answer is "the third market." However, if shares of GE or IBM are purchased/sold via the NYSE, that's still the first market.

To facilitate third market trading the industry developed a quotation system called the **Consolidated Quotation System (CQS)**. Although this quotation system operates between 9 AM and 6:30 PM Eastern time, the major action on the system is still during normal market hours.

The rules we looked at for excused withdrawals from the NASDAQ system also apply to market makers in the third market. If a market maker wants to withdraw indefinitely/permanently, as with NASDAQ, the firm just withdraws its quotes from the CQS. FINRA rules would require the firm to wait at least two business days before it can re-register as a market maker in that security. Remember that the wait time is 20 days for the NASDAQ system

Fourth Market

The fourth market, also known as the "ECN market," is an electronic trading system for institutional investors. Rather than using the services of a traditional broker-dealer, participants from insurance companies, pension funds, mutual funds, and other institutions trade electronically and directly with each other for both listed and unlisted securities.

The electronic communications networks used here are named, not surprisingly, **Electronic Communications Networks (ECNs)**. INSTINET is an example of an ECN used within the fourth market. ECNs are a form of Alternative Trading System (ATS) discussed and regulated by the SEC's Regulation ATS. An alternative trading system matches buyers and sellers electronically, usually those who trade in large quantities (institutional investors). SEC Regulation ATS imposes strict record keeping requirements on these trading systems and requires them to file a Form ATS. However, these systems do not have to go so far as to register as securities exchanges. As the SEC states, Regulation ATS allows "alternative trading systems to choose whether to register as national securities exchanges, or to register as broker-dealers and comply with additional requirements under Regulation ATS, depending on their activities and trading volume."

ECNs execute orders on an agency basis. They, therefore, are not obligated to maintain two-sided quotes, since they are not buying and selling for their own account.

Alternative Trading Systems

The Securities Exchange Act of 1934 requires SROs to maintain and enforce rules designed to keep trading in over-the-counter securities fair and honest. The specific section of "the Act" states:
Provisions governing the form and content of quotations relating to securities sold otherwise than on a national securities exchange which may be distributed or published by any member or person associated with a member, and the persons to whom such quotations may be supplied. Such rules relating to quotations shall be designed to produce fair and informative quotations, to prevent fictitious or misleading quotations, and to promote orderly procedures for collecting, distributing, and publishing quotations.

There are exchange rules designed to achieve the above goals. But, then there are "securities sold otherwise than on a national securities exchange," known as NMS securities. The SEC's Regulation NMS is concerned about access to timely market information on securities sold through other facilities, such as Electronic Communications Networks or ECNs. An ECN facilitates the electronic trading of securities that trade virtually everywhere. If they are a "linked ECN," they can report trades through the NASDAQ system. But if they are an "unlinked ECN," they need an alternative system to display quotes, compare trades, and report transactions to the market—everything but route and execute orders.

To satisfy the need for ECNs and other non-exchange trading facilities to display buying and selling interest and report transactions to the market, FINRA created the Alternative Display Facility or ADF. As its name suggests, this is a display-only facility, meaning that orders are not routed and executed through the ADF the way they are on NYSE or NASDAQ. Quotes are displayed through the ADF, but trades are not automatically routed for execution.

Rather, trades are routed and executed because broker-dealers are required to set up ADF Trading Centers that link to all other ADF Trading Centers and to any FINRA member who requests access. To set up an ADF Trading Center a member firm must set up an electronic system that provides electronic access to other members, meaning they must accept electronic orders from other members for execution, orders that do not require any voice communications. The ADF Trading Centers are referred to as Alternative Trading Systems (ATS). For a recent list of firms with an ATS, see http://www.finra.org/industry/equity-ats-firms.

Many firms see the quotes displayed through the ADF and enter orders through various Alternative Trading Systems. But, firms can enter quotes to buy and sell securities through the Alternative Display Facility only if they are a Registered Reporting ADF Market Maker or a Registered Reporting ADF ECN (Electronic Communications Network).

The ADF Trading Center must provide other registered broker-dealers access to the system and allow them to, in turn, provide access to their customers.

FINRA defines *indirect access* as:

> *"The ability to route an order through a FINRA member, subscriber broker-dealer, or customer broker-dealer of an ADF Trading Center that are not an affiliate of the ADF Trading Center, for execution against the ADF Trading Center's best bid or offer subject to applicable FINRA rules and the federal securities laws, including SEC Regulation NMS."*

The ADF Trading Center cannot determine or influence the prices charged by its customer broker-dealers who provide indirect access to the system to their customers, nor can they try to discourage or prevent indirect access from being provided. An ADF Trading Center must provide a level and cost of access to its quotations in an NMS stock displayed in that ADF at substantially equivalent levels to what SRO trading facilities provide and charge for that same stock. To be an ATS, the facility must demonstrate it has sufficient technology to update its quotes and immediately respond to orders for execution at the individual alternative trading system's best bid or offer.

Broker-dealers can only be denied access to the Alternative Display Facility as an ATS for failing to meet the requirements of the system and only through a carefully prescribed process

Automated trading centers must adopt reasonable standards that limit when their quotations can change from automated quotations to manual quotations, and vice versa, to specifically define circumstances that promote fair and efficient access to their automated quotations and are consistent with the maintenance of fair and orderly markets. What would be inconsistent with such a goal? How about a broker-dealer who waits for a lot of action on a thinly traded stock to suddenly become overloaded and starts executing orders manually and in a manner that customers are not able to follow? That would be a lack of transparency, what the regulators want to avoid.

Being able to enter automated quotations is critical. So is keeping the trading system up and running. As FINRA rules stipulate: in the event that an ADF Trading Center experiences three unexcused system outages during a period of five business days, the ADF Trading Center may be suspended from quoting in the ADF in all or certain issues for a period of twenty business days.

TRACE

TRACE is a trade reporting system for purposes of providing timely market information to participants and for providing documentation of trades for compliance purposes. The TRACE system does not accept quotes; it does not provide clearing/settlement of trades. It doesn't process trades at all—it merely reports them to the market and keeps a record for regulatory purposes. Also, while participation in other systems is voluntary, participation in the TRACE system is mandatory for member firms.

Transactions in corporate debt securities are reported through **TRACE,** which stands for the **Trade Reporting and Compliance Engine.** Trade reports are filed within 15 minutes of execution—nowhere near as fast as equity trades are reported through ACT (30 seconds). Securities eligible for and subject to TRACE reporting are called **TRACE-eligible securities.** These include:

- most corporate bonds
- church bonds
- agency bonds
- mortgage, asset-backed securities
- all securities issued by the Treasury Department except savings bonds

TRACE-eligible securities do not include:

- Debt issued by a foreign sovereign
- Money market instruments
- Debt securities in physical form/not "Depository Trust Company-eligible"
- Convertible bonds (these are reported through the ACT system)

To start using the TRACE system member firms must submit a TRACE Participant application agreement and comply with all provisions, plus all SEC and FINRA rules and operating procedures. If member firms do not comply with all requirements, they can end up having their TRACE service terminated by FINRA. Failing to comply would include failure to make timely payment to the system for its services.

The TRACE system displays the following information concerning a transaction in debt securities:

- execution date and time
- quantity
- price

- yield
- whether price includes a commission
- special settlement/conditions affecting price, if any
- whether trade reported late

For the trading systems involving equity trades, the seller reports. With TRACE, however, in a trade between two member firms, both the buy and sell side file a report. In a trade between a member and a non-member (including a customer) only the member firm files a report.

If securities are being underwritten, they are also about to be traded on the secondary market among investors. Therefore, the managing underwriter must provide notice to FINRA containing the following information:

- CUSIP # (or other identifying #)
- Name of issuer
- Coupon rate
- Maturity
- Whether 144A applies
- Time that new issue is priced
- Brief description of the issue (senior subordinated note, senior note, etc.)

Generally, this notice must be provided to FINRA Operations before the execution of the first transaction of the offering.

Municipal securities transactions are reported by dealers through an electronic reporting system known as RTRS for Real-Time Transaction Reporting System. As the **MSRB (Municipal Securities Rulemaking Board)** states, RTRS is a trade reporting facility "operated by the MSRB. RTRS receives municipal securities transaction reports submitted by dealers, disseminates price and volume information in real time for transparency purposes, and otherwise processes information."

Order Audit Trail (OATS)

Member firms execute orders for their customers and for their own accounts. Information on these orders is essential to regulatory efforts, which is why FINRA operates a system to capture basic order information from member firms. FINRA's **Order Audit Trail System** (OATS) captures order information reported by member firms and then integrates that order information with trade and quotation information from other systems that we just looked at.

This provides FINRA an accurate time sequenced record of orders and transactions for purposes of compliance. As they explain on their website, "FINRA uses this audit trail system to recreate events in the life cycle of orders and more completely monitor the trading practices of member firms." All FINRA member firms are required to report order information through this system in both NASDAQ and non-NASDAQ OTC equity securities. So, if it is a NASDAQ stock or a stock trading on the OTC Bulletin Board or the Pink Quote, the orders are reported to the system.

OATS combines the order information that firms report with transaction data reported through the ACT system and with quotation information entered through NASDAQ trading systems. This way, if

FINRA needs to roll back the clock to see if a market maker failed to honor a published bid at 17 seconds past 10:33 yesterday morning, the OATS system makes that possible. Member firms must record each order down to the hour/minute/second, like this: 13:21:59 (order executed at 59 seconds after 1:21 PM Eastern).

These time stamps are so important that firms must synchronize their business clocks according to FINRA guidelines so that regulators can go back to a single point of reference when sorting out what happened to determine who—if anyone—violated the rules. In other words, if Morgan Stanley's clock were a few seconds off from Merrill Lynch's clock . . . times several thousand firms . . . chaos. Some firms now have systems capable of recording transactions down to the millisecond. Such firms must add that extra decimal place in their reports through the trading facilities and to the OATS system.

But, while the clocks must be synchronized each day before the markets open, the order information reported to OATS is not done in real-time or even within 30 seconds. In fact, the order information simply must be provided by the next calendar day at 8 AM eastern. Remember it's an "audit trail" system, meaning the regulators want to see what happened yesterday—down to the hour/minute/second—as opposed to the quotes that are displayed in real-time through NASDAQ trading systems or the last-sale reports that are submitted to the market through the ACT platform within 30 seconds. Do all firms have to bear the burden/expense of synchronizing their clocks each day and throughout the day? No. If the firm only sells mutual funds and has no requirement to record market events, they do not have to synchronize their clock.

Whether the order is placed for a customer or the firm's proprietary trading account, the order information must be reported to the OATS system. Order information must be reported on the same day the order was executed—or modified, cancelled, received, or transmitted to another department within the firm. As with the ACT system, firms can sign an agreement with a third party to transmit order information on their behalf. In this case one Reporting Member agrees to fulfill the obligations of another, acting as a Reporting Agent to report information on the other firm's behalf. However, the firm that receives or originates the order remains ultimately responsible for making sure the order information is reported.

Orders that are partially executed are also reported. In that case the number of shares executed and the number of unexecuted shares remaining would be reported to the system.

A brokerage firm is a busy place to work. With registered representatives taking customer orders by telephone and/or reviewing the orders placed online, what are the odds that some of these transactions will end up going wrong? Pretty high. That's why every trade must be confirmed with the customer.

Best Execution, Trading Capacity and Quotation

A customer enters an order to buy 500 shares of SBUX through his online broker-dealer. The online broker-dealer routes the order to the best available market. Typically, that would be whichever market making firm were displaying the lowest ASK at the time.

The online broker-dealer is required to achieve **best execution** when filling customer orders. Typically, price determines the best execution, but FINRA allows firms to consider **execution quality**, as well. Execution quality includes the speed of execution and the % of orders that get filled by the market maker, called the "fill rate."

Price improvement doesn't happen often, but when it does the customer's order is filled at a better price than was displayed at the time of entry. For example, if the quote for ABC is Bid: $20.00, Offer: $20.05, let's say a customer places a market order to sell. That means he's willing to accept $20.00 for his shares. But, when his broker calls, the customer is informed he was filled at $20.04, 4 cents-per-share higher than the Offer/Ask at the time he placed the order.

Why this happens isn't clear. One explanation is that market makers earn profits on minute movements in a security's market price; therefore, sometimes they just act to keep the market for the security smooth, liquid. It's also possible that in a fast market, sometimes mistakes are made that favor investors.

Although the price of execution is important, FINRA allows firms to consider speed of execution, fill rates and price improvements when routing customer trades to market makers. Therefore, if a market maker's fill rates and/or price improvements are superior, the broker-dealer routing orders to them would be conforming to best execution requirements even in those cases where another market maker was quoting a better price.

The word "broker-dealer" is hyphenated for a reason. In any transaction, a broker-dealer can "broker" the transaction or "deal" the security. FINRA members either get a customer order filled between the customer and a market maker, or they are market makers themselves. A firm is never acting in both roles on the same trade.

When acting as a broker in the trade, a FINRA member indicates to the customer they acted in an **agency** capacity. If the firm is a market maker, they act in a **principal** capacity in these trades, as they either buy from, or sell to, an investor.

Also, if the firm is a market maker, it may act as principal in a trade with a retail investor by adding a **markup** to a purchase order, or a **markdown** to a sale. In these trades, the firm adds a few pennies to the ask when a customer buys (markup), or subtracts a few pennies from the bid when a customer sells (markdown). These are referred to as "net transactions."

Either way, the firm must give the customer a fair and reasonable price, and disclose in which role they acted. When acting in an agency capacity, the firm adds a commission. When making markets, the firm earns the difference between their Bid and Ask, known as the **spread**. And, when acting in a principal capacity with their retail customers, the firm earns a markup or markdown.

Trader Corrections "as/of" and Past Settlement Date

Sometimes trades are reported incorrectly. When that happens, the back office makes a bona fide correction. If the correction is made after the trade date, it is entered "as/of" the date the correction is entered. That day is known as the processing date. The trade is marked as of the trade date that was reported. The settlement date is calculated from the trade, or "as/of" date rather than the processing date.

That's how it works for trades corrected after the trade date but before settlement. For corrections entered after settlement, a similar procedure is used, except that the processing date becomes the settlement date.

Error Accounts

Trading mistakes happen. For example, a customer enters a limit order to buy 500 shares of ABC at $30, but the firm's trader buys shares at that price or better for the proprietary account before filling the customer's order. Or, on that same order, maybe the trader buys 800 shares rather than the 500 indicated.

In either case, the broker dealer moves such trades to its error account. From here, the broker-dealer buys or sells on the open market to complete the erroneous trade. The error account is a short-term account that is not to be used for regular proprietary trading activities.

Basic Knowledge of Settlement

Clearing broker-dealers that are members of the National Securities Clearing Corporation clear and settle transactions efficiently through the NSCC.

Trade Comparison

Trades among clearing broker-dealers are automatically compared and locked-in by the NSCC. This guarantee eliminates counterparty risk, meaning the sell side will be paid for the transaction, no matter what.

The final stage of the process is **settlement.** This happens at the related entity called the DTC or Depository Trust Company. Like the NSCC, the DTC is also a subsidiary of the Depository Trust Clearing Corporation (DTCC).

Settlement occurs when payment is made and securities are delivered to the accounts of both sides of the trade.

Continuous Net Settlement

Rather than settling with the other side on a per-trade basis, the NSCC's **Continuous Net Settlement (CNS) system** computes a net-long or net-short amount of either money or securities owed by a member firm on the settlement date. For ABC common stock, Broker-Dealer A is either net-long or net-short. If Broker-Dealer A is net-long, they owe money. If they are net-short, they owe shares of ABC to their NSCC account.

The ACT system used by broker-dealers trading through NASDAQ is a web-based system allowing member firms to submit up to 500 trades in a single computer file.

Trades are locked in by two different methods in the system: trade-by-match, and trade acceptance. A trade-by-match involves both sides of the transaction entering trade reports to the system, with the system automatically matching them. A trade acceptance involves a reporting party entering a trade on behalf of the other side of the trade, called the "contra party." In the second case, the contra party has 20 minutes to review the trade in the ACT system's browse function. If the trade is accepted, it becomes locked in. But, if it is rejected, it is purged from the system.

Once a trade has been accepted by both sides of the transaction, it is locked in. Locked in trades are sent to the NSCC and are considered a firm obligation of both the buy and sell side. That means the trade must be honored on the scheduled settlement date. Locked.

If a trade is canceled, the cancellation report must be filed to the ACT system by the party responsible for filing the original trade report.

Don't Know (DK) Trade

Trades are compared for accuracy on the following aspects:

- Buy/sell side
- Security
- Contra party
- Quantity
- Price
- (If applicable) accrued interest

When one side of the trade does not recognize a transaction, or disagrees with the details of a transaction reported by the other side, they **DK (Don't Know) Notice** the transaction electronically. Perhaps the number of shares is incorrect, or the stock symbol doesn't match the issuer.

Ex-Clearing Transactions

Most trades are settled among broker-dealers electronically through ACT and/or the NSCC. But, some transactions still settle outside of these systems. For example, when-, as-, and if-issued contracts are settled ex-clearing, or outside the typical ACT/NSCC method.

For ex-clearing transactions:

- Interdealer paper confirmations sent no later than next-day
- When the confirming member sends a confirmation but does not receive one in return, the confirming member must send a DK notice to the non-confirming member after 4 business days from the trade date
- After receipt of the DK, the non-confirming member has 4 business days to either confirm or DK the trade
- If no response is received from the non-confirming member, the confirming member can consider the lack of response as a DK, and can drop the trade

Settlement Service Providers

The Depository Trust & Clearing Corporation, with its subsidiary the National Securities Clearing Corporation, was established in 1976 with the goal of eliminating the need for paper certificates for clearing and settlement of broker-to-broker trades. The DTCC provides clearing, settlement, and guarantee-of-completion for transactions in equities, ETFs, UITs, corporate and municipal debt securities.

Available through the DTCC are services including:

- ACATS
- Continuous Net Settlement (CNS)
- Trade Comparison and Reporting
- Settlement Services
- Stock Borrow Program

Like FINRA, the Depository Trust & Clearing Corporation and National Securities Clearing Corporation are registered with the SEC as SROs. The Depository Trust & Clearing Corporation has 10 subsidiaries. Each one serves a different segment or purpose for the securities industry, including:

- National Securities Clearing Corporation (NSCC)
- Depository Trust Company (DTC)
- Fixed Income Clearing Corporation (FICC)
- DTCC Derivatives Repository Ltd.

Methods of Settlement

Most terms used in the industry are not fancy.

Regular Way

For example, the regular way of settling a transaction is known as **regular-way settlement.** Some securities settle regular way at T + 2. Others settle regular way at T + 1. A T + 2 settlement means if the customer buys stock Tuesday, the trade settles Thursday. If the security settles regular-way at T + 1, the trade settles Wednesday.

As with wire transfers through a bank, weekends and holidays are not counted. If a trade is executed Friday, it settles Monday, unless Monday is a holiday, at T + 1. A trade entered Friday settles at T + 2 on Tuesday.

To a customer, settlement refers to the day the funds become available for withdrawal for the sell-side. The buy-side must make full payment by settlement. Some broker-dealers allow buyers to pay for the transaction after it is entered. Many require the funds to be available when the trade is entered. Either way, full payment must be made by the settlement date to keep things running smooth.

Cash Settlement

A **cash settlement** settles "**same day,**" meaning the day it is traded is the day it settles. If the trade happens before 2:00 p.m., it settles by 2:30 p.m. If the trade happens after 2:00 p.m., it settles within 30 minutes.

Next Day

For a **next-day settlement,** the cash and securities must be available by the next day following the trade. Another way of saying next-day is "T + 1." Securities that settle regular-way at T + 1 include Treasury securities and options.

Seller's Option

The seller's option is used when the seller likes the price he can get today but—for whatever reason—won't be able to come up with the securities for a while. In this case the seller specifies the date on which he will be able to deliver the securities and may not deliver sooner than the third business day following the trade. If the seller specifies a certain date but ends up wanting to deliver the securities earlier, he must give the buyer a one-day written notice of his intention.

Buyer's Option

The buyer could also specify the date when payment will be made for securities and accept delivery, which is known as a buyer's option.

RVP/DVP

Certain institutional accounts avoid the risk of delivering securities before payment has been made by setting up a **DVP/RVP** account that uses **Delivery Versus Payment** settlement. As the name implies, payment must be made when or before the securities purchased are delivered. That is from the buyer's perspective. From the seller's perspective, the process is **Receive Versus Payment.** The DVP system ensures that securities will be delivered only if payment is made.

When-, As-, and If-Issued Contracts

New offers of municipal securities are frequently sold to investors before the securities have been issued. In these transactions, investors receive when-, as-, and if-issued confirmations. The confirmations must contain a description of the security with the yield to the customer and the trade date.

Because the securities have not been issued, the settlement date is not known. Therefore, if there is accrued interest due to the underwriters, the total price cannot yet be determined. When the bonds are issued, investors receive updated confirmations showing the settlement date and the total purchase price.

Standard Settlement for Various Products

Regular-way settlement is $T + 2$ for listed stocks, corporate bonds, and municipal bonds.

Options and U.S. Treasury Securities, on the other hand, settle regular-way on $T + 1$, or next-day.

So, a corporate bond purchased on a Tuesday settles Thursday. A T-Bond purchased on a Tuesday settles Wednesday.

Although the purchase or sale of an option settles $T + 1$, when an options holder exercises the contract, the underlying stock that changes hand settles $T + 2$. If a call buyer exercises the call, his payment is due, and the securities must be delivered by the seller, within the usual $T + 2$ settlement cycle. When a put is exercised, the holder delivers the stock to the writer, and the writer delivers payment to the put buyer within the usual $T + 2$ cycle.

U.S. Treasuries trading among investors settle $T + 1$. But, when they are auctioned by the Federal Reserve Board, those transactions settle $T + 2$. T-Bills are auctioned each Monday. Notes and Bonds have rarer, scheduled auctions.

As we saw, mutual fund trades for the shareholders of the fund execute once per day, only after the markets close. If an investor misses the trading deadline for that day, the trade is not executed until the close of the next trading day.

Most open-end mutual funds settle customer transactions on the next business day. Occasionally, a fund has provisions in its shareholder agreement allowing it more time to settle transactions. However long the settlement period is, fund buyers must have cash available by settlement, and fund sellers are unable to use cash proceeds for other purposes until the trade settles.

Money-market mutual fund transactions settle same-day. That is why customers often use money market mutual funds as sweep options, giving them fast access to funds without having to wait an extra day to clear transactions.

Other types of funds governed by similar rules to open-end funds have different settlement rules. For example, ETFs are like mutual funds, but follow the same rules as stocks. Therefore, they settle regular-way T + 2. Closed-end funds also trade like any other share of common stock, with a regular-way settlement period of T + 2.

Close-Outs

On some transactions, either the buy or sell side does not come through with their part of the obligation. Either the seller fails to deliver the securities sold in the trade or the buyer fails to transmit the funds to pay for the trade.

Buy-Ins

Failure to deliver securities does not force a cancellation of the trade. Rather, after proper procedures have been followed, the broker-dealer whose customer purchased the securities completes a buy-in to obtain the securities for the customer.

If both firms are members of a registered clearing agency, notice is sent through the NSCC, FICC, etc. If not, notice can be sent by fax, computer system, or any system providing return receipt capability. The firm transmitting the buy-in is required to maintain the return receipt with the buy-in notice on its books and records.

The buying broker-dealer may close out the position no sooner than the third business day following the settlement date. The firm must provide written notice to the other side by noon two business days before executing the buy-in. The notice informs the sell-side of the buyer's intention to purchase securities not delivered by the seller for the account and expense of the seller. If the market price of the securities not delivered hasn't moved, the sell-side will pay back the funds already delivered by the buy-side. If the market price has risen, the sell-side will realize a loss.

After executing the buy-in, the broker-dealer must notify the party for whose account the securities were bought as to the quantity purchased and the price paid. This notice is due by 6 PM on the date the buy-in is executed and must, again, be sent through a system providing return receipt capabilities.

When the sell-side receives the initial buy-in notice, the member can claim "no fault." This means the failure to deliver is due to a third party—typically, another member—not delivering to them. The seller in this case re-transmits the written notice to the third party. This extends the proposed buy-in date by up to seven calendar days.

Also, the firm may effect partial delivery by the proposed due date to extend the process.

Sell-Outs

Buy-Ins follow a complicated procedure in which the sell-side can get an extension, or can complete a partial delivery before the proposed buy-in date to buy some time.

With a sell-out, on the other hand, things are simple. If a member fails to pay for securities sold by another member by settlement, the sell-side can execute a sell-out any time after settlement. Unlike with the buy-in, no written notice is required before effecting a sell-out.

As with a buy-in, if the sale price is lower, the loss is borne by the other side—the contra party to the trade.

Aged Securities Fails

If a customer has a fail to deliver after selling stock, the firm must set up a fail to deliver account on its books in the amount of the sales proceeds for the transaction. Surprisingly, at this point the position is still an allowable asset. However, the longer the fail-to-deliver drags on, the bigger the required haircut.

On the fifth business day following settlement the fail-to-deliver must be aged for purposes of computing net capital. The position would now be marked to the market with a 15% haircut taken on that. Even though the asset has been aged, it is still an allowable asset. It just needs to get itself an extra-short haircut to be counted in the firm's net capital.

Securities Transfers

When stocks and bonds are bought and sold, the securities ownership is transferred from the seller to the buyer. No matter how the securities are held, the customer's broker-dealer will either assist with or complete the process.

Both stocks and bonds are evidenced by certificates. A bond certificate is a paper or electronic document stating the details of the bond:

- issuer's name
- par value or face amount
- interest rate
- maturity date
- call date (if any)

There are four different forms that a bond can take in terms of the certificate itself. In olden days, bonds were issued as bearer bonds, which meant that whoever had possession of the bond was assumed to be the owner. No owner name at all on the certificate. The bond certificate said, "pay to the bearer," so whoever presented the bond at maturity received the principal. To receive the interest, investors holding bearer bonds used to clip coupons attached to the bond certificate every six months.

There was no name on the interest coupon, either, so the IRS had no way of tracking the principal or the interest income. Bonds haven't been issued in bearer form for many years. That doesn't mean they don't exist. A few are out there in safe-deposit boxes surely.

Bonds also used to be registered as to principal only. That meant we had a name on the bond certificate—the person who would receive the principal amount at maturity. But, again, we had the unnamed interest coupons. Therefore, only the principal was registered, thus the name "registered as to principal only."

Eventually, issuers started registering the name of the owner [principal] and automatically making an interest payment every six months for the interest. We call these bonds fully registered, because both pieces of the debt service (interest, principal) are registered.

Book entry/journal entry bonds are also fully registered. It's just that it's done on computer, rather than on paper. The investor keeps the trade confirmation as proof of ownership, but the issuer's paying agent has an owner name on computer, and automatically pays interest to the registered owner. Book entry/journal entry is how virtually all securities are issued these days. But, since bonds often have 30-year maturities, there are investors out there with bond certificates in their possession.

Private companies often issue paper certificates to their investors, and transferring these securities is also subject to federal and state securities law. If you are a business owner with a corporation, your corporate books contain stock certificates. You would be wise to consult a business/securities attorney before offering any of them.

Good Delivery

After a trade is executed, the buy side must remit the funds to the clearing agency, while the sell side must deliver securities. Some customers still choose to have their securities "transferred and shipped," so when they sell stock, they are in possession of the certificates and must deliver them. Or, they must direct their bank to do so. Either way, if the stock or bond certificate is registered to Joe B. Kuhl, it must be signed exactly as: Joe B. Kuhl. If he signs it *Joey Kuhl*, the transfer agent will reject it.

Also, a security registered to more than one individual must be signed properly by all owners, and a security registered to a trust, an estate, a corporation, etc. must be properly signed by an executor, trustee, or corporate officer.

The back of the certificate often has a **stock power** form the owner fills out and signs. If the security is a bond, we refer to the form as a **bond power.** If the certificate lacks such a form, the broker-dealer provides a separate form for the customer to fill in and sign.

These forms are also known as **powers of substitution.** It is usually the power of substitution that is signed, rather than having the customer fill in and sign the back of the stock or bond certificate. That way, if the customer messes up the signature, they haven't destroyed anything of value. They can always try again until they get it right.

To complete the transfer of securities, the transfer agent first must accept the signature as valid. Therefore, a medallion signature guarantee is required.

The transfer agent would reject the following signatures:

- Signature of a minor child
- Signature of an individual now deceased

- Signature of just one person in a joint account

If a sale were executed, with the securities endorsed by a person who has since died, the securities must be re-issued by the transfer agent in the name of the estate or trust, with the executor or trustee properly signing after that has been taken care of.

Bond certificates delivered between broker-dealers must be $1,000 or $5,000 par value. If there are coupons (bearer, principal-only) missing, that's a problem. The receiving broker-dealer would cop such an attitude that if the missing coupon represented $60 of interest, they would deduct $60 from the money they send to the other firm. So there. If it's a municipal bond, the legal opinion must be attached. If there was no legal opinion obtained, the certificate needs to be stamped "ex-legal." Ex- means "without," as in "ex-dividend," which means the stock is trading without the dividend.

Delivery can be rejected by the firm representing the buyer if:

- Certificates are mutilated
- Certificates don't comply with the round and odd lot requirements
- All attachments are not present (affidavit of domicile, stock power, etc.)
- Signature is invalid
- Signatures are not guaranteed
- Securities are delivered prior to the settlement date

If a stock is purchased on or after the ex-dividend date, the seller is entitled to the dividend, and if the stock is purchased before the ex-date, the buyer is entitled to the dividend. Sometimes things get screwed up. The buyer purchases the stock before the ex-date, but the seller still ends up getting the dividend. In this case, the customer's broker-dealer would send a **due bill** for the dividend to the other broker-dealer and would expect them to fork over the cash that is due.

When securities are sent to a broker-dealer and are not in good delivery form, the broker dealer should file a **reclamation** with the other side. As the name indicates, it's time to reclaim things here and get them right.

Shares of Common Stock

A corporation files its articles of incorporation with the state where they are organized. These articles disclose the name and purpose of the business, its address, and how many shares of stock the corporation is authorized to issue, known as the **authorized** shares. If a public company is authorized to issue 1,000,000 shares of common stock, they will probably not sell all of them at once. When they first sell shares to the public during their IPO, the number they issue is known as **issued** shares. Let's say this corporation could issue 1 million, but they only issue 600,000 shares. If so, there would be 600,000 issued shares after the public offering. And, at that point, the **shares outstanding** would also be the 600,000 that were issued in the IPO.

For many reasons, the corporation might buy back some of those shares. These shares, which were issued but repurchased, are called **treasury stock**. Treasury stock has no voting rights and pays no dividends. The benefit to the shareholders who remain is that the value of their existing stock tends to rise when the company is reducing the number of shares on the secondary market. If this corporation had issued 600,000 shares and then purchased 200,000 for the treasury, they would have 400,000 shares outstanding.

600,000	Issued
-200,000	Treasury
400,000	Outstanding

When we look at a company's earnings per-share, or EPS, on the income statement, we only count the **outstanding shares**. That's why the company can boost its earnings per-share (EPS) by repurchasing their outstanding stock on the secondary market. Even if the company's total earnings stayed the same, the earnings per-share would rise if the company were reducing the number of outstanding shares. For example, if the company earned $1 million in net income, that is an earnings per-share of $1.67 when there were 600,000 shares outstanding. However, after the company buys back 200,000 shares for the treasury, that same $1 million profit would be $2.50 of earnings per-share.

Treasury stock doesn't vote, so the officers and directors of the company, who own large positions in the stock, end up with more influence during corporate elections after a large share buyback. Also note that the cash used buying back shares is reflected on the company's statement of cash flows under financing activities.

Common stock is easy to transfer to another party. It can be sold, donated, gifted, or inherited. The issuer of the stock hires a financial institution to keep track of the transfers of ownership, and they're called the **transfer agent**. The transfer agent keeps the ownership records of the company's stock. They deal with issuing and validating stock and bond certificates, recording name changes when investors sell their certificates, and re-issuing lost, stolen, or destroyed certificates. If there's a problem with the ownership records of the security, contact the transfer agent. They can validate or re-issue certificates, for a fee.

With just one share of some stocks worth thousands of dollars, most investors don't want the responsibility of protecting the certificates from damage, theft, or misplacement. So, rather than having the securities shipped, transfer the securities into their vault. That method is called safekeeping. The firm would most investors do is have the **street name**. This way, the  they could have the broker-dealer name and then hold them in the firm's either "transfer and hold" or likely charge a fee to do that. So, what broker-dealer hold the securities in broker-dealer is the named or nominal owner of the securities and the customer is the beneficial owner of the securities.

As we're about to see, shareholders can now also use the direct registration method.

But, whatever the customer chooses, the fact is most customers these days have never seen a stock or bond certificate because their broker-dealer holds them in street name and may have them on deposit at centralized "depositories" such as the **Depository Trust Company (DTC)**. From there, the securities are transferred through electronic entries only, which explains why many registered representatives have also never seen a stock or bond certificate. From the Depository Trust Company's website at www.dtc.org we see how things currently work:

With the implementation of direct registration, investors have three securities ownership options:

Physical Certificates: Certificates are registered and issued in the investor's name. The investor will receive all mailings directly from the issuer or its transfer agent, including dividend or interest payments, annual reports, and proxies.

Street Name Registration: Securities are registered in the street name of the investor's broker-dealer. While no physical certificate will be issued to the investor, the broker-dealer will issue, at least quarterly, account statements of the investor's holdings. The broker-dealer will pay dividends or interest to the investor, as well as provide the investor with mailing material from the issuer or transfer agent.

Direct Registration: This option allows the investor to be registered directly on the books of the transfer agent without the need of a physical certificate to evidence the security ownership. While the investor will not receive a physical certificate, he or she will receive a statement of ownership and periodic (at least yearly) account statements. Dividend or interest payments, proxy materials, annual reports, etc., will be mailed from the issuer or its transfer agent.

Handling Lost Certificates

If a security is lost or stolen, the owner should immediately contact the transfer agent and request that a "stop transfer" be placed to prevent ownership from improperly transferring to someone else. If an investor was expecting certificates through the mail directly from the issuer, he should take the same steps if the certificates do not arrive when anticipated.

In either case, should the owner then locate lost certificates, he must contact the transfer agent again to remove the stop transfer. Otherwise, he may later find it difficult to sell the securities.

The transfer agent contacts the SEC's lost and stolen securities program to file a report. Or, if the customer uses a broker-dealer, he can contact them to see if they have a record of his purchase. If not, they will typically file notice with the SEC.

To have stock certificates reissued, the transfer agent and issuer require:

- The owner must state the facts surrounding the loss in an affidavit
- The owner must buy an indemnity bond to protect the corporation and the transfer agent against the possibility that the lost certificate may be presented later by an innocent purchaser
  - Usually costs between 2 or 3% of the market value of the missing certificates
- The owner must request a new certificate before an innocent purchaser acquires it

The SEC's website recommends that investors with certificates make a photocopy of the front and back, keeping the copies separate from the originals. Without such a record, it is possible that someone could fraudulently transfer the securities on the transfer agent's books to another party without the owner's being able to prove they were ever his.

And, as we just saw, this can all be eliminated by using either direct registration or the street-name method.

If someone has reason to believe he owns stocks or bonds but has no records or broker-dealer to help prove it, the SEC informs investors of the escheatment process we looked at. There are several websites available to help such people or entities verify if they own securities held as abandoned accounts.

Legends

A certificate with a **legend** stamped or printed on it provides notice to the owner that the unregistered security may not be transferred unless it is registered or sold through an exemption under the Securities Act of 1933. The legend is a contract between the issuer and the securities holders, an agreement they will not sell their stocks or bonds before the holding period expires.

Therefore, many restrictive legends are removed by the issuer's transfer agent only if the owner provides an opinion by a qualified attorney. Some require the issuer's counsel to issue an opinion before the legend may be removed and the security sold or otherwise transferred to another party.

Restricted Stock

The term **restricted stock** means the owner's ability to sell or transfer the stock is restricted because of a required holding period. Stock purchased in a private placement is restricted stock, restricted in terms of the investor's ability to sell it to another party. Officers and key employees may also receive restricted shares subject to a holding period as opposed to stock options that can be exercised right away. When purchasing restricted securities, investors typically receive a certificate with a legend stamped on it indicating the securities may not be resold in the marketplace unless they are registered with the SEC or are exempt from the registration requirements. If the securities are electronic/book entry, the electronic record contains the legend.

Either way, the SEC does not want people acting like underwriters and funneling unregistered stock to the securities markets in a way that bypasses the Securities Act of 1933's concerns for full disclosure. **Rule 144** provides a safe harbor exemption for those who want to sell restricted stock without violating securities law. And, though a registered representative will perhaps never own restricted stock, if he executes a sale for a customer who does, he could get in trouble if he doesn't know and follow the rules.

The text of a restrictive legend typically looks something like this:

> THIS SECURITY HAS NOT BEEN REGISTERED OR QUALIFIED UNDER
> THE SECURITIES ACT OF 1933 OR THE SECURITIES OR BLUE SKY
> LAWS OF ANY STATE AND MAY BE OFFERED AND SOLD ONLY IF
> REGISTERED AND QUALIFIED PURSUANT TO THE RELEVANT
> PROVISIONS OF FEDERAL AND STATE SECURITIES OR BLUE SKY

> LAWS OR IF AN EXEMPTION FROM SUCH REGISTRATION OR
> QUALIFICATION IS APPLICABLE.

Typically, the legend is stamped or printed on the back of the certificate, with notice on the front such as:

> TRANSFER OF THE SHARES REPRESENTED BY THIS CERTIFICATE IS
> RESTRICTED. SEE LEGEND ON REVERSE SIDE.

The first requirement for selling restricted stock is that the issuer must have been a reporting company under the Securities Exchange Act of 1934 for at least 90 days immediately before the sale. And, the issuer cannot have missed filing any of the reports they were required to file during the preceding 12 months. Without this requirement, worthless securities in companies no one knows anything about could be dumped onto the securities markets at great harm to investors.

So, first, the issuer must be someone about whom investors can receive material information. Even if the issuer is an insurance company or a company not subject to reporting (non-reporting company) under the Securities Exchange Act of 1934, the SEC requires that certain basic information on these issuers be available including information on the nature of its business, the identity of the officers and directors, and financial statements.

Otherwise, no sale.

Restricted stock is subject to a holding period. If the issuer is a reporting company subject to reporting requirements at least 90 days, purchasers must hold the securities a minimum of six months before reselling them. If the issuer is not a reporting company, the minimum holding period is one year.

Once the holding period is met, a non-affiliate can sell his shares if he wants to.

For affiliates of the company, Rule 144 has further requirements, whether selling restricted or control stock. Restricted stock is unusual because of the way it was offered to investors. For control stock, on the other hand, it's the owner who triggers the requirements, not the securities. Control stock is held by investors who can control the issuer or could harm the market price of the stock by selling a large amount. So, whether selling restricted or control stock, affiliates must file a Form 144 with the SEC no later than at the time of the sale. The filing is good for 90 days.

Also, if the transaction is not larger than 5,000 shares and $50,000, the sale can be made without filing a Form 144.

Typically, affiliates sell large amounts of securities, but they must comply with the volume limits under Rule 144. For exchange-traded securities, affiliates can sell the issuer's stock provided they sell no more than the greater of 1% of the outstanding shares or the average weekly trading volume over the four most recent weeks. If the company has 1 billion shares outstanding, the affiliate could sell whichever is greater over the next 90 days—10 million shares or the average weekly trading volume going back four weeks. For stocks that either don't trade or trade on the OTC Bulletin Board or Pink Quote, only the 1% figure is used.

That's the amount that can be sold. As for the method of sale the rule states, "If you are an affiliate, the sales must be handled in all respects as routine trading transactions, and brokers may not receive more than a normal commission. Neither the seller nor the broker can solicit orders to buy the securities."

Also, affiliates can never sell the company's stock short. And, although control stock is not subject to a holding period, an affiliate can't take a profit on their company's stock held less than 6 months. This is called a short-swing profit, which must be turned back over to the company with the gain being taxed by the IRS.

FINRA is concerned that agents and their firms sometimes help customers sell unregistered restricted securities, which violates federal securities law. If the customer does not conform to all the stipulations we just went over, but wants to take his unregistered restricted shares and sell them, firms must be sure they don't help him skirt securities law in this manner. FINRA alerts its member broker-dealers that some customers are companies trying to sell their shares illegally. If the customer deposits certificates representing a large block of thinly traded or low-priced securities, that's a red flag. If the share certificates refer to a company or customer name that has been changed or that does not match the name on the account, that's another red flag. If a customer with limited or no other assets under management at the firm receives an electronic transfer or journal transactions of large amounts of low-priced, unlisted securities, that's another red flag.

Broker-dealers must do a reasonable inquiry to ensure they are not helping people get around securities law.

Corporate Actions

Many companies remain private to avoid filing reports with the SEC and shareholders. Full disclosure of material facts to the public is not attractive to many businesses. It is also a great expense to prepare reports required under the Securities Exchange Act of 1934.

The quarterly reports contain financial statements that have not been audited by an outside accounting firm. They are called 10Q reports, and the issuer files three per year. The annual report contains financials which are audited, or "certified," by an independent auditing firm. The annual report is called a 10K. Rather than filing a fourth 10Q, the issuer files their 10K. The 10K contains the most information, and the most accurate information, of the four required reports.

The annual report is issued in conjunction with the annual shareholder meeting. At the annual meeting, important matters are voted on. The routine matters include electing the board of directors and ratifying the independent auditor. Shareholder and board of director proposals are often voted on, too.

Shareholders may inform themselves about the upcoming annual meeting and the issues to be voted on by reading the **proxy statement.** In the proxy statement, the issuer provides all material information about the board of directors running for election and the proposals to be decided. Management typically indicates how they feel shareholders should vote on each item. But, shareholders are free to vote as they see fit.

Investors are not required to attend the annual meeting to cast their votes. In fact, that is a rare thing these days. Then again, Berkshire Hathaway's annual meeting attracts more people than many rock concerts, so, as usual, general statements fail to hold up in this industry.

A shareholder planning to attend the meeting revokes the proxy. That means he is not going to appoint a third party to cast his vote. Most shareholders, however, fill out their voting instructions on the proxy card or proxy form. From there, the broker-dealer or their third-party service provider assures the shareholder's vote is cast by proxy before polling closes during the annual meeting.

Special shareholder meetings are also called when corporations are merged with, or acquired by, other companies. Public companies must alert the SEC and give shareholders sufficient notice when a corporate action is proposed. The party interested in acquiring a large position or all the issuer's outstanding stock makes what is known as a tender offer. They are required to follow many requirements under SEC rules and the Exchange Act to prevent the market for the stock from becoming overrun by rumor, panic, volatility, etc.

After management for the target company explains the proposal to their shareholders—often giving their opinion of the terms—shareholders vote to accept or reject the deal. For example, if the common stock trades around $50 and the acquirer offers $55 per share, the shareholders might turn down the first offer. It is not uncommon for two or three offers to be made before shareholders accept what they feel is a fair price.

It is also not uncommon for such proposed actions to fall apart. Or, management might express their opinion that merging with any company is a bad idea, and the shareholders vote no from the start.

In many cases, a public or private company offers to buy all the common stock of an issuer. For example, a few years ago a European private investment group offered to buy all the common stock of Krispy Kreme (KKD) at a premium to what it then traded for. Management liked the deal, the shareholders voted to accept, their shares were turned into cash, and from then on, the company was private.

Not that anything changed about the donuts or the stores themselves. These corporate actions are about shifting ownership, the realm of attorneys and investment bankers. Making the donuts and running the stores involves different departments.

Sometimes, a tender offer is for a stated percentage of the common stock. The acquiring party sets a deadline for successfully purchasing a percentage of the common stock from all those who tender (offer up) their stock for the stated price.

If enough shares are tendered, the deal is successfully completed. If not, money is returned, and the deal is canceled.

Another type of corporate action is called a spin-off. Large public companies occasionally take a business unit and "spin it off" into a separate entity that will trade on the public markets. For example, many years ago AT&T Wireless was spun off from the parent company in an extremely large offer of common stock.

Shareholders of the parent company receive their fair share of the new entity when this happens. Maybe a shareholder with 1,000 shares of the parent company receives 200 shares of the entity being spun off.

Cash dividends are taxable because they involve a payment to the shareholder. Stock dividends, on the other hand, are not payments. Rather, investors end up with more shares in the company, with the shares worth less per-share. So, the big idea behind **stock splits** and **stock dividends** is that even when the investor ends up with more shares, the total value of his investment is unchanged. If he had 100 shares at $10 before, that was worth $1,000. No matter how many shares he has after the split or the stock dividend, the total value is $1,000. So, when a corporation does a 2:1 stock split, the investor would have twice as many shares. What would the price per-share be?

Half as much. The investor has $1,000 worth of stock both before and after the split. He used to have 100 shares worth $10 each. Now he has 200 shares worth $5 each. $1,000 worth, either way. The test might want you to work with an uneven split, like a 5:2 ratio. This is where the company gives investors five shares for every two that they own. So, let's say the question tells you the investor holds 100 shares of ABC, which she purchased for $50 each. What happens after a 5:2 stock split? All we do is multiply the number of shares by 5 and then divide that by 2. So, 100 times 5 equals 500, and 500 divided by 2 shows us the investor will have 250 shares after the split. Her cost basis is a total of $5,000 (100 shares @50), so take that $5,000 total and divide it by the new number of shares, which is 250. Her new cost basis is 250 ABC @20.

It's important to keep an investor's cost basis so that capital gains can be reported accurately in the future. But that is all that really happened in both examples—the investor's cost basis changes along with the lowered per-share price of the stock.

A stock dividend works the same way in terms of more shares/lower price. If an investor receives a 20% stock dividend, that's 20% more shares of stock, but the total value of the investment is the same. It's just divided among more shares. So, an investor with 200 shares of XYZ common stock @40 would have $8,000 of XYZ stock. If XYZ declared a 20% stock dividend, she would then have 240 shares. Her $8,000 would then be divided among 240 shares, with a per-share price of $33.33. Companies in a growth phase are more likely to pay stock dividends than more established companies, who are more likely to pay cash dividends compared to small, growing companies.

Either way, nothing really changes for the investor after a stock dividend or a stock split. The investor has more shares at a lower price, which means her cost basis in the stock changes. 100 shares @50 might become 125 shares @40. Just keep track of your cost basis so that when you sell someday you can tell the IRS how much of a capital gain or loss you realized on the stock. But whether you have 100 shares @50 or 125 shares @40, you've paid $5,000 for a certain percentage of ownership. And, we'll deal with concerns such as "cost basis" and "capital gains" later in the book.

A forward stock split means investors end up with more shares. A 2:1, 3:2, or 5:4 split is a forward split that pushes the share price down.

Sometimes companies have the opposite problem. Their share price is so low that institutional investors won't touch it. These entities usually won't buy a stock trading below $5, so if our company's stock is trading for $1, we might need to increase that price. One way to do it is to perform a reverse stock split.

If JoAnne owns 100 shares of ABCD @$1, we might find ABCD doing a reverse split of 1:10. That means for every 10 shares she owns now, she'll end up with only one really big share. She'll have 10 shares when it's all over. If the shares were trading for $1 before the split and everybody now has shares that are 10 times bigger, the share price becomes $10 a share. JoAnne now owns 10 ABCD @$10.

Shareholders vote on stock splits, whether forward (5:4, 2:1, 3:2) or reverse (1:7, 1:10, etc.). Shareholders do not vote on dividends, whether cash or stock.

Sometimes a public company performs a type of "divestiture" known as a spin-off in which shareholders receive shares of a subsidiary or division of the company. For example, when Abbott Labs decided to make their business unit Hospira a separate company, they performed a spin-off in which ABT shareholders received a certain number of shares of HSP, which has since traded and operated as a separate company. If a company wants to exit a business line to concentrate on other areas, a spin-off may be completed. Usually, there are no tax consequences when the shareholders merely receive the shares of the spin-off. Rather, they have a cost basis, and are taxed on a capital gain if they sell the shares someday for a profit.

Another way investors receive shares of stock is through mergers & acquisitions. If a larger company offers to give, for example, .75 shares of their stock for each share investors currently hold of the target company, shareholders end up with a completely different holding. When they receive cash in an acquisition, shareholders record a capital gain or loss. But, if they're receiving shares of one company when turning in shares of their existing holding, investors record their cost basis in the shares for now. Someday, when they transfer those shares through a sale or gift, the tax consequences will be realized.

Whether it's a proposed merger, a special shareholder meeting, or a stock split, shareholders must receive sufficient formal notice, with a deadline for action far enough into the future to allow them to inform themselves of the matter or matters at hand.

Customer Accounts and Compliance Considerations

Registered representatives meet with prospects and customers and help them invest through the broker-dealer they represent. Much of the documents and procedures required to open and maintain the accounts are handled by back-office professionals.

Types of Accounts

Some accounts are taxable, some are tax-deferred. Some accounts are owned by individuals, some by entities including estates, trusts, and corporations.

Individual Account

When the account is owned by an individual, a registered representative may only discuss the account with and take orders from the individual owner. For an **individual account,** the only way a registered representative could take orders from another party is if the individual account owner grants **power of attorney** or **trading authorization** to him, and the firm keeps the signed authorization on file. Both the customer and the person who will enter transactions on his behalf must sign the form.

Pay-On-Death

A **transfer on death** or **pay-on-death account** provides a way to transfer assets without the hassle and cost of probate. If an investor sets up an account this way, the executor or administrator of the estate will not have to take any action to ensure that the securities transfer to the designated beneficiaries when the account owner passes away. With TOD registration, the investor maintains complete control of the assets during his lifetime. The named beneficiaries have no access to or control over the assets while the account owner is alive. A "POD" or "payable on death" account is the same idea applied to a bank or credit union account. A pay-on-death bank account can also be referred to as a "Totten trust."

A related idea is the **durable power of attorney** that an individual can grant to someone else. A durable power of attorney stays in force even after the individual is declared mentally incompetent. The person granted this durable power of attorney can make healthcare, financial, and legal decisions for someone who is incapacitated.

So, if a customer were in a coma after a motorcycle accident, an agent could accept orders from the person granted durable power of attorney, after verifying that the person has been granted that power by the customer.

The durable power of attorney goes into effect if the individual becomes incapacitated. The power ends when the individual dies.

Joint Accounts

When two or more individuals jointly own the assets in the account, we call it a **joint account**. All the owners sign a joint account agreement. We can accept orders from any of the parties, and we can send mail to any of the parties. But, when we cut a check or distribute securities, they must be made out to all names on the account. If the account is entitled Barbara Williams and JoAnne Stevens, **Joint Tenants in Common,** do not cut the check to Barbara and tell her to settle with JoAnne next time they have lunch. Cut the check to "Barbara Williams and JoAnne Stevens, as Joint Tenants in Common."

A **Joint Tenants with Rights of Survivorship** (JTWROS or JTROS) account gives the survivor rights to all the assets. When one account owner dies, the assets pass directly and equally to the surviving owner(s).

However, if the account is a Joint Tenants in Common (JTIC) account, when one party dies, part of the assets go to that person's estate. For JTIC accounts, the account owners indicate what % each party owns in the account agreement. For JTWROS, that wouldn't matter, as all assets go to the survivor.

Married couples often use either joint tenants in common or joint tenants with rights of survivorship accounts. However, such accounts also do not require the account owners to be married and may have more than two owners. On the other hand, a tenancy in the entirety account can only be established by a married couple. What separates these accounts from the other two is that while they are alive neither spouse can sell or give away his interest in the property without the consent of the other spouse, and creditors of either spouse cannot attach and sell one debtor spouse's interest in the property--only creditors of the married couple can do that.

If a customer has an individual account at your firm and is now deceased, know that in a "common law" state, his wife only has a claim on half the assets if she is listed as an account owner. On the other hand, if we're in a "community property" state, the wife owns half of whatever the customer earned while they were married, whether he thought to name her on the account or not. In a transfer-on-death account, the deceased customer would have named a beneficiary, but that is subject to challenge, especially in "community property" states. Assets the now deceased husband had before the marriage would generally not be subject to a claim by the wife.

Discretionary Accounts

When a registered representative can trade the customer's account without talking to the customer first, we call this a **discretionary account**. In other words, what is purchased and sold for the customer is up to the agent's and firm's discretion. That means if the registered representative decides to buy 1,000 shares of MSFT, he can do so without first contacting the customer. The customer must sign a discretionary authorization form to grant this authority to the agent and firm, and the account must be reviewed more frequently, but that's about it. From then on, the registered representative can buy or sell securities for the customer without first talking to him.

On the other hand, unless the account is a discretionary account, the only thing that can be determined for the customer is the time or price at which to execute a specific transaction. If a customer calls and says, "Buy some computer chip manufacturers today," do we need discretionary authority before you buy 100 shares of Intel?

Yes. If the registered representative chooses the security (or the number of shares), that requires discretionary authority. If a customer calls up and says, "Buy 1,000 shares of Intel today," does the registered representative need discretionary authorization? No, the customer told him what to buy and how much of it to purchase. The only thing left to decide is the best time and price at which to do it, and time/price discretion does not require discretionary authorization over the account.

These market orders that don't have to be placed immediately are called "market not held orders." They are only good for that day and may not be executed tomorrow or the next day without talking to the customer again.

When entering a discretionary order, the registered representative marks the order ticket "discretionary" at the broker-dealer, and a principal is assigned to make sure the securities purchased are appropriate and that the agent isn't churning the account.

Having the power to choose investments is often convenient, but the securities professional still must purchase what is suitable for the customer given her objectives, time horizon, risk tolerance, and capital resources. If a registered representative purchases unsuitable investments for a discretionary account, it's not just a bad idea—it's a violation of SEC, SRO, and state securities regulations.

Investment Advisory Accounts

Investment advisers typically have the discretion to enter trades for their clients' accounts, and those accounts are often held in custody by a broker-dealer independent of the advisory firm. The broker-dealer must verify that the investment adviser has discretionary authorization to enter transactions in those accounts. It would be the broker-dealer sending customers their account statements, at least monthly, by the way, rather than the adviser. And, the broker-dealer can pay the adviser the customer's advisory fee, provided the adviser sends a billing statement to both the broker-dealer and the customer.

Health Savings Accounts

As nice as it is to take money out of a Roth IRA tax-free, there was no tax deduction back when that money went in. With the Health Savings Account (HSA), on the other hand, contributions are deductible and withdrawals used to pay medical expenses are tax-free.

The account receives favorable tax treatment and is tied to an insurance policy called a high deductible health plan (HDHP). To be eligible for one of these accounts the individual can be covered under no other plan and must be below the eligibility age for Medicare. HSAs are owned by the individual, even though these plans are frequently offered through an employer. If an employee changes jobs, his HSA is portable—it's his account. There is no pressure to spend any amount of money from one's health savings account each year. Even if there is money in the account, the individual is not required to use the account to pay for medical expenses. Many people choose instead to pay expenses out-of-pocket and let the account balance continue to grow tax-deferred until they really need it in their golden years.

Saving for Education

529 Savings Plan

The **529 savings plan** allows investors to save/invest for education. Usually it is a family member putting money away for a child's education, but the beneficiary does not have to be a child, or even a blood relative of the donor. In fact, an individual can set up a 529 plan for him or herself. The person who opens the account is the owner. The beneficiary is the person who will use the money for education. For 529 savings plans, the owner controls the assets.

Contributions are made after-tax (non-deductible), but the withdrawals used for qualified education expenses are tax-free at the federal level. Notice how we said, "federal level." The plans are state-specific, so some states may tax the withdrawals. That means that if Grandma lives in New Jersey and buys a Wisconsin plan, New Jersey could end up taxing the money that the grandkids use for college. Then again, New Jersey might allow Grandma to deduct her contributions for purposes of state income taxes. So, you don't want to buy into a 529 savings plan without first checking how it will be taxed by the state.

And, even with the federal taxation, the withdrawals for education must be qualified withdrawals that cover tuition, room & board, books, etc. The expenses must be directly related to education; otherwise, the account owner will be subject to a 10% penalty plus ordinary income tax on any earnings withdrawn. If the beneficiary decides he doesn't need the money, the account can name a second beneficiary without tax problems, if the second beneficiary is related to the first.

And there is one area that can lead to confusion. When setting up a 529 plan, it makes no difference whether the account owner is related to the beneficiary. It's just that if an individual starts a 529 plan for a beneficiary and then discovers that the child has no intention of going to college, then if he wants to avoid tax implications, he can only change the beneficiary to a blood relative of the beneficiary. If he wants to change beneficiaries to someone not related, he would have to deal with the 10% penalty and ordinary income tax ramifications.

When the donor is putting money into a 529 savings plan on behalf of her granddaughter, she is making a gift. Gifts over a certain amount are taxable to the one making the gift. With a 529 savings plan, this grandmother can contribute up to the gift tax exclusion without incurring gift taxes, and can even do a lump-sum contribution for the first five years without incurring gift tax hassles. In other words, if the annual gift tax exclusion is $14,000, she can put in $70,000 for the next five years. If she and Grandpa are married-filing-separately, they could put in twice that amount, or $140,000, without any gift tax issues. Note that if someone uses the five-year-up-front method, they can't make any more gifts to the beneficiary for the next five years without dealing with gift taxes.

Each plan has a maximum lifetime contribution limit, rather than an annual limit.

The owner of the plan maintains control over the assets, deciding when withdrawals will be made. The money can be withdrawn to cover higher education expenses, such as tuition, books, and room and board. College is one type of institution covered by these plans. Vocational schools are another.

Prepaid Tuition

If you're sure that Junior won't mind going to college in-state, you might want to lock him in as a future Boilermaker, Hoosier, or Sycamore through a plan whereby you pay for his tuition credits now for any public school in the fine state of Indiana. I didn't say you were locking him into being accepted at IU or Purdue, but he would get to go to a state school with a certain number of credits already paid for. Parents worried about the ever-rising cost of tuition, then, can pay today's prices and redeem the credits more than a decade into the future.

These tuition credits cover tuition and fees only. If the child gets a scholarship or doesn't need the money because of something tragic like death or disability, a refund is typically provided plus a modest rate of interest. The exam could refer to prepaid tuition plans as "defined benefit plans." You pay for the tuition credits now, and then you hope the state can afford to provide the benefit of education when your child needs it.

Coverdell Education Savings Account

A **Coverdell Education Savings Account** (CESA) also allows for after-tax contributions (non-deductible), but the current maximum is only a few thousand dollars per year per child. While the 529 Plan is for higher education only, the Coverdell plan can be used for elementary, secondary, and higher education expenses. The distributions are tax-free at the federal level if used according to the plan guidelines. As with the 529 plan, the Coverdell ESA account can be used for education expenses, including tuition, books, and room and board. In a Coverdell, contributions must stop on the beneficiary's 18th birthday, and the assets must be used for education or distributed to him by age 30. Also, there are income limits on the donors of a CESA, like the limits placed on people trying to fund their Roth IRAs.

So, should you use a 529 plan or a CESA? Generally, it would come down to the amount of money you want to contribute. If you're going to contribute only a few thousand dollars, you might as well use the CESA. If you want to put large sums away, you'll have to use the 529 plan. Either way, you'll get tax deferral and tax-free withdrawals at the federal level, assuming you do everything according to plan.

UGMA/UTMA Accounts

If a donor wants to donate money for the benefit of a minor, all she has to do is set up the account as either an **UGMA** or **UTMA** account. UGMA stands for "Uniform Gifts to Minors Act" and UTMA stands for "Uniform Transfers to Minors Act." All states except Vermont and South Carolina have now adopted UTMA laws, which supersede UGMA laws. Either way, the child is going to eventually be in control of the assets, either at age 18 in a few states or age 21 in most states. There are even a few states that allow the transfer to happen as late as age 25, but that is the maximum and not typical. The state used is typically where the minor resides, although it could be where the custodian resides.

Setting up the account requires no supporting documentation. The donor needs the minor's social security number and provides the tax ID number of the custodian. The donor often manages the account as the **custodian,** although the two could be different parties, as well. If the donor is trying to minimize the size of his estate to avoid estate taxes, he will typically appoint another party as the custodian. Otherwise, the assets would be counted under his estate.

Either way, the account is opened as UGMA or UTMA, with just one adult custodian and one minor child per account. You can't have two adults as custodians, and you can't have more than one minor child per account. You also can't have a corporation or a partnership acting as the custodian. Only an adult human being can serve in that role. And, that adult is a fiduciary, meaning if he "invests" the money at the racetrack or tries to engage in naked options, he could be forced to refund any losses caused by his lack of prudence.

If the exam asks what happens if you want to establish an UTMA for your niece, whose parents oppose the gift, tell it that if you have the minor's social security number, you can open the account. The minor's parents have no access to the account that you will set up and/or manage as custodian. In fact, one could probably keep the minor in the dark about the existence of the account.

A proper title for an UTMA account would look like this: Mark Michelson, as Custodian for Michael Michelson under the Illinois Uniform Transfers to Minors Act. The adult custodian is the "nominal owner" while the beneficiary is the "beneficial owner" of this account. The gifts are considered "irrevocable and indefeasible," which means they cannot be taken back or treated as loans to be repaid.

When the beneficiary reaches the state's age of majority (adulthood), there is nothing the donor or custodian can do to stop him from selling off all the securities and buying a Corvette. In a formal trust account that sort of thing can be avoided. But an UTMA/UGMA account is a "trust" whose terms are drawn up in state law, as opposed to a formal trust account in which the trust documents stipulate the terms.

Of course, there is no reason to assume all young adults would be foolish with the account assets. Parents might set up an UTMA account so that the child at age 21 has money to make a down payment on a house or start a business. But, what the parents intended as a down payment on a house could, again, be spent on anything the new adult wants, instead.

Since the child won't need the money for, say, eight years, surely the adult custodian can sort of "borrow" from the account from time to time as needed, if she repays it eventually, with interest, right?

Wrong. These accounts receive special tax consideration, so if the custodian is pretending the account is an UTMA account, but uses it to get interest-free loans, the IRS might start talking about tax fraud, back taxes, and penalties-plus-interest.

If the question asks if room and board would be a legitimate expense to be covered by an UTMA account, the answer is no. Room and board is something parents are expected to provide to their children, and not through some tax-advantaged account.

Setting up UTMA/UGMA accounts requires no legal work, making it much cheaper than establishing a formal trust account. These days, investors typically use 529 Plans to save for college rather than custodial accounts, because assets in an UTMA/UGMA count against the child's chances of receiving financial aid more so than assets in a 529 Savings Plan.

Retirement Plans

In a taxable account, the principal is reduced each year when the investor is taxed on interest, dividends, and capital gains. In a tax-deferred account, however, the principal is not taxed until the

individual takes distributions. The account balance grows faster when it is growing tax-deferred.

Tax-deferral is an advantage offered by deferred annuities and retirement accounts. Whether one's contribution is tax-deductible, the fact that the interest, dividends, and capital gains will not be taxed each year is an advantage to the investor. That's why so many individuals participate in at least one retirement plan.

Some retirement plans are started by the individual, and some are offered through an employer.

Let's start with the plans an individual can open, provided he has **earned income**. Earned income includes salary, bonuses, tips, alimony, and any income derived from actively participating in a business. It does not include passive income such as rental income from an apartment building or portfolio income such as bond interest, dividends, or capital gains.

Individual Plans

An **IRA** is an **Individual Retirement Account**, or an Individual Retirement Arrangement.

Traditional

To contribute to a **Traditional IRA** the individual must be younger than 70 ½ and have earned income for the year. If the individual's income consists solely of dividends and bond interest, he can't make an IRA contribution for that year.

Contributions to an IRA are tax-deductible. If the individual contributes $5,000 to his IRA this year, that $5,000 no longer counts as taxable income. If he was going to pay tax on $52,000, now it's only $47,000 of taxable income for the year.

If he does have earned income for the year, an individual can contribute 100% of that amount up to the current maximum. So, if she earns $1,800, then $1,800 is her maximum IRA contribution for that year. People 50 years and older can add a **catch-up contribution**. That amount is currently an extra $1,000.

At the time of writing, the maximum contribution to a Traditional IRA is $5,500, $6,500 for those 50 or older.

Penalties

Over-funding an IRA results in a 6% penalty on the amount above the maximum contribution for the year and any earnings associated with it. If the individual realizes she has over-funded her IRA for the year, she can remove the excess by the tax filing deadline the following year, or re-characterize the excess as part of the following year's contributions. If it's March 17, 2019 when she realizes she has over-funded her IRA by $1,000 for 2018, she can remove the $1,000 to avoid a penalty or fill out a form to re-characterize it as part of her 2019 contributions. If she does nothing, she pays a 6% penalty on the $1,000 ($60) plus any earnings associated with it.

Money withdrawn from a Traditional IRA is taxable at ordinary income rates. While we can pull the money out any time, if we take it out before age 59½, we'll pay a 10% penalty, on top of income taxes on the full amount. However, the following are qualifying exemptions to the 10% penalty. Although the withdrawal is taxable, the 10% penalty is waived for withdrawals made pursuant to:

- Death
- Permanent disability
- First home purchase for residential purposes
- A series of substantially equal periodic payments under IRS Rule 72-t
- Medical expenses
- Higher education expenses

A withdrawal pursuant to death means that the IRA owner has died and someone else is receiving the account balance as a named beneficiary. The beneficiary will be taxed but will not be penalized because the account owner died before age 59 ½.

So, an individual can't have the money until he's 59½ without paying a penalty unless he uses one of the exemptions above. That's on the front end.

On the back end, he also is required to start taking it out by the time he's 70½. If not, the IRS will impose a 50% insufficient distribution penalty. We're talking about RMDs here, or **required minimum distributions**. When someone turns 70½, he has until April 1st of the following year to take out at least the required minimum distribution. If not, the IRS will levy a 50% penalty.

That's 50% of what he should have taken out at this point, not half the account value.

The absolute latest date that an individual can take his first withdrawal from a Traditional IRA without penalty is April 1st following the year he turns 70 ½. However, if he does that, he must take *two* distributions that year, which can push him into a higher tax bracket and make more of his social security benefits taxable. So, it's easier to take the first distribution in the year the individual turns 70½.

Unlike the Roth IRA, no contributions can be made into the Traditional IRA after age 70½.

Roth

The **Roth IRA** is funded with non-deductible contributions. However, the money comes out tax-free in retirement if the individual is 59½ years old and has had the account at least 5 years. That means if the individual starts the account at age 56, he'll have to wait until age 61 to take tax-free withdrawals.

The withdrawals we take from a Traditional IRA are taxable income. If we withdraw $30,000, we might only keep $22,000 after-tax. A withdrawal of $30,000 from our Roth IRA, on the other hand, leaves us with $30,000 to spend.

Unlike the Traditional, for the Roth IRA there is no requirement to take a distribution by age 70½. Since the IRS isn't going to tax that money, they couldn't care less when or even if it is withdrawn. In fact, individuals can keep contributing if they have earned income. So, a 72-year-old can refrain from taking Roth IRA withdrawals and can keep making contributions into the account if she has earned income. Neither option is available, on the other hand, for her Traditional IRA.

If the individual or married couple have adjusted gross incomes above a certain amount, they cannot contribute to their Roth IRAs. Period. So, get those Roth IRA accounts started while you're young and before you strike it rich. The money you contribute in your 20s and 30s can compound for decades, even if the IRS cuts off new contributions by age 40 based on your income.

If an individual has both a Traditional and a Roth IRA, the contribution limit is the total allocated among the two accounts.

Also, the Roth IRA allows the individual to remove her cost basis, or the amount she has contributed, after five years without penalty. So, if the account owner has contributed $25,000 to a Roth IRA and seven years later the account is worth $40,000, he could take the $25,000 out without a penalty and keep the remainder of $15,000 in the account. He could not put that $25,000 back in, however, and would not earn the tax-deferred and tax-free returns going forward.

But, as always, it's his money.

Rollovers and Transfers

To move an IRA from one custodian to another, the best bet is to do a **direct transfer**. Just have the custodian cut a check to the new custodian. The IRA owner can do as many of these direct transfers as he wants. If, however, he does a **rollover**, things get tricky. First, he can only do one per year, and, second, it must be completed within 60 days to avoid tax ramifications.

In a rollover, the custodian cuts a check in the individual's name. The account owner cashes it and then sends the money to the new custodian, but any shortfall is subject to taxes and a 10% penalty. If the individual withdrew $50,000 but could only come up with $10,000 sixty days later, that $40,000 difference is taxed as ordinary income, plus a penalty tax of $4,000.

Employer-Based Plans

Plans offered through an employer either define the benefit to be received when the employee retires or the contributions made into the account. Usually, it is only the contributions that are defined.

Defined Contribution Plans

A **defined contribution plan** only defines the contributions the employer and/or the employee can make into the plan. The employer is not promising any benefit at retirement. We'll talk about **defined benefit pension plans** in a bit, but let's focus first on the more familiar defined contribution plans.

At many companies, new employees receive paperwork to fill out concerning the **401(k) plan** sponsored by the employer as an employee benefit. The employees choose mutual funds, and tell the HR department to deduct X amount from their paychecks to go into the 401(k) account. This way, part of their salary goes straight into a retirement fund and is not taxable currently, just like the money that goes into a Traditional IRA. Pretty attractive, especially if the employer matches what the employees elect to defer from each paycheck.

The amount of the employee's contribution is known as an **elective deferral**. Employers generally match all or part of an employee's elective deferral up to a certain percentage of compensation, as stipulated in their plan literature. But, they are not required to make **matching contributions**. Why might someone choose to participate in a 401(k) even if the company was not matching contributions? Maybe he likes the higher maximum contribution limit vs. the IRA or Roth IRA.

The advantage to a business owner setting up a 401(k) plan is that a vesting schedule can be laid out over several years, meaning that the employer's contributions don't belong to the employee until he is fully vested. However, 401(k) plans come with complicated **top-heavy** rules, which means the plan cannot provide benefits to just the key, highly compensated employees. A plan in which 60% of the benefits go to key employees is a plan that shows signs of being "top-heavy," and will need to adjust things or deal with tax problems.

For-profit companies offer 401(k) plans to their employees. Non-profit organizations such as schools and hospitals offer **403(b) plans** to their employees. As with a 401(k) plan, the employee indicates how much of her paycheck should go into the 403(b) account, which simultaneously gives her a tax break now and helps her save up for retirement later. As with a 401(k) plan, the contributions go in pre-tax but come out taxable when the participant starts taking distributions.

While a 401(k) plan might offer participants the ability to purchase stocks and bonds a la carte, a 403(b) plan only offers annuities and mutual funds as investment vehicles. The 403(b) plans can also be referred to as Tax-Sheltered Annuities or TSAs.

Some states and cities have begun to shift the burden of funding retirement benefits to their employees. These so-called **457 plans** are for state and local government employees, e.g., police and fire workers. Contributions are tax-deductible, and the plans use the same maximum contribution limits used by 401(k) and 403(b) plans.

Profit sharing plans are also defined contribution plans, but the contributions are never required. If the company does contribute, it must be made for all eligible employees based on a predetermined formula. For example, maybe all workers receive up to 10% of their salaries when the company has a banner year. The profit-sharing plan uses much higher maximum annual contributions than the 401(k), 403(b) or Section 457 plans. Of course, that would only matter if you happened to work for a profitable and generous employer.

A **money purchase plan** is not flexible the way a profit sharing plan is. The money purchase plan requires the employer to make a mandatory contribution to each employee's account, based on his/her salary, whether the company feels like it or not. The exam might say something like "in a money purchase plan, contributions are mandatory on the part of the employer and discretionary on the part of the employee."

Keogh plans are for individuals with self-employment income or for those working for a sole proprietorship with a Keogh plan in place. They're not for S-corps, C-corps, LLCs, etc.—only sole proprietors. If the individual in the test question has side income or is self-employed, he or she can have a Keogh. They can contribute a certain percentage of their self-employment income into the Keogh.

How much? A lot. As with the SEP-IRA, the business owner can put 20% of her compensation into a Keogh, and she can put in 25% of her employees' compensation.

Also, Keogh plans are for sole proprietorships only; we did not say that sole proprietorships can only have a Keogh plan. A SEP-IRA or SIMPLE IRA would also be available to a sole proprietor, for example.

A small business can establish a **SEP-IRA**, which stands for "Simplified Employee Pension" IRA. This allows the business owner to make pre-tax contributions for herself and any eligible employees. Twenty-five percent of wages can be contributed to an employee's SEP, up to the current maximum. SEP contributions are not mandatory on the part of the business owner. It's just that if the business makes any contributions, they must be made to all eligible employees as stipulated in the plan agreement. Same as for a profit sharing plan.

Also like a profit sharing plan, the employer makes the contributions, not the employees. So, if you're self-employed, you can contribute to your own SEP-IRA, but if you're an employee at a company with a SEP-IRA, it's the company who will make the contributions on your behalf. To establish a SEP, the employer uses a model agreement put out by the IRS (download it from www.irs.gov) that they and the employees sign. It does not have to be filed with the IRS, which does not issue an opinion or approval.

A **SIMPLE** plan can be either an IRA or a 401(k). The SIMPLE plan is for businesses with no more than 100 employees and with no other retirement plan offered. In a SIMPLE plan, business owners choose to either match the employee's contributions up to 3% of compensation, or to contribute 2% of the employee's compensation if he does not make an elective deferral from his paycheck. A SIMPLE plan is ideal at a small company where, say, only 3 of 12 employees want to put money away for retirement. When the other 9 make no elective deferrals, the employer makes no matching contributions. And for the three who do choose to invest part of their paychecks, the company matches the elective deferrals up to just 2% of compensation. That means for an employee earning $40,000, the employer's matching contributions would stop at $800.

Unlike with a 401(k) plan, employees are immediately vested in a SEP-IRA or SIMPLE plan. That means the employer's contributions belong to the employee as soon as they are made.

Many companies reward key employees by offering them **employee stock options**. These options do not trade among investors but are essentially free call options that allow employees to buy the company's stock at a set strike/exercise price. To keep the employee around a while, the company usually awards the options to buy the stock on a vesting schedule by which the employee gradually receives options. An **ESOP** or **employee stock ownership plan** is what it sounds like. Through these plans the company allows all workers to purchase company stock at a discount and through a payroll deduction. The stock and the dividends/cap gains generated on it grow tax-deferred, like a 401(k) plan.

Defined Benefit Plans

Defined benefit pension plans are the opposite of defined contribution plans. In a defined contribution plan the employer puts in some money and then wishes employees the best of luck with retirement. For a defined benefit plan, the employer bears all the risk and, therefore, must earn sufficient returns on their investments to pay a defined benefit to retirees and their survivors.

Maybe that defined benefit is 70% of average salary figured over the employee's last three years of service, paid out each year in retirement, plus maybe a benefit to a spouse or children if he dies within a certain time.

A defined benefit pension plan is established as a trust and does not pay tax on the income it generates. In fact, the company gets to deduct the contributions it makes into the pension fund from taxable income. Therefore, these plans do not typically invest in municipal securities, since they are already tax-advantaged accounts.

Because corporations typically try to fund these plans only as much as required, defined benefit plans require an actuary to certify that funding levels are sufficient to cover future pension fund obligations.

Margin Accounts

Most retail brokerage accounts are retirement accounts. Retirement accounts are cash accounts in which customers must pay in full either at the time of the transaction or no later than 2 days after settlement. Because retirement accounts cannot be approved for margin trading, no short sales are executed in IRA or 401(k) accounts, either. And, that makes sense, as selling short involves potentially unlimited risk.

Investing on **margin** is a high-risk strategy that involves buying securities on credit, hoping to make more on the securities positions than the interest the broker-dealer charges on the margin loan. Another use of such accounts is to profit when a stock's market price drops by **selling short**.

Broker-dealers offer **margin accounts** to earn interest on the loans and to encourage more trading activity. Institutional traders including hedge funds utilize margin or leverage at high levels. Some retail customers also have their taxable accounts approved for margin. A new account number is not provided when they do. The account is simply approved for margin trading and borrowing after careful review of suitability by the member firm.

In a margin account, customers pledge the securities they buy on credit to the lender, the broker-dealer. If things go wrong, the broker-dealer can sell the stock or bond to recover the money they lent. So, the interest rate they charge is lower than what we pay on a credit card, since the broker-dealer has collateral backing the loan.

People talk about the equity in their houses. Maybe they bought the house for $200,000 and borrowed $180,000 to do that. If so, their account starts out like this:

$200,000 Market Value

-$180,000 Money Owed

$20,000 Equity

Equity is the difference between what someone owns and owes. If the value increased 15% three years running, while the principal was being reduced, the account now looks like this:

$304,175 Market Value

-$170,000 Money Owed

$134,175 Equity

What can these homeowners do with that equity? They can borrow against it.

In a margin account, we don't buy houses on credit. Rather we buy stocks and bonds on credit. If their market value rises, we win. What if their market value drops? Then, we have a problem. This is where margin accounts get their bad name.

Regulation T

The Securities Exchange Act of 1934 gave the Federal Reserve Board the authority to regulate margin accounts. The Fed regulates credit, and one form of credit is the margin account, in which the broker-dealer advances the customer half the purchase price of a security. **Regulation T** also covers cash accounts, preventing customers from freeriding or being late to pay for securities transactions.

To purchase stock on margin, the broker-dealer follows Regulation T (Reg T), which states that a margin-eligible stock can be pledged as collateral by the customer in exchange for a loan from the broker-dealer up to a maximum percentage of its value. Reg T tells broker-dealers how much credit they can extend to their customers. That percentage is 50%. The industry sometimes refers to the amount a customer puts down as the "Fed call."

When a customer buys $200,000 of stock, he puts down ½ or $100,000. The other $100,000 is provided by the broker-dealer, who charges interest on that debit balance for as long as the customer owes them. The amount the customer puts down is referred to as "the margin." The margin refers to the money the investor is required to deposit. The rest of the market value is extended on credit.

Regulation T requires 50% of the purchase price to be deposited by the customer within two business days after the settlement date of the transaction. Any market price change between the purchase of the security and the required payment does not affect the amount of the deposit the customer is required to make. If the stock purchased on margin rises from, say, $50 to $60, or drops from, say, $50 to $40, the margin call is based on $50 per-share. It is figured at the time of purchase.

Long Positions

Say a customer bought 1,000 shares @40 and made the required Reg T deposit of half or $20,000. At that point, the customer's account looks like this:

$$LMV \quad - \quad Dr \quad = \quad Equity \quad \quad Reg\ T\ Deposit$$

$$\$40,000 - \$20,000 = \$20,000 \quad \quad \$20,000$$

LMV stands for "long market value." It could be referred to as "market value" or "current market value." The "Dr" stands for "debit register," which can also be called the "debit balance." This is the amount the customer borrowed and owes his broker-dealer, like the mortgage balance that the homeowner owes the lender.

So, the long market value of the stock he bought is $40,000. He made the required Reg T deposit of half, or $20,000. The broker-dealer advanced him the other half, so it's a debit to the client's account until he pays it off.

The customer now owns an asset worth 40K but he owes 20K to the lender. That's why his equity is $20,000. Just like if you owed $80,000 on your mortgage when your house was worth $100,000—the difference of $20,000 would be your equity.

Equity, Excess Equity

If the stock rises, to $50 a share, the account looks like this:

$$\text{LMV} \quad - \quad \text{Dr} \quad = \quad \text{Equity}$$

$$\$50,000 \quad - \quad \$20,000 \quad = \quad \$30,000$$

The amount owed to the broker-dealer didn't change. The long market value of the stock went up, increasing the equity dollar-for-dollar. Now, let's compare the equity of $30,000 to Reg T, which is 50% of the market value. Half of 50K is $25,000. The customer has $30,000 of equity.

That's **excess equity** of $5,000:

$$\text{LMV} \quad - \quad \text{Dr} \quad = \quad \text{Equity} \quad - \quad \text{Reg T} \quad = \quad \text{Excess Equity}$$

$$\$50,000 - \$20,000 = \$30,000 - \$25,000 = \quad \$5,000$$

Since this customer has excess equity of $5,000, $5,000 is credited to a special line item called "SMA." SMA, which stands for Special Memorandum Account, is a line of credit the customer can tap. So, he can withdraw $5,000 of his cash, like in a savings account?

No. The $5,000 is just a number. But, if the customer wants to borrow that amount of money, he can. And whenever he borrows from SMA, that amount is added to the debit balance. The customer can just tell the broker-dealer to cut him a check for $5,000, which will be added to his tab, like this:

$$\text{LMV} \quad - \quad \text{Dr} \quad = \quad \text{Equity}$$

$$\$50,000 - \$25,000 = \$25,000$$

Borrowing the cash didn't affect the long market value of the securities. We added the amount borrowed to the debit balance, which reduced equity and wiped out the SMA. SMA can be used as a cash advance that will be repaid with interest.

Or, SMA can be used as an initial margin requirement for the purchase of more stock. So, instead of borrowing the cash, the customer could have used the $5,000 SMA credit to purchase $10,000 of stock.

If so, the account would have looked like this:

$$\text{LMV} \qquad \text{Dr} \qquad \text{Equity} \qquad \text{SMA}$$

$60,000 $30,000 $30,000 $0

If the customer buys more stock, that adds to the market value of securities held long in the account. Why did his debit balance go up by $10,000? Because the customer in our example used his line of credit as his margin deposit, and the broker-dealer fronted him the other half, or $5,000, which is also added to the Debit. So, he borrowed $5,000 from his line of credit (SMA), plus $5,000 that the broker-dealer fronted him for the additional stock purchase.

When dividends, interest, or capital gains distributions from mutual funds come into the account, that income is applied to the debit balance. Therefore, SMA is affected by such income being applied to the debit.

Reg T requires that a customer put up 50% of the long market value initially. After that, what happens if the customer's equity dips below 50%?

Not much. Even though the account is called "restricted," there really aren't many restrictions. The customer is required to put up ½ to buy more stock. If the customer sells stock, he can borrow ½ the proceeds. He can do that provided it doesn't bring him below the minimum equity of $2,000, that is.

Surprisingly, when the market value of a securities position drops, that does not affect SMA. It reduces the market value of the stock and, therefore, the equity, but SMA is just a line of credit. It does not get taken away. The customer can always use SMA so long as using it does not take him below the minimum maintenance requirement, which we're about to look at.

Minimum Maintenance

Reg T dictates what to put down on an initial transaction, and any excess above Reg T gives the customer excess equity. But excess equity is a term used when the market is cooperating with the margin customer.

What happens when the market goes the wrong way? Suddenly, the customer's equity is deficient, and he either must throw more cash on the fire or put the fire out by liquidating securities. Broker-dealers do not have to consult with customers before selling positions to pay down debit balances. Unlike a mortgage lender foreclosing on a property with notice, the broker-dealer just sells the depressed property if the market price is dropping fast.

Reg T requirements apply initially and then help us figure if the customer has excess equity or buying power. But, the customer's larger concern is the SRO minimum maintenance requirement. The regulators say that a customer's equity cannot go lower than 25% of the long market value. If it does, the customer gets a maintenance call to bring the equity up to the minimum 25%. If the customer can't deliver the cash, the firm sells securities equal to four times the amount of the maintenance call:

LMV	Dr	Equity	Minimum	Call	Liquidate
40,000	20,000	20,000	10,000	0	0

At this point, the customer has twice as much equity as the minimum (25% of long market value).

If the stock goes from 40K down to 30K, he is okay:

LMV	Dr	Equity	Minimum	Call	Liquidate
30,000	20,000	10,000	7,500	0	0

But, if the market value falls to 24K, he is in trouble:

LMV	Dr	Equity	Minimum	Call	Liquidate
24,000	20,000	4,000	6,000	2,000	8,000

The SROs demand $6,000 in equity, which is ¼ of $24,000. The customer has only $4,000. So, the customer gets a maintenance call informing him that he must deliver $2,000. If the customer does that, the account looks like this:

LMV	Dr	Equity	Minimum	Call	Liquidate
24,000	18,000	6,000	6,000	0	0

He paid down the debit by $2,000 and now has $6,000 in equity, the bare minimum of 25% of market value.

If he didn't have the cash, the firm would have liquidated $8,000 worth of securities. If so, the account would have looked like this:

LMV	Dr	Equity	Minimum Maintenance
16,000	12,000	4,000	4,000

Whereas, it used to look like this:

LMV	Dr	Equity	Minimum Maintenance
24,000	20,000	4,000	6,000

Selling the $8,000 worth of securities reduced the market value and the debit by an equal amount, leaving the customer with exactly 25% equity.

Also, the 25% requirement is the minimum maintenance. Many broker-dealers require a higher minimum maintenance than just 25% to protect themselves. For example, 33% is often used, the difference between $1/4^{th}$ and $1/3^{rd}$ the stock's market value. The regulators are fine with that, so long as the firm does not let equity drop below 25%.

Account at Maintenance

In the example above the investor received a maintenance call when the market value dropped to

$24,000. Luckily, he doesn't have to wait for such a drastic outcome before realizing the phone is about to ring. Back when he established the long position the market value was $40,000 and the debit balance $20,000.

At that point, we can calculate the account at maintenance by dividing the debit by .75.

When we divide $20,000 by .75, we see that the lowest account value allowed before a maintenance call is $26,667. To double check that, we can take the equity that would be in the account--$6,667-- and see if that is 25% of $26,667. It is. But any further drops will lead to more calls.

Short Positions

When a customer sells short, he sells borrowed securities in anticipation he can replace them at a lower price. So, if he wants to sell short $10,000 worth of securities, he must deposit half that value, $5,000, to meet the Reg T requirement. If he did, his account would look like this:

Cr	$15,000
SMV	– $10,000
Equity	$5,000

The "Cr" stands for the "credit" and the "SMV" stands for "short market value," or, perhaps, we could just call it the "market value." In any case, when the customer sells short $10,000 worth of securities, that $10,000 is credited to the customer's account. Remember, he sold some stock— someone paid him $10,000.

So, our investor gets the proceeds from the sale, and deposits another 50% of that to meet the Reg T requirement. The $10,000 he took in for selling the stock, plus a $5,000 cash deposit, equals a total credit of $15,000.

If the "SMV" goes down, as the investor hopes, he'll have more equity. For example, if the SMV dropped to just $5,000, the customer's equity would increase by $5,000, like this:

Cr	$15,000
SMV	– $5,000
Equity	$10,000

The credit didn't change. He started with a credit of $15,000, and that's all the credit he's going to have. It's the market value (SMV) that changed, dropping in the desired direction for our short seller.

And if the market value of the securities sold short were to increase, his equity would shrink, like this:

Cr	$15,000

$$\frac{\text{SMV} \quad - \quad \$11{,}000}{\text{Equity} \quad \$4{,}000}$$

How high can the SMV go before a customer gets one of those nasty maintenance calls? For most short positions, customers need 30% of their SMV as equity. If the customer's SMV is $11,000, he needs at least $3,300 in equity. You can find the highest SMV at maintenance by taking the "Cr" and dividing it by 1.3. Since the customer has a credit of $15,000, just divide that by 1.3, and you see that the highest SMV without a maintenance call is $11,538. If the securities' value doesn't exceed that number, his account will remain properly margined.

Combined Equity

To find combined equity, find the equity for the long positions and add it to the equity for the short positions. You can also remember that the formula for combined equity is:

$$\text{LMV} + \text{Cr} - \text{Dr} - \text{SMV}$$

Which is just another way of saying, "Add the two things that go on top and subtract the two things that go on the bottom." So, if a customer had an LMV of $20,000, a Cr of $20,000, a Dr of $10,000, and SMV of $10,000, his combined equity is $20,000:

$$\text{LMV} \quad + \quad \text{Cr} \quad - \quad \text{Dr} \quad - \quad \text{SMV}$$

$$20{,}000 + 20{,}000 - 10{,}000 - 10{,}000$$

He has $10,000 equity on the long positions, and $10,000 equity on the short positions. He must have 25% equity for the long, and 30% for the short. This customer is okay on both fronts. Each day the markets are open, the margin department recalculates requirements by marking to the market. If market values have gone the wrong way, the customer might receive a margin call. If market values have gone the right way, the customer might see SMA increase.

Marginable Securities, Accounts

Not everything can be purchased "on margin," but that doesn't mean it can't be purchased within a margin account. A "margin account" is an account that has been approved for margin. The following securities are "marginable," meaning they can be purchased using margin:

- NYSE, NASDAQ, AMEX stocks
- OTC securities on the FRB's approved list
- Exempted securities: Treasuries, municipal securities

The following can be purchased inside a margin account, but must be paid in full:

- Non-NASDAQ OTC securities not on the FRB's approved list
- Options
- IPOs or any new issue for 30 days
- Mutual fund shares

If the exam question asks if options can be purchased "on margin," the answer is no. If the question asks if options can be purchased "in a margin account," the answer is yes.

Maintenance Requirements

Regulation T requires the initial margin a customer must deposit, either in cash or securities. For example, when purchasing $20,000 of stock on margin, the customer must deposit either $10,000 or fully paid stock with a market value of $20,000. Fully paid stock has a loan value of 50%, so whatever amount the customer is buying, that's the amount the stock must be worth when used to meet the Fed call.

If the Reg T requirement is less than $2,000, the customer must deposit $2,000. For example, if he purchases $3,500 of stock on margin, he deposits $2,000 rather than $1,750. $2,000 is the minimum equity for a long account. Just as a customer cannot borrow money if it would take the equity below $2,000, he must deposit at least that much initially.

With one exception. If the total amount of the purchase is less than $2,000, the customer pays in full. If the stock is worth just $1,500, he pays $1,500. He does not pay more than the stock is worth. He has an account approved for margin. He hasn't used the feature yet.

For a short position, the customer deposits 50% of the proceeds from the short sale initially.

That addresses the initial margin. Going forward, the margin account is subject to maintenance margin. For margin-eligible stocks held long, the minimum maintenance is $1/4^{th}$ or 25% of the current market value. For any equity security that is not margin-eligible, the customer must pay in full to establish a long position.

Reg T does not apply to exempt securities such as U.S. Treasuries and municipal bonds. FINRA rules establish the maintenance margin for such securities based on their maturity and current market price. The following applies to bills, notes, bonds, and STRIPS issued by the Treasury.

Maturity	Percent of Current Market Value
Less than one year to maturity	1%
One year but less than 3 years to maturity	2%
Three years but less than 5 years to maturity	3%
Five years but less than 10 years to maturity	4%
Ten years but less than 20 years to maturity	5%
Twenty years or more to maturity	6%

Although the above applies to zero coupons such as STRIPS, there is also a requirement for any zero coupon with 5+ years to maturity. The rule states, "Notwithstanding the above, on zero coupon bonds with five years or more to maturity the margin to be maintained shall not be less than 3 percent of the principal amount of the obligation."

For other exempted securities besides Treasuries, the maintenance margin is 7% of the current market value, for both long and short positions.

Securities Lending

FINRA requires that customers receive a margin disclosure document explaining how interest is charged and pointing out many of the things we've considered. For example, customers are informed they can lose more than they initially deposit in some cases and the firm can liquidate securities without notice or consultation with the customer.

The customer signs a margin agreement. The margin agreement either includes a hypothecation agreement, or a separate document is signed. To hypothecate means to pledge securities as collateral to secure the loan. Without the customer's written consent, a broker-dealer cannot hypothecate a customer's securities. And, the firm only hypothecates enough to secure the loan, called the margin securities. The excess of that are the excess margin securities, separated clearly on the firm's books and records.

More correctly, the customer hypothecates his margin securities to the broker-dealer. The broker-dealer then re-hypothecates them to the bank providing the margin loan.

Some customers also opt into the firm's securities lending program. Typically, these are customers with account balances of $250,000 or more. Short sales require cash collateral, and the broker-dealer earns interest on this cash. Therefore, customers in the lending program providing their fully-paid securities to short sellers share in some of that interest as an incentive to make their shares available.

There are also disadvantages, which must be disclosed to customers signing the **loan consent** agreement for the securities lending program. For example, securities loaned out confer voting rights to the borrower, rather than the owner. The borrower must pay any dividends to the lender of the stock, but the tax code treats such payments less favorably than a typical dividend received from the issuer. Also, securities loaned out are typically not protected by SIPC.

The agreements here can be combined into one margin agreement provided they are made clear to the customer before he signs. And, the hypothecation, margin, and lending agreements can be incorporated into the customer agreement signed when he opens an account at the broker-dealer, provided nothing is slipped by him in small print or opaque language.

Locating and Borrowing

The SEC does not like it when short sellers sell shares that don't exist. Allowing them to do so would distort the downward (bearish) pressure on a stock by distorting the laws of supply & demand that determine the stock's market price. Therefore, under **Regulation SHO**, broker-dealers must locate the shares their customers are selling short and document it before effecting the short sale.

That means they reasonably believe the securities can be delivered by the settlement date as required. Such securities are located through the lending programs we just looked at.

The regulators have other concerns about short selling and its potential impact on the market. Many years ago, a short sale could only be executed at a price that was higher than the previous price for the security, or at the same price if the price before had been an "uptick."

In May 2010 **Reg SHO** was updated to impose a temporary version of the old uptick rule that applies when a "circuit breaker" is tripped for a security. Starting in May of that year if a security dropped during the day by 10% or more below its most recent closing price, short sellers would not be able to sell short at or below the current best bid price for the security. In other words, people "selling long," which means selling the shares they own, will have priority and will be able to liquidate their holdings before short sellers can jump onto the pile.

As the SEC states:

> a targeted short sale price test restriction will apply the alternative uptick rule for the remainder of the day and the following day if the price of an individual security declines intra-day by 10% or more from the prior day's closing price for that security. By not allowing short sellers to sell at or below the current national best bid while the circuit breaker is in effect, the short sale price test restriction in Rule 201 will allow long sellers, who will be able to sell at the bid, to sell first in a declining market for a particular security. As the Commission has noted previously in connection with short sale price test restrictions, a goal of such restrictions is to allow long sellers to sell first in a declining market. In addition, by making such bids accessible only by long sellers when a security's price is undergoing significant downward price pressure, Rule 201 will help to facilitate and maintain stability in the markets and help ensure that they function efficiently. It will also help restore investor confidence during times of substantial uncertainty because, once the circuit breaker has been triggered for a particular security, long sellers will have preferred access to bids for the security, and the security's continued price decline will more likely be due to long selling and the underlying fundamentals of the issuer, rather than to other factors.

As we see from that passage, there is a difference between a customer sell order marked "long" and a sell order marked "short." That is why Reg SHO requires all sell orders to be marked properly. When a customer "sells long," he is liquidating shares that he owns. To sell short, he borrows shares that will be sold and then replaced later by the customer.

Short sales take place only in margin accounts, not cash accounts. Cash accounts do not involve borrowed money.

Many broker-dealers earn a substantial part of their revenue and profits from day-trading customers. Institutional customers are free to day-trade without the broker-dealer having to protect the investor from himself. But, for retail customers, broker-dealers follow stringent rules for opening and handling day-trading accounts.

As FINRA stipulates, "to approve a customer's account for a day-trading strategy, a member shall have reasonable grounds for believing that the day-trading strategy is appropriate for the customer. In making this determination, the member shall exercise reasonable diligence to ascertain the essential facts relative to the customer." FINRA then lists 7 specific items:

(1) Investment objectives;
(2) Investment and trading experience and knowledge (e.g., number of years, size, frequency and type of transactions);
(3) Financial situation, including: estimated annual income from all sources, estimated net worth (exclusive of family residence), and estimated liquid net worth (cash, securities, other);
(4) Tax status;
(5) Employment status (name of employer, self-employed or retired);
(6) Marital status and number of dependents;
(7) And age.

Does that mean if the broker-dealer knows this customer is married, self-employed and has no day-trading experience, that day-trading might be an appropriate strategy to recommend? Probably not. If the investor is in the top two tax brackets, does it make sense for him to generate short-term capital gains, taxed as high as almost 40%? Again, probably not.

Because there is so much risk involved with day-trading, FINRA does not allow member firms to open non-institutional day-trading accounts without providing required disclosures.

As the rules state: no member that is promoting a day-trading strategy, directly or indirectly, shall open an account for or on behalf of a non-institutional customer, unless, prior to opening the account, the member has furnished to the customer the risk disclosure statement and has:

(1) approved the customer's account for a day-trading strategy in accordance with the procedures set forth in paragraph (b) and prepared a record setting forth the basis on which the member has approved the customer's account; or
(2) received from the customer a written agreement that the customer does not intend to use the account for the purpose of engaging in a day-trading strategy, except that the member may not rely on such agreement if the member knows that the customer intends to use the account for the purpose of engaging in a day-trading strategy.

At the time of this writing, the full text of the Day-Trading Risk Disclosure Statement was available at: http://finra.complinet.com/en/display/display.html?rbid=2403&element_id=8832

The main bullet points this document makes to the customer include:

- Day-trading can be extremely risky
- Be cautious of claims of large profits from day-trading
- Day-trading requires knowledge of securities markets
- Day-trading requires knowledge of a firm's operations
- Day-trading will generate substantial commissions, even if the per-trade cost is low
- Day-trading on margin or short selling may result in losses beyond your initial investment

The term "day trading" is defined by FINRA as, "the purchasing and selling or the selling and purchasing of the same security on the same day in a margin account." The exceptions to the definition include purchasing a stock held overnight if the position is sold before buying any more of that stock, or if a short-seller keeps a short-position open overnight, covering it before selling any more of those shares short.

The term "pattern day trader" is defined as, "any customer who executes four or more day trades within five business days. However, if the number of day trades is 6 percent or less of total trades for the five-business-day period, the customer will not be considered a pattern day trader and the special requirements will not apply."

Day traders are in margin accounts, and their buying power is significantly higher than the typical retail margin account.

FINRA defines *day trading buying power* as:

> "The equity in a customer's account at the close of business of the previous day, less any maintenance margin requirement, multiplied by four for equity securities."

If the customer's long positions are worth $100,000, and his debit balance is $30,000, he has $70,000 of equity. According to FINRA's definition, his buying power is four times his equity of $70,000, or $280,000.

What happens when a customer's minimum equity is insufficient under these rules? FINRA explains that, "when the equity in a customer's account is not sufficient to meet the day trading requirements of this paragraph, additional cash or securities must be received into the account to meet any deficiency within five business days of the trade date."

Pattern day traders have special requirements. The minimum equity requirement for pattern day traders is $25,000. That equity "must be deposited in the account before the customer may continue day trading and must be maintained in the customer's account at all times."

Opening Accounts

You have heard their names on TV or seen them in magazine ads: Charles Schwab, TD Ameritrade, E-trade, Goldman Sachs, Fidelity, etc. Maybe you've seen branch offices for such firms at the mall, or on one of the floors at your office building. What is happening inside these offices?

Customers are investing in the stocks, bonds, mutual funds, and options we have looked at earlier. Maybe the customer was pulled in by an advertisement on TV or the car radio. Maybe she was recommended by a friend. Maybe she received a form letter from one of the agents at the firm.

Whatever pulled her toward the front door, an agent's job is to sign her up for a new account.

New Account Form

Typically, a registered representative fills out the new account form, often over the telephone. Often, customers complain the forms through the member firm's website.

Either way, member firms should obtain from the new customer:

> Full name and address
> Home and work phone numbers
> Social security or Tax ID number
> Employer, occupation, employer's address
> Net worth
> Investment objectives (speculation, growth, income, growth & income, preservation)
> Estimated annual income
> Bank/brokerage firm reference
> Whether employed by a bank or broker-dealer
> Third-party trading authorization (if any)
> Citizenship (doesn't must be an American)
> Whether the customer is of legal age (not a minor child)
> How account was obtained (referring broker-dealer, investment adviser)
> Whether customer is an officer, director, or 10% shareholder of a publicly traded company

A registered representative for a broker-dealer is supervised by **principals**. A principal has sign-off power over important matters, and one thing a principal must always sign off on is a new account. So, the registered representative is listed on the new account form, but it's the principal/branch manager who must sign it to accept the new account. Surprisingly, there is no rule that says the customer must sign it. And, of course, that statement is always true except when it isn't. What we mean is that the customer can open a **cash account** without signing the new account form, but if she's opening a **margin account** or wants to trade options, she must sign it.

And, even though the customer is not required to sign the new account form for a pay-as-you-go cash account, she does need to verify that the information recorded is accurate, and she must sign that acknowledgment. The firm is required to send the customer a copy of the new account form within 30 days of opening the account and within 30 days of any major change in the information. Every 36 months the firm must verify the customer's information, too. Why? Making suitable recommendations to customers is your main job. If you're looking at customer information that is no longer accurate, your recommendations will most likely be unsuitable.

For example, one of your customers used to trade speculative penny stocks and call options. That made sense when she was single, but in the past few years she got married and had twins. So, if you're still recommending high-risk strategies, you're probably making unsuitable recommendations.

It might be time to set up a tax-advantaged education plan for the kids and tone down the aggressive posture of her existing account.

Unsuitable recommendations frequently lead to fines and suspensions from FINRA, and customers have been known to recover the money they lost by filing an arbitration claim. So, as the NYSE has been saying for centuries, the first rule for the registered representative is to "know thy customer." Since customers' situations change frequently, you and your firm need to keep up with the changes.

Even though a firm can send correspondence to the customer's PO Box, they still need to get a street address from the customer. What if the customer refuses to provide a social security or other tax ID number?

The account can still be opened, but the firm must notify him that the IRS is going to demand that a certain percentage of any interest, dividends, or capital gains must be withheld by the broker-dealer, known as a **backup withholding**. If the customer sells 100 shares of ABC for a profit, he won't be able to pull all of it out in cash at this time. Rather, a percentage will go to the IRS.

Surprisingly, even in today's climate, customers can open **numbered accounts**. This does not mean the customer remains anonymous. Rather, it means the customer does not want people at the firm talking about his or her financial business. The customer would need to sign a written statement acknowledging she owns the account identified only with a number or symbol, and your firm must keep that on file.

Whether an account is identified by a name, number or symbol, remember that account information is considered confidential. This is the customer's personal business, and you know how touchy some people get over financial matters. So, the information you obtain on a customer can only be released with the customer's written permission, or if there is a legal requirement to turn it over—the SEC, FINRA, a divorce or probate court, or your state regulator, for example, has subpoenaed the information. But, if somebody calls up claiming to be the customer's fiancée and just wants to know how much dividend income she should expect this month, do not release any information to him.

Unfortunately, sometimes customers end up losing money by following the recommendations of their registered representatives. Sometimes, the customer assumes the rep was not at fault. Other times, this being America, the customer demands her money back. FINRA has a system in place to handle such disputes, called **arbitration**. Members of the securities industry are automatically required to use arbitration to handle disputes between firms or between registered representatives and their employing broker-dealers. But a customer only must use arbitration if she has signed a pre-dispute arbitration agreement. If your firm failed to get her signature on that agreement, the customer would be free to sue you and your firm in civil court, where her attorneys could keep filing appeal after appeal until you cry uncle. To avoid the lengthy and expensive process of civil court, broker-dealers use arbitration. The pre-dispute clause must make it clear that the customer generally gets only one attempt at arbitration—no appeals—and that the arbitrators are not required to explain their decisions, and that many of them come from the industry.

So, if she loses, say, $100,000 following her registered representative's recommendations, the arbitrators could decide a range of outcomes. Maybe she gets $100,000, maybe she shares half the blame and gets $50,000. Maybe she gets nothing at all, and the arbitrators won't even explain why they decided against her. You can probably see why this arbitration thing needs to be clearly explained before the firm tries to hold the customer to the process by signing on the dotted line.

Finally, if the test asks about the customer's educational background, that it is not relevant. Educated people frequently do the dumbest things with their money, and less educated people have been known to make money in the market even as all the MBAs, CFAs, and CFPs consistently lose their shirts. So, we won't ask for the customer's educational level or record it on the new account form.

Options Account

Here are the steps for opening an options account:

1. Registered rep discusses suitability issues with the customer: net worth, experience with options, types of options trades anticipated.
2. Registered rep sends OCC Disclosure Brochure either now or at the time the Options Principal approves the account. Registered rep also indicates when the **OCC Disclosure Brochure** called "Characteristics and Risks of Standardized Options" was sent/delivered to customer.
3. As soon as the Options Principal approves account, first options trade may occur.
4. Customer has 15 days to return a signed options agreement. If not, only closing transactions would be allowed—no new positions.

Instructions for Securities, Cash, and Mail

Securities

When a customer buys securities, someone must hold them. There are three basic ways this can happen:

- Transfer and ship
- Transfer and hold in safekeeping
- Hold in street name

Maybe Grandma wants to put the cute, colorful Disney stock certificates right over the baby crib in the spare bedroom. If so, she'll request that you register the certificates in her name and ship them—**transfer and ship**.

Some investors have the broker-dealer transfer the securities into the name of the investor and then hold them in the firm's vault (**transfer and hold**). The firm would likely charge a fee to do that. So, most investors have the broker-dealer hold the securities in **street name**. The exam might say that the firm in this case is the "nominal owner" and the customer is the "beneficial owner" of the securities.

And, as we're about to see, shareholders can now use the **direct registration** method.

Whatever the customer chooses, most customers these days have never seen a stock or bond certificate because their broker-dealer holds them in street name (name of the firm) and may have them on deposit at centralized "depositories" such as the **Depository Trust Company (DTC)**. From there, the securities are transferred through electronic book/journal entries only, which explains why many registered representatives have also never seen a stock or bond certificate. It also explains why good record keeping is such a concern for your firm's principals and for FINRA. From the Depository Trust Company's website at www.dtc.org we see how things currently work in terms of how a customer can register/hold securities:

> With the implementation of direct registration, investors have three securities ownership options:
>
> *Physical Certificates*: Certificates are registered and issued in the investor's name. The investor will receive all mailings directly from the issuer or its transfer agent, including dividend or interest payments, annual reports, and proxies.
>
> *Street Name Registration*: Securities are registered in the street name of the investor's broker-dealer. While no physical certificate will be issued to the investor, the broker-dealer will issue, at least quarterly, account statements of the investor's holdings. The broker-dealer will pay dividends or interest to the investor, as well as provide the investor with mailing material from the issuer or transfer agent.
>
> *Direct Registration*: This option allows the investor to be registered directly on the books of the transfer agent without the need of a physical certificate to evidence the security ownership. While the investor will not receive a physical certificate, he or she will receive a statement of ownership and periodic (at least yearly) account statements. Dividend or interest payments, proxy materials, annual reports, etc., will be mailed from the issuer or its transfer agent.

Direct registration, then, is a relatively new development. The website referenced here mentions that since the NYSE allowed their listed companies to issue spin-off stock and stock-split shares as book-entry statements instead of certificates, some 300 companies have decided to allow shareholders to use direct registration with the transfer agent, rather than via their broker-dealer under the street name method.

Cash

Brokerage accounts contain securities and cash. The cash in customer accounts earns interest for the broker-dealer, and for some firms this represents most of their profits. The trading commissions cover expenses, but the spread between the high rate of interest they earn on customer cash and the low rate paid to customers is how they make their money.

Then again, it's not really their money. Customer cash is referred to as a **free credit balance** and is a liability of the broker-dealer that must be paid on demand. As the SEC rule explains, "The term 'free credit balances' means liabilities of a broker or dealer to customers which are subject to immediate cash payment to customers on demand, whether resulting from sales of securities, dividends, interest, deposits or otherwise."

As with a bank, a broker-dealer being able to honor customer requests for withdrawals is important. It is why the broker-dealer's minimum net capital is regularly monitored both internally and by the securities regulators.

Customers indicate on the new account form what the firm should do with their free credit balance. Some customers choose to have the cash "swept" into a money-market account, others into FDIC-insured deposit accounts. Either way, the industry calls these accounts sweep accounts.

Alternatively, the cash can be sent to the customer, or, it can be credited to her cash balance until she decides how to reinvest the proceeds into more securities.

Mail

The firm will be sending the customer monthly or (at least) quarterly **account statements** confirming the positions in the account and the value of the securities and the cash. Also, any time the customer buys or sells, a **trade confirmation** will be mailed to the customer's address of record. These days, statements and confirmations are often sent by email, but a customer must sign off on this method, which is much faster and cheaper for the firm to use. Confirmations and statements must be sent to the customer, unless the customer has instructed the firm in writing to send them elsewhere, e.g., his financial planner/investment adviser. Or, if the customer gives written instructions to hold back on delivering such mail while she is traveling, the firm can hold it for a reasonable length of time as instructed by the customer.

Standing Settlement Instructions (SSI)

Regular way is the typical method used to settle securities transactions, but for many institutional accounts, DVP/RVP is the default method. Customers, especially institutional investors, complete documents called standing settlement instructions to be used for all transactions. As we see from this explanation at a large financial firm's website, "These Standard Settlement Instructions are to be used for all transactions with HSBC Bank plc ("HSBC"), in the products denoted, unless otherwise specified at transaction level. Please follow carefully the instructions within the attached documents to ensure correct payment/delivery."

As it states, the customer can specify a different method on any transaction. But, otherwise, the standing settlement instructions are used by default. At the same HSBC website (http://www.hsbcnet.com/gbm/products-services/trading-sales/standard-settlement-instructions-document.html) we see that settlement instructions vary based on where the investor is located and the type of security or commodity being traded. Among many, there is a form for "USA: Options," one for "USA: Fixed Income – Mortgage-Backed Securities," and one for "USA: Precious Metals."

Protecting Seniors and Other Vulnerable Adults from Financial Exploitation

FINRA rules protect certain investors from caregivers or family members who might try to exploit their assets held by a broker-dealer. These rules apply both to senior investors and any adult with a physical or mental impairment that renders him unable to protect his own interests. Member firms must make reasonable efforts to obtain the name and contact information for a trusted contact person upon opening a customer's account. Then, if the firm ever suspects that financial exploitation could be occurring, they will notify the customer's trusted contact. Although firms are not required to spot potential exploitation and prevent it, they will be granted safe harbor for putting a temporary hold on an account if they suspect financial exploitation is going on.

As their website explains, "On April 20, 2015, FINRA launched a toll-free senior hotline – 1-844-57-HELPS – to provide older investors with a supportive place to get assistance from knowledgeable FINRA staff related to concerns they have with their brokerage accounts and investments. To date, FINRA has received over 1500 calls on issues including how to find information on their brokers, calls from children of deceased parents trying to locate assets or having difficulty moving assets from a brokerage firm, concerns from seniors ranging from routine poor service complaints to routine sales practice issues at firms, and fraud raised by a senior and/or child on behalf of senior investors."

Maintenance of Accounts

One way a broker-dealer could get in trouble financially is if too many customers fail to pay for securities purchases by the settlement date. In those cases, the firm's net capital takes a hit.

Account Restrictions

Therefore, under **Regulation T**, customer accounts are frozen if they don't make prompt payment for securities purchases. Regulation T is enforced by the Federal Reserve Board. It covers both margin accounts and cash accounts.

Broker-dealers don't have to allow customers to buy stock without having sufficient cash in the account to cover it. But, if they decide to carry such transactions in their "good faith account," customers must make payment by no later than 2 business days after settlement. Although firms can request extensions from FINRA, a slow-paying customer is eventually subject to an **account freeze**.

That term sounds harsher than it is. All it prevents the customer from doing is making further purchases over the next 90 days without having or depositing the funds prior to entering the trade. If they wire the funds or deliver a cashier's check personally, then they can enter a purchase order up to the amount. But, they can't enter the purchase order and then promise to come up with the funds.

At least, not until the freeze is lifted.

Another action that leads to an account freeze is a customer purchasing the stock without having the funds in the account. Then, rather than sending payment promptly, the customer sells the stock to cover the buy side. The broker-dealer fills the order, but this "freeriding" violation of Reg T leads to a 90-day customer account freeze.

We looked at other account restrictions, including that officers, directors, and large shareholders of public companies are subject to volume limits when selling the company's common stock. Such people are also subject to lock-up periods if they buy the issuer's securities in a primary offer. And, if they purchase the issuer's stock through a private placement, they are subject to holding periods under Rule 144.

We'll look at margin accounts elsewhere. A margin account extends a line of credit to customers, but they can't access that line if doing so brings the account's equity below the minimum maintenance, which is $2,000.

In an options account, a new customer must return the signed options agreement no later than 15 business days after receiving account approval. If he fails to do so, he can enter no new purchases but can only liquidate any positions he has already opened.

Transactions for or by Associated Persons

On the new account form, we ask if the customer is associated with a member firm. If your broker-dealer knows that the customer is associated with a member firm, or if an associate of a member firm has discretion over the account, your firm must:

- notify the employer member in writing, prior to the execution of a transaction for such account, of the executing member's intention to open or maintain such an account;
- upon written request by the employer member, transmit duplicate copies of confirmations, statements, or other information with respect to such account; and
- notify the person associated with the employer member of the executing member's intention to provide the notice and information required

If you want to open an investment account with another firm, remember that FINRA rules state:

> *A person associated with a member, prior to opening an account or placing an initial order for the purchase or sale of securities with another member, shall notify both the employer member and the executing member, in writing, of his or her association with the other member; provided, however, that if the account was established prior to the association of the person with the employer member, the associated person shall notify both members in writing promptly after becoming so associated.*

Transactions Involving FINRA Employees

FINRA has approximately 3,400 employees, and surely some of them have investment accounts. Because FINRA is the regulator of the broker-dealer and agent dealing with such an employee's account, there are rules designed to prevent members from trying to buy favor with their regulator. When the member has actual knowledge that the account is partly or wholly owned by an employee of FINRA, they must promptly provide duplicate account statements to FINRA. Also, other than normal margin loans or loans between family members, no member can make any loans to an employee of FINRA. And, if an employee of FINRA has responsibility for any regulatory matter concerning the member, the firm would be in serious trouble if they tried to start providing expensive gifts to that employee. Anything more than, say, a key chain or pen would probably raise red flags for FINRA.

As in Major League Baseball, disputes in this industry are settled through arbitration. In other words, member firms can't sue each other in civil court if an underwriting turns sour and one member of the syndicate is convinced they are owed an additional $1 million from another member, who acted as syndicate manager in the IPO. That sort of dispute must be submitted to arbitration. That means you get one shot, no appeals. As we saw earlier, firms get their customers to sign pre-dispute arbitration agreements, but they must be very upfront about what that means in the document they're getting the customer to sign. The rule stipulates that the warning must look like this:

> This agreement contains a pre-dispute arbitration clause. By signing an arbitration agreement, the parties agree as follows:
>
> (A) All parties to this agreement are giving up the right to sue each other in court, including the right to a trial by jury, except as provided by the rules of the arbitration forum in which a claim is filed.
>
> (B) Arbitration awards are generally final and binding; a party's ability to have a court reverse or modify an arbitration award is very limited.
>
> (C) The ability of the parties to obtain documents, witness statements and other discovery is generally more limited in arbitration than in court proceedings.
>
> (D) The arbitrators do not must explain the reason(s) for their award.
>
> (E) The panel of arbitrators will typically include a minority of arbitrators who were or are affiliated with the securities industry.
>
> (F) The rules of some arbitration forums may impose time limits for bringing a claim in arbitration. In some cases, a claim that is ineligible for arbitration may be brought in court.
>
> (G) The rules of the arbitration forum in which the claim is filed, and any amendments thereto, shall be incorporated into this agreement.

Only by getting the customer to sign this agreement would your firm know that when somebody loses money, that somebody will not be able to drag them through civil court, with appeal after appeal. Arbitration is faster and cheaper for all involved.

FINRA rules make sure that your firm provides the registered representative with the same written disclosure that he is bound by FINRA Arbitration when asked to sign a U4 or U5 form.

Position Limits

The customer's signature on the options agreement means he understands the risks associated with options and will follow the rules of the options exchange. For example, he won't take the electronic quotes and re-sell them on a website. He won't write calls and then flee the country whenever they go deep in-the-money. And, he will abide by any position limits that may be in place.

A **position limit** means that a customer, or a group of customers "acting in concert," will not try to corner the market, so to speak. If a standardized option has a position limit of 25,000, that means that an investor can have no more than 25,000 bull or bear positions in that option. If he buys 20,000 calls, there are 5,000 bull positions left. He could, therefore, buy 20,000 calls and write 5,000 puts. I'm talking about "per class" here, meaning all MSFT calls or puts, not all MSFT Oct 30 calls, which would be a series. He could also establish 25,000 bear positions (buy puts, sell calls) on an underlying security.

The same numbers used for position limits are used for exercise limits. That means if the option is subject to a limit of 25,000, 25,000 represents the maximum number of open bull or bear positions a trader can have at one time on a class of options and also the maximum number of contracts he can exercise over five consecutive business days. The CBOE regularly publishes a list of position limits associated with options.

The Escheatment Process

Escheatment involves accounts that have been abandoned or are unclaimed and inactive. As the SEC explains, "All states require financial institutions, including brokerage firms, to report when personal property has been abandoned or unclaimed after a period of time specified by state law — often five years. Before a brokerage account can be considered abandoned or unclaimed, the firm must make a diligent effort to try to locate the account owner. If the firm is unable to do so, and the account has remained inactive for the period of time specified by state law, the firm must report the account to the state where the account is held. The state then claims the account through a process called escheatment, whereby the state becomes the owner of the account.

As part of the escheatment process, the state will hold the account as a bookkeeping entry, against which the former account owner may make a claim. States tend to sell the securities in escheated accounts and treat the proceeds as state funds. When a former account owner makes a valid request, however, the states will normally provide the former owner with cash equaling the value of the account at the time of escheatment. This amount of cash does not include any dividends or interest covering the time after escheatment."

There are websites, both free and commercial, that allow people to check for any unclaimed accounts in their name. One free site allows visitors to search for accounts by state, at https://www.unclaimed.org/.

Anti-Money Laundering (AML)

Criminals pulling in millions in cash must be careful not to draw the attention of both the police and the IRS. If one drives a $95,000 Cadillac Escalade™ while holding no job or owning no business that could explain it, soon stern professionals in dark suits show up asking questions and seizing documents or assets.

Therefore, criminals use elaborate schemes to take their "dirty" money and make it "clean." Maybe they buy a car wash and write up phony receipts for non-existent customers to match that up with a few hundred thousand dollars of illegal profits that end up being "cleaned" in the wash so to speak.

Money laundering is the process of taking illegal profits and disguising them as clean money. The three distinct phases of money laundering are:

- Placement

- Layering
- Integration

Placement is the first stage in the cycle in which illegally generated funds are placed into the financial system or are smuggled out of the country. The goals of the money launderer are to remove the cash from where it was acquired to avoid detection from the authorities, and to then transform it into other assets, e.g., travelers' checks, money orders, etc.

Layering is the first attempt at disguising the source of the ownership of the funds by creating complex layers of transactions. The purpose of layering is to disassociate the dirty money from the source of the crime through a complicated web of financial transactions. Typically, layers are created by moving money in and out of offshore bank accounts of shell companies, through electronic funds transfers (EFTs). Because there are over 500,000 wire transfers circling the globe every day, most of which are legitimate, there isn't enough information disclosed on any single wire transfer to know how clean or dirty the money is. This provides an excellent way for money launderers to move their dirty money.

Other forms used by launderers are complex dealings with stock, commodity and futures brokers. Given the sheer volume of daily transactions, and the high degree of anonymity available, the chances of transactions being traced are insignificant. In other words, broker-dealers are great places to launder money, which is why broker-dealers need to help the federal government clamp down on terrorists and other criminals trying to layer dirty money through a flurry of trading activity.

Integration is the final stage in the process. In this stage, the money is integrated into the legitimate financial system. Integration of the now-clean money into the economy is accomplished by making it appear to have been legally earned. By this stage, it is very difficult to distinguish "clean" financial assets from "dirty."

Broker-dealers are required to design AML programs based on the unique aspects of their business. Firms are expected to take a proactive approach to their AML programs, too. Those who treat it like an afterthought have been fined millions of dollars by FINRA, many also having their licenses revoked.

From a recent speech by Kevin W. Goodman, from the SEC's Broker-Dealer Examination Program:

> While at first blush AML obligations may seem to be the mechanical process of monitoring and reporting cash flows and securities transactions, AML programs are actually much more. When implemented well, they provide protections against misuse of the nation's financial system for criminal activity – activity that ranges from financial fraud (endangering people's financial security) to profiting from drug businesses to funding terrorist activities. For example, federal authorities have used filed suspicious activity reports ("SARs") to identify fraud schemes such as purported investments in non-existent high yield investments, Ponzi or pyramid schemes, and market manipulation.

AML has a direct connection to investor protection. "Purported investments in non-existent high-yield investments" means that investors were duped into turning over their money to financial criminals, who then got away with it through illegal money laundering activities.

So, in cases like that, regulators would be one problem. Another would be explaining to the customer what happened. Another would be making the customer whole with the firm's own funds.

FINRA lays out the rules for member firms' AML programs:

> *Anti-Money Laundering Compliance Program*
>
> *On or before April 24, 2002, each member shall develop and implement a written anti-money laundering program reasonably designed to achieve and monitor the member's compliance with the requirements of the Bank Secrecy Act, and the implementing regulations promulgated thereunder by the Department of the Treasury. Each member's anti-money laundering program must be approved, in writing, by a member of senior management.*

Broker-dealers are required to report large cash transactions and retain records on wire transfers, whether any potential criminal activity is suspected.

FINRA-member firms must also monitor suspicious activity and report it to the U.S. Treasury's Financial Crimes Enforcement Network. Suspicious activity includes financial activity with no business or apparent lawful purpose. This includes not just money laundering by violent criminals, but also non-violent felonies such as Ponzi schemes and insider or other forms of manipulative trading.

If a transaction involves at least $5,000, and the broker-dealer knows, suspects, or has reason to suspect that it has no apparent lawful purpose, the member must file a **Suspicious Activity Report (SAR)** with FinCEN. The $5,000 figure covers any one transaction or series of transactions.

An SAR must be filed if the transaction falls within one of four classes:

- the transaction involves funds derived from illegal activity or is intended or conducted to hide or disguise funds or assets derived from illegal activity;
- the transaction is designed to evade the requirements of the Bank Secrecy Act
- the transaction appears to serve no business or apparent lawful purpose or is not the sort of transaction in which the customer would be expected to engage and for which the broker/dealer knows of no reasonable explanation after examining the available facts; or
- the transaction involves the use of the broker/dealer to facilitate criminal activity

As a FINRA notice to members announces, "To help the government fight the funding of terrorism and money laundering activities, federal law requires financial institutions to obtain, verify and record information that identifies each person who opens an account." The notice explains obligations under the **Customer Identification Program (CIP)** for financial institutions including banks and broker-dealers. The first thing member firms must do is establish a written policy for establishing and documenting the identity of each customer for whom the firm opens an account.

Under the Customer Identification Program, broker-dealers must obtain an individual's name, date of birth, residential address, citizenship, and social security/taxpayer ID. If the customer is not a U.S. citizen, the firm will need:

- taxpayer identification number
- passport number and country of issuance
- alien identification card number or government-issued identification showing nationality, residence and a photograph of the customer.

Even the U.S. citizen may need to show a photo ID, just as you do when you take your Series 99 exam.

The federal government maintains an **Office of Foreign Asset Control (OFAC)** designed to protect against the threat of terrorism. This office maintains a list of individuals and organizations viewed as a threat to the U.S. Broker-dealers and other financial institutions must be sure they aren't setting up accounts for these organizations, or—if they are—must block/freeze the assets.

As the Department of Treasury explains, "As part of its enforcement efforts, OFAC publishes a list of individuals and companies owned or controlled by, or acting for or on behalf of, targeted countries. It also lists individuals, groups, and entities, such as terrorists and narcotics traffickers designated under programs that are not country-specific. Collectively, such individuals and companies are called 'Specially Designated Nationals' or 'SDNs.' Their assets are blocked and U.S. persons are generally prohibited from dealing with them."

Currency Transaction Reports

FinCEN is the U.S. Treasury's Financial Crimes Enforcement Network. Broker-dealers, banks, casinos, and check-cashing/wire transfer firms file various FinCEN forms when handling certain transactions.

Under the Bank Secrecy Act (BSA), FinCEN requires that for transfers of funds of $3,000 or more, broker-dealers obtain and keep certain specified information concerning the parties sending and receiving those funds. In addition, broker-dealers must include this information on the transmittal order itself.

For example, if a customer sends an electronic funds transfer (EFT) to his father's bank account from his own brokerage account, detailed records are required if the amount is $3,000 or more.

Cash transactions over $10,000 require that broker-dealers file a **Currency Transaction Report (CTR)**, FinCEN Form 104.

Why? Because terrorist and criminal organizations fund their operations through money laundering. Since broker-dealers are financial institutions, they're included with banks, casinos, check-cashing services, etc., and required to keep records helping the government prevent these operations.

The form is available at https://www.irs.gov/pub/irs-tege/fin104_ctr.pdf. Detailed information is required and provided on the parties involved in the transaction, the financial institution involved, and the amount and source of funds.

A test question could say a customer brings in $5,000 over his lunch break and $6,000 at 3:30 PM, all to be deposited in his account. Because the total exceeds $10,000, a CTR is required.

The transactions just discussed require recordkeeping and retention based on the amount of the transaction. On the other hand, any suspicious transaction requires them to file an SAR (Suspicious Activity Report).

A test question could involve a scenario in which a customer endorses a check made payable to him from a third party for $10,025. The bank charges a $30 fee to cash large 3rd-party checks same-day; therefore, the customer receives $9,995 in an envelope from the teller. Must the bank fill out a CTR?

No. The cash amount was not > $10,000. But, if they have reason to believe the customer is involved in illegal activities, they are required to file an SAR. And, if he consistently receives as close to $10,000 in cash without going over, it might appear he is trying to avoid any FinCEN forms from being filed.

Which would be suspicious.

Confirmations and Account Statements

A **trade confirmation** confirms a transaction for the customer's review:

Account #	Transaction #	Capacity	Account Executive	
26597-5	006530698	Agent	GH	
Activity	Quantity	CUSIP	Price	Principal Amt.
Bought	10,000	3890227	$25.49	254,900.00
Trade Date	Settlement Date	Interest	Commission	Net Amount

04/22/2003	04/25/2003	N/A	$10.99	254,910.99
Symbol	Trade Description			
LGTO	Legato Systems, Inc.			

This document is called a trade confirmation because it confirms the trade, showing the customer everything material about the transaction: the stock, the number of shares, the price of the stock, the commission, and the total price paid or received on the transaction, etc. It is the invoice for the transaction.

Trade confirmations must be delivered no later than settlement, which is the completion of the transaction (T + 2 regular-way for stock, corporate bonds, and municipal bonds).

Confirmations are often delivered by email, a faster and cheaper method. Whether on paper or PDF, customers should save their trade confirmations. If the broker-dealer fails, SIPC protection may require investors to prove they held positions with the firm.

An SEC rule under the Securities Exchange Act of 1934 requires that a customer trade confirmation contain:

The date and time of the transaction (or the fact that the time of the transaction will be furnished upon written request to such customer) and the identity, price, and number of shares or units (or principal amount) of such security purchased or sold by such customer

For a transaction in an NMS stock, a statement of whether payment for order flow is received by the broker or dealer and a statement that the source and nature of the compensation will be provided upon request

In the case of any transaction in a debt security subject to redemption before maturity, a statement to the effect that such debt security may be redeemed in whole or in part before maturity, that such a redemption could affect the yield represented and the fact that additional information is available upon request

That the broker or dealer is not a member of the Securities Investor Protection Corporation (SIPC), or that the broker or dealer clearing or carrying the customer account is not a member of SIPC, if such is the case

Whether the broker or dealer is acting as agent for such customer, as agent for some other person, as agent for both such customer and some other person, or as principal for its own account; and if the broker or dealer is acting as principal, whether it is a market maker in the security

If the broker or dealer is acting as agent for such customer, for some other person, or for both such customer and some other person:

- The name of the person from whom the security was purchased, or to whom it was sold, for such customer or the fact that the information will be furnished upon written request of such customer
- The amount of any remuneration received or to be received by the broker from such customer in connection with the transaction unless remuneration paid by such customer is determined pursuant to written agreement with such customer, otherwise than on a transaction basis
- If acting in a principal capacity and not a market maker, the firm must disclose:

- the difference between the price to the customer and the dealer's contemporaneous purchase (for customer purchases) or sale price (for customer sales) when executing riskless principal transactions
- for stocks trading on an exchange or subject to last sale price reporting, the difference between the price to the customer and the last reported price

We mentioned account statements earlier and compared them to the performance reports an investment adviser provides its clients. At the least, a broker-dealer must send account statements to their customers quarterly. It would only be that infrequently if there had been no activity in the account—an inactive account. If any of the following had occurred, a monthly statement would be sent:

- Purchases or sales of securities
- Dividend and/or interest received
- Addition or withdrawal of cash or securities
- Margin interest charged to a margin account

The account statement shows:

- All positions in the account
- All activity since the last statement
- All credit and debit balances

Account statements must contain a message to customers asking them to verify the statement and promptly report any discrepancy or error. This way, unauthorized transactions or mistakes can be spotted and fixed sooner. Some firms take the position that after 10 days of the account statement being received the customer is bound by the positions revealed in the statement.

Prospectus Delivery Requirements

An offer of securities involves publishing and delivering a prospectus to interested investors. The Securities Act of 1933 states that a prospectus must "contain the information contained in the registration statement."

The Securities Act of 1933 and the rules thereunder guide the registration process for issuers, as does Regulation S-K. Regulation S-K provides guidance on forward-looking statements made by an issuer and lays out the information required in various types of securities registration statements. Regulation S-K makes it clear that to file full disclosure of risks and business plans an issuer necessarily must make projections. While such projections can provide clarity, the issuer also must have a reasonable basis for making projections about, say, a proposed merger, or projections of earnings for a key business unit.

Aiding investor understanding is key, and the SEC explains their concerns like this, "When management chooses to include its projections in a Commission filing, the disclosures accompanying the projections should facilitate investor understanding of the basis for and limitations of projections. In this regard investors should be cautioned against attributing undue certainty to management's assessment, and the Commission believes that investors would be aided by a statement indicating management's intention regarding the furnishing of updated projections."

To give investors an idea of how big a gap could exist between management's previous projections and reality, the SEC stipulates that, "Management also should consider whether disclosure of the accuracy or inaccuracy of previous projections would provide investors with important insights into the limitations of projections. In this regard, consideration should be given to presenting the projections in a format that will facilitate subsequent analysis of the reasons for differences between actual and forecast results."

Most American companies use a Form S-1 to register an offer of common stock. When completing this registration statement, the issuer is required to provide:

FORM S-1

A general description of their business: Describe the general development of the business of the registrant, its subsidiaries and any predecessor(s) during the past five years, or such shorter period as the registrant may have been engaged in business.

Description of property: State briefly the location and general character of the principal plants, mines and other materially important physical properties of the registrant and its subsidiaries. In addition, identify the segment(s), as reported in the financial statements, that use the properties described.

Legal proceedings: Describe briefly any material pending legal proceedings, other than ordinary routine litigation incidental to the business, to which the registrant or any of its subsidiaries is a party or of which any of their property is the subject.

Mine safety disclosure: companies involved in mining must disclose the total number of violations of mandatory health or safety standards that could significantly and substantially contribute to the cause and effect of a coal or other mine safety or health hazard for which the operator received a citation from the Mine Safety and Health Administration.

Securities of the registrant: identify the principal United States market or markets in which each class of the registrant's common equity is being traded. Where there is no established public trading market for a class of common equity, furnish a statement to that effect. Also indicate the approximate number of shareholders and any dividends paid over the previous two years.

Description of registrant's securities: provide legal description of the securities in terms of rights of holders of common stock, preferred stock, debt securities, etc.

Financial information: provide financial information (balance sheet, income statement, cash flow, etc.) for the previous five years or life of operations.

Management's discussion and analysis of financial condition and results of operations: discuss registrant's financial condition, changes in financial condition and results of operations.

Changes in and disagreements with accountants on accounting and financial disclosure: provide disclosure on any auditing accountants who were removed, resigned, etc.

Quantitative and qualitative disclosures about market risk: discuss market risk and risk factors for the registrant's securities.

Management and certain security holders: list the names and ages of all directors of the registrant and all persons nominated or chosen to become directors; indicate all positions and offices with the registrant held by each such person. List the names and ages of all executive officers of the registrant and all persons chosen to become executive officers; indicate all positions and offices with the registrant held by each such person; state his term of office as officer and the period during which he has served as such and describe briefly any arrangement or understanding between him and any other person(s) (naming such person) pursuant to which he was or is to be selected as an officer. Identify certain significant employees who are not officers and disclose the same information required of corporate officers.

Executive compensation: provide details of executive officers' compensation, cash, stock, options, etc.

Security ownership of certain beneficial owners and management: options and shares held by management and large shareholders.

Corporate governance: discuss whether directors are independent.

The issuer must also provide:

Name of registrant
Title and amount of securities
Offering price of the securities
Market for the securities
Risk factors
State legend: Any warnings required of state regulators.

Commission legend: A legend that indicates that neither the Securities and Exchange Commission nor any state securities commission has approved or disapproved of the securities or passed upon the accuracy or adequacy of the disclosures in the prospectus and that any contrary representation is a criminal offense.

Underwriting: information on underwriters of the securities.

Date of prospectus

Prospectus subject to completion legend: if a preliminary prospectus.

Use of proceeds: what will the issuer do with the proceeds of the offering? As the SEC states, "State the principal purposes for which the net proceeds to the registrant from the securities to be offered are intended to be used and the approximate amount intended to be used for each such purpose. Where registrant has no current specific plan for the proceeds, or a significant portion thereof, the registrant shall so state and discuss the principal reasons for the offering."

Selling security holders: if any of the securities are being offered by security holders, provide information on each one.

Issuers must provide a table of contents on either the inside front or outside back cover of the prospectus to help investors navigate the document. As the SEC states, "It must show the page number of the various sections or subdivisions of the prospectus. Include a specific listing of the risk factors section required by Item 503 of this Regulation S-K."

Dealers have prospectus delivery requirements, so the SEC requires that, "On the outside back cover page of the prospectus advise dealers of their prospectus delivery obligation, including the expiration date specified by . . . the Securities Act of 1933."

The final prospectus must be delivered to all buyers of an IPO no later than completion of the transaction. It also must be delivered to buyers on the secondary market—the investors buying from the IPO investors—for a certain amount of time, depending on which market it trades on. Since there isn't much required of or known about Pink Quote or OTCBB stocks, the prospectus for an IPO must be delivered for 90 days on the secondary market, even after the offering period closes. For additional offerings of these stocks, the prospectus must be provided on the secondary market for 40 days. For NYSE and NASDAQ securities IPOs require the prospectus be delivered for 25 days, but for additional offers there is no requirement to deliver the prospectus on the after- or secondary market.

Broker-dealers must respond promptly to any written request for a preliminary or final prospectus. Any associated persons expected to solicit sales must be provided with copies of the preliminary prospectus and the final prospectus—if the information is materially different from the preliminary prospectus. If the broker-dealer is the managing underwriter, they must provide sufficient copies of these documents to all syndicate and selling group members requesting them. Because of prospectus delivery requirements after the offering period, the managing underwriter also must provide copies of these disclosure documents to firms who will make a market in or trade heavily in the security.

The prospectus for an IPO is often retired soon after the offering is completed. But, the prospectus for a mutual fund or variable annuity would be subject to regular updates. Therefore, if a prospectus is used more than 9 months after the effective date, the information cannot be more than 16 months old. The SEC has the authority to permit issuers to omit any item of information by their rules if they feel it's not necessary for the protection of investors to include it. By the same token the SEC has the authority to decide that a prospectus must contain whatever they stipulate through their rulemaking process and authority.

There are many different types/forms of "prospectuses," which is why the Securities Act of 1933 states, "the Commission shall have authority to classify prospectuses according to the nature and circumstances of their use or the nature of the security, issue, issuer, or otherwise, and, by rules and regulations and subject to such terms and conditions as it shall specify therein, to prescribe as to each class the form and contents which it may find appropriate and consistent with the public interest and the protection of investors."

A "prospectus" can come in the form of a TV or radio broadcast, which is why the Securities Act of 1933 also states, "In any case where a prospectus consists of a radio or television broadcast, copies thereof shall be filed with the Commission under such rules and regulations as it shall prescribe."

Proxies and Annual Statements

Back in olden days small shareholders weren't likely to cast votes at the annual meeting, unless they happened to live near corporate headquarters. The Securities Exchange Act of 1934 covered a whole lot of ground, and part of the ground covered had to do with public corporations/issuers letting shareholders vote by proxy. This way, we don't have to travel to Redwood Shores, California, just to cast our votes at the Oracle annual shareholder meeting. Instead, shareholders can fill out the form received from our broker-dealers and let them vote per our instructions. Usually these **proxy statements** indicate how management thinks shareholders should vote.

Of course, we can vote however we want with our number of shares. Or if we sign the proxy and fail to indicate how we want to cast my votes, then the board of directors/management of the company gets to use those votes as they see fit. If the matter is of no major importance, the broker-dealer can cast the votes on behalf of their customer, if the customer has failed to return the proxy at least 10 days prior to the annual meeting. A major issue, such as whether two companies should merge, would be a different matter. We're talking more like the decision to retain KPMG as the firm's auditor.

The Securities Exchange Act of 1934 also requires public companies to report quarterly and annually. So, the broker-dealer forwards those reports as well as proxy materials to their customers, but they don't charge the customers. This is all a cost that the issuer must bear. Another name for a proxy is an "absentee ballot," by the way.

Prohibited Activities

Let's look at the industry from a regulatory perspective, starting with the conduct of registered representatives.

Outside Business Activities

Many students seem shocked to learn they'll need to notify their employing broker-dealer before doing any type of work outside the firm. As this rule stipulates:

> *No person associated with a member in any registered capacity shall be employed by, or accept compensation from, any other person as a result of any business activity, other than a passive investment, outside the scope of his relationship with his employer firm, unless he has provided prompt written notice to the member. Such notice shall be in the form required by the member.*

Although the rule does not require permission be granted, it functions the same way. Member firms can restrict or reject any plans to work outside the firm for compensation. Therefore, associated persons must give their employing firm notice, and then wait to see if the firm has questions or concerns before engaging in that activity.

The rule covers any work for compensation, not just work in the financial services industry. Giving golf or piano lessons for compensation are examples of outside business activities subject to disclosure to the firm.

The rule does not cover volunteer work, since that is not for compensation.

Private Securities Transactions

FINRA wants all activities of a registered representative monitored, so if the registered representative is sitting in his office offering investors a chance to invest in his sister's new LLC without telling his firm, there is no way the firm could monitor his sales activities, which poses a threat to investors. That could even be the answer to a question that asks why **selling away** is a violation—because it gives your principal/firm no opportunity to supervise your activities. So, principals and registered representatives cannot offer securities to investors that their firm knows nothing about. As this rule makes clear:

> *No person associated with a member shall participate in any manner in a private securities transaction except in accordance with the requirements of this Rule.*
>
> *(b) Written Notice*
>
> *Prior to participating in any private securities transaction, an associated person shall provide written notice to the member with which he is associated describing in detail the proposed transaction and the person's proposed role therein and stating whether he has received or may receive selling compensation in connection with the transaction.*

Once the associated person has provided written notice to the employing member firm, the firm can either approve or disapprove the activities. If they disapprove, the associated person would be subject to disciplinary action by FINRA and termination by the firm if he went ahead and sold the securities, anyway.

The member firm must follow different procedures based on whether the associated person will receive selling compensation. If the transactions involve compensation and the firm approves the activity, the member must record the transactions on their regular books and records as well as supervise the registered representative (or principal) as if the transactions were being done on their behalf.

On the other hand, if the transactions will not involve selling compensation, the employing firm must provide the associated person prompt written acknowledgment of receiving notification. The member firm may then, at its discretion, require the person to adhere to specified conditions.

However, if the associated person fails to provide prior written notice, this violates the rule above whether any selling compensation is received or not. For purposes of this rule, FINRA defines selling compensation as, "Any compensation paid directly or indirectly from whatever source in connection with or as a result of the purchase or sale of a security, including, though not limited to, commissions; finder's fees; securities or rights to acquire securities; rights of participation in profits, tax benefits, or dissolution proceeds, as a general partner or otherwise; or expense reimbursements."

Customers' Securities or Funds

> *c) Authorization to Lend*
>
> *No member shall lend, either to himself or to others, securities carried for the account of any customer, which are eligible to be pledged or loaned unless such member shall first have obtained from the customer a written authorization permitting the lending of securities thus carried by such member.*

Margin customers sometimes sign a loan consent, which allows the broker-dealer to use the securities when lending to short sellers. The above rule requires the firm to have the customer's consent first. But, FINRA does not require separate forms here. As a recent notice to member firms states, "FINRA Rule 4330(a) requires a firm to obtain a customer's written authorization prior to lending securities that are held on margin for a customer and that are eligible to be pledged or loaned. Supplementary Material .02 permits a firm to use a single customer account agreement/margin agreement/loan consent signed by the customer as written authorization under Rule 4330(a), provided such customer account agreement/margin agreement/loan consent includes clear and prominent disclosure that the firm may lend either to itself or others any securities held by the customer in its margin account."

The firm must keep their assets separate from the assets that clearly belong to the customer, and their books and records must make it clear which securities belong to which customers. A failure to do so is a violation called commingling:

> *d) Segregation and Identification of Securities*
>
> *No member shall hold securities carried for the account of any customer which have been fully paid for or which are excess margin securities unless such securities are segregated and identified by a method which clearly indicates the interest of such customer in those securities.*

FINRA rules require members to segregate and identify by customers both fully paid and "excess margin" securities. "With regard to a customer's account which contains only stocks, it is general practice for firms to segregate that portion of the stocks having a market value in excess of 140% of the debit balance therein."

So, if the "Dr" or "debit register" in a margin account is $5,000, 140% of that would be $7,000, and anything above that would be considered "excess margin" securities. So, the broker-dealer pledges $7,000 of the securities as collateral to the bank, and the rest is/are "excess margin securities."

Agents and broker-dealers do not guarantee customers against losses:

Prohibition Against Guarantees

> *No member or person associated with a member shall guarantee a customer against loss in connection with any securities transaction or in any securities account of such customer.*

Some securities are guaranteed, but neither broker-dealers nor agents may guarantee customers against investment losses. A Treasury Bond is guaranteed against default by the US Treasury. But, agents and broker-dealers cannot shield customers against investment losses should they purchase T-Bonds just before interest rates rise.

Treasury securities are safe, but they are not the only debt securities that may be guaranteed. A corporate bond may be guaranteed as to interest and principal by a third party. This means if the issuer is unable to pay, the third party has promised to at least try to make good on the interest, principal or both. Often, the issuer is a subsidiary of the guarantor in these cases.

Paying Commissions to Unregistered Persons
Broker-dealers and associated persons are prohibited from paying individuals and entities not registered or associated with a member firm referral fees or any form of compensation for helping them increase their sales efforts.

The same prohibition applies to unregistered employees of the broker-dealer. An assistant without the appropriate license cannot share in any revenues connected to securities transactions with a registered representative.

IPO shares in a hot company could be used as rewards, or to threaten people. The prohibited practice of spinning occurs when underwriting broker-dealers allocate shares of popular IPO stocks to investors who can then direct securities business to the firm as a thank-you. To prevent spinning, FINRA prohibits the practice of allocating IPO shares to officers and directors of companies if the company is an investment banking customer of the broker-dealer or becomes an investment banking customer in the next three months.

Clearly, it is not okay for an underwriting broker-dealer to force someone to buy 100,000 shares of an IPO by threatening to withhold shares of future offerings. Similarly, it would be a violation for the managing underwriter to offer to allot 1 million shares to a broker-dealer who first writes a favorable research report on the stock. These violations could get the regulators to start using fancy phrases like "quid pro quo," which means you-scratch-my-back-I'll-scratch-yours in the original Latin.

Quid pro quo allocations of IPO shares are not allowed. Why should the public investor be exposed to some bogus "research report" that is overly enthusiastic due to the conflict of interest? Turns out they shouldn't be and that's why quid pro quo allocations are not allowed. You've likely noticed that virtually anything that threatens the integrity of the securities markets is not allowed by the SEC, FINRA or both.

To make sure public offerings of stock have integrity FINRA has rules that will prevent you, dear reader, from buying IPO shares, period. The FINRA rules apply only to initial public offerings of common stock—not to debt securities, preferred stock, mutual funds, or even additional offers of common stock.

So, we're only talking about the companies coming out-of-the-starting-gates with an IPO here. Even if it's a bond that converts to common stock—not subject to this rule.

Who is defined as a **restricted person** and, therefore, restricted from buying IPOs?

- broker-dealer member firms
- employees of broker-dealer member firms
- anyone/any entity owning 10% or more of a broker-dealer member firm
- finders and fiduciaries acting on behalf of the managing underwriter (e.g., attorneys, accountants, financial consultants)
- portfolio managers (mutual funds, banks, pension funds, insurance company, etc.) buying for their own account
- any immediate family member of anyone above

So, if you own 10% or more of a FINRA member broker-dealer, or if you are a broker-dealer, or if you merely work for a broker-dealer, or have someone in your immediate family who fits any of those descriptions, you are basically not buying into an initial public offer of common stock. What does "immediate family member" include? First, it includes anyone who receives material financial support from a restricted person. Then, it includes: parents and in-laws, spouses, siblings, and children of a restricted person. So, if your sister works for Morgan-Stanley, you are a restricted person as an immediate family member.

On the other hand, the following family members are considered too distant to worry about: aunts and uncles, grandparents, cousins. What if you have one of those old college buddies that just can't seem to catch a break? Whether he lives with you is irrelevant; remember that, among other reasons, you might want to keep your financial support to under 25% of his income. Yes, "material support" means providing more than 25% of an individual's personal income for the prior year.

While a receptionist for a member firm is a restricted person, if that individual is in a joint account, and that individual's ownership is no more than 10%, then the account can buy an equity IPO under the "de minimis rule." You can see why broker-dealers who engage in underwriting activities need initial and annual statements obtained in the past 12 months or sooner from their customers verifying that they either are or are not a "restricted person". These are known as pre-conditions for sale of an equity IPO.

Nothing is ever simple in this business. Even though we just said that broker-dealers are not allowed to buy shares of an equity IPO, there are exceptions. If a broker-dealer—usually one of the underwriters—signs an agreement to act as a standby purchaser, then they can help an offering that is selling weakly by promising to buy any shares the public doesn't want. This arrangement must be in writing; it must be disclosed in the final prospectus; and the managing underwriter must state in writing that it was unable to find any other purchasers for the stock.

So, can a broker-dealer buy an equity IPO? No, except when they can—e.g., by acting as a standby purchaser with a bona fide agreement in writing that is disclosed in the prospectus. Securities purchased through a standby agreement may not be re-sold to investors for at least three months.

Also, it's not the underwriters' fault if the public just isn't that into this IPO. Therefore, if the managing underwriter or other syndicate members end up buying the unsold shares of an undersubscribed offering and hold them in their investment account, that is not only okay, but is also common. The idea is that they can't pretend they couldn't sell all the good IPOs to end up keeping them for themselves—that, as we saw, is a violation.

FINRA rules state: the book-running managing underwriter of a new issue shall be required to file the following information in the time and manner specified by FINRA with respect to new issues:

- the initial list of distribution participants and their underwriting commitment and retention amounts on or before the offering date; and
- the final list of distribution participants and their underwriting commitment and retention amounts no later than three business days after the offering date.

A "distribution participant" is "an underwriter, prospective underwriter, broker, dealer, or other person who has agreed to participate or is participating in a distribution."

An IPO is not to be treated as a quick buy-and-flip opportunity. If some investors are immediately selling their shares on the secondary market, that can push the market price of the stock downward. This is what FINRA must say about the process:

> *The term "flipping" refers to the practice of selling new issues into the secondary market at a profit within 30 days following the offering date. Because these sales create downward pressure on the secondary market trading price, underwriters and selling group members may seek to discourage such sales. Under most syndicate selling agreements, a managing underwriter is permitted to impose a "penalty bid" on syndicate members to reclaim the selling concession for allocations that were flipped. Separately, and independent of any syndicate penalty bid, some firms have sought to recoup selling concessions from brokers when their <u>customers</u>— typically retail customers—flip a new issue. [FINRA rules prohibit] any member from recouping any portion of a commission or credit paid or awarded to an associated person for selling shares of a new issue that are subsequently flipped by a customer, unless the managing underwriter has assessed a penalty bid on the entire syndicate. FINRA believes that it is only appropriate for a firm to recoup a broker's compensation for selling a new issue in connection with a customer's decision to flip a security when the firm itself is required to forfeit its compensation to the managing underwriter(s).*

Prohibited Activities Related to Trading

Broker-dealers and their agents are not allowed to take advantage of customers through churning, excessive mark-ups, breakpoint sales, front-running, market manipulation, and the improper sharing in profits and losses with customers.

Churning

Agents and their broker-dealers are paid to execute trades. Therefore, the more trading a customer does, the better for the agent and the firm he represents.

However, frequent trading has not shown to benefit retail investors. As Professor Brad Barber and Terrence Odean found by studying the habits of U.S. retail investors, investors who were in the bottom 20% for trading activity had an average annual portfolio return of 18.5%, while those in the top 20% had an average annual return of just 11.4%. (Source: Brad Barber and Terrence Odean (1999) 'The courage of misguided convictions' Financial Analysts Journal, November/December, p. 50.).

Recommending the customer engage in excessive trading is a violation known as **churning**. Based on the investment profile of the account, if the trading activity is excessive, both the agent and the broker-dealer risk being disciplined by FINRA. Not many investors are suitable candidates for frequent trading. If the firm determines an investor is interested in high-risk trading strategies, understands them, and can bear the risks associated, then frequent trading may be suitable.

But, when FINRA discovers that small IRA accounts with $20,000 balances experience $200,000 worth of trading activity over the year, they tend to take disciplinary action. That would be a "turnover rate" of 10, while regulators typically see a rate of 6 or higher as a red flag.

Broker-dealers who make markets in securities trade with other institutional investors at their Bid and Ask prices. Some of these firms fill orders in the same securities for their retail investors at those prices, adjusted by either a **markup** or a **markdown**. When the retail customer buys, the broker-dealer fills the order at the Ask plus a few cents per share. That net price is known as a markup. When the retail customer sells, the broker-dealer fills the order at the Bid minus a few cents per share. That net price is known as a markdown.

Markups and markdowns are associated with principal transactions, while commissions are associated with agency transactions. Firms either receive a markup/markdown or a commission, because they act in only one capacity in a trade. However they compensate themselves, the compensation must be reasonable. It is up to the firm to determine a fair and reasonable price to the customer based on factors including:

- The size of the order
- The price of the security
- The liquidity of the security
- The services provided by the firm

If a broker-dealer charges a per-share fee, FINRA expects the fee to go down on larger orders, not up. Volume in any industry tends to lead to better pricing for the customer, after all. If the security trades inactively, the customer does not receive as good a price as on actively traded securities. And, if the broker-dealer offers more services than a discount online broker, their charges are typically higher.

FINRA provides only guidelines for commissions and markups/markdowns. Member firms who charge excessively are disciplined by FINRA. And, FINRA tends to make the fines larger than any benefit the firm tried to make through excessive charges to customers.

Charges for Services

Member firms not only must be fair and equitable in securities transactions with their customers, but also, if they charge for other services, those charges must also be reasonable and fair. FINRA states that, "Charges, if any, for services performed, including miscellaneous services such as collection of moneys due for principal, dividends, or interest; exchange or transfer of securities; appraisals, safe-keeping or custody of securities, and other services, shall be reasonable and not unfairly discriminatory between customers."

Breakpoint Sales

Most open-end funds these days are no-load. However, many funds charge front-end sales charges. Let's say, a small investment into a stock fund involves a sales charge of 5%. If so, a customer investing $10,000 only invests $9,500. The other $500 is taken out of his initial investment as a sales charge.

Funds with sales charges also have breakpoint schedules. For example, the Growth Fund of America™ by American Funds charges 5.75% on the front end for investments up to $24,999. From $25,000 to $49,999, the sales charge drops to 5.0%. From $50,000 to $99,999, the sales charge is just 4.5%. And, investments of $1 million or more are charged no sales charge at all.

These quantity discounts are illustrated in the prospectus, but the registered representative must not try to sell shares just below the next breakpoint. If the customer has close to $50,000 to invest in the Growth Fund of America™, the registered representative would commit the violation known as **breakpoint selling** if he didn't mention the breakpoint, or if he tried to talk the customer into investing just under that amount.

Let's see how a breakpoint sale would harm the customer. If he were to invest $50,000, the sales charge of 5.0% would equal $2,500. On the other hand, an investment of $49,000 would involve a 5.75% charge, which is $2,817.50.

Not many customers would notice the difference, making it a tempting sales practice. As we can see, it's manipulative and fraudulent.

If the agent informs the customer of the breakpoints, but the customer declines to utilize them, he should make notes of this. The firm might also request the customer's signature on an acknowledgement that he was made aware of all quantity discounts before making the investment.

Sharing in Accounts

Agents and their broker-dealers execute trades for their customers. They make money to do so, whether the customer wins or loses on the investment. To show how confident he is in a recommendation, an agent might want to offer to go "halvsies" on the trade. He'll put up as much as the client wants to, up to $5,000. If the stock goes up, they split the gain. If it drops, they split the loss.

How does that sound? To a lot of investors, it probably sounds great. To FINRA, however, it sounds like a violation. Agents and broker-dealers do not partner on a trade with the customer.

FINRA rules state:

> *(1)(A) Except as provided in paragraph (f)(2) no member or person associated with a member shall share directly or indirectly in the profits or losses in any account of a customer carried by the member or any other member; provided, however, that a member or person associated with a member may share in the profits or losses in such an account if (i) such person associated with a member obtains prior written authorization from the member employing the associated person; (ii) such member or person associated with a member obtains prior written authorization from the customer; and (iii) such member or person associated with a member shares in the profits or losses in any account of such customer only in direct proportion to the financial contributions made to such account by either the member or person associated with a member.*

Maybe the agent and the customer are married. Or the customer is the agent's mother. Whatever the reason, both the customer and the broker-dealer must give their written authorization for the agent to share or participate in the account. And, the agent can only benefit in the same proportion that he invests.

As usual, though, there is an exception:

> *(B) Exempt from the direct proportionate share limitation of paragraph (f)(1)(A)(iii) are accounts of the immediate family of such member or person associated with a member. For purposes of this Rule, the term "immediate family" shall include parents, mother-in-law or father-in-law, husband or wife, children or any relative to whose support the member or person associated with a member otherwise contributes directly or indirectly.*

The test could ask a few questions about borrowing from or lending to customers. Those words make the regulators a nervous—how, exactly, does that registered representative define "borrowing" from a customer? Is this like an actual loan from a bank that happens to be his customer? Or, is this like a little old lady who seldom monitors her account and, therefore, probably won't even notice that the $50,000 was missing for a few weeks?

➤ Borrowing from or Lending to Customers

FINRA has many concerns about registered representatives borrowing money from customers or lending money to them. The main point to know is, before doing either, the registered representative must check his firm's written supervisory procedures to see what is allowed and what is required. As the rule states:

> *(a) No person associated with a member in any registered capacity may borrow money from or lend money to any customer of such person unless: (1) the member has written procedures allowing the borrowing and lending of money between such registered persons and customers of the member; and (2) the lending or borrowing arrangement meets one of the following conditions: (A) the customer is a member of such person's immediate family; (B) the customer is a financial institution regularly engaged in the business of providing credit, financing, or loans, or other entity or person that regularly arranges or extends credit in the ordinary course of business; (C) the customer and the registered person are both registered persons of the same member firm; (D) the lending arrangement is based on a personal relationship with the customer, such that the loan would not have been solicited, offered, or given had the customer and the associated person not maintained a relationship outside of the broker/customer relationship; or (E) the lending arrangement is based on a business relationship outside of the broker-customer relationship.*

How do they define "immediate family" here? Quite broadly:

> *(c) The term immediate family shall include parents, grandparents, mother-in-law or father-in-law, husband or wife, brother or sister, brother-in-law or sister-in-law, son-in-law or daughter-in-law, children, grandchildren, cousin, aunt or uncle, or niece or nephew, and shall also include any other person whom the registered person supports, directly or indirectly, to a material extent.*

As with sharing, the most important thing is to get your firm's permission before borrowing or lending with any customer. A registered representative who borrows money "under the table" from a customer will likely be suspended by FINRA.

Front-running

Some trades are large enough to push the price of the stock up or down. If a buy order for 10,000 shares is entered by a customer, the agent might be tempted to first buy calls on the stock, and then enter the large purchase order. Or, he could buy shares of the stock himself. That way, he makes an easy profit, while the customer pays more than he needed to.

This is a violation known as **front-running**. The firm itself would engage in front-running if they took advantage of large customer orders for their proprietary account.

As usual, the rules are stricter for transactions with retail customers than with institutional. Still, the rules apply in both situations.

Market manipulation is prohibited under the Securities Exchange Act of 1934 and various SEC and FINRA rules. If a few cheaters can manipulate the markets for their own advantage, the entire financial system suffers. Therefore, the exam might bring up terms such as painting the tape, a technique whereby individuals acting together repeatedly sell a security to one another without changing ownership of the securities. This is intended to give an impression of increased trading volume that can drive up the market price of their holdings.

FINRA has a specific rule that says, "no member shall publish or circulate, or cause to be published or circulated, any…communication of any kind which purports to report any transaction as a purchase or sale of any security unless such member believes that such transaction was a bona fide purchase or sale of such security." So, if a member firm is publishing transactions designed to merely inflate the price of a security, such market manipulation would be a serious infraction that could get the member expelled from FINRA altogether.

However, these days firms have such sophisticated, rapid-fire, electronic trading desks generating orders based on algorithms that they sometimes end up accidentally completing "self trades" in which the firm or in which related firms end up as both the buyer and seller on the same transaction.

And, that of course violates the rule against reporting trades that did not involve an actual change in beneficial ownership. Therefore, FINRA states in a notice to members that "firms must have policies and procedures in place that are reasonably designed to review trading activity for, and prevent, a pattern or practice of self-trades resulting from orders originating from a single algorithm or trading desk, or related algorithms or trading desks."

Other forms of **market manipulation** include capping and pegging. Capping is the illegal technique of trying to depress a stock price while pegging involves trying to move a stock up to a target price. A shady call option writer, for example, might want to help ensure that the calls expire by artificially conspiring to keep the price of the underlying stock from rising (capping). Or, the writer of a put might engage in pegging to push the put contracts out-of-the-money in his favor.

It's tough to manipulate a stock with billions of shares outstanding, but it's not so hard to do it with microcap stocks where the entire float is worth perhaps just $10 million. A few shady operators could easily manipulate the share price by forming secret joint accounts that allow them to drive up price and volume without any legitimate sales taking place. If all ten investors jointly own all 10 accounts, all the purchases and sales among these accounts would be bogus. That's a form of market manipulation that could end up being prosecuted in criminal court, apart from whatever the securities regulators do. The exam could refer to that form of market manipulation as "engaging in securities transactions that involve no effective change in beneficial ownership."

Another form of market manipulation occurs when traders spread rumors designed to move the stock price. Maybe they purchase put options on a stock trading on the OTC Bulletin Board and then start an ugly rumor about the company on social media to help push down the price. Or, they could buy call options on a small drug maker and then start a false rumor that the company has just developed the cure for ALS. The possibilities are endless, but if a registered representative were caught engaging in this type of activity, that would be the end of a career.

Although the Securities Exchange Act of 1934 talked about insider trading, apparently it didn't quite get the message across. So, in 1988 Congress passed the **Insider Trading & Securities Fraud Enforcement Act** of 1988 and raised the penalties for insider trading, making it a criminal offense with stiff civil penalties as well.

If you are married to an attorney working on an unannounced merger involving one or two public companies, you must pretend you know nothing about the deal. If you share that information, or if you use it to your advantage, you could face federal criminal charges. More likely, the SEC would merely sue you in federal court and try to extract a civil penalty of three times the amount of the profit made or loss avoided.

Any material information the public doesn't have is inside information. If you are the CFO of a large public company, you may know the numbers to be announced a few days before the rest of the world. It would be tempting to sell your stock if you knew the news was bad, or buy more shares if the news was good. But, the SEC has no sense of humor about such things. The CFO is a fiduciary to the shareholders. He or she cannot profit at the expense of shareholders, and is a position of trust where we expect him/her to put the interests of the shareholders first. Even though he or she is almost certainly a shareholder, too.

People who violate the act can be held liable to what they call "contemporaneous traders." That means that if you're dumping your shares based on an inside tip, and that hurts me, we might need to have a little talk with our attorneys.

The investment banking arm of a broker-dealer has access to all kinds of material non-public information. To prevent that sensitive information from flowing to other areas of the firm, the broker-dealer is required to create a Chinese wall around departments that obtain such information. No, they don't build an actual wall. They just try to prevent the investment bankers working on a merger from revealing some good trading tips to the registered representatives working the telephones.

Communications with the Public

Before we distinguish the types of communications, let's understand the main points:

- A principal (compliance officer) must approve the firm's communications and file them.
- The communications cannot be misleading in any way.

(1) Standards Applicable to All Communications with the Public

(A) All member communications with the public shall be based on principles of fair dealing and good faith, must be fair and balanced, and must provide a sound basis for evaluating the facts in regard to any security or type of security, industry, or service. No member may omit any material fact or qualification if the omission, in the light of the context of the material presented, would cause the communications to be misleading.

(B) No member may make any false, exaggerated, unwarranted or misleading statement or claim in any communication with the public. No member may publish, circulate or distribute any public communication that the member knows or has reason to know contains any untrue statement of a material fact or is otherwise false or misleading.

(C) Information may be placed in a legend or footnote only in the event that such placement would not inhibit an investor's understanding of the communication.

(D) Communications with the public may not predict or project performance, imply that past performance will recur or make any exaggerated or unwarranted claim, opinion or forecast. A hypothetical illustration of mathematical principles is permitted, provided that it does not predict or project the performance of an investment or investment strategy.

(E) If any testimonial in a communication with the public concerns a technical aspect of investing, the person making the testimonial must have the knowledge and experience to form a valid opinion.

Okay. Seems fair enough—don't mislead investors through any of your communications regardless of the format. The exam may also want you to know the types of communication. Understand that all communications must be at least monitored by the firm, but that your **correspondence** with retail investors would not be approved before it went out. It would just be monitored, with filters and red-flag words built into the automatic monitoring system. If you send out, say 50 letters to existing retail investors, this is now considered retail communications, while in the past it would have been correspondence. The difference between correspondence—which does not have to be pre-approved—and retail communications—which do—has to do with the number 25. Up to 25 retail investors = correspondence. Over 25 retail investors = retail communications.

If the communications are for only institutional investors, they are considered **institutional communications.** For institutional communications, each member firm simply must, "establish written procedures that are appropriate to its business, size, structure, and customers for the review by an appropriately qualified registered principal of institutional communications used by the member and its associated persons. Such procedures must be reasonably designed to ensure that institutional communications comply with applicable standards. When such procedures do not require review of all institutional communications prior to first use or distribution, they must include provision education and training of associated persons as to the firm's procedures governing institutional communications, documentation of such education and training, and surveillance and follow-up to ensure that such procedures are implemented and adhered to."

So, correspondence is not pre-approved but is monitored. Institutional communications may be pre-approved or not, depending on how the firm sets up its supervisory and training system. Retail communications are subject to pre-approval before being first used or filed with FINRA.

Regardless of what we call it, the communication had better not be misleading. Any statement of the benefits of an investment or strategy, for example, needs to be balanced out with the associated risks involved.

Any materials that are subject to review, approval and filing are subject to this:

> *(1) Date of First Use and Approval Information*
>
> *The member must provide with each filing under this paragraph the actual or anticipated date of first use, the name and title of the registered principal who approved the advertisement or sales literature, and the date that the approval was given.*

This is also self-explanatory:

> *(7) Spot-Check Procedures*
>
> *In addition to the foregoing requirements, each member's written and electronic communications with the public may be subject to a spot-check procedure. Upon written request from the Department, each member must submit the material requested in a spot-check procedure within the time frame specified by the Department.*

FINRA recently changed some definitions and procedures involving communications with the public. First, they added some new definitions:

> *"Retail communication" means any written (including electronic) communication that is distributed or made available to more than 25 retail investors within any 30 calendar-day period.*
>
> *"Retail investor" means any person other than an institutional investor, regardless of whether the person has an account with a member.*

Then, to protect "retail investors," FINRA requires that any "retail communication" that has not already been filed with FINRA must be approved by a principal either before its first use or before filing it with FINRA's Advertising Regulation Department. And, for new member firms retail communications must be filed with FINRA at least 10 days prior to first use. This includes the content of the firm's website, and any other communication with retail investors (radio, newspaper, magazine, etc.). A retail communication could come in the form of a group email, a form letter, a chat room, or a webinar—provided it involves more than 25 retail investors, it is probably a form of retail communications subject to prior principal approval.

A recent change says that firms who are intermediaries in selling investment company products (e.g., mutual funds, annuities) are not required to approve or file sales material that was already filed by someone else, usually the distributor of the fund. The intermediary selling the products could not alter the material significantly; otherwise, they would have changed it enough to require re-approval and re-filing, which is what they're trying to avoid in the first place. So, the many broker-dealers selling the American Funds™ are acting as intermediaries. Provided they don't alter the materials, they can just use the materials that have already been created and filed by the distributor of the funds, American Funds Distributors.

Members use television and other video formats to communicate with investors. Therefore, FINRA stipulates that, "If a member has filed a draft version or 'story board' of a television or video retail communication pursuant to a filing requirement, then the member also must file the final filmed version within 10 business days of first use or broadcast."

Specific Communications Rules

We just explored rules on communications in general. FINRA then has specific rules based on the investment being offered by the member.

Investment Company Products

As we just saw, new FINRA members must pre-file their retail communications at least 10 business days before first use with the Advertising Regulation Department of FINRA. That applies during their first year of association and applies to all retail communications other than freewriting prospectuses filed with the SEC—those can be filed with FINRA within 10 days but after-the-fact. Also, if a member firm has problems getting their advertising up to regulatory standards, FINRA can require that firm to pre-file all their retail communications or just the types that are causing the problems.

After their first year of registration member firms file most of their retail communications with FINRA, but within 10 days after they have already been used. On the other hand, retail communications concerning certain investments still must be pre-filed. Not only must some of these communications be pre-filed, but also members must wait to see if any changes are demanded by FINRA and must withhold using the communications until they have been approved by the regulators. As the rule states:

> *At least 10 business days prior to first use or publication (or such shorter period as the Department may allow), a member must file the following retail communications with the Department and withhold them from publication or circulation until any changes specified by the Department have been made*

The communications subject to this heightened requirement are:

> *Retail communications concerning registered investment companies that include or incorporate performance rankings or performance comparisons of the investment company with other investment companies when the ranking or comparison category is not generally published or is the creation, either directly or indirectly, of the investment company, its underwriter or an affiliate. Such filings must include a copy of the data on which the ranking or comparison is based.*

The rule defines "registered investment companies" as "including mutual funds, exchange-traded funds, variable insurance products, closed-end funds and unit investment trusts." So, if there is a ranking that did not come from, say, Lipper or Morningstar, but, rather, by the fund or its underwriter—FINRA wants to look at that sort of publication, before it goes out.

Specific Retail Communications

Retail communications for investment company securities that contain a ranking or performance comparison used to require members to file a copy of the ranking or comparison used when filing the retail communication with FINRA. The rule was created back when FINRA staff did not have ready access to such rankings or comparisons. Now that such information is readily available online, members simply need to maintain back-up materials supporting what was cited in their retail communications.

FINRA also used to require any retail communication involving bond mutual fund volatility to be filed 10 days prior to first use. Also, any such communication had to be preceded or accompanied by a prospectus when delivered to an investor. Now, FINRA allows these retail communications to be filed within (after) 10 days of first use and has eliminated the prospectus-delivery requirement for these communications.

Members offering and providing investment analysis tools allowing customers to make their own investment decisions used to be required to provide access to the tools to FINRA staff. Now, members simply must provide such access upon FINRA's request. Members also no longer must file report templates and the retail communications themselves with FINRA.

Communications Regarding Variable Contracts

Communications about variable contracts are subject to the FINRA standards for communications generally, as well as a few that are specific to these products. First, a statement to a customer or, say, a full-page advertisement in Forbes magazine must be clear that what is being offered or advertised is a variable annuity or variable life insurance (VLI) policy and not a traditional insurance product. Liquidity is not available on deferred variable contracts, so if a customer is sold an annuity or variable life policy thinking it makes a good short-term investment that can be liquidated for a good price, that's a problem if it turns out to be a lie. Remember that cashing in or "surrendering" a deferred variable annuity can subject the investor to a 10% penalty tax plus surrender charges/contingent deferred sales charges to the annuity company. If the customer didn't realize that, we're looking at securities fraud.

There are "guarantees" offered in variable contracts, but these guarantees are subject to the insurance company's ability to pay claims. That needs to be made clear to investors, and it needs to be made clear that "backed up by the insurance company" and "you can't lose money" are not the same thing.

Even though variable life insurance ties cash value and death benefit values to the ups and downs of the investment markets, it must be presented primarily as a life insurance product as opposed to a security. If the regulators feel that you're selling VLI as a way to invest in the stock and bond market while barely considering the more important insurance protections, you could have problems. To that end, don't compare VLI to mutual funds, stocks or bonds; compare it to other types of insurance, including term, whole life, or variable universal life (VUL) insurance.

Unlike with a mutual fund —where you never even imply what future results might be—when selling insurance, illustrations are routinely used. Chances are an agent will show illustrations of a whole life insurance policy compared to a VLI and perhaps a VUL policy. The illustrations are not guarantees, and the insurance company must be careful how they present this information. They can show a hypothetical illustration as high as a "gross rate" of 12%, provided they also show how things would work out with a "gross rate" of 0%. Whatever the maximum rate used, it must be reasonable given recent market conditions and the available investment options. Since mortality and expense charges reduce returns, illustrations must be figured using the maximum charges. Current charges may also be included.

Research Reports

If you're a big Wall Street broker-dealer the **research reports** your analysts put out encouraging customers to buy or sell a security can have an impact on the price of the stock. So, if your research department is about to issue a "strong buy" recommendation and a glowing report on Google tomorrow morning, why not buy a boatload of Google shares today, and then release the report tomorrow? Won't that be fun? Your customers will want to buy the stock tomorrow at higher and higher prices and, heck, you'll be right here to sell it to them, at higher and higher prices. FINRA defines a research report as:

> *any written (including electronic) communication that includes an analysis of equity securities of individual companies or industries, and that provides information reasonably sufficient upon which to base an investment decision.*

FINRA states:

In the old days research analysts often functioned as cheerleaders for a company's stock to drum up investment banking business for the firm. Basically, the firms were just drawing in suckers willing to prop up the stock of a company whose CEO would become so giddy he would then do mergers and acquisitions, as well as stock and bond offerings through the firm's investment banking department. To put an end to those days, FINRA now stipulates:

240

> *No research analyst may be subject to the supervision or control of any employee of the member's investment banking department, and no personnel engaged in investment banking activities may have any influence or control over the compensatory evaluation of a research analyst.*

Research analysts cannot participate in efforts to solicit investment banking business. Accordingly:

> *No research analyst may, among other things, participate in any "pitches" for investment banking business to prospective investment banking customers, or have other communications with companies for the purpose of soliciting investment banking business.*

Also:

> *No member may pay any bonus, salary or other form of compensation to a research analyst that is based upon a specific investment banking services transaction.*

So, the research analysts can't put out positive reports just to help the investment banking or trading departments. Surely, they can buy a few shares of the stock for themselves, their family, and friends, right?

Wrong.

> **Restrictions on Personal Trading by Research Analysts**
>
> *(1) No research analyst account may purchase or receive any securities before the issuer's initial public offering if the issuer is principally engaged in the same types of business as companies that the research analyst follows.*
>
> *(2) No research analyst account may purchase or sell any security issued by a company that the research analyst follows, or any option on or derivative of such security, for a period beginning 30 calendar days before and ending five calendar days after the publication of a research report concerning the company or a change in a rating or price target of the company's securities; provided that:*
>
> *(A) a member may permit a research analyst account to sell securities held by the account that are issued by a company that the research analyst follows, within 30 calendar days after the research analyst began following the company for the member*

So, the research analyst who's working on a "strong buy" research report on XYZ can't receive bonuses if XYZ then does investment banking through the firm, and can't go on the "road shows" for IPOs designed to drum up interest in the new issue. Also, the firm can't establish a large inventory position in XYZ to then sell it to their customers all excited by the glowing research report. And, the analyst can't buy any XYZ ahead of releasing his research report. But, surely, as the guy's golfing buddy, with an office right next door, you can look at it before the firm releases it, right?

FINRA saw that problem coming a mile away and, therefore, now stipulates that:

> *Non-research personnel may review a research report before its publication as necessary only to verify the factual accuracy of information in the research report or identify any potential conflict of interest, provided that (A) any written communication between non-research personnel and research department personnel concerning the content of a research report must be made either through authorized legal or compliance personnel of the member or in a transmission copied to such personnel; and (B) any oral communication between non-research personnel and research department personnel concerning the content of a research report must be documented and made either through authorized legal or compliance personnel acting as intermediary or in a conversation conducted in the presence of such personnel.*

But, other than that:

> *...no employee of the investment banking department or any other employee of the member who is not directly responsible for investment research ("non-research personnel"), other than legal or compliance personnel, may review or approve a research report of the member before its publication.*

The research report can also not be sent to the subject company except according to this:

> *A member may submit sections of such a research report to the subject company before its publication for review as necessary <u>only to verify the factual accuracy</u> of information in those sections, provided that:*
>
> *(A) the sections of the research report submitted to the subject company do not contain the research summary, the research rating or the price target;*
>
> *(B) a complete draft of the research report is provided to legal or compliance personnel before sections of the report are submitted to the subject company; and*
>
> *(C) if after submitting the sections of the research report to the subject company the research department intends to change the proposed rating or price target, it must first provide written justification to, and receive written authorization from, legal or compliance personnel for the change. The member must retain copies of any draft and the final version of such a research report for three years following its publication.*
>
> *(3) The member may notify a subject company that the member intends to change its rating of the subject company's securities, provided that the notification occurs on the business day before the member announces the rating change, after the close of trading in the principal market of the subject company's securities.*

Research reports are subject to a "quiet period," meaning firms cannot publish a research report on a newly public company until 10 days after the IPO. Some smaller firms don't have their own research analysts, so they use third parties to provide reports on various securities and then deliver them to their customers. If that is the case, the member firm needs to disclose that the research was/is provided by someone else and is third-party research. Finally, research analysts are regulated by Regulation AC, which requires them to certify that their research accurately reflects their own objective, non-cash-influenced views. To that end, they also need to disclose if they or any of their immediate family members received any type of compensation (cash, options, warrants, what-have-you) for making this recommendation. This regulation applies to both research reports and public appearances by research analysts.

Websites and BrokerCheck

FINRA requires member firms to include a prominent reference to FINRA's BrokerCheck and a hyperlink to it on the initial web page intended to be viewed by retail investors, as well as on any page containing a professional profile of any registered person conducting business with retail investors. Clearly, FINRA wants to encourage investors to check out their registered representatives both before and after they start investing through them. A few minutes with BrokerCheck will confirm—or not—whether the individual is licensed and with which firm, as well as any disciplinary reports or arbitration awards of $15,000 or more paid out to disgruntled customers.

Public Appearances

Registered representatives frequently attract customers by holding seminars, or speaking to a local chamber of commerce, for example. This activity is called a public appearance. Member firms must establish written supervisory procedures to appropriately handle public appearances through education and training, documentation, and surveillance. Evidence that the firm has implemented such procedures must be maintained and made available to FINRA staff upon request.

If the agent uses PowerPoint slides or gives attendees a handout or DVD, these communications are subject to principal review and approval according to the rules on retail communications and correspondence.

Agents who make securities recommendations through public appearances must have a reasonable basis to believe the recommendation is suitable. And, if the agent has a conflict of interest such as receiving compensation from sales of the security, these must be clearly disclosed.

Independently Prepared Reprint

Broker-dealers and agents are not allowed to write or commission a favorable publication about the firm and then pass it off as positive press. They are also not allowed to hire English majors to churn out favorable press through fake magazines and websites like a propaganda machine.

On the other hand, if the firm or an agent wants to use a reprint of an article published by an unaffiliated third party, such activity is allowed subject to FINRA rules. For example, if Forbes or Bloomberg publish a favorable article about the broker-dealer, the firm can distribute this independently prepared reprint. They may not alter the article other than to correct facts or to make it confirm to FINRA rules.

And, the publisher must be an independent third party.

Recordkeeping and Filing Requirements

Member firms must maintain a separate file containing retail communications and independently prepared reprints. The file must include the names of the persons who prepared and approved the communication's first use and must be maintained for 3 years from the date of its last use.

Members must also maintain records of its registered representatives' correspondence. A file showing the persons who prepared and approved the correspondence must be maintained for 3 years. Firms typically have all emails route to a central mailbox, where they can be reviewed and archived.

During its first year of operation, a FINRA member pre-files retail communications 10 business days before first use. After that, assuming the firm does not have problems getting their communications in compliance, the firm files such communications within 10 business days after first use. We explored some communications that are always subject to prefiling, as well. And, a firm with a history of misleading communications may be required to pre-file with FINRA for a stated time or indefinitely.

FINRA may send a written request for records concerning retail communications over a stated time. Members must comply with such spot checks within the required time frame.

Gifts and Gratuities

FINRA does not allow member firms and their associated persons to buy influence at other firms with gifts of cash or gifts with resale value over a certain amount. Currently the amount is $100 but is expected to rise to $175 in the near future. Why would someone at your firm want to give someone at another firm a $1,000 set of titanium golf clubs? Maybe your firm would like to start getting invited to join certain municipal securities underwritings that they run as syndicate manager. Or, maybe your firm would just like the other firm to start throwing some of the smaller accounts they don't want your way? Maybe a case of expensive scotch would do the trick?

While gifts and business entertainment are not completely prohibited, we are now entering a gray area that can either be considered normal business expenses or a violation of FINRA rules on influencing or rewarding the employees of other member firms.

Here is how FINRA states the rule:

> *No member or person associated with a member shall, directly or indirectly, give or permit to be given anything of value, including gratuities, in excess of one hundred dollars per individual per year to any person, principal, proprietor, employee, agent or representative of another person where such payment or gratuity is in relation to the business of the employer of the recipient of the payment or gratuity. A gift of any kind is considered a gratuity.*

FINRA then makes it clear that what they are prohibiting here is more along the lines of a $1,000 set of golf clubs, as opposed to legitimate contracts of employment where one member employs another member's employee for legitimate purposes. As the rule then states:

> *This Rule shall not apply to contracts of employment with or to compensation for services rendered provided that there is in existence prior to the time of employment or before the services are rendered, a written agreement between the member and the person who is to be employed to perform such services. Such agreement shall include the nature of the proposed employment, the amount of the proposed compensation, and the written consent of such person's employer or principal.*

As with most sensitive issues, FINRA requires records surrounding these activities to be kept:

> *A separate record of all payments or gratuities in any amount known to the member, the employment agreement referred to in paragraph (b) and any employment compensation paid as a result thereof shall be retained by the member for the period specified by SEA Rule 17a-4.*

Note that "SEA" means "Securities Exchange Act of 1934" and "SEA Rule 17a-4" would be that SEC Rule promulgated under the Securities Exchange Act of 1934.

Non-cash Compensation

Associated persons may not accept compensation from anyone other than the member firm. The only exception here is if there is an arrangement between you and the other party that your member firm agrees to, and your firm deals with a bunch of other requirements. Associated persons (you) may not accept securities from somebody else in exchange for selling variable contracts. The only non-cash compensation that can be offered or accepted is:

- gifts that do not exceed an annual amount per person fixed periodically by the Association, and that are not preconditioned on achievement of a sales target. The gift limit is still $100, by the way.
- an occasional meal, a ticket to a sporting event or the theater, or comparable entertainment that is neither so frequent nor so extensive as to raise any question of propriety and is not preconditioned on achievement of a sales target
- payment or reimbursement by offerors in connection with meetings held by an offeror or by a member for the purpose of training or education of associated persons of a member

For that last bullet, the associated person must get the firm's permission to attend and his attendance and reimbursement of expenses cannot be preconditioned on meeting a sales target. Only he—not a guest—can have expenses reimbursed. The location of the meeting must be appropriate, too, meaning if the offeror's office is in Minneapolis, it looks suspicious when the meeting is held in Maui.

And, the rule states that the "member firm shall maintain records of all compensation received by the member or its associated persons from offerors. The records shall include the names of the offerors, the names of the associated persons, the amount of cash, the nature and, if known, the value of non-cash compensation received."

A firm can give their registered representatives non-cash compensation for selling variable contracts, but they can't compensate them more for selling one variable contract than for another. This rule states that the non-cash compensation arrangement requires that the credit received for each variable contract security is equally weighted.

Political Contributions

Municipal securities are issued by states, cities, counties, school districts, etc. Therefore, many elected officials are in a position to influence which firms get to underwrite certain offerings. They could either rig the bidding process for a competitive, sealed bid, or they could manipulate the negotiated underwritings in a way that benefits those firms willing to donate to their campaign funds.

Fortunately, the securities regulators are interested in maintaining the integrity of the municipal bond underwriting process. The tax payers supporting all the school bond issues should not have to worry that some politically-connected broker-dealer is gouging them every time another bond is sold.

Therefore, if any firm makes a large political contribution, they are prohibited from doing securities business with the related issuer for a period of two years. So, if your broker-dealer is a municipal bond underwriter in New Orleans, and you make a $10,000 donation to the mayor's reelection campaign, not only must you disclose the contribution, but also you are not to do any municipal securities business with the City of New Orleans for two years.

The same would apply if a political action committee controlled by your firm funneled the money to the mayor's campaign, or if one of your "municipal finance professionals" made the contribution with her own money. For purposes of this rule, a "municipal finance professional" includes principals, registered representatives, and any paid solicitors who help firms land underwriting deals.

Firms must keep records on all contributions by the firm, their municipal finance professionals, and any associated PACs (political action committees). And, they must refrain from doing business with an issuer if large donations are made, or if donations are made to politicians that the firm and its personnel are not even in a position to vote for. To that end, if the municipal finance professional making the contribution is eligible to vote for the mayor, governor, etc. *and* the contribution does not exceed $250, then provided the firm keeps records of this there is no reason to refrain from doing business with the related issuer. In other words, if one of the principals lives in New Orleans and is eligible to vote for the mayor, he or she could contribute up to $250 and provided the firm disclosed this to regulators in their regular reports on such contributions, the firm could continue to underwrite securities for the City of New Orleans. So, we're not allowing the firm or one of their PACs to make such a contribution; only the individuals working for the firm who are eligible to vote for that official. And, only up to a small amount—currently $250.

Quarterly, members who engage in municipal securities activities must file reports disclosing to FINRA the following information:

- the name and title (including any city/county/state or political subdivision) of each official of an issuer and political party receiving contributions or payments during such calendar quarter, listed by state
- the contribution or payment amount made and the contributor category of each person and entity making such contributions or payments during such calendar quarter
- a list of issuers with which the broker, dealer or municipal securities dealer has engaged in municipal securities business during such calendar quarter, listed by state, along with the type of municipal securities business
- records on contributions to any "bond ballot campaign" beyond the allowed $250 contribution by eligible municipal finance professionals

When a customer complaint is received by a broker-dealer, the appropriate personnel at the member firm must promptly be notified. This is also the case when a red flag is spotted concerning a customer account. Personnel who may require notification include the account representative, the principal over that account, the branch manager, or member of the compliance team. The process of alerting the appropriate "higher ups" is referred to as escalation. Like an escalator, this process raises something to a higher level.

A complaint is a written statement by a customer—or a person acting on behalf of a customer—that alleges any grievance or dispute connected to a securities transaction or the handling of the account. Maybe a customer was recommended an investment that has suffered a large loss, an investment she now feels was unsuitable. Or, maybe the customer checks her monthly account statement and sees three purchases she doesn't recognize, with the agent claiming she told him to execute the trades.

If no resolution is reached, the firm must report the complaint to FINRA's director of arbitration. And, if the complaint involves an allegation of theft, forgery, or misappropriation of customer assets, it must be reported within 10 business days at the latest.

Broker-dealers must maintain files for customer complaints, with notes indicating what happened and how it was resolved, endorsed by a principal. Copies of customer complaints are maintained at the supervising OSJ. Within 15 days after the end of each calendar quarter member firms must electronically file information on all customer complaints to FINRA.

Copies of customer complaints, and the quarterly filings, are required to be maintained for three years, as are many broker-dealer records.

Red flags include anything that looks suspicious to broker-dealer personnel. For example, excessive customer complaints against a registered representative often signal a pattern that should be brought to the attention of the firm's management. Any suspicious activity involving the movement of funds or securities should be taken as a red flag. And, if the account of a deceased individual shows any activity, that is another example of a red flag.

Also, if the back office finds discrepancies between the address where customer account documents are delivered and the street address provided by the customer, they should treat this is a red flag. In such a case, a registered representative engaging in excessive or inappropriate transactions may be trying to mail all documents to a PO box he controls. Maybe he is engaging in expensive annuity switches he doesn't want his customer to know about. If he signs the customer's name to the paperwork and sends all the paperwork to his own PO box, he might get away with it.

For a while. The broker-dealer's procedures for handling red flags, including the proper steps for escalation to the appropriate supervisors, are designed to prevent and detect such fraudulent sales practices.

Chapter 3 Review Exercises
DIRECTIONS: underline the word or phrase that completes each statement.

1. A long stock position is (bullish/bearish).

2. A short stock position is (bullish/bearish).

3. Short sales are executed exclusively in (cash/margin) accounts.

4. The NYSE is (an auction/a negotiated) market.

5. The OTC market is (an auction/a negotiated) market.

6. When registering as a market maker through the NASDAQ system, the firm is assigned (a CUSIP/an MPID) number.

7. The TRACE system is associated with (equity/debt) securities.

8. TRACE is a (reporting/quotation) system.

9. When executing a transaction on behalf of a customer, a broker-dealer acts in (an agency/a principal) capacity.

10. When executing a transaction with a customer, a broker-dealer acts in (an agency/a principal) capacity.

11. When trading a Treasury Note on the secondary market, investors should know that regular-way settlement occurs at (T + 1/T + 2).

12. When trading a corporate bond on the secondary market, investors should know that regular-way settlement occurs at (T + 1/T + 2).

13. Shares of common stock that were issued and repurchased by the issuer are known as (treasury/outstanding) shares.

14. The difference between the shares originally issued and those subsequently repurchased are known as (treasury/outstanding) shares.

15. After a forward stock split, the number of outstanding shares (increases/decreases), while the market price for the stock (increases/decreases).

16. Within a Joint Tenants in Common account, when one account owner dies, his or her share passes to (his or her estate/the other account owners equally).

17. Within a Joint Tenants with Rights of Survivorship account, when one account owner dies, his or her share passes to (his or her estate/the other account owners equally).

18. If a registered representative without discretionary authorization enters a transaction without discussing it first with the customer, he has engaged in a violation known as (unsuitable recommendations/unauthorized transactions).

19. The maximum contribution amounts to a 529 Savings Plan are based on (an annual amount per-beneficiary/a lifetime amount per-account).

20. If the parents wish to use the account assets to fund tuition at a private middle or high school, they should open a (529 Savings Plan/Coverdell Education Savings Account).

21. If the individual seeks tax deductions on his contributions to the account, he should open a (Traditional/Roth) IRA.

22. If the individual wants to take tax-free distributions in retirement, he should open a (Traditional/Roth) IRA.

23. Employee elective deferrals are associated with (SEP-IRA/SIMPLE Plans).

24. A registered representative selling investments his broker-dealer is unaware of is engaging in a violation known as (selling away/painting the tape).

25. Before performing work outside the employing broker-dealer for compensation, an associated person must (notify the employer in writing/receive the employer's written permission).

Answers

1. A long stock position is (<u>bullish</u>/bearish).
2. A short stock position is (bullish/<u>bearish</u>).
3. Short sales are executed exclusively in (cash/<u>margin</u>) accounts.
4. The NYSE is (<u>an auction</u>/a negotiated) market.
5. The OTC market is (an auction/<u>a negotiated</u>) market.
6. When registering as a market maker through the NASDAQ system, the firm is assigned (a CUSIP/<u>an MPID</u>) number.
7. The TRACE system is associated with (equity/<u>debt</u>) securities.
8. TRACE is a (<u>reporting</u>/quotation) system.
9. When executing a transaction on behalf of a customer, a broker-dealer acts in (<u>an agency</u>/a principal) capacity.
10. When executing a transaction with a customer, a broker-dealer acts in (an agency/<u>a principal</u>) capacity.
11. When trading a Treasury Note on the secondary market, investors should know that regular-way settlement occurs at (<u>T + 1</u>/T + 2).
12. When trading a corporate bond on the secondary market, investors should know that regular-way settlement occurs at (T + 1/<u>T + 2</u>).
13. Shares of common stock that were issued and repurchased by the issuer are known as (<u>treasury</u>/outstanding) shares.
14. The difference between the shares originally issued and those subsequently repurchased are known as (treasury/<u>outstanding</u>) shares.
15. After a forward stock split, the number of outstanding shares (<u>increases</u>/decreases), while the market price for the stock (increases/<u>decreases</u>).
16. Within a Joint Tenants in Common account, when one account owner dies, his or her share passes to (<u>his or her estate</u>/the other account owners equally).
17. Within a Joint Tenants with Rights of Survivorship account, when one account owner dies, his or her share passes to (his or her estate/<u>the other account owners equally</u>).
18. If a registered representative without discretionary authorization enters a transaction without discussing it first with the customer, he has engaged in a violation known as (unsuitable recommendations/<u>unauthorized transactions</u>).
19. The maximum contribution amounts to a 529 Savings Plan are based on (an annual amount per-beneficiary/<u>a lifetime amount per-account</u>).
20. If the parents wish to use the account assets to fund tuition at a private middle or high school, they should open a (529 Savings Plan/<u>Coverdell Education Savings Account</u>).
21. If the individual seeks tax deductions on his contributions to the account, he should open a (<u>Traditional</u>/Roth) IRA.
22. If the individual wants to take tax-free distributions in retirement, he should open a (Traditional/<u>Roth</u>) IRA.
23. Employee elective deferrals are associated with (SEP-IRAs/<u>SIMPLE Plans</u>).
24. A registered representative selling investments his broker-dealer is unaware of is engaging in a violation known as (<u>selling away</u>/painting the tape).
25. Before performing work outside the employing broker-dealer for compensation, an associated person must (<u>notify the employer in writing</u>/receive the employer's written permission).

1. Your customer has read an enticing article touting the many advantages of investing in real estate; therefore, she calls and says, "I want you to buy as many REITs as you think I can afford." This is an example of
   A. painting the tape
   B. an unauthorized transaction
   C. a discretionary order
   D. a non-discretionary order

2. Issuers with securities traded through which of the following are required to remain current in their SEC filings under the Securities Exchange Act of 1934?
   A. NYSE
   B. NASDAQ
   C. OTCBB
   D. All choices listed

3. The Third Market is accurately associated with which of the following?
   A. NYSE-listed stocks traded over-the-counter
   B. The aftermarket for open-end fund shares
   C. The aftermarket for closed-end fund shares
   D. After-hours trading of NASDAQ securities

4. Electronic Communications Networks (ECNs) are accurately associated with which of the following?
   A. First market
   B. Second market
   C. Third market
   D. Fourth market

5. Transactions in which of the following securities are subject to TRACE reporting requirements?
   A. Agency bonds
   B. Asset or mortgage-backed securities
   C. Treasury Notes
   D. All choices listed

6. A member firm charges a markdown when buying securities in which of the following capacities?
   A. Principal
   B. Agency
   C. Fiduciary
   D. Passive

7. Transactions in which of the following securities settle regular-way at T + 1?
A. Corporate bonds
B. Listed options
C. Municipal bonds
D. Listed stock

8. An issuer's transfer agent would accept which of the following signatures in connection to a sale or transfer of securities?
A. Signature of a minor child who is the named beneficiary of an UTMA account
B. Signature of an individual now deceased
C. Signature of one party in a joint account
D. Signature of the executor of an estate for a deceased customer

9. ABC has issued 10 million shares of common stock. Currently, there are 2 million shares in treasury. Therefore, the number of shares outstanding is
A. 12 million
B. 10 million
C. 8 million
D. 2 million

10. When calculating Earnings Per Share (EPS), which of the following shares are included?
A. Issued
B. Treasury
C. Outstanding
D. All choices listed

11. A legend on a stock or bond certificate signifies which of the following?
A. The transfer of the security is restricted.
B. The security is considered high-risk by either a state securities Administrator or the SEC.
C. The security pays dividends which are a higher obligation than the interest payable to their bondholders and other creditors.
D. The issuer's "story" is considered "speculative" by the SEC and must, therefore, be laid out in bullet-point format on the certificate itself.

12. An investor who wishes to sell or otherwise transfer a restricted security will be able to if which of the following determines the holding period has been met or does not apply do to a transactional exemption?
A. The issuer's transfer agent
B. The issuer's board of directors
C. The broker-dealer holding the securities
D. The clearing facility in control or possession of the securities

13. Issuers of publicly traded stock perform forward stock splits to:
A. Lower the stock's market price and reduce its liquidity
B. Lower the stock's market price and increase its liquidity
C. Increase the stock's market price and reduce its liquidity
D. Increase the stock's earnings per share and increase its liquidity

14. Which of the following is a FALSE statement concerning Transfer on Death (TOD) accounts?
A. When the account owner dies, the assets pass to the beneficiary outside the probate process
B. The named beneficiaries receive income from—but have no control over—the account as soon as they are formally named
C. The named beneficiaries have no control over the account until the owner dies
D. The beneficiaries can be changed at any time during the life of the account owner

15. A durable power of attorney goes into effect when the individual is declared mentally incompetent and remains in effect until:
A. The individual dies
B. The individual's estate is settled
C. The individual's spouse formally revokes it
D. The individual's executor files notice with the appropriate probate court

16. Contributions must stop on the beneficiary's 18th birthday for which of the following accounts?
A. UTMA
B. Coverdell Education Savings Account
C. 529 Savings Plan
D. All choices listed

17. From which of the following accounts must the individual begin taking distributions at age 70?
A. Roth IRA
B. Traditional IRA
C. Non-qualified annuity
D. All choices listed

18. A 45-year-old customer of a broker-dealer leaves a job where she had a 401(k) account, with an account balance of $25,000. Upon leaving her job, she instructs the plan custodian to issue a check payable to her. 60 days later, she opens an IRA with a deposit of $15,000. Therefore,
A. $25,000 will be considered an early distribution, subject to both taxes and penalties.
B. $10,000 will be considered an early distribution, subject to both taxes and penalties.
C. $15,000 will be her cost basis in the newly opened IRA.
D. The customer has another 30 days to deposit $10,000 to the newly opened IRA and avoid both taxes and penalties.

19. If only 3 of 15 full-time employees express interest in saving/investing for retirement, a small business owner would most likely benefit by starting which of the following plans?
A. Defined benefit pension
B. Money purchase
C. SEP-IRA
D. SIMPLE Plan

20. A minimum contribution is required of the employer in which of the following plans?
A. Money purchase
B. SEP-IRA
C. Profit sharing
D. Defined benefit pension

21. In a margin account a customer holds 1,000 shares of XYZ valued at $50 per share. FINRA requires the customer have a minimum maintenance of what amount for this position?
A. $25,000
B. $20,000
C. $15,000
D. $12,500

22. In a new margin account the customer purchase 100 shares of ABC, trading at $30 per share. The customer's initial deposit, then, is
A. $1,500
B. $2,000
C. $3,000
D. $4,500

23. Which of the following is an accurate statement?
A. No security may be described by an agent as "guaranteed."
B. Agents and broker-dealers may only guarantee customers against investment losses on direct obligations of the United States Treasury.
C. Securities that are "guaranteed" are still subject to investment risk.
D. US Treasury—but not corporate—debt obligations may be guaranteed as to interest and principal.

24. The "turnover rate" of an investment account is related to a FINRA rule violation known as
A. Churning
B. Breakpoint selling
C. Unauthorized transactions
D. Selling away

25. An agent of a member firm may borrow money or securities from a customer of the member provided
A. The customer is a bank or similar lending institution
B. The customer is an immediate family member
C. The customer has a preexisting business or personal relationship with the agent outside the broker-dealer relationship
D. The member allows such borrowing in its written supervisory procedures

Answers

1. C
2. D
3. A
4. D
5. D
6. A
7. B
8. D
9. C
10. C
11. A
12. A
13. B
14. B
15. A
16. B
17. B
18. B
19. D
20. A
21. D
22. B
23. C
24. A
25. D

Chapter 4: Overview of the Regulatory Framework

Federal Securities Acts

The securities markets are regulated under a handful of federal securities Acts of the United States Congress. The Securities and Exchange Commission also makes rules under these federal securities acts.

Securities Act of 1933

The Securities Act of 1933 aims to ensure that investors have all the material information they need before buying stocks and bonds issued on the primary market and that this information is accurate and not misleading.

As the SEC explains on their website:

> Often referred to as the "truth in securities" law, the Securities Act of 1933 has two basic objectives:
>
> • require that investors receive financial and other significant information concerning securities being offered for public sale; and
>
> • prohibit deceit, misrepresentations, and other fraud in the sale of securities.

The scope of this securities law is narrower than the far-reaching Securities Exchange Act of 1934. The Securities Act of 1933 focuses solely on the offering of securities to public investors for the first time. The Act requires issuers to register an offering of securities with the SEC before the issuer can offer or sell their securities to the public. Because of this securities law an investor must be provided with a disclosure document that discloses everything he might need to know about the company issuing the security before the issuer or underwriters take his money and close the deal. Investors can read about the issuer's history, its board of directors, its products and services, its chances for success, and its chances for failure. They'll still be taking a risk if they buy, but at least they'll be able to make an informed decision because of this full and fair disclosure.

When a corporation wants to raise capital by selling securities, they get a group of underwriters together and fill out paperwork for the federal government in the form of a **registration statement**. Part of this registration statement will become the **prospectus**, which is the disclosure brochure that investors are provided with. An underwriter is just a broker-dealer that likes to take companies public. Another name for an underwriter is investment banker, but they don't act like a traditional bank. No deposits or checking offered here. Their job is to raise money for their clients, other people's money.

Once the underwriters file the registration statement on behalf of the issuer, the process goes into a cooling off period, which will last 20 days or longer for most offerings. This process can drag on and on as the SEC reviews the paperwork, but no matter how long it takes, the issuer and underwriters can only do certain things during this "cooling off" period. Number one, they can't sell anything. They can't do any general advertising of the securities offering. They can announce that a sale is going to take place by publishing a **tombstone** ad in the financial press, because a tombstone ad is just a rectangle with some text. It announces that a sale of securities will take place at a particular offering price (or yield) and informs the reader how he/she can obtain a prospectus. But it is neither an offer to sell nor a solicitation to buy the securities. The underwriters can find out if anyone wants to give an "indication of interest," but those aren't sales. Just names on a list.

If someone gives an indication of interest, he must receive a preliminary prospectus, which contains everything the final prospectus will contain except for the effective date and the final/public offering price or "POP." The registered rep may not send a research report along with the preliminary prospectus and may not highlight or alter it in any way.

The preliminary prospectus is also referred to as a "red herring," due to the red-text warning that information may be added or altered. The release date and the final public offering price are two pieces of information yet to be added to what's in the red herring to make it a final prospectus. But, the preliminary prospectus has virtually all the material information a potential investor would need before deciding to invest or not.

The issuer and the underwriters attend a due diligence meeting toward the end of the cooling-off period to try and make sure they provided the SEC and the public with accurate and full disclosure. Nothing gets sold until the SEC grants the release date/effective date. Starting on that date, the prospectus must be delivered to all buyers of these new securities for a certain length of time.

And, even though the SEC makes issuers jump through all kinds of hoops, the SEC doesn't approve or disapprove of the security. They don't guarantee accuracy or adequacy of the information provided by the issuer and its underwriters. In other words, if this whole thing goes horribly wrong, the liability still rests squarely on the shoulders of the issuers and underwriters, not on the SEC. For that reason, there must be a disclaimer saying basically that on the prospectus. It usually looks like this:

> The Securities and Exchange Commission has not approved or disapproved of these securities. Further, it has not determined that this prospectus is accurate or complete. Any representation to the contrary is a criminal offense.

So, how does the SEC feel about the investment merits of the security? No opinion whatsoever. They just want to make sure you receive full and fair disclosure to make an informed decision to invest or to take a pass.

Securities Exchange Act of 1934

As mentioned, the Securities Exchange Act of 1934 is broader in scope than the Securities Act of 1933. As the SEC explains on the same page of their website:

> With this Act, Congress created the Securities and Exchange Commission. The Act empowers the SEC with broad authority over all aspects of the securities industry. This includes the power to register, regulate, and oversee brokerage firms, transfer agents, and clearing agencies as well as the nation's securities self-regulatory organizations (SROs). The various securities exchanges, such as the New York Stock Exchange, the NASDAQ Stock Market, and the Chicago Board of Options are SROs. The Financial Industry Regulatory Authority (FINRA) is also an SRO.
>
> The Act also identifies and prohibits certain types of conduct in the markets and provides the Commission with disciplinary powers over regulated entities and persons associated with them.
>
> The Act also empowers the SEC to require periodic reporting of information by companies with publicly traded securities.

The Securities Exchange Act of 1934 gave the SEC broad powers over the securities markets. The Act gave the Federal Reserve Board the power to regulate margin. It also requires public companies to file quarterly and annual reports with the SEC. If a material event occurs before the next regular report is due, the issuer files an 8-K. There are reports filed when the officers and members of the board sell their shares. Mergers and acquisitions must be announced through various filings. And, broker-dealer net capital requirements are also covered in this legislation.

Trust Indenture Act of 1939

The SEC describes the **Trust Indenture Act of 1939** like so:

> This Act applies to debt securities such as bonds, debentures, and notes that are offered for public sale. Even though such securities may be registered under the Securities Act, they may not be offered for sale to the public unless a formal agreement between the issuer of bonds and the bondholder, known as the trust indenture, conforms to the standards of this Act.

As we see above, the Trust Indenture Act of 1939 is all about protecting bondholders. If a corporation wants to sell $5,000,000 or more worth of bonds that mature outside of one year, they must do it under a contract or indenture with a trustee, who will enforce the terms of the indenture to the benefit of the bondholders. In other words, if the issuer stiffs the bondholders, the trustee can get a bankruptcy court to sell off the assets of the company so that bondholders can recover some of their hard-earned money. Sometimes corporations secure the bonds with specific assets like airplanes, securities, or real estate. If so, they pledge title of the assets to the trustee, who just might end up selling them off if the issuer gets behind on its interest payments.

Investment Company Act of 1940

The SEC summarizes this federal securities law like so:

This Act regulates the organization of companies, including mutual funds, that engage primarily in investing, reinvesting, and trading in securities, and whose own securities are offered to the investing public. The regulation is designed to minimize conflicts of interest that arise in these complex operations. The Act requires these companies to disclose their financial condition and investment policies to investors when stock is initially sold and, subsequently, on a regular basis. The focus of this Act is on disclosure to the investing public of information about the fund and its investment objectives, as well as on investment company structure and operations. It is important to remember that the Act does not permit the SEC to directly supervise the investment decisions or activities of these companies or judge the merits of their investments.

So, mutual funds must register their securities and provide a prospectus to all investors under the Securities Act of 1933. The Investment Company Act of 1940 requires the investment company itself to register and then lays out an exhaustive array of dos and don'ts for their operations. The Investment Company Act of 1940 classified investment companies as face amount certificate companies, unit investment trusts, or management companies. As we saw in an earlier chapter, the management companies are either open-end or closed-end funds. The distinguishing factor is that the open-end funds are redeemable, while the closed-end shares trade on the secondary market among investors. The unit investment trust has no investment adviser managing the portfolio and is sometimes linked with "having no board of directors." Note that the separate account for a variable annuity is registered under this Act, too, either as an open-end fund or as a UIT.

To fit the definition of "investment company," the shares must be easily sold and the number of shareholders must exceed 100. Hedge funds go the other way to avoid fitting the definition of "investment company." That is, they don't let people sell their investment freely and they keep the number of investors under 100, because if you can escape the definition of "investment company," you can escape the hassle of registering the investments and providing lots of disclosure to the SEC and the public markets. As usual, under the Act of 1940 the average investor is protected more than the sophisticated investor. Mutual funds and variable annuities are for the average investor; therefore, they need to be registered and watched closely by the SEC. Hedge funds are for the sophisticated investor primarily, so maybe things don't need to be watched so closely with them.

Investment Advisers Act of 1940

If you want to give people your expert securities advice based on their specific investment situation and receive compensation for doing so, you must register under the Investment Advisers Act of 1940 or under your state securities law. Portfolio managers, financial planners, pension fund consultants, and even many sports and entertainment agents end up having to register to give investment advice to their customers. All open- and closed-end funds are managed by registered investment advisers, and pension funds typically farm out their assets to many different investment advisory firms. Because the role they play is so important and so potentially dangerous, all investment advisers must be registered unless they qualify for some type of exemption.

Federal covered advisers are subject to the provisions of the Investment Advisers Act of 1940. A federal covered investment adviser with offices in various states only complies with the recordkeeping requirements and the net capital requirements set by the SEC.

The SEC promulgates rules under the Investment Advisers Act of 1940, and the state regulators often write their own rules in reference to the rules the SEC has already made. For example, the SEC is very specific on the dos and don'ts for investment advisers putting out advertisements. Most states tell advisers not to do anything that would violate that particular SEC rule.

The SEC doesn't care whether an investment adviser is subject to registration or not. Either way, if the person fits the definition of "investment adviser," he is at least subject to the anti-fraud section of the Investment Advisers Act of 1940. If the investment adviser qualifies for an exemption, he may get to skip various filing requirements, but he would still be subject to the anti-fraud provisions of the Act. That also means that if the person is not an investment adviser, he is not subject to the Investment Advisers Act of 1940, period.

The SEC can discipline federal covered investment advisers through administrative hearings to determine if a license is to be denied, suspended or revoked. They can also represent the U.S. Government in federal court and ask a judge to issue an injunction/restraining order against an investment adviser violating various sections of the "Advisers Act."

FINRA

The Securities and Exchange Commission has authority over broad aspects of the securities industry. They are granted this authority under the Securities Exchange Act of 1934. Under this landmark securities legislation the SEC requires securities exchanges such as NYSE and CBOE to register. These self-regulatory organizations in turn register and regulate their own member firms and the associated persons of those firms.

Securities have long traded both on the New York Stock Exchange and the Over-The-Counter (OTC) market. In 1938 Congress passed the **Maloney Act**, a law providing for the regulation of the OTC securities markets through national associations registered with the SEC. The National Association of Securities Dealers (NASD) then registered under the act. In 2007 the NASD and the regulatory arm of the NYSE formed FINRA, which stands for the **Financial Industry Regulatory Authority**. FINRA, along with NYSE and CBOE, is a self-regulatory organization (SRO) registered with the SEC under the Securities Exchange Act of 1934.

FINRA is organized along four major bylaws:

- rules of fair practice
- uniform practice code
- code of procedure
- code of arbitration

The rules of fair practice describe how to deal with customers. Commissions, markups, recommendations, advertising, sales literature, etc., are covered here. These are often referred to as "member conduct rules." The uniform practice code is the code that keeps the practice uniform.

Settlement dates, delivery of securities, the establishment of the ex-date, ACAT transfers, etc. are covered here. The exam might refer to the uniform practice code as "promoting cooperative effort" among member firms.

If your firm wants to join FINRA, it must:

- meet net capital requirements
- have at least two principals to supervise the firm
- have an acceptable business plan detailing its proposed activities
- attend a pre-membership interview

If your firm becomes a member of FINRA, they must agree to:

- abide by the rules of the "Association"
- abide by all federal and state laws
- pay dues, fees, and membership assessments

What are these fees the firm must pay?

- Basic membership fee
- Fee for each rep and principal
- Fee based on gross income of the firm
- Fee for all branch offices

Membership, Registration and Qualification Requirements

FINRA's **Central Registration Depository (CRD)** is the electronic registration system for member firms, principals, and registered representatives. FINRA reminds their member firms not to file misleading information. As the FINRA Manual says:

> *Filing of Misleading Information as to Membership or Registration*
>
> *The filing with the Association of information with respect to membership or registration as a Registered Representative which is incomplete or inaccurate so as to be misleading, or which could in any way tend to mislead, or the failure to correct such filing after notice thereof, may be deemed to be conduct inconsistent with just and equitable principles of trade and when discovered may be sufficient cause for appropriate disciplinary action.*

Filing misleading information with FINRA is a major violation. Firms also must not use their association with FINRA in a way that is misleading, as we see with this rule:

Member firms may not use the FINRA logo in any manner; however, a firm may refer to itself as a "FINRA Member Firm" or "Member of FINRA." Also, if a firm refers to its FINRA membership on its website, it must provide a hyperlink to FINRA's website, which is www.finra.org.

> *Failure to Register Personnel*
>
> *The failure of any member to register an employee, who should be so registered, as a Registered Representative may be deemed to be conduct inconsistent with just and equitable principles of trade and when discovered may be sufficient cause for appropriate disciplinary action.*

As we can see above, it is a violation to use an individual in a position that requires registration unless and until the individual is registered. Who "should be so registered"?

> **Definition of Representative**
>
> *Persons associated with a member, including assistant officers other than principals, who are engaged in the investment banking or securities business for the member including the functions of supervision, solicitation or conduct of business in securities or who are engaged in the training of persons associated with a member for any of these functions are designated as representatives.*

There are different categories of "registered representative," too. A General Securities Representative has a Series 7 and can sell individual stocks, bonds, municipal securities, options…generally just about anything. A person with a Series 6 is called a Limited Representative–Investment Company and Variable Contracts Products. This allows the individual to sell only mutual funds and variable contracts.

So, if you fit the definition of "representative," you must be registered:

> **All Representatives Must Be Registered**
>
> *All persons engaged or to be engaged in the investment banking or securities business of a member who are to function as representatives shall be registered as such with FINRA in the category of registration appropriate to the function to be performed as specified in Rule 1032. Before their registration can become effective, they shall pass a Qualification Examination for Representatives appropriate to the category of registration as specified by the Board of Governors.*

As basic as that rule seems, you might be surprised how often member firms try to use an unlicensed employee to function as a registered representative. Bad idea. Unless and until the individual is licensed by FINRA and the state securities regulators, he must not perform any of the functions of a registered representative.

As we said, firms, principals, and registered representatives submit their registration information to FINRA's Central Registration Depository (CRD). An individual trying to become a registered representative submits information to the CRD through a Form U4, which asks questions about residential history and professional background, etc. A principal must sign the U4 application and certify that he or she has reviewed the information, which is why it's not a good idea to use a fictional work history—they check that stuff.

The CRD system is used for many different purposes. FINRA uses the information to determine whether the applicant is subject to statutory disqualification or presents a risk for the firm and its customers. Member firms use the information to determine if a candidate is subject to statutory disqualification or special heightened supervision. Firms also use the information reported to check the backgrounds of candidates. Maybe most important, the information released to the public through BrokerCheck protects investors from serial offenders in the securities industry.

Candidates for registered representative and principal positions often try to conceal their criminal or regulatory problems when completing Form U4. When FINRA finds out, they usually bar the representative permanently from association with any member firm, because if the individual can't be trusted when applying, why let him meet with customers?

In a notice to members FINRA explains that firms have the responsibility to review the information their candidates submit on Form U4 and conduct thorough background checks. Member firms are not supposed to just run candidates through the CRD system and see which ones get past the regulators. FINRA requires that "each member firm ascertain by investigation the good character, business reputation, qualifications and experience of an applicant before the firm applies to register that applicant with FINRA and before making a representation to that effect on the application for registration."

If the applicant has already been registered, member firms are required to review his most recent U5 information—the form filed when an associated person ends employment with a member firm—within 60 days of filing the candidate's U4.

When a principal or registered representative leaves a member firm or ceases to function as a principal or registered representative at the firm, a U5 must be submitted to FINRA within 30 days. The firm the associated person is leaving completes a U5, and the firm that is hiring him completes a U4. If the exam uses the phrase "termination for cause," that means the registered rep gave the firm a good reason to fire him, including:

- Violating the firm's policies
- Violating the rules of the NYSE, FINRA, SEC, or any other industry regulator
- Violating state or federal securities laws

If the registered representative is the subject of an investigation by any securities industry regulator, the firm cannot terminate the rep until the investigation is completed.

FINRA requires firms to adopt written procedures on how they verify the information on a candidate's U4, and to complete that verification process within 30 calendar days of filing the U4. If the member finds information that doesn't match what the candidate disclosed, the firm must file an amended U4 within 30 calendar days. While FINRA encourages firms to complete this process before filing the U4, the firm can also just pay the Late Disclosure Fee involved with filing the amended U4.

Not surprisingly, the filing of an amended U4 often leads to FINRA deciding they might need to deny this one. For example, an amended U4 is often where a "no" answer to felony convictions and charges becomes two very embarrassing "yes" answers, with detailed explanations and court records detailing the unfortunate incident.

It used to be that if a customer wanted to win an arbitration claim, it was sort of understood that they needed to name the firm—not the individual representative—in the claim. This way, when the customer got paid, the registered representative had nothing to report on a U4 or U5 form.

Now, the firm must add the arbitration or civil litigation (lawsuit) award to the registered representative's U4/U5 form even if he or she isn't specifically named in the arbitration award. But, the threshold is $15,000 for the firm to report the settlement. FINRA and the SEC are also especially concerned about "willful violations" of securities law, and the new questions under the disclosure section are specifically designed to find out about those.

As you might expect, if your U4 contains information about "willful violations" of securities law— maybe executing transactions that your customers don't even know about, or misleading people about the mutual funds you sold them—it can be very tough to stay in the business. FINRA uses "statutory disqualification," which means that by statute you are disqualified.

After becoming a registered representative, you will also need to put in some time earning continuing education requirements. Let's see what FINRA must say about that:

> **_Continuing Education Requirements_**
>
> _This Rule prescribes requirements regarding the continuing education of certain registered persons subsequent to their initial qualification and registration with FINRA. The requirements shall consist of a Regulatory Element and a Firm Element as set forth below._

The Regulatory Element is described like so:

> *Each registered person shall complete the Regulatory Element on the occurrence of their second registration anniversary date and every three years thereafter, or as otherwise prescribed by FINRA. On each occasion, the Regulatory Element must be completed within 120 days after the person's registration anniversary date.*

What if you don't complete the Regulatory Element in that time frame?

> **Failure to Complete**
>
> *Unless otherwise determined by the Association, any registered persons who have not completed the Regulatory Element within the prescribed time frames will have their registrations deemed inactive until such time as the requirements of the program have been satisfied. Any person whose registration has been deemed inactive under this Rule shall cease all activities as a registered person and is prohibited from performing any duties and functioning in any capacity requiring registration.*

The Firm Element is described like this by the FINRA Manual:

> **Standards for the Firm Element**
>
> *(A) Each member must maintain a continuing and current education program for its covered registered persons to enhance their securities knowledge, skill, and professionalism. At a minimum, each member shall at least annually evaluate and prioritize its training needs and develop a written training plan.*

Active Military Duty

What happens when a registered representative volunteers or is called into active military duty? FINRA and the SEC are accommodating when a registered representative or principal is called away from the firm to serve in the armed forces. Here are the basic facts:

- license is placed on "inactive status"
- continuing education requirements waived
- dues, assessments waived
- two-year expiration period does not apply—exam might refer to this as "tolling"
- can earn commissions, usually by splitting them with another rep who will service the book of business
- the "inactive" rep cannot perform any of the duties of a registered rep while on inactive status

For a "sole proprietor" called into active military duty the same bullet points above apply.

When you complete your Series 7 requirements, you will become licensed to sell securities. You will not, however, be automatically registered to provide investment advice for compensation. To open a financial planning business or manage portfolios for a percentage of assets, you must pass your Series 65 or 66 exam and register your firm as an **investment adviser** or associate with an investment adviser as an **investment adviser representative**. If an agent opened either type of sideline without informing her employer and/or getting registered, disciplinary action could be taken by FINRA and his or her state securities regulator.

As a securities agent/registered representative, some of your customers will be investment advisers entering trades on behalf of their customers. But you yourself can only work the advisory side of the financial services business if you are properly licensed.

Principals

Member firms need principals who review correspondence, approve every account, initial order tickets, handle written customer complaints, and make sure there's a procedural manual for the office to use. In other words, somebody at the firm is ultimately responsible for the business of the firm—that person is the principal.

FINRA says:

> **All Principals Must Be Registered**
>
> *All persons engaged or to be engaged in the investment banking or securities business of a member who are to function as principals shall be registered as such with FINRA in the category of registration appropriate to the function to be performed as specified in Rule 1022. Before their registration can become effective, they shall pass a Qualification Examination for Principals appropriate to the category of registration as specified by the Board of Governors.*

Here is how FINRA defines a principal:

> **Definition of Principal**
>
> *Persons associated with a member who are actively engaged in the management of the member's investment banking or securities business, including supervision, solicitation, conduct of business or the training of persons associated with a member for any of these functions are designated as principals.*

Also, note that, in general, each member must have at least two principals taking care of:

- New accounts
- Trades (transactions)

- Communications
- Written Customer Complaints
- Updating the Written Supervisory Procedures (WSPs)

Research Analysts

A research analyst prepares the research reports put together by a member firm. To become a research analyst, one generally must earn the Series 7 and then pass another license exam specifically for research analysts (Series 86 and 87).

A supervisory analyst must approve all research reports.

> **Registration of Research Analysts**
>
> *(a) All persons associated with a member who are to function as research analysts shall be registered with FINRA.*

More on Registration Requirements

Many people in the industry ask, "If I stop selling for a while, can I just park my license at the firm until I'm ready to use it again?"

Here is how FINRA answers that:

> *A member shall not maintain a representative registration with FINRA for any person (1) who is no longer active in the member's investment banking or securities business, (2) who is no longer functioning as a representative, or (3) where the sole purpose is to avoid the examination requirement prescribed in paragraph (c).*

So, if the registered representative is out for two years or more, he must take his Series 6 or Series 7 exam again. Item (3) is saying that a member firm had better not pretend the agent is associated just so he can skip the requirement to requalify by exam.

A broker-dealer also could not sponsor someone for the Series 7 exam just so the person could sit for the test and maybe tell the rest of the candidates what to expect. As the rules say:

> *A member shall not make application for the registration of any person as representative where there is no intent to employ such person in the member's investment banking or securities business.*

Exemptions from Registration

Not every employee of a broker-dealer must register. The following have been granted exemptions from the painful process you're undergoing right now:

> ### *Persons Exempt from Registration*
>
> *(a) The following persons associated with a member are not required to be registered with the Association:*
>
> *(1) persons associated with a member whose functions are solely and exclusively clerical or ministerial;*
>
> *(2) persons associated with a member who are not actively engaged in the investment banking or securities business;*
>
> *(3) persons associated with a member whose functions are related solely and exclusively to the member's need for nominal corporate officers or for capital participation; and*
>
> *(4) persons associated with a member whose functions are related solely and exclusively to:*
>
> *(A) effecting transactions on the floor of a national securities exchange and who are registered as floor members with such exchange;*
>
> *(B) transactions in municipal securities;*
>
> *(C) transactions in commodities; or*
>
> *(D) transactions in security futures, provided that any such person is registered with a registered futures association.*

So, if he is just doing filing/temp work, not involved with underwriting or trading securities, just sitting on the board or investing in the firm, or is a member of a futures or stock exchange filling orders for the firm, that individual is not required to register as a registered representative.

Supervision

FINRA requires principals to supervise registered representatives. The member firm must establish and maintain written procedures to supervise the types of business it's engaged in and must supervise the activities of registered representatives. They must also designate a principal responsible for supervising each type of business in which the firm engages, and they must designate an "OSJ" (Office of Supervisory Jurisdiction).

The firm must perform internal inspections:

> *Each member shall conduct a review, at least annually, of the businesses in which it engages, which review shall be reasonably designed to assist in detecting and preventing violations of and achieving compliance with applicable securities laws and regulations, and with the Rules of this Association. Each member shall review the activities of each office, which shall include the periodic examination of customer accounts to detect and prevent irregularities or abuses and at least an annual inspection of each office of supervisory jurisdiction. Each branch office of the member shall be inspected according to a cycle which shall be set forth in the firm's written supervisory and inspection procedures.*

This is how FINRA defines office of supervisory jurisdiction (OSJ) and **branch office**:

> *Branch office: any location identified by any means to the public or customers as a location at which the member conducts an investment banking or securities business*
>
> *OSJ: "Office of Supervisory Jurisdiction" means any office of a member at which any one or more of the following functions take place:*
>
> *(A) order execution and/or market making;*
>
> *(B) structuring of public offerings or private placements;*
>
> *(C) maintaining custody of customers' funds and/or securities;*
>
> *(D) final acceptance (approval) of new accounts on behalf of the member;*
>
> *(E) review and endorsement of customer orders*
>
> *(F) final approval of advertising or sales literature for use by persons associated with the member*
>
> *(G) responsibility for supervising the activities of persons associated with the member at one or more other branch offices of the member.*

Gifts and Gratuities

FINRA does not allow member firms and their associated persons to buy influence at other firms with gifts of cash or gifts with resale value over a certain amount. Currently the amount is $100 but is expected to rise to $175 in the near future. Why would someone at your firm want to give someone at another firm a $1,000 set of titanium golf clubs? Maybe your firm would like to start getting invited to join certain municipal securities underwritings that they run as syndicate manager. Or, maybe your firm would just like the other firm to start throwing some of the smaller accounts they don't want your way? Maybe a case of expensive scotch would do the trick?

While gifts and business entertainment are not completely prohibited, we are now entering a gray area that can either be considered normal business expenses or a violation of FINRA rules on influencing or rewarding the employees of other member firms.

Here is how FINRA states the rule:

> *No member or person associated with a member shall, directly or indirectly, give or permit to be given anything of value, including gratuities, in excess of one hundred dollars per individual per year to any person, principal, proprietor, employee, agent or representative of another person where such payment or gratuity is in relation to the business of the employer of the recipient of the payment or gratuity. A gift of any kind is considered a gratuity.*

FINRA then makes it clear that what they are prohibiting here is more along the lines of a $1,000 set of golf clubs, as opposed to legitimate contracts of employment where one member employs another member's employee for legitimate purposes. As the rule then states:

> *This Rule shall not apply to contracts of employment with or to compensation for services rendered provided that there is in existence prior to the time of employment or before the services are rendered, a written agreement between the member and the person who is to be employed to perform such services. Such agreement shall include the nature of the proposed employment, the amount of the proposed compensation, and the written consent of such person's employer or principal.*

As with most sensitive issues, FINRA requires records surrounding these activities to be kept:

> *A separate record of all payments or gratuities in any amount known to the member, the employment agreement referred to in paragraph (b) and any employment compensation paid as a result thereof shall be retained by the member for the period specified by SEA Rule 17a-4.*

Note that "SEA" means "Securities Exchange Act of 1934" and "SEA Rule 17a-4" would be that SEC Rule promulgated under the Securities Exchange Act of 1934.

Government entities use the services of investment advisers, and these advisers often use broker-dealers to solicit business on their behalf. This type of service is typically called either soliciting or acting as the investment adviser's placement agent. A recent FINRA rule change prohibits a covered member from engaging in distribution or solicitation activities for compensation with a government entity on behalf of an investment adviser that provides or is seeking to provide investment advisory services to that government entity within two years after a contribution to an official of the government entity is made by the covered member or a covered associate. And, this includes a person who becomes a covered associate within two years after the contribution is made.

The rule also prohibits a member or associate from "soliciting or coordinating any person or political action committee (PAC) to make any contribution to an official of a government entity in respect of which the covered member is engaging in, or seeking to engage in, distribution or solicitation activities on behalf of an investment adviser, or to make any payment to a political party of a state or locality of a government entity with which the covered member is engaging in, or seeking to engage in, distribution or solicitation activities on behalf of an investment adviser."

Contributions made by a covered associate who is a natural person to government entity officials for whom the covered associate was entitled to vote at the time of the contributions, provided the contributions do not exceed $350 to any one official per election, are allowed. Unlike the earlier rule, if the covered associate was not entitled to vote for the official at the time of the contribution, the contribution must not exceed $150 per election. Primary and general elections are considered separate for purposes of the rule.

For a newly hired covered associate, FINRA will not preclude the member from engaging in placement activities if the individual made a contribution > 6 months ago and will not engage directly in solicitation activities with government entities on behalf of investment advisers.

As with the previous rule, member firms are required to keep information on political contributions and solicitation activities in their books and records so that FINRA can verify that members are not buying undue influence for their clients.

Exam Confidentiality

How serious is FINRA about protecting the surprise element in their exams?

> *FINRA considers all of its Qualification Examinations to be highly confidential. The removal from an examination center, reproduction, disclosure, receipt from or passing to any person, or use for study purposes of any portion of such Qualification Examination, whether of a present or past series, or any other use which would compromise the effectiveness of the Examinations and the use in any manner and at any time of the questions or answers to the Examinations are prohibited and are deemed to be a violation of Rule 2110.*

FINRA also explains that:

> *An applicant cannot receive assistance while taking the examination. Each applicant shall certify to the Board that no assistance was given to or received by him during the examination.*

Code of Procedure (COP)

FINRA investigates violations of the conduct rules through **Code of Procedure**. When we mentioned words such as "suspend, expel, bar, and censure," those are all part of the Code of Procedure. Maybe a staff member of FINRA found out some disturbing information during a recent routine examination of a firm, or maybe a customer is upset about losing 90% this year and then found out her agent was breaking rules along the way.

Either way, the respondent is notified and asked to respond to the charges in writing. All requests for information must be met within 25 days. All registered persons must cooperate with the investigation, producing documents or testimony as required. And if it's decided that the respondent broke a rule, he could be censured, fined, suspended, expelled, or barred.

Respondents receive an offer from FINRA to use what they call "summary complaint procedure," and if they want to avoid a hearing, they must accept it within 10 business days. Acceptance, waiver, and consent is the term used when the respondent accepts this outcome.

On the other hand, if the respondent rejects their offer, there will be a hearing. Although not held in a court of law, the respondent typically is represented by an attorney in these proceedings.

A third method of handling disciplinary charges is for the respondent to make an offer of settlement, in which he or they propose their own penalties.

Whether acceptance, waiver and consent (AWC), an offer of settlement, or a contested hearing is used, FINRA can hand down any of the following penalties:

- Censure
- Fine
- Suspension (up to 1 year) from the member firm or all member firms
- Expelled (up to 10 years, for firms only)
- Barred

What is the maximum fine FINRA can impose? Trick question—for a major violation, they've never set a cap. If it's a minor rule violation, there is a maximum fine (which changes from time to time), but no maximum will ever be set for the big violations.

Under COP, if the respondent is unhappy with the outcome of his hearing, he may appeal the decision, first, to FINRA's National Adjudicatory Council (NAC), then, to the SEC, and, finally, to the appropriate Federal appellate court.

That would also involve significant legal fees, and we would not find a lot of overturned disciplinary decisions through this process. But, unlike under Code of Arbitration—up next—there is an appeal process under Code of Procedure.

Code of Arbitration

When broker-dealers are arguing over money, they must take it to arbitration. Under the **Code of Arbitration** members of FINRA must resolve disputes with an arbitrator or arbitration panel, which cuts to the chase and makes their decision quickly. There are no appeals to arbitration. If they say your firm owes the other side one million dollars, your firm must cut a check for one million dollars. End of story.

A customer is free to sue a firm or registered rep in civil court unless the customer signs the arbitration agreement. Once that's signed, the customer is also bound by the Code of Arbitration, which means they can't sue their agent of broker-dealer in civil court. Which is why most firms get their customers to sign arbitration agreements when the new account is opened. Civil court is too costly and time-consuming. Arbitration can be very painful, but at least it's quick.

If the arbitration claim is for a small amount of money, Simplified Industry Arbitration is used. Here there is just one "chair-qualified" arbitrator and no hearing. The claims are submitted in writing, and the arbitrator reaches a decision.

Larger amounts of money are handled by three or five arbitrators, some from the industry and some from outside the industry. Evidence and testimony is examined, and the arbitration panel makes a final determination. Maybe they say the lead underwriter owes your firm $1 million. Maybe they say they owe nothing. Either way, all decisions are final and binding in arbitration, unlike civil court where the appeal process can go on and on.

So, if the arbitration panel says a firm owes somebody $250,000, they must pay them, promptly. Failure to comply with the arbitration decision could lead to disciplinary proceedings under Code of Procedure, which is always bad.

The bylaw doesn't specifically mention the word "money." The precise wording is:

> *any dispute, claim, or controversy arising out of or in connection with the business of any member of the Association, or arising out of the employment or termination of employment of associated person(s) with any member*

While arbitrators generally don't explain their decision, FINRA requires arbitrators to explain their decision if both parties make a joint request. The parties to the arbitration are required to submit any joint request for an explained decision at least 20 days before the first scheduled hearing date. The chairperson of the arbitration panel writes the explained decision and receives an additional honorarium of $400 for doing so.

An alternative method for resolving disputes is called **mediation.** Let's see how FINRA describes the difference between the two processes at http://www.finra.org/ArbitrationMediation/Parties/Overview/OverviewOfDisputeResolutionProcess/:

> *Dispute resolution methods, including mediation and arbitration, are non-judicial processes for settling disputes between two or more parties. In mediation, an impartial person, called a mediator, assists the parties in reaching their own solution by helping to diffuse emotions and keeping the parties focused on the issues. In arbitration, an impartial judge, called an arbitrator, hears all sides of the issue, studies the evidence, and then decides how the matter should be resolved. The arbitrator's decision is final....*
>
> *The mediator's role is to guide you and the other party toward your own solution by helping you to define the issues clearly and understand each other's position. Unlike an arbitrator or a judge, the mediator has no authority to decide the settlement or even compel you to settle. The mediator's "key to success" is to focus everyone involved on the real issues of settling--or the consequences of not settling. While the mediator may referee the negotiations-- defining the terms and rules of where, when, and how negotiations will occur--he or she never determines the outcome of the settlement itself.*

Okay, so what if the parties try to mediate the issue but can't come to a resolution?

When it seems that other efforts to resolve your dispute are not working, it is then time to decide whether you will file a claim to arbitrate. Even if you choose, or are required to use, arbitration rather than a lawsuit as a means of resolving your dispute, you should consider hiring an attorney who will provide valuable instruction and advice.

Arbitrators are people from all walks of life and all parts of the country. After being trained and approved, they serve as arbitrators when selected to hear a case. Some arbitrators work in the securities industry; others may be teachers, homemakers, investors, business people, medical professionals, or lawyers. What is most important is that arbitrators are impartial to the case and sufficiently knowledgeable in the area of controversy. Potential arbitrators submit personal profiles to FINRA; the profiles detail their knowledge of the securities industry and investment concerns. If accepted, their names and backgrounds go into a pool from which arbitrators are selected for any given case. Arbitrators do not work for FINRA, though they receive an honorarium from FINRA in recognition of their service.

FINRA also warns investors:

Caution. *When deciding whether to arbitrate, bear in mind that if your broker or brokerage firm goes out of business or declares bankruptcy, you might not be able to recover your money-even if the arbitrator or a court rules in your favor.* ***Over 80 percent of all unpaid awards involve a firm or individual that is no longer in business.***

(That is one of the reasons why it is so important to investigate the disciplinary history of your broker or brokerage firm before you invest. For tips on how to do this, please read the SEC publication entitled Check Out Your Broker located on the SEC Investor Education Web site. Through FINRA's BrokerCheck Program, investors, and others, can find out background information about brokers and brokerage firms.)

If a registered representative violates sales practice rules, and a customer makes an arbitration claim after losing money, the firm must report it on the registered (or formerly registered) representative's U4/U5 forms. As mentioned, if the amount of the award is $15,000 or more, the public will be able to find out about it, even if the plaintiff (customer) names the firm and not the registered rep specifically.

The exam could also mention that broker-dealer customers are not prevented from joining a class of plaintiffs in a class-action lawsuit. Meaning, if a large broker-dealer with offices all over the nation is found to be gouging customers on mutual fund sales through hidden charges, there could be a class-action lawsuit filed that all customers could join. Also, if an agent has a sexual harassment or civil rights case to file, that is also outside the scope of arbitration.

Chapter 4 Review Exercises

DIRECTIONS: underline the word or phrase that completes each statement.

1. Public companies must file quarterly and annual reports with the SEC under (The Securities Act of 1933/The Securities Exchange Act of 1934).

2. The information required in a prospectus is found within (The Securities Act of 1933/The Securities Exchange Act of 1934).

3. A preliminary prospectus discloses (the final public offering price/audited financial statements).

4. The Securities and Exchange Commission was formed under legislation passed in (1933/1934).

5. The Trust Indenture Act of 1939 applies to corporate bond offerings of (up to $5 million par value/$5 million par value or more) with maturities of (up to 1 year/more than 1 year).

6. Under the Investment Company Act of 1940, a (closed-end fund/Unit Invest Trust) is defined as a "management company."

7. The Investment Company Act of 1940 does not permit the SEC to directly supervise the investment decisions or activities of these companies or judge the merits of their investments. The previous statement is (true/false).

8. Open- and closed-end funds register their securities under (The Securities Act of 1933/The Investment Company Act of 1940).

9. Open- and closed-end funds register their investment companies under (The Securities Exchange Act of 1934/The Investment Company Act of 1940).

10. Investment advisers subject to SEC registration actively manage (no more than $100 million/at least $100 million) of assets.

11. FINRA's electronic registration system for member firms, principals, and registered representatives is known as the (CRD/IARD) system.

12. A registered representative terminates his association with a member firm, with both he and the member filing a Form (U4/U5) with FINRA.

13. Under FINRA rules, "Each registered person shall complete the Regulatory Element on the occurrence of their (second/third) registration anniversary date and every (two/three) years thereafter."

14. Under FINRA rules, "Any registered persons who have not completed the Regulatory Element within the prescribed time frames will have their registrations (suspended/deemed inactive) until such time as the requirements of the program have been satisfied.

15. Violations of FINRA rules are handled under (Code of Procedure/Code of Arbitration).

16. Disputes between two members of an underwriting syndicate would be handled under (Code of Procedure/Code of Arbitration).

17. A member or associated person's failure to honor an arbitration award to a disgruntled customer would be handled under (Code of Procedure/Code of Arbitration).

18. Decisions under Code of Procedure are reviewed by the National Adjudicatory Council, to whom appeals can be filed. If the NAC fails to overturn or modify the original decision, the affected party can then appeal to the (SEC/Federal court system).

19. An individual who is removed from the industry by FINRA over rule violations is (barred/expelled), while a member firm so removed is (barred/expelled).

20. If the amount of the award is at least ($5,000/$15,000) FINRA rules require the member firm to name the associated person(s) involved in the dispute.

Answers

1. Public companies must file quarterly and annual reports with the SEC under (The Securities Act of 1933/<u>The Securities Exchange Act of 1934</u>).
2. The information required in a prospectus is found within (<u>The Securities Act of 1933</u>/The Securities Exchange Act of 1934).
3. A preliminary prospectus discloses (the final public offering price/<u>audited financial statements</u>).
4. The Securities and Exchange Commission was formed under legislation passed in (1933/<u>1934</u>).
5. The Trust Indenture Act of 1939 applies to corporate bond offerings of (up to $5 million par value/<u>$5 million par value or more</u>) with maturities of (up to 1 year/<u>more than 1 year</u>).
6. Under the Investment Company Act of 1940, a (<u>closed-end fund</u>/Unit Invest Trust) is defined as a "management company."
7. The Investment Company Act of 1940 does not permit the SEC to directly supervise the investment decisions or activities of these companies or judge the merits of their investments. The previous statement is (<u>true</u>/false).
8. Open- and closed-end funds register their securities under (<u>The Securities Act of 1933</u>/The Investment Company Act of 1940).
9. Open- and closed-end funds register their investment companies under (The Securities Exchange Act of 1934/<u>The Investment Company Act of 1940</u>).
10. Investment advisers subject to SEC registration actively manage (no more than $100 million/<u>at least $100 million</u>) of assets.
11. FINRA's electronic registration system for member firms, principals, and registered representatives is known as the (<u>CRD</u>/IARD) system.
12. A registered representative terminates his association with a member firm, with both he and the member filing a Form (U4/<u>U5</u>) with FINRA.
13. Under FINRA rules, "Each registered person shall complete the Regulatory Element on the occurrence of their (<u>second</u>/third) registration anniversary date and every (two/<u>three</u>) years thereafter."
14. Under FINRA rules, "Any registered persons who have not completed the Regulatory Element within the prescribed time frames will have their registrations (suspended/<u>deemed inactive</u>) until such time as the requirements of the program have been satisfied.
15. Violations of FINRA rules are handled under (<u>Code of Procedure</u>/Code of Arbitration).
16. Disputes between two members of an underwriting syndicate would be handled under (Code of Procedure/<u>Code of Arbitration</u>).
17. A member or associated person's failure to honor an arbitration award to a disgruntled customer would be handled under (<u>Code of Procedure</u>/Code of Arbitration).
18. Decisions under Code of Procedure are reviewed by the National Adjudicatory Council, to whom appeals can be filed. If the NAC fails to overturn or modify the original decision, the affected party can then appeal to the (<u>SEC</u>/Federal court system).
19. An individual who is removed from the industry by FINRA over rule violations is (<u>barred</u>/expelled), while a member firm so removed is (barred/<u>expelled</u>).
20. If the amount of the award is at least ($5,000/<u>$15,000</u>) FINRA rules require the member firm to name the associated person(s) involved in the dispute.

1. FINRA's Conduct Rules prohibit which of the following?
A. choosing the price paid for a security after a non-discretionary customer has named the action, asset, and amount of shares
B. splitting commissions with another registered representative of the employing member
C. choosing the security to be bought/sold in the absence of discretionary authority
D. all choices listed

2. You are a registered representative at a branch office with five registered representatives. One of the other representatives is an active member of the U.S. Army Reserve. If he is called up for active military duty overseas for a period of three years, which of the following statements is accurate?
A. His license is automatically revoked
B. His license remains valid provided he completes any continuing education requirements online and on time
C. After two years he must requalify by examination
D. He cannot perform any of the duties of a registered representative while on inactive status

3. Self-Regulatory Organizations or SROs include all the following EXCEPT:
A. FINRA
B. CBOE
C. SEC
D. NASDAQ

4. Securities—other than exempted securities or securities offered and sold through an exempt transaction—are subject to registration under the Securities Act of 1933. Which of the following is subject to registration under this act?
A. An offer of common stock by an Iowa-based company to Iowa investors only
B. Any offer of a municipal security wherein the issuer is a political subdivision below the county level
C. A weekly auction of United States Treasury Bills by the Federal Reserve Board
D. An IPO in which the shares are authorized for NYSE listing

5. Which TWO of the following are accurately associated with the Securities Act of 1933?

I.   10K report
II.   Preliminary prospectus
III.   8K release
IV.   Tombstone

A. I, III
B. II, III
C. I, IV
D. II, IV

6. Persons associated with a member who are actively engaged in the management of the member's investment banking or securities business, including supervision, solicitation, conduct of business or the training of persons associated with a member for any of these functions are defined by FINRA as which of the following?

A. Officers
B. Principals
C. Directors
D. Chief Compliance Officers

7. If a brokerage customer claims that her substantial loss on two mutual funds was caused by the inappropriate recommendations and deceptive sales tactics of her registered representative, which of the following is typically utilized in her attempt to recover damages?

A. Code of Procedure
B. Code of Arbitration
C. Civil Court
D. All choices listed

8. A dissatisfied brokerage customer files an arbitration claim against the broker-dealer employing her agent. The agent has since been fired for cause and is no longer in the securities industry. If the arbitrator hands down an award of at least what amount, the member firm must add the event to the former agent's Form U5 information in the CRD system?

A. $5,000
B. $10,000
C. $15,000
D. $20,000

9. Some of these professionals manage mutual and pension fund portfolios. Some manage portfolios for individuals and large trusts. Others provide financial planning services. Such professionals are known as which of the following?
A. Registered Investment Advisers
B. Registered Fiduciaries
C. Registered Portfolio Consultants
D. Registered Investment Managers

10. Which of the following statements is accurate?
A. Member firms may not use the FINRA logo in any manner
B. If a member firm refers to its FINRA membership on its website, it must provide a hyperlink to FINRA's website
C. A firm may refer to itself as a "FINRA member firm"
D. All choices listed

Answers

1. C
2. D
3. C
4. D
5. D
6. B
7. B
8. C
9. A
10. D

1.   Which of the following accounts can be opened without supporting documentation?

A.   UTMA

B.   Guardian

C.   Trust

D.   Estate

2.   Broker-dealer member firms must obtain and maintain all the following signatures connected to a customer account EXCEPT:

A.   Dated manual signature of each party authorized to exercise discretion over any discretionary account

B.   Signature of the registered representative with responsibility over the account

C.   Signature of the principal approving the account

D.   Signature of the branch manager of the customer's provided bank reference

3.   Which statement below is accurate concerning an UTMA/UGMA account?

A.   Upon death of the minor, the assets pass to the minor's estate

B.   Earnings grow tax-deferred until the beneficiary reaches the state's age of majority

C.   The custodian must be related to the beneficiary as an "immediate family" member

D.   All these statements are accurate

4.   Identify the one accurate statement below regarding individual accounts opened for a customer at a member firm.

A.   Such accounts may be opened only with the signature of an impartial witness

B.   Such accounts are for tax-advantaged accounts only

C.   Only orders from the account owner may be accepted

D.   Only orders from the account owner or a duly authorized third party may be accepted

5.   Which of the following types of account ownership allow(s) assets to transfer outside the probate court process?

A.   Transfer on Death (TOD)

B.   Joint Tenants in Common (TIC)

C.   Both choices

D.   Neither choice

6.   What should a registered representative do if she receives a call from the executor for the estate of an elderly customer, and the executor informs her that his grandmother has died, with detailed instructions as to which securities to liquidate immediately?

A.   Ignore the instructions and inform a principal of the call upon receipt of proper court documents

B.   Inform the executor that your firm will require a death certificate, letters of office, and various other documents before executing any transactions upon his instructions

C.   Upon receipt of a photo ID verifying the executor's identity, follow his instructions

D.   Upon receipt of a photo ID verifying the executor's identity and principal approval, follow the executor's instructions

7.   If a registered representative lacks written discretionary authorization over the account, which of the following customer orders could be accepted?

A.   Allocate this $20,000 among three different mutual funds

B.   Allocate this $20,000 among three different large cap growth funds

C.   Buy 1,000 shares of ABC sometime this week when you think the price is right

D.   Buy 1,000 shares of ABC this afternoon

8.   A true statement regarding a Currency Transaction Report (CTR) is that it would be filed

A.   For any wire transfer exceeding $3,000

B.   For any incoming wire transfer exceeding $5,000

C.   For any cash transaction or series of transactions exceeding $10,000 in a single day

D.   For any cash transaction or series of transactions under $10,000 in a single day

9. Which of the following is an accurate statement of brokerage procedures in connection to the Bank Secrecy Act (BSA)?

A. Special forms and recordkeeping are required for all wire transmittals of $3,000+

B. Broker-dealers are exempt from all requirements unless affiliated with a retail bank

C. FinCEN, a subdivision of the Securities and Exchange Commission (SEC), must be alerted of all wire transmittals by or for non-U.S. citizens regardless of the amount involved

D. Because of Dodd-Frank, broker-dealers may opt-in or opt-out of compliance with requirements under the Bank Secrecy Act

10. The stage in the money laundering process in which a series of complex transactions is used to obscure the origin of the illicit funds is known as

A. Layering

B. Placement

C. Integration

D. Obfuscation

11. A brokerage customer would request that her previous broker-dealer move her account assets to your firm through which of the following?

A. ACT

B. ACAT

C. SIPC

D. SARS

12. FINRA member broker-dealers routinely forward all the following mail to their customers EXCEPT:

A. Account statements

B. Proxy statements

C. IRS Form 1040

D. 10K Reports

13.   Which of the following statements accurately addresses the process of updating personal information associated with a customer account?

A.   Only the customer may make such a change, and not more often than annually

B.   Only the customer may make such a change, and not more often than quarterly

C.   Personal information is updated no more frequently than annually when the customer responds to a request from a registered broker-dealer

D.   Personal information should be updated whenever the customer informs the registered representative of relevant changes

14.   Which of the following requires that a principal sign off on the information being changed or recorded?

A.   A customer calls to inform the firm that her husband has lost his job

B.   A customer calls to inform the firm that she and her husband are switching to a JTIC (Joint Tenants in Common) account designation

C.   A customer calls to inform the firm that she has lost her job

D.   A customer calls to request information about a tax-exempt bond fund not sponsored by the firm

15.   Which of the following is an accurate statement of individual accounts?

A.   Orders may only be accepted from the individual listed as the account owner

B.   Orders may only be accepted from the individual listed as the account owner and anyone granted power of attorney orally by the customer

C.   Orders may only be accepted from the individual listed as the account owner and anyone granted power of attorney in writing by the customer

D.   Orders may be accepted from immediate family members of the customer only

16.   If an employee transfers a 401(k) to a rollover IRA upon leaving a job,

A.   The employee must pay tax on the excess above cost basis

B.   There will be no penalties or taxation to pay at this time

C.   The employee must be 59 ½ to avoid penalties

D.   The employee may only perform one transfer per year

17.   A 1035 contract exchange may not take place in which of the following ways?

A.   one annuity to another offered by a different company

B.   one annuity to a life insurance policy issued by the same company

C.   one insurance policy to another issued by a different company

D.   one insurance policy to another issued by the same company

18.   A teacher participated in a tax-sheltered annuity for 20 years. During her employment she and the school district contributed $30,000 into the plan. At retirement the teacher takes a lump-sum distribution of $50,000. What is the tax treatment of the distribution?

A. $20,000 taxed at long-term capital gains rates

B. $50,000 taxed as ordinary income

C. $50,000 taxed at long-term capital gains rates

D. $20,000 taxed as ordinary income

19.   JoAnn originally invested $10,000 into the Argood Value Fund. She has since reinvested dividend distributions of $1,000 and capital gains distributions of $500. If JoAnn currently holds 1,000 shares of the Argood Value Fund, her cost basis per-share is

A. $10.00

B. $11.00

C. $11.50

D. $10.50

20.   Doris contributed $60,000 into a non-qualified variable annuity at age 41. Nine years later Doris takes a random withdrawal of $15,000 with the account value at $85,000. Her tax liability on the withdrawal is

A.   Ordinary income tax on $15,000

B.   Ordinary income tax on $15,000, plus a $1,500 penalty tax

C.   None, as this represents a tax-free return of cost basis

D.   Ordinary income tax on $25,000

21.　　Which of the following statements accurately describe(s) the tax implications of insurance contracts?

A.　　death benefits are not taxable to the beneficiary, but are includable in the insured's estate for purposes of estate taxes

B.　　loans against the policy are charged interest, and both the principal and interest reduce the contract values

C.　　the policyholder may surrender the part of cash value representing net premiums paid into the contract tax-free

D.　　all choices listed

22.　　Which of the following are available only to sole proprietors?

A.　　SIMPLE IRA

B.　　SEP-IRA

C.　　Keogh

D.　　Non-qualified annuity

23.　　Which of the following may a 72-year-old not do regarding a Roth IRA account?

A.　　Change the beneficiary

B.　　Elect to take no distributions

C.　　Continue to make contributions from earned income

D.　　Make deductible contributions from earned income

24.　　Which of the following offers annual downside protection to an investor?

A.　　U.S. Treasury Bond

B.　　Equity indexed annuity

C.　　Variable annuity

D.　　All choices listed

25.　　Which of the following statements accurately describes SIMPLE Individual Retirement Arrangements?

A.　　Employees are immediately vested

B.　　SIMPLE IRAs are for businesses with more than 100 employees

C.　　SIMPLE IRAs are for businesses with at least one other retirement plan option

D.　　Contributions are non-tax-deductible

26. FINRA requires a reasonable-basis suitability standard for investment recommendations. Which of the following exemplifies a broker-dealer meeting this standard?

A. An agent of the firm recommends a transaction that is suitable based on an inquiry of the customer's needs

B. The firm performs due diligence to determine that a new securities product may be suitable for some investors

C. An agent of the firm recommends a deferred annuity to an elderly client with high liquidity needs

D. The firm reviews the transactions within an agent's book of business to verify that an excessive number of transactions has not been executed, making otherwise suitable recommendations unsuitable when taken as a whole

27. When a large state needs to raise capital to improve the highway system, the services of which of the following would be used?

A. Retail bank

B. Investment banker

C. Investment adviser

D. The state must raise capital internally, and may not use the services of an outside party to raise capital for such projects

28. ABC Industries completed its IPO several years ago. If the company offers shares to investors this year, the offering could be accurately referred to as a/an

A. Subsequent primary offering

B. Secondary offering

C. Combined offering

D. Reg D offering

29. Which of the following securities issued by a corporation pays an income stream that is fixed as to the minimum but not as to the maximum?

A. Straight preferred stock

B. Participating preferred stock

C. Callable preferred stock

D. Cumulative preferred stock

30. Which of the following positions allows the investor to force another investor to buy her stock at a stated price?

A. Buy a call

B. Buy a put

C. Sell a call

D. Sell a put

31. GNMA (Government National Mortgage Association) pass-through securities make payments to investors in which of the following ways?

A. Interest is paid semi-annually with all principal paid at a stated maturity date

B. Interest is paid monthly with all principal paid on an uncertain maturity date

C. Interest and principal are paid monthly

D. Interest is paid monthly, principal is paid annually

32. Which of the following securities is offered with a relatively low rate of income but with potential capital appreciation/purchasing power protection?

A. Participating preferred stock

B. Callable preferred stock

C. Adjustable-rate preferred stock

D. Convertible preferred stock

33. A 69-year-old annuitant would likely receive the highest monthly payment if choosing which of the following payout options?

A. Straight life

B. Life with 15-year period certain

C. Join-and-last survivor

D. All choices would lead to equal monthly payouts

34.   You could accurately inform a customer that the death benefit offered through a deferred variable annuity contract works in which of the following ways?

A.   During the accumulation phase the beneficiary would receive at least what the annuitant contributed to the contract upon his/her death

B.   Once annuitized the beneficiary will receive at least what the individual contributed to the account

C.   Once annuitized the beneficiary will receive a minimum number of payments

D.   During the accumulation period the beneficiary is assured of receiving a minimum rate of return on the annuitant's purchase payments

35.   What is true of the investment options offered to the policyholder of a variable life insurance contract?

A.   The policyholder may invest no more than 50% of net premiums in the separate account

B.   The policyholder may invest no more than 50% of net premiums in equity-based subaccounts

C.   The policyholder may invest among the subaccounts as she sees fit

D.   During the first 24 months net premiums are automatically allocated to the general account

36.   Companies typically finance their short-term operations with the issuance of which of the following types of securities?

A.   Commercial paper

B.   Banker's acceptances

C.   Treasury Bills

D.   Treasury stock

37.   Which of the following is potentially a dis-advantage of automatically investing $100 into a mutual fund each month?

A.   Dollar cost averaging

B.   Avoiding timing risk

C.   Triggering wash sales

D.   There are no dis-advantages to this practice

38.   Investors who re-invest dividend distributions from a mutual fund should be aware of which of the following?

A.   Reinvested dividends are taxable and do not add to the investor's tax basis

B.   Reinvested dividends are not taxable but are added to the investor's tax basis

C.   Reinvested dividends are taxable and are added to the investor's tax basis

D.   Reinvested dividends reduce the investor's tax basis by the amount reinvested

39.   What is true of surrenders of cash value on a variable life insurance policy?

A.   The policyholder is taxed on any surrenders of cash value similar to the tax consequences on a non-qualified variable annuity

B.   Surrenders up to the amount of premiums paid are not taxable to the policyholder

C.   Surrenders must be for the full cash value of the policy in order to avoid tax consequences

D.   Surrenders of cash value do not impact the amount of the policy's death benefit

40.   Several weeks after one of your elderly customers passed away you are meeting with the executor of the estate, who is also the sole beneficiary of a variable life insurance policy you sold to the now-deceased customer. All the following statements to the executor are accurate EXCEPT:

A.   The death benefit is not taxable to the executor

B.   The death benefit is includable in the value of the deceased customer's estate

C.   The securities account can only be re-titled in the name of the estate after receipt of a death certificate, letters of office, affidavits, etc.

D.   The death benefit is not includable in the value of the deceased customer's estate because the executor and beneficiary are one-in-the-same

41.   Individuals frequently take distributions from annuities and retirement plans prior to age 59 ½ and avoid penalties under which section of the tax code?

A.   1035

B.   1031

C.   72(t)

D.   401(k)

42.   Contract owners of annuities and insurance policies can transfer contract values tax-free by utilizing which of the following sections of the tax code?

A.   1031

B.   1035

C.   1099

D.   72(t)

43.   If a registered representative of a FINRA-member firm borrows money from a customer without violating FINRA rules, the most likely reason is that

A.   The member's written supervisory procedures permitted the activity

B.   The customer was a bank

C.   The customer was an immediate family member

D.   The customer was a registered representative of an unaffiliated brokerage firm

44.   On vacation recently, you met a registered representative working for a different broker-dealer than yours and discovered that while the registered representative does not sell variable annuities, you do not like to sell open-end mutual funds. In order to work together, which of the following are you allowed to do without violating industry rules?

A.   Make an annual payment to the registered representative of $500

B.   Make an annual payment to the registered representative of $500 only after receiving principal approval

C.   Set up a referral arrangement and split the commissions 50/50

D.   Make a gift of cash or goods not to exceed FINRA's annual limit

45.   One of your customers is 55 years old and ready to retire in the next few months. She owns a non-qualified variable annuity with a cost basis of $300,000 and a contract value of $442,000. Which of the following statements could you accurately make to this customer?

A.   A lump-sum withdrawal of $442,000 will be taxed as ordinary income in its entirety

B.   If you annuitize the contract, the first two years of payments will be tax-free

C.   A random withdrawal of $75,000 would be subject to a penalty of $7,500

D.   There is no way to avoid either income taxes or penalties on any withdrawal from this account due to your age

46.   An annuitant in her 40's is receiving generous dividend and capital gains distributions from the various subaccounts of her variable annuity to which her purchase payments have been allocated. What is true of the tax implications of these distributions?

A.   They will be reinvested into more accumulation units of the separate account

B.   They may be received constructively currently without tax implications

C.   The dividend distributions are tax-exempt while the capital gains distributions are taxed at long-term capital gains rates

D.   The dividends are tax-exempt if the purchase payments are allocated to any municipal bond subaccounts

47.   Which of the following is an accurate statement of guarantees as they relate to the securities industry?

A.   No securities are guaranteed

B.   U.S. Treasury—but not corporate—bonds may be described as "guaranteed"

C.   Broker-dealers and agents may not guarantee customers against investment loss

D.   All choices given

48.   For purposes of determining the suitability of an annuity switch transaction which of the following facts about the customer or the proposed transaction would most likely make the switch suitable?

A.   The customer is 53 years old

B.   The customer is female

C.   The existing contract will charge a 6% surrender fee

D.   The annuity offered will waive all surrender charges after two years

49.   Your Aunt Allie Mae originally invested $25,000 into the ABC Balanced Fund. Over the years, she has reinvested $3,000 in dividends and $1,500 in capital gains distributions. When she dies, you inherit the shares, with the investment worth $48,000. What are the tax implications on your inheritance?

A.   None currently except to establish a cost basis of $48,000

B.   None currently except to establish a cost basis of $29,500

C.   None currently except to establish a cost basis of $25,000

D.   Long-term capital gains tax rates on $17,500

50.   Which of the following correctly describes the FINRA violation called "breakpoint selling"?

A.   Trying to guide investors toward investing in mutual fund shares at a higher dollar amount

B.   Intentionally trying to guide investors to combine investments within one family of funds

C.   Intentionally trying to entice investors to buy shares of a mutual fund to receive an upcoming dividend distribution

D.   Selling mutual funds in a way that prevents investors from receiving available breakpoints

51.   The one accurate statement below of mutual fund sponsors is that

A.   They are federal covered investment advisers

B.   They may offer educational seminars to registered representatives based on their sales volume

C.   They may offer educational seminars to registered representatives, reimbursing their expenses as well as the reasonable expenses of one guest

D.   They must be FINRA-member firms in good standing

52.   Under the Securities Act of 1933 the SEC is responsible for all the following EXCEPT:

A.   Promotion of market efficiency

B.   Fostering capital formation through the primary market

C.   Encouraging competition among market participants

D.   Reducing paperwork for brokerage firms

53.   FINRA would have regulatory concerns over which of the following compensation arrangements?

A.   Janet and Jill, registered representatives of ABC Brokerage Services, plan to do joint work and split commissions on mutual fund sales

B.   David, age 67 and retired, pursuant to a written agreement with his former employing member firm receives commissions on annuity business written several years ago

C.   Donna, registered with a Series 7 and Series 24, receives a percentage of the commissions received by the registered representatives under her supervision

D.   Myrtle agrees to rebate 1/3 of the commissions paid on a large variable annuity sale to the customer after receiving principal approval

54. An example of market manipulation, prohibited under Rule 10b-5 of the Securities Exchange Act of 1934, is which of the following?

A. An institutional trader sells 1,000 shares of ABC short without attempting to pay for the stock immediately

B. A broker-dealer executes > 25 agency cross transactions on the same trading day

C. A retail investor establishes five separate LLCs under diverse names and stated purposes and spends the day trading an illiquid stock at progressively higher price and volume levels among the various controlled entities

D. Seven retail investors form an investment club for the express purpose of pooling their capital, knowledge, and experience

55. While making a sales presentation to a wealthy customer, you discover that the customer's business is about to be acquired by a much larger player, with the announcement to come out the following afternoon after markets close for regular trading. At this point, what can you do concerning this information?

A. Use it for your own personal trading, but not for recommendations to your customers

B. Do not use it for your own personal trading or for recommendations to your customers but inform investors who are not customers of your firm in the interest of full and fair disclosure

C. Contact FINCen immediately and/or complete a Suspicious Activity Report

D. Do not use the information for your personal trading, and do not divulge it to any other investor until it has been publicly released

56. If a retail investor reads the summary prospectus for the ABC Value Fund and sees that no more than 15% of the fund's assets may be invested in companies that are neither domiciled in the U.S. nor included in the S&P 500. This policy exists as stated because

A. The board of directors has established this policy

B. The SEC requires that funds invest no more than 20% in such companies

C. FINRA requires that funds invest no more than 1/3 of total assets in such companies

D. The investment adviser has determined that this is a prudent investment policy

57.   One of your customers is a 31-year-old single woman who is about to purchase a condominium. Which of the following statements could you accurately make to her concerning her Traditional IRA and this transaction?

A.   She can perform a qualifying rollover from her existing IRA to a new account if she completes it within 180 calendar days

B.   She can withdraw up to $10,000 from the account and use it as a down payment without any tax implications

C.   If she were purchasing a detached, single-family home she could withdraw up to $10,000 from the account and use it as a down payment without penalty

D.   If this is her first purchase of a primary residence, she can avoid penalties on a withdrawal of up to $10,000 for a down payment on the property

58.   One of your mutual fund customers is ready to retire. She would like to receive $500 monthly through a systematic withdrawal plan. Which of the following statements is accurate of this situation?

A.   She should choose a fixed-share withdrawal plan

B.   She should choose a fixed-dollar withdrawal plan to be certain of her money lasting a minimum amount of time

C.   She should choose a fixed-dollar withdrawal plan provided she can live with the uncertain time frame implied by this choice

D.   She should choose a fixed-percentage withdrawal plan

59.   An investor holding shares of a non-diversified open-end fund could accurately be informed of which of the following?

A.   Sales charges and management fees are operating expenses deducted against fund assets

B.   Management fees, transfer agent fees, and 12b-1 fees are operating expenses deducted against fund assets

C.   No-load open-end funds do not impose operating expenses on their investors

D.   Only front-end-loaded open-end fund shares impose operating expenses on their investors

60.   How would you explain to a customer the significance of a "frozen account"?

A.   An account that cannot buy or sell securities for 90 days

B.   An account that can sell but cannot purchase securities for 90 days

C.   A margin account that is under-collateralized

D.   An account whose credit has been cut off for 90 days

61.	Which of the following customer actions will lead to an account freeze under Regulation T?

A.	A customer requests the full amount of the proceeds of a large stock sale within 5 business days of the transaction

B.	A customer enters an order to buy 500 shares of ABC, making payment for the purchase from the proceeds of the sale executed on the next business day

C.	A customer writes a covered call within 4 business days of purchasing the underlying stock within a cash account

D.	All choices listed

62.	Marcy purchases 300 shares of ABC common stock on the ex-dividend date; therefore, which of the following will occur?

A.	Marcy will receive the declared dividend on the payable date

B.	The seller will receive the declared dividend on the record date

C.	The seller will receive the declared dividend on the payable date

D.	Marcy will receive the declared dividend on the record date

63.	If a brokerage customer wants to see the dividends and interest received on her account over the previous month, she should consult which of the following?

A.	Form 1041

B.	Account statement

C.	Trade confirmation

D.	Proxy statement

64.	A trade confirmation sent to a customer who has sold $100,000 par value of a corporate bond issue would list all the following information EXCEPT:

A.	Commission if executed on an agency basis

B.	Net price if executed on a principal basis

C.	CUSIP number of the bond

D.	Credit rating of the bond

65.   If a registered representative engages in excessive trading of a customer account, which of the following is accurate?

A.   The registered representative is subject to disciplinary action only

B.   The registered representative is subject to arbitration only

C.   The registered representative is subject to arbitration and FINRA disciplinary action but may not be fired for cause by his employing broker-dealer

D.   The registered representative is subject to arbitration, FINRA disciplinary action, and being fired for cause by his employing broker-dealer

66.   Which of the following represents appropriate conduct by an agent of a FINRA-member broker-dealer responding to a written customer complaint?

A.   Call the customer and invite him or her to a business lunch in which you will attempt to rectify the situation amenably

B.   Offer to refund the purchase price, plus interest, for the security involved in the complaint

C.   Immediately forward the complaint to the appropriate principal

D.   All choices listed

67.   FINRA's Code of Procedure (COP) would be used in which of the following situations?

A.   An agent works outside the firm without written notification provided to his employing member

B.   An agent claims that his employer owes him $10,000 in promised commissions

C.   The member of a syndicate claims that the managing underwriter owes the firm $50,000 and/or 1,000 more shares of a recent securities offering

D.   A customer feels that she is owed $45,000 due to poor recommendations from an inexperienced agent

68.   A registered representative of a FINRA member broker-dealer must update which of the following upon executing a "short sale" on his personal residence?

A.   Form U4

B.   Form U5

C.   None, as this is a non-securities-related misdemeanor

D.   None, as this is a non-investment-related property

69.	A new-hire of a FINRA member broker-dealer is completing her Form U4. Seven years ago, she was convicted of misdemeanor shoplifting and subsequently had the conviction expunged. How should she answer the question asking if she has ever been charged with a misdemeanor that is investment-related?

A.	No

B.	Yes

C.	Nolo contendere

D.	Pass

70.	A registered representative must update her Form U4 information for which of the following?

A.	Completion of her college degree (baccalaureate) from an accredited university

B.	Receiving her certification as a massage therapist

C.	Agreeing to satisfy a debt by paying $11,000 of a $19,000 balance

D.	Executing a call or put purchase transaction for any retail customer

71.	Which of the following activities may a registered representative engage in without notification to her firm?

A.	Coaching a youth basketball team on a volunteer basis

B.	Opening a brokerage account with another member firm

C.	Opening a checking account with an unaffiliated bank

D.	Giving piano lessons for modest remuneration

72.	An agent of a FINRA member firm could engage in which of the following activities without notifying her employing member firm?

A.	Helping her sister find 10 investors—none of whom have accounts with the employing broker-dealer—for a bakery she is opening formed as an LLC

B.	Helping her brother-in-law find 9 investors—5 of whom have accounts with the employing broker-dealer—for an auto body repair business formed as an S-Corporation

C.	Directing a church choir for no more than $100 weekly

D.	Joining a local health club when the firm has equal-or-greater facilities on premises

73.   Identify the one accurate statement below concerning securities accounts/transactions for agents of FINRA member firms?

A.   Agents must notify their employer of their intention to open an account and the executing member of their affiliation with their employing firm

B.   Agents may not open accounts except with their employing broker-dealer

C.   While employed with a member firm, agents may purchase only mutual funds and annuities if they hold a Series 6 license, and only through an independent firm

D.   Agents may not engage in options transactions unless the account is held by a non-FINRA-member firm

74.   Marcy was hired as an agent of a FINRA-member firm two years ago. She recently opened a "total financial planning business" at a local strip mall to boost sales of the annuities and mutual funds she sells on behalf of her broker-dealer. Which of the following is a true statement of this situation?

A.   Provided Marcy has the CFP distinction, no notification to the employing broker-dealer is required, but she would have to pass the exams required of investment advisory personnel

B.   Marcy may open a financial planning business, provided she first informs her broker-dealer in writing, without further securities licensing requirements

C.   Provided Marcy has the CFP distinction, no registration as an investment adviser is required, but notification to her employer would still be required

D.   Marcy must meet registration requirements for investment advisers and notify her broker-dealer in writing, who would have the ability to restrict or prohibit this activity

75.   If a customer asked what a Self-Regulatory Organization (SRO) is, you could accurately list all the following as examples of SROs EXCEPT:

A.   The SEC

B.   FINRA

C.   CBOE (Chicago Board Options Exchange)

D.   NASDAQ

Answers

1. ANSWER: A

EXPLANATION: the other three accounts are opened when certain legal documents are presented, e.g. letters of office for the executor of an estate.

2. ANSWER: D

EXPLANATION: the customer typically does provide a bank reference, but there is no requirement to obtain a signature of a bank officer or employee.

3. ANSWER: A

EXPLANATION: such accounts are associated with a limited amount of tax-free income per-year but are not tax-deferred. The custodian must be an adult.

4. ANSWER: D

EXPLANATION: the customer can grant trading authorization/power of attorney to others. Otherwise, only orders from the customer may be accepted.

5. ANSWER: C

EXPLANATION: joint accounts and TOD accounts allow assets to travel without the probate process being involved. This makes the transfer much faster, easier, and less costly.

6. ANSWER: B

EXPLANATION: although the executor would also be required to verify his identify, several other documents are required to retitle the account in the name of the estate or transfer the assets to a new account at another financial institution.

7. ANSWER: D

EXPLANATION: without discretionary authority, a registered representative can take a buy or sell order for a specified amount of a specified security and execute it at an unspecified time that same day. He cannot accept such an order and hold it for more than a day.

8. ANSWER: C

EXPLANATION: a CTR must be filed for any cash transaction or series of transactions exceeding $10,000 in a single day.

9. ANSWER: A

EXPLANATION: broker-dealers are included with banks and other financial institutions under the BSA. FinCEN is a division of the US Treasury Department.

10. ANSWER: A

EXPLANATION: in order, the three stages are placement, layering, and integration.

11. ANSWER: B

EXPLANATION: ACAT is an abbreviation for Automated Customer Account Transfer. Most transfers of securities and cash between broker-dealers are completed through this system.

12. ANSWER: C

EXPLANATION: tax forms are routinely mailed to customers, perhaps, by the CPA who prepares their taxes. Broker-dealers deliver annual 1099s that assist the customer or his CPA in preparing tax filings.

13.   ANSWER: D

EXPLANATION: personal information should be updated whenever the customer informs the registered representative of relevant changes.

14.   ANSWER: B

EXPLANATION: changing to designation/ownership of the account requires principal approval.

15.   ANSWER: C

EXPLANATION: immediate family members are not authorized to place orders or discuss the account. Orders may only be accepted from the individual listed as the account owner and anyone granted power of attorney in writing by the customer.

16.   ANSWER: B

EXPLANATION: moving a 401(k) into an existing or new IRA does not affect the amount the individual can contribute to the account, and is not taxable. Tax problems occur only if the individual takes an early distribution of funds from either a 401(k) or Traditional IRA, which can occur by failing to complete a rollover within 60 days.

17.   ANSWER: B

EXPLANATION: although life insurance policies can be annuitized,

annuities may not be turned into life insurance policies, whether issued by the same or another insurance/annuity company.

18.   ANSWER: B

EXPLANATION: all contributions are assumed to have gone in pre-tax, so all distributions are taxable as ordinary income for the year in which they are withdrawn. Capital gains tax rates are applied only to investments held in taxable accounts.

19.   ANSWER: C

EXPLANATION: reinvested dividends and capital gains distributions are both taxable and added to the investor's cost basis. If the mutual fund has a front-end load, investors avoid those when reinvesting these payments into more shares.

20.   ANSWER: B

EXPLANATION: the first $25,000 Doris takes as a distribution is taxable. Then, because she is many years shy of 59 ½, there is also a 10% penalty on the amount withdrawn, up to the $25,000 of excess over cost basis.

21.   ANSWER: D

EXPLANATION: unlike in a non-qualified annuity, the policyholder may surrender the part of cash value representing net premiums paid into the contract tax-free.

22.   ANSWER: C

EXPLANATION: while sole proprietors have many plan options, the only business entity that may establish a Keogh plan is the sole proprietorship, as opposed to an LLC or corporation.

23.   ANSWER: D

EXPLANATION: contributions to a Roth IRA are non-deductible. Unlike in a Traditional IRA, a person older than 70 can continue to make contributions to the account.

24.   ANSWER: B

EXPLANATION: unlike most investments, the indexed annuity guarantees a minimum rate of return to the contract value annually.

25.   ANSWER: A

EXPLANATION: the SIMPLE plan offers tax-deductible contributions and is open to companies with no other plan and no > 100 employees.

26.   ANSWER: B

EXPLANATION: when an agent of the firm recommends a transaction that is suitable based on an inquiry of the customer's needs, he is meeting his customer-specific obligation. When an agent learns the details, risks, and rewards of an investment, he is meeting his reasonable-basis obligation, as is a broker-dealer vetting new products to assure they may be suitable for at least some investors.

27.   ANSWER: B

EXPLANATION: investment bankers are broker-dealers who raise capital for issuers of securities, including both corporate and municipal government issuers.

28.   ANSWER: A

EXPLANATION: when the issuer receives the proceeds, it is a primary transaction. When any other party receives the proceeds, it is a secondary transaction, or part of a combined offering.

29.   ANSWER: B

EXPLANATION: participating preferred stock pays the stated rate of return as a minimum. Then, if the Board increases dividends to common stock, dividends are also raised for holders of participating preferred shares.

30.   ANSWER: B

EXPLANATION: the holder of a put option has the right to sell the underlying security to the seller of the option at the strike price. Another way to say that is the holder can force the other side to buy the underlying stock at the stated exercise price.

31.   ANSWER: C

EXPLANATION: just as the homeowners in the pool pay their monthly mortgage payments, investors receive payments that are part interest and part principal. In the early years, most of the payments represent interest; later payments represent more and more principal.

32.   ANSWER: D

EXPLANATION: holders of convertible securities accept a lower income payment in exchange for potential upside should the issuer's common stock price increase.

33.   ANSWER: A

EXPLANATION: with the straight-life or life-only settlement option, payments stop when the annuitant dies, unlike when the annuity company guarantees payments for certain period or to more than one individual.

34.   ANSWER: A

EXPLANATION: while there are several settlement options for receiving distributions on the way out, during the accumulation phase the beneficiary receives what the annuitant contributed to the contract upon his/her death or the current contract value, whichever is higher.

35.   ANSWER: C

EXPLANATION: as with a variable annuity contract, the VLI policyholder may invest among the subaccounts as she sees fit.

36.   ANSWER: A

EXPLANATION: banker's acceptances are associated with financing importing/exporting. The U.S. Government issues Treasury Bills. Treasury stock has been repurchased on the open market by the issuer.

37.   ANSWER: C

EXPLANATION: wash sales occur within taxable accounts when a purchase is made 30 days before or after the investor sells the same shares at a loss, triggering a wash sale. So, if investments are made every month, it is likely any sales at a loss will end up being deemed wash sales.

38.   ANSWER: C

EXPLANATION: because they are taxable for the year in which received, reinvested dividends and capital gains distributions are taxable and are added to the investor's cost basis.

39.   ANSWER: B

EXPLANATION: unlike taking distributions from a non-qualified annuity, in a VLI contract surrenders up to the amount of premiums paid are not taxable to the policyholder.

40.   ANSWER: D

EXPLANATION: while the death benefit paid to the beneficiaries is not taxable, the amount is factored into the value of the deceased customer's estate.

41.   ANSWER: C

EXPLANATION: 72(t) allows an individual younger than 59 ½ to take a series of substantially equal payments/distributions and avoid the 10% penalty. Distributions must continue for either 5 years or until the individual is 59 ½, whichever occurs last.

42.   ANSWER: B

EXPLANATION: a 1035 exchange allows the holders of annuities and life insurance to switch policies/contracts without incurring taxation or penalties.

43.   ANSWER: A

EXPLANATION: member firms often allow registered representatives to borrow money from customers who happen to be banks, but the main idea is that the registered rep must follow the firm's written supervisory procedures, which may or may not allow such borrowing.

44.   ANSWER: B

EXPLANATION: such an arrangement must be approved by a principal, and, typically, the firms are related.

45.   ANSWER: C

EXPLANATION: because she is not yet 59 ½, the withdrawal is subject to an additional 10% penalty. The first $142,000 of growth is taxable upon withdrawal; then, the rest is considered a return of cost basis.

46.   ANSWER: A

EXPLANATION: this is why an answer to a test question could say that "accumulation units vary both in number and in value."

47.   ANSWER: C

EXPLANATION: some securities are guaranteed, and agents must be careful to explain the many limits of this feature. On another note, persons in the industry may not guarantee customers a certain profit or against a loss.

48.   ANSWER: D

EXPLANATION: the switch is less suitable if there are fees involved. If surrender charges will be quickly waived, with the individual still several years from retirement, that makes the recommendation more suitable.

49.   ANSWER: A

EXPLANATION: unless you sell, you only establish your cost basis at this point, which is the fair market value as of her date of death.

50.   ANSWER: D

EXPLANATION: Selling mutual funds in a way that prevents investors from receiving available breakpoints is a violation called "breakpoint selling." Just below the next breakpoint, the sales charge would be a higher amount than an on an investment at or slightly above the breakpoint.

51.   ANSWER: D

EXPLANATION: educational seminars may not be based on agents reaching sales targets, and expenses may be reimbursed for the attendee only.

52.   ANSWER: D

EXPLANATION: if anything, the SEC and FINRA have created more paperwork for broker-dealers over the years.

53.   ANSWER: D

EXPLANATION: agents can share commissions if the arrangement is approved by a principal, but agents may not share commissions with customers are any other unregistered person.

54.   ANSWER: C

EXPLANATION: selling short requires broker-dealers to locate the shares to be borrowed, but the short seller typically waits days or weeks before buying to cover. Broker-dealers execute agency transactions among customers regularly.

55.   ANSWER: D

EXPLANATION: this is material inside information. Do not share or use it.

56.   ANSWER: A

EXPLANATION: the BOD establishes the investment policies and restrictions followed by the investment adviser to the fund.

57.   ANSWER: D

EXPLANATION: all withdrawals from a Traditional IRA are taxable. Withdrawals before age 59 ½ are also subject to a 10% penalty, which can be avoided by using the funds in this way, or subject to permanent disability, educational and medical expenses, etc.

58.   ANSWER: C

EXPLANATION: the customer requires a fixed dollar amount monthly. Because we can't predict the value of the shares going forward, we can't predict how long the money will last.

59.   ANSWER: B

EXPLANATION: all mutual funds have operating expenses. Management, transfer agent, and 12b-1 fees are examples of operating expenses. A sales charge is a one-time event based on what the investor does when buying or selling shares of the fund.

60.   ANSWER: D

EXPLANATION: the assets are not frozen, nor is the customer unable to enter trades. When the account is frozen, the customer may not buy on credit for 90 days.

61.   ANSWER: B

EXPLANATION: if a customer sells the stock to pay for the buy side of the transaction, he never sent payment for the purchase. This will lead to a frozen account.

62.   ANSWER: C

EXPLANATION: on the ex-dividend date, purchases are made without the dividend included in the price. The dividend goes to the seller, which is why the buyer doesn't pay for it.

63.   ANSWER: B

EXPLANATION: account statements show all activity in the account, including dividends, interest, deposits, withdrawals, purchases, and sales. They also show the current securities positions and their market values.

64.   ANSWER: D

EXPLANATION: credit ratings are assigned by at least three ratings agencies, who do not always agree on the rating. The CUSIP doesn't change, and the other information is directly connected to the transaction.

65.   ANSWER: D

EXPLANATION: excessive trading is a violation of FINRA rules, so disciplinary action is possible, as is being fired for cause. Customers usually lose money due to churning; therefore, an arbitration claim is also likely.

66.   ANSWER: C

EXPLANATION: agents must forward all written complaints promptly to the appropriate principal/supervisor.

67.   ANSWER: A

EXPLANATION: working outside the firm without their knowledge is a violation of FINRA conduct rules. The other matters are resolved through arbitration.

68.   ANSWER: A

EXPLANATION: making a compromise with a creditor is a reportable event. Failure to update U4 information leads to disciplinary action.

69.   ANSWER: B

EXPLANATION: if the conviction is expunged, she can answer "No" concerning the conviction, but she was still charged with the crime.

70.   ANSWER: C

EXPLANATION: making a compromise with a creditor is a reportable event. Failure to update U4 information leads to disciplinary action, even though the event itself would not have.

71.   ANSWER: A

EXPLANATION: the rule covers work for compensation performed outside the employment with the member firm, not volunteer work.

72.   ANSWER: D

EXPLANATION: joining a health club is outside the scope of the rule.

73.   ANSWER: A

EXPLANATION: agents must notify their employer of their intention to open an account and notify the executing member of their affiliation with their employing firm. They must also notify both sides promptly if the account was opened before the agent became an agent of the member firm.

74.   ANSWER: D

EXPLANATION: if she tried to do this without registration or notification to her firm, she would face several disciplinary problems all at once.

75.   ANSWER: A

EXPLANATION: under the Securities Exchange Act of 1934 SROs register with the SEC. The SEC has authority over SROs; it is not an SRO itself.

1.   All the following statements of custodial accounts (UGMA/UTMA) are accurate EXCEPT:

A.   The original gift to the account is typically treated as a loan to the beneficiary

B.   At the age of adulthood, the former minor controls all assets in the account

C.   The gifts are irrevocable and indefeasible

D.   If the parents object to the opening of the account, it may still be opened by an adult

2.   One of your customers is the custodian for an UTMA (Uniform Transfers to Minors Act) account. The custodian tells you to liquidate 100 shares of ABC preferred stock so that he can fund the purchase of some landscaping equipment for his business, a business which frequently provides financial benefit to the minor named as beneficiary on the account. What should you do at this point?

A.   Execute the unsolicited order without adding any commentary

B.   Inform the custodian that withdrawals are to be used only for the benefit of the minor on the account

C.   Immediately contact the parents of the beneficiary named on the account

D.   Execute the transaction, but inform the custodian that your firm will be forced to represent the child in family court if any funds are used to benefit his business

3.   Which of the following retirement plans allows for the least flexible contributions on behalf of the employer?

A.   Profit sharing

B.   Defined benefit pension

C.   SIMPLE IRA

D.   Money purchase

4.   Which of the following securities is offered with a relatively low rate of income but with potential capital appreciation/purchasing power protection?

A.   Participating preferred stock

B.   Callable preferred stock

C.   Adjustable-rate preferred stock

D.   Convertible preferred stock

5.   In an additional offering of common stock for ABC both the issuing company and early investors will be selling shares to the public for the first time. This offering is known as which of the following?

A.   Primary offering

B.   Secondary offering

C.   Combined offering

D.   Standby offering

6.   When the Securities and Exchange Commission gives an issuer a release or effective date for an offer of securities, this signifies which of the following?

A.   The SEC has deemed the registration statement to be complete

B.   The SEC has deemed the registration statement to be accurate and complete

C.   The SEC has verified the data provided in the financial statements attached to the registration statement

D.   The SEC has allowed the issuer to complete the transaction after reviewing the registration statement

7.   An investment banker acts in a principal capacity in which of the following types of underwriting agreements?

A.   Standby

B.   All or None

C.   Mini-Max

D.   Best Efforts

8.   Best efforts and all-or-none underwritings are also known as which of the following?

A.   Contingency offerings

B.   Secondary offerings

C.   Combined offerings

D.   Shelf offerings

9. Under the Securities Act of 1933 a general obligation bond issued by a state, city, or county government is which of the following?

A. An exempt security

B. An exempt transaction

C. Exempt from anti-fraud regulations

D. An exempt, reporting issuer

10. The rate that banks pay when borrowing from other banks is known as which of the following?

A. The discount rate

B. The fed funds rate

C. The prime rate

D. The lender rate

11. Six-month T-Bills currently yield 2%. If the yield curve is normal, the yield on 5-year T-Notes would most likely be which of the following?

A. 1.5%

B. 2.0%

C. 3.5%

D. 9.0%

12. Six-month T-Bills currently yield 2%. If the yield curve is flat, the yield on 5-year T-Notes would most likely be which of the following?

A. 1.5%

B. 2.0%

C. 3.5%

D. 9.0%

13. Which of the following indicates the risk premium investors demand to purchase debt securities of lesser quality?

A. Yield curve

B. Credit spread

C. Puts/call ratio

D. Case-Shiller Index

14. In terms of the business cycle, which of the following represents the most profoundly bad and sustained economic conditions?

A. Contraction

B. Recession

C. Depression

D. Trough

15. To stimulate the economy, the FOMC would most likely take which of the following actions?

A. Increase marginal tax rates

B. Purchase Treasury securities

C. Increase the reserve requirement

D. Raise the discount rate

16. The claims paying ability of the insurance company's general account is LEAST important when purchasing which of the following?

A. Whole life insurance

B. Variable life insurance

C. Term life insurance

D. Fixed annuity

17. Typically, an individual in his 40s would purchase which of the following?

A. Immediate annuity

B. Fixed annuity

C. Deferred annuity

D. Variable annuity

18. An annuitant chooses a life-with-15-year-period-certain settlement option. If the annuitant lives 17 years, which of the following will result?

A. The contract will pay the annuitant for 15 years

B. The contract will pay the annuitant for 17 years

C. The contract will pay the beneficiary for 2 additional years

D. The beneficiary will receive the death benefit

19.	A tax-exempt money market mutual fund would most likely hold which of the following in its portfolio?

A.	Commercial paper

B.	T-Bills

C.	T-Notes

D.	Tax Anticipation Notes (TANs)

20.	Bowers County School District 207-U will offer a $50,000,000 issue of general obligation bonds in which a portion of the bonds will mature each year over the next 20 years. This type of maturity is known as which of the following?

A.	Term maturity

B.	Series maturity

C.	Serial maturity

D.	Balloon maturity

21.	A so-called "guaranteed bond" is most likely which of the following?

A.	A Treasury Bond

B.	A corporate bond in which the parent of the issuer promises to pay interest, principal, or both if the issuer is unable to

C.	A Treasury Note

D.	A municipal bond

22.	Assessed values and millage rates are associated with which of the following?

A.	Revenue bonds

B.	Treasury bonds

C.	General obligation bonds

D.	Real Estate Investment Trusts

23.	To finance the construction of, or improvement to, which of the following would a revenue—as opposed to a general obligation—bond be issued?

A.	Public high school

B.	Airport

C.	Highway

D.	Library

24.   A fixed-income investor holds $100,000 par value of a corporate bond with a 4% nominal yield. The interest is paid semiannually. Therefore, each year the investor receives income payments of

A. $2,000

B. $4,000

C. $20,000

D. $40,000

25.   A fixed-income investor holds a large position of ABC debentures, which have a nominal yield of 5%. These bonds would trade at a discount if their yield to maturity were which of the following?

A.   4.0%

B.   4.5%

C.   5.0%

D.   5.5%

26.   When a bond is purchased on the secondary market for more than face value, which of the following yields is lowest?

A.   Nominal yield

B.   Current yield

C.   Yield to maturity

D.   Yield to call

27.   When a bond is purchased on the secondary market for less than face value, which of the following yields is lowest?

A.   Nominal yield

B.   Current yield

C.   Yield to maturity

D.   Yield to call

28. Minority shareholders of a public company benefit under which of the following methods of voting?

A. Statutory

B. Cumulative

C. Open outcry

D. Laissez-faire

29. Owners of which type of preferred stock receive increased dividends if the Board of Directors increases the dividend paid to holders of common stock?

A. Cumulative

B. Participating

C. Convertible

D. Adjustable-rate

30. The only type of preferred stock tied to the increased profits of the issuer is

A. Participating

B. Cumulative

C. Convertible

D. Adjustable-rate

31. When portfolio securities are sold within an open-end fund, which of the following is responsible for delivering them?

A. Board of directors

B. Investment adviser

C. Transfer agent

D. Custodian

32. When shares of an open-end fund are inherited and retitled in the name of the deceased's estate, which of the following is responsible for making this change?

A. Board of directors

B. Investment adviser

C. Transfer agent

D. Custodian

33. Which of the following is associated with a closed-end—but not an open-end—fund?

A. Board of directors

B. Investment adviser

C. Use of leverage

D. Daily calculation of NAV

34. Which of the following is a portfolio NOT managed by an investment adviser?

A. Diversified open-end fund

B. Diversified closed-end fund

C. Unit Investment Trust

D. Non-diversified closed-end fund

35. Which of the following direct participation programs is LEAST associated with tax shelter?

A. Oil exploration program

B. Apartment rental program

C. Raw land program

D. New construction program

36. Including warrants with the issuance of a corporate bond benefits the issuer in which of the following ways?

A. It allows them to offer a higher nominal yield on the bonds.

B. It allows them to offer a lower nominal yield on the bonds.

C. It raises the rating on the bonds, typically.

D. It stabilizes the market price of the bonds going forward.

37. Engaging in which of the following options transactions can lead to the investor being forced to purchase shares of stock for more than they are currently trading?

A. Buying call options

B. Selling call options

C. Buying put options

D. Selling put options

38. An investor buys an ABC Apr 45 call @2 when ABC common stock trades @46.50. Therefore,

A. The call is in-the-money

B. The call is out-of-the-money

C. The investor is out-of-the-money

D. The investor is at-the-money

39. How would a registered representative best explain interest rate risk to a fixed-income investor?

A. It is the risk that as interest rates drop, investors reinvest at lower rates.

B. It is the risk that as interest rates rise, bond market prices drop.

C. It is the risk that interest rates will remain flat over the investor's holding period.

D. It is the risk that as interest rates drop, callable bonds will be redeemed early.

40. Zero coupon bonds allow investors to avoid _____ risk, but also are associated with more _____ risk than coupon bonds.

A. Reinvestment, Call

B. Reinvestment, Interest Rate

C. Purchasing Power, Credit

D. Default, Interest Rate

41. The risk common to investing in either developed or emerging markets is, primarily, which of the following?

A. Political

B. Business

C. Currency exchange

D. Legislative

42.   An investor holding shares of an intermediate-term investment-grade corporate bond fund is most exposed to which of the following risks?

A.   Interest rate risk

B.   Default risk

C.   Reinvestment risk

D.   Purchasing power risk

43.   Which of the following investment risks is reduced through diversification?

A.   Market risk

B.   Purchasing power risk

C.   Legislative risk

D.   Interest rate risk

44.   Investors may execute short sales within which of the following?

A.   Cash accounts

B.   Margin accounts

C.   Retirement accounts

D.   All choices listed

45.   Which of the following presents the greatest risk to the investor?

A.   Establishing a long stock position within a margin account

B.   Purchasing a put option without owning the underlying stock

C.   Purchasing stock and writing a covered call position against it

D.   Establishing a short stock position within a margin account

46.   Common stock trading for less than $1 per share is associated with which of the following?

A.   New York Stock Exchange

B.   NASDAQ

C.   OTC Bulletin Board

D.   The secondary market for closed-end funds

47.   The requirements for an issuer to have its stock traded through the OTC Bulletin Board include which of the following?

A.   A minimum price of $4 per share

B.   A minimum of 3 market makers

C.   Remaining current in SEC filings

D.   All choices listed

48.   Transactions in all the following debt securities must be reported to TRACE except:

A.   Government agency bonds

B.   US Treasury securities (other than savings bonds)

C.   Convertible bonds

D.   Mortgage-backed securities

49.   When acting in a principal capacity with a retail customer, a broker-dealer is compensated by

A.   Selling securities to the customer at the bid

B.   Purchasing securities from the customer at a markdown

C.   Purchasing securities from the customer at a markup

D.   Buying securities from the customer at the ask

50.   Secondary market transactions in all the following currently settle regular-way at "T + 2," EXCEPT:

A.   General obligation bonds

B.   Treasury bonds

C.   Corporate bonds

D.   Common stock

51.   Secondary market transactions in which of the following currently settle regular-way at "T + 2"?

A.   Listed options

B.   Treasury Notes

C.   Municipal bonds

D.   Treasury Bonds

52.   When calculating the earnings per share for common stock, which of the following shares are included in the calculation?

A.   Issued

B.   Treasury

C.   Outstanding

D.   All choices listed

53.   Which of the following reports required under the Securities Exchange Act of 1934 are audited by an independent CPA?

A.   8K

B.   10Q

C.   10K

D.   All choices listed

54.   An investor holds 1,000 shares of ABC purchased for $50 per share. If ABC declares a 3:1 split, the investor's position will be which of the following?

A.   3,000 shares @50

B.   1,000 shares @50

C.   3,000 shares @16.67

D.   1,000 shares @150

55.   Which of the following is NOT true concerning discretionary accounts?

A.   Each transaction entered pursuant to discretionary authority must be first approved by the customer.

B.   The manual signatures of anyone with discretion over the account must be maintained by the member.

C.   Discretionary authorization must be signed by the customer and received by the member before the first transaction made using the authority may be entered.

D.   Such accounts must be scrutinized for suitability and other regulatory concerns.

56. For which of the following account types is a limit placed on annual contributions?

A. UTMA or UGMA

B. Coverdell Education Savings Account

C. 529 Savings Plan

D. Options Trading Account

57. To the employer, which of the following plans leaves the greatest flexibility for contributions?

A. Defined benefit pension plan

B. Profit sharing plan

C. SIMPLE plan

D. Money purchase plan

58. Which of the following retirement plans requires an annual certification by an actuary that funding levels are sufficient?

A. 401(K)

B. Defined benefit pension

C. Money purchase

D. All choices listed

59. A customer in a new margin account buys 1,000 shares of ABC, making the required Reg T deposit. ABC now trades for $24 a share, and the debit balance in the account is $10,000. What is the lowest price per-share that ABC could fall to without triggering a maintenance call?

A. $20.00

B. $27.00

C. $10.50

D. $13.33

60. What is the minimum maintenance for a short position in a margin account?

A. 75% of the market value

B. 50% of the market value

C. 30% of the market value

D. 25% of the market value

61.   When a customer buys or sells securities through a member firm, a trade confirmation must be delivered

A.   By the end of the trading day

B.   By the settlement date

C.   By the end of the next business day

D.   By the fifth day following execution of the trade

62.   For a transaction in a debt security that is subject to redemption before maturity (callable), the trade confirmation must contain which of the following?

A.   a statement to the effect that such debt security may be redeemed in whole or in part before maturity

B.   a statement that such a redemption could affect the yield represented

C.   a statement that additional information is available upon request

D.   all choices listed

63.   A registered representative of a member firm helps to identify and persuade 10 investors to buy into an LLC run primarily by a friend of his. Which of the following statements is correct relating to this activity?

A.   Because LLC interests are not securities, no notification to the employing member is required.

B.   The registered representative must provide notification to the employer, including whether compensation is or was received for his activities.

C.   Only if receiving compensation for this activity is the registered representative required to notify the employing member.

D.   Provided the securities are not publicly traded, no notification to the employing member is required.

64.   Which of the following securities may be guaranteed as to interest, principal, or dividends?

A.   A US Treasury bond

B.   A corporate bond

C.   A municipal bond

D.   Any of these choices

65. Why are rules against "breakpoint selling" necessary?

A. Because breakpoint schedules are not required to be disclosed in the prospectus for the open-end fund

B. Because at certain dollar amounts just below the next breakpoint the investor would pay a higher sales charge than if investing just a few dollars more

C. Because most investors are unsophisticated

D. Because the amount invested does not affect the registered representative's compensation either way

66. The preliminary prospectus or "red herring" typically lacks which of the following information, which will be finalized in the final prospectus?

A. Where the security will be listed for trading

B. Whether the security will be listed for trading

C. The public offering price

D. Important risks to securities holders

67. The Securities Exchange Act of 1934 grants the SEC all the following EXCEPT

A. Authority to pursue violators of insider trading and other anti-manipulation rules in civil court

B. Authority to require the registration of stock exchanges and national securities associations

C. Authority to require investment advisers receiving compensation to register

D. Authority to require public companies to file reports disclosing material information connected to their securities

68. You would expect which of the following types of management company to be associated with the highest risk to the investor?

A. Diversified open-end fund

B. Non-diversified open-end fund

C. Diversified closed-end fund

D. Non-diversified closed-end fund

69. In which of the following cases has the individual filed or updated his U4 information with the Central Registration Depository (CRD) properly?

A. An applicant answers "No" to questions concerning criminal charges and convictions based on a conviction of misdemeanor shoplifting that occurred 12 years earlier

B. A registered representative updates his U4 information 60 days after making a formal compromise with a creditor

C. An applicant answers "No" to questions concerning criminal charges and convictions based on a felony conviction that was expunged

D. An applicant answers "Yes" to questions concerning criminal charges and convictions based on a misdemeanor conviction of possession of stolen property that occurred 15 years earlier

70. If an associated person is barred by FINRA and fined $90,000, what would most likely happen if the individual refused or was unable to pay the fine?

A. The case would be referred to the appropriate district attorney or attorney general for criminal prosecution

B. FINRA would pursue the individual in civil court

C. The individual would be unable to re-enter the securities industry without satisfying the demand for payment

D. FINRA would pursue the individual via arbitration

71. If an associated person or member firm is disciplined and fined by FINRA, the maximum fine to be imposed is

A. $2,500

B. $100,000

C. Three times the amount involved but no > $1 million

D. Unlimited

72. What is the most severe disciplinary action FINRA can take against a member firm?

A. Indictment

B. Suspension

C. Denial

D. Expulsion

73.   If the SEC determines that an offer of securities has or will operate as a fraud on investors, they may take all the following actions EXCEPT:

A.   Seek an injunction/restraining order against the issuer in the appropriate court of law

B.   Issue a Cease & Desist order against the issuer

C.   Order the forcible liquidation of the issuer's assets

D.   Initiate administrative action against the issuer

74.   Under Code of Procedure, rule violations are handled under all the following EXCEPT:

A.   Offer of Settlement

B.   Mediation

C.   Acceptance, Waiver and Consent

D.   Contested Hearing

75.   A respondent appeals the decision to fine him $75,000 and suspend his registration for 6 months to the National Adjudicatory Council (NAC). If he is dissatisfied with their decision, his next appeal would be to the

A.   SEC

B.   Federal courts

C.   FINRA Code of Arbitration

D.   Any of these choices

Answers

1.   ANSWER: A

EXPLANATION: contributions to UGMA/UTMA accounts are not to be revoked or paid back as loans.

2.   ANSWER: B

EXPLANATION: the account is to be used only for the benefit of the minor.

3.   ANSWER: D

EXPLANATION: the money purchase plan requires the employer to make a specified contribution each year. A defined benefit pension plan must be sufficiently funded, as verified by an actuary.

4.   ANSWER: D

EXPLANATION: in exchange for the possible capital appreciation, holders of convertible preferred stock accept a lower rate of income, as do holders of convertible bonds.

5.   ANSWER: C

EXPLANATION: if the issuer receives the proceeds, it is a primary offer. If anyone other than the issuer receives the proceeds, it is a secondary offer. If both are happening, it is a combined offer.

6.   ANSWER: D

EXPLANATION: the SEC neither approves nor disapproves of any securities or offer of securities, and this disclaimer must be included with a preliminary or final prospectus.

7.   ANSWER: A

EXPLANATION: a standby underwriting is associated with a rights offering in which an underwriter promises to subscribe to any shares that remain outstanding to ensure all offered securities will be sold.

8.   ANSWER: A

EXPLANATION: in these contingency offerings, money may be returned to investors if a specified amount is not raised. Broker-dealers, therefore, must segregate these payments from their own assets.

9.   ANSWER: A

EXPLANATION: an exempt security is offered without any paperwork being filed. An exempt transaction requires some notice to be filed concerning the basic details of the transaction.

10.   ANSWER: B

EXPLANATION: banks borrow from the Federal Reserve at the discount rate. Banks lend funds to each other at the fed funds rate. The prime rate is offered to creditworthy borrowers on unsecured loans.

11.   ANSWER: C

EXPLANATION: in a positive/normal yield curve, yields rise with maturities. A yield of 9%, however, would make the curve unrealistically steep, which is why the question used the phrase "most likely."

12.   ANSWER: B

EXPLANATION: when yields are similar across all maturities, the yield curve is said to be flat.

13.   ANSWER: B

EXPLANATION: with the same maturities, bonds of different credit quality have different yields. The difference is known as a yield spread or credit spread. For example, if 10-year A-rated corporate bonds yield 5% when 10-year Treasury Notes yield 2.5%, the credit spread is 2.5%.

14.   ANSWER: C

EXPLANATION: depressions are less common and more severe than recessions. Both represent diminished economic activity, unemployment, deflation, and falling interest rates.

15.   ANSWER: B

EXPLANATION: increasing the discount rate or the reserve requirement are actions taken to fight inflation. Increasing marginal tax rates is not only the wrong policy action, but also part of fiscal—rather than monetary—policy and outside the Fed's authority.

16.   ANSWER: B

EXPLANATION: in both variable annuity and variable life insurance contracts purchase payments are allocated to investment accounts rather than the insurance company's general account.

17.   ANSWER: C

EXPLANATION: there is not enough information provided to choose either fixed or variable, but given his age, we can rule out an immediate annuity. An immediate annuity is for someone at least 59 ½ years old.

18.   ANSWER: B

EXPLANATION: the contract will pay for the longer of his life or 15 years. If he dies after 5 years, payments continue for 10 years. If he lives longer than 15 years, payments cease at his death.

19.   ANSWER: D

EXPLANATION: tax-exempt money market mutual funds purchase tax-exempt, short-term notes issued by municipalities.

20.   ANSWER: C

EXPLANATION: most municipal bonds are issued with this type of maturity. This way, if interest rates drop, they can refinance a large amount of principal at a lower rate, having paid off a small percentage of the principal up to that point.

21.   ANSWER: B

EXPLANATION: US Treasuries are not typically described as "guaranteed bonds," which are rare situations as described in the answer to the question.

22.   ANSWER: C

EXPLANATION: revenue bonds are self-supporting, backed by revenues from the project being built with the proceeds of the bonds. GO bonds are backed by property (local), income and sales taxes (state), primarily.

23. ANSWER: B

EXPLANATION: of these choices, only an airport would generate sufficient revenues to service the debt.

24. ANSWER: B

EXPLANATION: 4% of $100,000 = $4,000 of interest income. The "paid semiannually" detail was designed to distract.

25. ANSWER: D

EXPLANATION: yields/interest rates are inverse to bond prices. For the bond price to be down, the yield/interest rate must be up, and vice versa.

26. ANSWER: D

EXPLANATION: the yields are always in this order—nominal, current, YTM, YTC. For a premium bond, that is given in descending order; opposite for a discount bond, in which the yields rise in that same order.

27. ANSWER: A

EXPLANATION: discount bonds are associated with yields that rise from nominal to current yield, YTM, and, finally, YTC.

28. ANSWER: B

EXPLANATION: if minority shareholders nominate a candidate and pool all their votes for that one candidate, abstaining on the rest, they can sometimes get one of their own on the Board of Directors. The shareholders with bazillions of shares prefer statutory voting, where votes cannot be stacked for one candidate.

29. ANSWER: B

EXPLANATION: participating preferred stockholders receive increased dividends if the BOD raises the dividend paid to common stockholders. Note that the words "cumulative" and "adjustable-rate" are tempting to one who doesn't know their definitions. Cumulative preferred stock has dividends go in arrears if missed. Adjustable-rate preferred pays a dividend rate tied to an interest rate, a payment which, therefore, fluctuates.

30. ANSWER: C

EXPLANATION: as a rule, preferred stock has no stake in increased profits of the issuer. The exception is convertible preferred stock, whose value is tied to the value of the issuer's common stock. This makes the preferred stock less sensitive to interest rates, and explains the lower dividend paid to the investor. Hybrid securities are another name for convertible preferred stock and convertible bonds.

31. ANSWER: D

EXPLANATION: the custodian maintains possession/control of a mutual fund's cash and securities. The transfer agent deals with shareholders of the fund.

32. ANSWER: C

EXPLANATION: the transfer agent handles name changes and processes all redemption and purchase orders entered by shareholders of the fund.

33.   ANSWER: C

EXPLANATION: closed-end funds often issue preferred shares and bonds, trying to increase the return for the common shareholders. This is a form of leverage, which is not used by open-end funds.

34.   ANSWER: C

EXPLANATION: a UIT is supervised by the trustee but unmanaged—not traded the way mutual fund portfolios are.

35.   ANSWER: C

EXPLANATION: raw land is about appreciation. There are no tax advantages to holding raw land.

36.   ANSWER: B

EXPLANATION: this feature makes the bonds more attractive. Therefore, investors accept lower yields.

37.   ANSWER: D

EXPLANATION: the seller of a put option agrees to buy the stock at the strike price if the holder of the put exercises his option. A put is exercised only if the market price is below the strike price.

38.   ANSWER: A

EXPLANATION: the premium does not determine whether the call is in the money. The call is in the money as soon as the market price exceeds the exercise/strike price of the call. Investors have gains or losses; they do not go in or out of the money.

39.   ANSWER: B

EXPLANATION: interest rate risk is the risk that rates will rise, pushing bond prices down. Reinvesting at lower rates = reinvestment risk.

40.   ANSWER: B

EXPLANATION: there are no coupon payments to reinvest at varying rates, but zero-coupon bonds are highly sensitive to interest rate changes.

41.   ANSWER: C

EXPLANATION: either way, the currency of the issuing companies is not the US dollar.

42.   ANSWER: D

EXPLANATION: the "intermediate-term" reduces interest rate risk, and the "investment-grade" reduces default risk. Bonds are always subject to purchasing power/inflation risk.

43.   ANSWER: C

EXPLANATION: unsystematic risks, including legislative and business risk, are reduced through diversification.

44.   ANSWER: B

EXPLANATION: short sales are executed exclusively in margin—not cash, retirement, or UTMA— accounts.

45.   ANSWER: D

EXPLANATION: short sales subject the investor to unlimited loss, as do naked calls. When buying a security, 100% of the price paid is the maximum the investor can lose.

46.   ANSWER: C

EXPLANATION: NYSE and NASDAQ de-list stocks trading below a certain price, while stocks trading on the non-NASDAQ OTC often trade for pennies, or fractions-of-pennies per-share.

47.   ANSWER: C

EXPLANATION: the performance of the company is not relevant when trading on the OTCBB. The issuer must only stay current in its SEC filings required under the Securities Exchange Act of 1934.

48.   ANSWER: C

EXPLANATION: transactions in the other three securities must be reported to TRACE.

49.   ANSWER: B

EXPLANATION: in these transactions the BD buys securities at a markdown, or sells them at a markup. These are prices based on the inside market but representing a profit to the broker-dealer.

50.   ANSWER: B

EXPLANATION: secondary market trades in US Treasuries settle T + 1 or next-day.

51.   ANSWER: C

EXPLANATION: common stock, corporate bonds, and municipal bonds settle currently at T + 2 (which was T + 3 for many years).

52.   ANSWER: C

EXPLANATION: the only shares that matter are the outstanding shares, whether we're talking about dividends, EPS, or voting.

53.   ANSWER: C

EXPLANATION: of the four reports over the year, only the annual or 10K report is audited. An 8K is used to release material information in between scheduled 10Q and 10K reports.

54.   ANSWER: C

EXPLANATION: the total amount does not change. Rather, the position changes to reflect more shares at a lower cost basis.

55.   ANSWER: A

EXPLANATION: the customer grants discretionary authority over the account. Then, until she revokes it, the agent may enter transactions without first discussing them with her.

56.   ANSWER: B

EXPLANATION: for the CESA, an annual contribution limit is imposed. For a 529 Savings Plan, a lifetime contribution limit is imposed.

57.   ANSWER: B

EXPLANATION: the SIMPLE offers flexibility, too, but the profit sharing plan always involves discretionary contributions from the employer.

58.   ANSWER: B

EXPLANATION: in a defined benefit pension plan, an actuary certifies annually that funding levels are sufficient to pay expected benefits in the future.

59.   ANSWER: D

EXPLANATION: to calculate the account at maintenance divided the debit balance by .75.

60.   ANSWER: C

EXPLANATION: 30% for a short position; 25% for a long position.

61.   ANSWER: B

EXPLANATION: trade confirmations are delivered by settlement of the transaction.

62.   ANSWER: D

EXPLANATION: all three are required.

63.   ANSWER: B

EXPLANATION: if he fails to provide notification, he engages in a prohibited practice known as selling away, an abbreviation for "selling away from the firm."

64.   ANSWER: D

EXPLANATION: sometimes a third party guarantees the payment of interest, principal or dividends. GO and US Treasury bonds are guaranteed as to the payment of interest and principal.

65.   ANSWER: B

EXPLANATION: without this rule, many agents could game the system without the customer realizing she could have saved money by investing just a few dollars more.

66.   ANSWER: C

EXPLANATION: a range of possible Public Offering Prices is given on the cover of the preliminary prospectus. The final POP is given in the final prospectus only.

67.   ANSWER: C

EXPLANATION: the SEC requires investment advisers to register under the Investment Advisers Act of 1940.

68.   ANSWER: D

EXPLANATION: closed-end funds use leverage, which increases their risk. Then, a non-diversified fund is riskier than one that is diversified.

69.   ANSWER: D

EXPLANATION: even if a conviction is expunged, FINRA expects the applicant/registrant to answer "Yes" to the question of being charged with the crime. The questions ask if the applicant has ever been charged with, pled guilty or no contest to, or been convicted of any felony, or any misdemeanor related to the industry.

70.   ANSWER: C

EXPLANATION: FINRA would not allow such a person to re-enter the industry without satisfying the fine and, perhaps, waiting 10 years to re-apply.

71.   ANSWER: D

EXPLANATION: there is no limit to how high the fine could be.

72.   ANSWER: D

EXPLANATION: expulsion for a member firm, bar for an individual.

73.   ANSWER: C

EXPLANATION: the SEC is not a court of law. They could petition a judge to order liquidation of the firm's assets.

74.   ANSWER: B

EXPLANATION: mediation is used to avoid an arbitration proceeding.

75.   ANSWER: A

EXPLANATION: the appeals go, first, to the NAC, then, the SEC, and, finally, the federal courts.

Glossary

8K: a special report of a material event required under the Securities Exchange Act of 1934.

10Q: a quarterly report required under the Securities Exchange Act of 1934.

10K: an annual report required under the Securities Exchange Act of 1934.

100% no-load fund: a mutual fund charging neither a sales charge nor a 12b-1 fee.

1035 contract exchange: a tax-free exchange of one annuity contract for another, one life insurance policy for another, or one life insurance policy for an annuity. The contracts do not have to be issued by the same company.

1099-DIV: a tax form sent to investors showing dividends and capital gains distributions from a mutual fund for the tax year.

12b-1 fee: annual fee deducted quarterly from a mutual fund's assets to cover distribution costs, e.g., selling, mailing, printing, advertising. An operating expense, unlike the sales charge that is deducted from the investor's check.

200-day moving average: average closing price over the previous 200 days for a stock or an index.

401(k): qualified defined contribution plan typically offering employer-matched contributions.

403(b): qualified plan for tax-exempt, non-profit organizations.

(Section) 457 plan: qualified plan for state and municipal government employees.

529 Plans: education savings plans offering tax-deferred growth and tax-free distributions at the federal level for qualified educational expenses. Pre-paid tuition plans allow customers to purchase a certain number of tuition credits at today's prices to be used at a school within a state. 529 Savings Plans allow customers to contribute up to the current gift tax exclusion without paying gift taxes. Earnings grow tax-deferred and may be used for qualified education expenses (more than just tuition) later without federal taxation. States can tax the plans—so know the customer's situation!

72(t): an exemption under IRS tax code allowing people to take money from retirement plans including annuities without paying penalties, even though they aren't 59½ yet.

75-5-10 rule: diversification formula for an open- or closed-end fund advertising itself as "diversified." 75% of the portfolio must have no more than 5% of assets invested in any one security, and no more than 10% of a company's outstanding shares may be owned.

A

A-Shares: mutual fund shares sold with a front-end sales load/charge. Lower annual expenses than B- and C-shares.

Account at maintenance: the point at which a customer's equity in a margin account is just high enough to avoid a margin call.

Account Executive (AE): another name for a registered representative or agent.

Account Statement: document sent to a broker-dealer customer showing the recent value of all cash and securities, plus all recent activity in an investment account.

Accounts Payable: what the company owes its vendors, a current liability.

Accounts Receivable: what customers owe a corporation, a current asset.

Accredited Investors: large institutional investors, and individuals meeting certain income or net worth requirements allowing them to participate in, for example, a private placement under Reg D of the Securities Act of 1933, or hedge funds.

Accrued Interest: the interest that the buyer of a debt security owes the seller. Bond interest is payable only twice a year, and the buyer will receive the next full interest payment. Therefore, the buyer owes the seller for every day of interest since the last payment up to the day before the transaction settles.

Accumulation Stage/Period: the period during which contributions are made to an annuity, during which the investor holds "accumulation units."

Accumulation Units: what the purchaser of an annuity buys during the pay-in or accumulation phase, an accounting measure representing a proportional share of the separate account during the accumulation/deposit stage.

Ad Valorem: property tax. Literally "as to value."

Additional Takedown: the piece of the spread that goes to the various members of the syndicate when the bonds they've been allotted are sold.

Adjustable Rate Preferred Stock: preferred stock whose dividend is tied to another rate, often the rate paid on T-bills.

Adjusted Gross Income (AGI): earned income plus passive income, portfolio income, and capital gains. The amount upon which we pay income tax.

Adjustment Bond: another name for an "income bond," on which the issuer may skip interest payments without going into default.

Administrator: (1) the securities regulator of a state; (2) a person or entity authorized by the courts to liquidate an estate.

ADR/ADS: American Depository Receipt/Share. A foreign stock on a domestic market. Toyota and Nokia are two examples of foreign companies whose ADRs trade on American stock markets denominated in dollars. Carry all the risks of owning stocks, plus "currency exchange risk."

Advance Refunding/Pre-refunding: issuing new bonds and depositing part of the proceeds in escrow more than 90 days ahead of the first legal call date on the existing bond issue.

Affiliated Person or Affiliates: anyone in a position to influence decisions at a public corporation, including board members (directors), officers (CEO, CFO), and large shareholders (Warren Buffett at Coca-Cola or Wells Fargo) owning 10%+ of any class of the issuer's securities.

Age-Based Portfolio: also known as a lifecycle fund, a fund whose asset allocation shifts automatically over time to match the goal and time horizon of the investors in the fund. Many 529 Savings Plans offer age-based portfolios, similar to target-date retirement funds.

Agency Issue (Agency Bond): a debt security issued by an agency of the US Government such as GNMA or by a government sponsored enterprise, such as FNMA or FHLMC. Agency issues promote the public good through increased home ownership or increased credit to farmers.

Agency Transaction: a securities transaction in which the broker-dealer acts as an agent for the buyer or seller, completing the transaction between the customer and another party.

Agent: an individual representing a broker-dealer or issuer in effecting/completing transactions in securities for compensation. What you will be after passing your exams and obtaining your securities license.

Aggressive Growth: an investment objective associated with a willingness to bear a high amount of investment risk in exchange for potential appreciation in the value of the investment, e.g. emerging market or sector funds.

Agreement Among Underwriters: a document used by an underwriting syndicate bringing an issue of securities to the primary market. This document sets forth the terms under which each member of the syndicate will participate and details the duties and responsibilities of the syndicate manager.

AIR: Assumed Interest Rate. Used to determine the value of annuity units for annuities and the death benefit for variable life contracts.

All or None: a type of underwriting in which the syndicate will cancel the offering if a sufficient dollar amount is not raised as opposed to being responsible for the unsold shares (as in a "firm commitment"). Also, a type of order on the secondary market in which the investor wants the order to be canceled if the broker cannot acquire the full number of shares on one attempt.

A.M. Best: a ratings service for insurance company claims paying ability/financial strength.

American Stock Exchange (AMEX): a private, not-for-profit corporation that handles roughly 20% of all securities trades in the U.S. One of the big secondary markets, along with NYSE, and the various NASDAQ markets.

American Style: an option that can be exercised at any time up to expiration.

And Interest: term used for a debt security that trades subject to accrued interest, as opposed to "flat."

Annual Compliance Review: a broker-dealer's annual compliance review process that is mandatory for principals and registered representatives.

Annual Shareholder Report: a formal statement (10K) issued by a corporation to the SEC and shareholders discussing the company's results of operations, challenges/risks facing the company, any lawsuits against the company, etc. Required by the Securities Exchange Act of 1934.

Annuitant: the person who receives an annuity contract's distribution.

Annuitize: the process of changing the annuity contract from the "pay-in" or accumulation phase to the "pay-out" or distribution phase. Defined benefit pension plans generally offer their pensioners either a lump sum payment or the option to annuitize and receive monthly payments going forward.

Annuity Units: what the annuitant holds during the pay-out phase. Value tied to AIR.

Annuity: a contract between an individual and an insurance company that either guarantees income for the rest of the individual's life or allows him to invest his purchase payments into various subaccounts in return for a lump-sum or periodic payment to the insurance company.

Anticipation Notes: short-term obligations of a municipality often held by tax-exempt money market mutual funds.

Appreciation: the increase in an asset's value that is not subject to tax until realized.

Arbitrage: taking advantage of the disparity in pricing between two things. In a proposed merger, some traders bet against the acquiring company and bet on the company to be acquired in an arbitrage trade. Or, some specialized traders buy or sell convertible bonds versus the underlying security when there is a temporary price disparity.

Arbitration: settling a dispute without going to an actual court of law.

Arbitration Award: the decision rendered through FINRA Arbitration.

Articles of Incorporation: documents that a corporation files with the state disclosing the name and purpose of the business, its address, and how many shares of stock the corporation is authorized to issue.

Ask, Asked: the higher price in a quote representing what the customer would have to pay/what the dealer is asking the customer to pay. Ask/asked is also called "offer/offered."

Assessed Value: the value of property used to calculate property tax. For example, a home with a market value of $300,000 might have an assessed value of $150,000 against which the rate of tax is applied.

Asset Allocation: maintaining a percentage mix of equity, debt, and money market investments, based either on the investor's age (strategic) or market expectations (tactical).

Asset-Backed Securities: or ABS, bonds or notes backed by financial assets, e.g., credit card receivables or auto loans.

Asset Coverage: a measure from the balance sheet showing how well an issuer can meet its debt servicing obligations.

Assets: something that a corporation or individual owns, e.g., cash, investments, accounts receivable, inventory, etc.

Assignment Notice: what the seller of an option receives when the buyer exercises the contract.

Associated Person: a registered representative or principal of a FINRA member firm.

Assumed Interest Rate: see AIR.

At-The-Market: an offer of securities to be sold over time, often at different prices to different investors depending on when the investment is made.

Auction Market: the NYSE, for example, where buyers and sellers simultaneously enter competitive prices. Sometimes called a "double auction" market because buying and selling occur at the same time.

Auction Rate Securities: debt securities with a variable rate of interest or preferred stock with a variable dividend rate that is re-set at regular auctions.

Authorized Stock: the number of shares a company can issue by its corporate charter. Can be changed by a majority vote of the outstanding shares.

Automated Customer Account Transfer (ACAT): a system that provides instructions among broker-dealers for transfer and delivery of customer assets.

Automatic Reinvestment: a feature offered by mutual funds allowing investors to automatically reinvest dividend and capital gains distributions into more shares of the fund, without paying a sales charge.

Average Cost Basis: a method of figuring cost basis on securities for purposes of reporting capital gains and/or losses. The investor averages the cost for all purchases made in the stock, as opposed to identifying shares to the IRS when selling.

B

B-Shares: mutual fund shares charging a load only when the investor redeems/sells the shares. Associated with "contingent deferred sales charges." B-shares have higher operating expenses than A-shares by way of a higher 12b-1 fee.

Backdating: pre-dating a letter of intent (LOI) for a mutual fund to include a prior purchase in the total amount stated in the letter of intent. LOIs may be backdated up to 90 calendar days.

Back-end Load: a commission/sales fee charged when mutual fund or variable contracts are redeemed. The back-end load declines gradually, as described in the prospectus. Associated with "B-shares" and, occasionally, "C-shares."

Backing Away: a violation in which a market maker fails to honor a published firm quote to buy or sell a security at a stated price.

Backup Withholding: a required withholding from an investment account that results when the customer refuses/fails to provide a tax identification number.

Balance of Payments: imports versus exports and also financial transactions. A surplus = more $ coming into the country. A deficit = more $ flowing out of the country.

Balance of Trade: imports versus exports. A surplus= more exports than imports. A deficit = more imports than exports.

Balance Sheet: a financial statement of a corporation or individual showing financial condition (assets vs. liabilities) at a moment in time.

Balance Sheet Equation: Assets – Liabilities = Shareholders' Equity, or Assets = Liabilities + Shareholders' Equity.

Balanced Fund: a fund that maintains a mix of stocks and bonds. Close to an asset allocation fund except that an asset allocation fund would typically hold a larger % in money market instruments.

Balloon Maturity: a bond issue in which some principal is paid in the early years, with most due at end of the term.

Bank Qualified Municipal Bond: municipal bonds that allow banks to deduct 80% of the interest costs incurred to buy them.

Bankers' Acceptance (BA): money-market security that facilitates importing/exporting. Issued at a discount from face-value. A secured loan.

Bar: the most severe sanction that FINRA can impose on an individual, effectively ending his/her career.

Basis: a synonym for yield. A bond trading at a "550 basis" trades at a price making its yield to maturity 5.5%.

Basis Points: a way of measuring bond yields or other percentages in the financial industry. Each basis point is 1% of 1%. Example: 2% = .0200 = 200 basis points. 20 basis points = .2% or 2/10ths of 1%.

Basis Quote: the price at which a debt security can be bought or sold, based on the yield. A bond purchased at a "5.50 basis" is trading at a price that makes the yield 5.5%.

Bear Market: a market for stock or bonds in which prices are falling and/or expected to fall.

Bear Spread: a call or put spread in which the investor benefits if the underlying instrument's value drops. For example, an investor who buys the ABC Aug 50 call and sells the ABC Aug 45 call establishes a bear spread. The spread would also happen to be a "credit spread" in this case.

Bearer Bond: an unregistered bond that pays principal to the bearer at maturity. Bonds have not been issued in this way for over two decades, but they still exist on the secondary market.

Bearish, Bear: an investor who takes a position based on the belief that the market or a security will fall. Short sellers and buyers of puts are "bearish." They profit when stocks go down. Seriously.

Beneficiary: the one who benefits. An insurance policy pays a benefit to the named beneficiary. IRAs and other retirement plans, including annuities, allow the owner to name a beneficiary who will receive the account value when the owner dies. A 529 plan names a beneficiary, who will use the money for educational expenses someday.

Best Efforts: a type of underwriting leaving the syndicate at no risk for unsold shares, and allowing them to keep the proceeds on the shares that were sold/subscribed to. Underwriters act as "agents," not principals, in a best-efforts underwriting.

Best Execution: obligation to fill customer orders at the best available price, while considering other factors, e.g. execution quality.

Bid Form: document used to submit a competitive bid to the issuer of municipal securities.

Bid: what a dealer is willing to pay to a customer who wants to sell. Customers sell at the bid, buy at the ask.

Blend Fund: a fund that is neither a growth fund nor a value fund but a blend of both.

Blind Pool Offering: a direct participation program in which the sponsor does not identify the assets of the partnership.

Block: a large number of securities or dollar amount presented as one transaction. For purposes of different rules "block transactions" are defined differently.

Blue Chip: stock in a well-established company with proven ability to pay dividends in good economic times and bad. Lower risk/reward ratio than other common stock.

Blue Sky: state securities law, tested on the Series 63, 65, and 66 exams.

Board of Directors: the group elected by shareholders to run a mutual fund or a public company and establish corporate management policies.

Bona Fide: a Latin phrase meaning authentic, true. Or, made or presented without deception or fraud. A bona fide stock certificate, for example, as opposed to a bogus certificate made on a color laser printer.

Bond: a debt security that offers interest payments—but not a share of profits—to the investor.

Bond Anticipation Note (BAN): a short-term municipal debt security backed by the proceeds of an upcoming bond issue. Often found in tax-exempt money market funds.

Bond Buyer: daily publication covering the municipal securities industry.

Bond Certificate: a paper or electronic document stating the details of a bond, e.g., the issuer's name, par value or face amount, interest rate, maturity date, and call date (if any).

Bond Counsel: tax law firm that guides a municipal issuer through the legal process of issuing bonds and determines the tax treatment of the interest based on research and knowledge of the Internal Revenue Code.

Bond Fund: a mutual fund with an objective of providing income while minimizing capital risk through a portfolio of bonds.

Bond Indenture: the contract spelling out the rights of bondholders and the obligations of the bond issuer.

Bond Point: 1% of a bond's par value. 1 bond point = $10.

Bond Ratio: a measure from the balance sheet showing how leveraged the issuer is. Found by taking long-term debt and comparing to (dividing by) total capitalization to show what % of the issuer's capitalization was derived from borrowed money vs. equity.

Bond Rating: an evaluation of a bond issue's chance of default published by companies such as Moody's, S&P, and Fitch.

Bond Resolution: a document that legally authorizes the process of issuing municipal bonds for a specific purpose.

Bond Swap: taking a loss on a bond and replacing it with a substantially different bond to avoid a wash sale.

Bonus Annuity: an annuity with special riders/enhancements attached.

Book Entry: a security maintained as a computer record rather than a physical certificate. All U.S. Treasuries and many mutual funds are issued in this manner.

Box Counts: regular check of a broker-dealer's securities versus what is indicated on its stock record.

Brady Bonds: bonds issued by emerging-market nations and collateralized by U.S. Treasury securities to keep yields down and help such nations pay off their debt to the developed world.

Branch Office: any location identified by any means to the public or customers as a location at which the member conducts an investment banking or securities business. The small Charles Schwab or E-Trade office at the nearby mall or office complex is a "branch office." Registered with a Form BR.

Breakeven: the price at which the underlying security is above or below the strike price of the option by the amount of the premium paid or received. For example, an ABC Aug 50 call @2 has a "breakeven" of $52 for both the buyer and the seller.

Breakpoint: a discounted sales charge or "volume discount" on mutual fund purchases offered on A-shares at various levels of investment.

Breakpoint Selling: preventing an investor from achieving a breakpoint. A violation.

Broad-Based Index: an index such as the S&P 500 or the Value Line Composite Index that represents companies from many industries.

Broker: an individual or firm that charges a commission to execute securities buy and sell orders submitted by another individual or firm.

Broker Call Loan Rate: interest rate that broker-dealers pay when borrowing on behalf of margin customers.

Brokered CDs: certificates of deposit offered by selling agents and paying competitive yields among a larger universe of banks.

Broker's Broker: a firm that holds no inventory and executes securities transactions exclusively with other broker-dealers and not with public investors.

Broker-dealer: a person or firm in the business of completing transactions in securities for the accounts of others (broker) or its own account (dealer).

Bull Market: a market for stocks or bonds in which prices are rising and/or expected to rise.

Bulletin Board: OTC stocks too volatile and low-priced for NASDAQ. Stocks trading on the OTCBB do not have to meet requirements for profitability or number of shares and shareholders.

Bullish, Bull: an investor who takes a position based on the belief that the market or a security will rise. Buyers of stock and call options are bullish.

Business Cycle: a progression of expansions, peaks, contractions, troughs, and recoveries for the overall (macro) economy.

Business Risk: the (unsystematic) risk that the company whose stock or bond you own will not be successful as a business. Competition, poor management, obsolete products/services are all examples of business risk.

Buy Limit: an order to buy a security at a price below the current market price, executable at a specified price or lower/better.

Buy Stop: an order to buy a security at a price above the current market price triggered only if the market price hits or passes through the stop price.

Buy-to-Cover: a purchase order entered by a short seller to close out the short stock or options position.

C

C-corporation: a business entity that does not provide for flow-through to the owners but, rather, is associated with the double taxation of profits/dividends.

C-Shares: often called "level load" because of the high 12b-1 fee. Usually involve no front-end load, sometimes have a contingent deferred sales charge for 1 or 1.5 years. Appropriate for shorter-term investing only.

Call (n.): a contract that gives the holder the right to buy something at a stated exercise price.

Call (v.): to buy.

Call Premium: the price paid and received on a call option. Or, the amount above the par value paid by the issuer to call/retire a bond.

Call Protection: the period during which a security may not be called or bought by the issuer, usually lasting five years or more.

Call Provision: agreement between the issuer and the bondholders or preferred stockholders that gives the issuer the ability to repurchase the bonds or preferred stock on a specified date or dates before maturity.

Call Risk: the risk that a callable bond or preferred stock will be forcibly called when interest rates fall, reducing the investor's total return.

Call Spread: buying and selling a call on the same underlying instrument where the strike price, the expiration, or both are different.

Callable: a security that may be purchased/called by the issuer as of a certain date, e.g., callable preferred, callable bonds. Generally, pays a higher rate of return than non-callable securities, as it gives the issuer flexibility in financing.

Cancel and rebill: fixing a trade error by placing the transaction in the proper customer account.

Cap: the maximum that an equity indexed annuity contract's value can rise in a year.

Capital: money raised from investors by issuing stocks, bonds, etc.

Capital Appreciation: the rise in an asset's market price. The objective of a "growth stock investor."

Capital Appreciation Bond: another name for a zero-coupon bond.

Capital Assets: items of value including securities, real estate, artwork, collectibles, etc.

Capital Gain: the amount by which the proceeds on the sale of a stock, bond, or other capital asset exceed your cost basis. If you sell a stock for $22 and have a cost basis of $10, the capital gain or profit is $12.

Capital Gains Distribution: distribution from fund to investor based on net capital gains realized by the fund portfolio. Holding period determined by the fund and assumed to be long-term.

Capital Loss: loss incurred when selling a capital asset for less than the purchase price. Capital losses offset an investor's capital gains and can offset ordinary income to a certain amount.

Capital Preservation: a conservative investment goal placing safety-of-principal above all else. Associated with U.S. Treasuries, GNMA securities, and bank CDs.

Capital Risk: the risk that an investor will lose some or all his invested principal.

Capital Structure: the make-up of a corporation's financing through equity (stock) and debt (bonds) securities.

Capping: a form of market manipulation that involves trying to decrease the value of a security, often so that call sellers will not be called. A violation.

Carrying Broker: a firm that acts as an introducing broker-dealer's back office, handling customer assets and clearing transactions through a clearing broker-dealer.

Cash Account: an investment account in which the investor must pay for all purchases no later than 2 business days following regular way settlement. Not a margin account.

Cash Dividend: money paid to shareholders from a corporation's current earnings or accumulated profits.

Cash Equivalent: a security that can readily be converted to cash, e.g., T-bills, CDs, and money market funds. Listed with cash as a current asset on a company's balance sheet.

Cash Flow: the cash provided or used by a business over a reporting period through operating, investing, and financing activities.

Cash Settlement: same-day settlement of a trade requiring prior broker-dealer approval. Not the "regular way" of doing things.

Cash Value: the value of an insurance policy that may be accessed by the policyholder through a loan or a surrender.

Catastrophic Call: a provision in a municipal bond issue providing for an automatic call of the bonds due to a disaster, e.g., hurricane, flood, or loss of tax-exempt status, etc.

Catch-Up Contribution: the extra amount that a person 50 or older can contribute annually to a retirement account.

Central Registration Depository or **CRD:** the central licensing and registration system for the U.S. securities industry and its regulators, operated by FINRA. Agents, principals, and member firms are assigned CRD numbers. Broker-Check provides disclosure information from a registrant's CRD information.

CEO: chief executive officer. Individual ultimately responsible for a corporation's results.

Certificate of Deposit or **CD:** a (usually) longer-term deposit with a bank or other financial institution that typically offers compounded interest.

Certificate of Limited Partnership: a document filed by the general partner of a direct participation program with a state disclosing who the partnership is and what it does.

Certificate of Participation: or "COP," a municipal security paying a share of lease revenues to the investor as opposed to a bond backed by such revenues from a project.

CFO: chief financial officer. Individual in charge of a corporation's financial activities.

Check Kiting: financial crime in which the criminal exploits the lag time involved with clearing checks by writing bogus checks on two or multiple accounts.

Check-writing Privileges: a privilege offered by mutual funds, especially money market funds, by which investors can automatically redeem shares by writing checks.

Chinese Wall: the separation that is supposed to exist between the investment banking department and the traders and registered representatives to prevent insider trading violations.

Churning: excessive trading in terms of frequency and size of transactions designed to generate commissions without regard for the customer.

Class: for example, all MSFT calls, or all IBM puts.

Clean-Up Price: a price outside the current quote for a security that is used to execute a block transaction.

Clearing Agencies: firms that clear/process transactions between clearing member firms. Includes both clearing agencies and depositories.

Clearing Broker: a member of the clearing agencies who clears trades for itself and other firms.

Clearing Corporation: a financial institution that compares member transactions (or reports to members the results of exchange comparison operations), clears those trades and prepares instructions for automated settlement of those trades, and often acts as an intermediary in making those settlements. For example, the Options Clearing Corporation or the National Securities Clearing Corporation.

Clearing Rate: the interest rate established by auction in connection with auction rate securities.

CLN: construction loan note, a type of municipal note backed by the proceeds from a construction loan for a new building project.

Closed-end Fund: an investment company that offers a fixed number of shares that are not redeemable. Shares are traded on the secondary market at a price that could be higher or lower than NAV (or even the same as NAV).

CDO: Collateralized Debt Obligation. A structured asset-backed security paying cash flows to investors in a predetermined sequence, based on how much cash flow is collected from the package of assets owned

CMO: Collateralized Mortgage Obligation: A complicated debt security based on a pool of mortgages or a pool of mortgage-backed securities. Pays interest monthly but returns principal to one tranche at a time.

Code of Arbitration: FINRA method of resolving disputes (usually money) in the securities business. All decisions are final and binding on all parties.

Code of Procedure: FINRA system for enforcing member conduct rules.

Collateral Trust Certificate: a bond secured by a pledge of securities as collateral.

Collection Ratio: the amount of taxes collected by a municipality divided by the amount of taxes assessed.

Combination Privilege: allows investors to combine purchases of many funds within the mutual fund family to reach a breakpoint/reduced sales charge.

Combined Offering: an offering of securities in which both the issuer and other large shareholders will be selling to the public.

Commercial Paper: a short-term unsecured loan to a corporation. Issued at a discount from the face value. See "money market securities."

Commissions: a service charge an agent earns for arranging a security purchase or sale.

Common Stock: the most "junior security," because it ranks last in line at liquidation. An equity or ownership position that usually allows the owner to vote on major corporate issues such as stock splits, mergers, acquisitions, authorizing more shares, etc.

Competitive, Sealed Bids: process used for most general obligation bonds in which the underwriting business is awarded to the syndicate that turns in the lowest cost of borrowing to the issuer.

Compliance Department: the principals and supervisors of a broker-dealer responsible for making sure the firm adheres to SEC, exchange, and SRO rules.

Concession: the amount that the seller of a new issue of municipal bonds receives, whether a syndicate member or a selling group member.

Conduct Rules: an SRO's rules for member conduct that, if violated, may lead to sanctions and fines.

Conduit Theory (Tax Treatment): a favorable tax treatment achieved if a company (REIT, mutual fund) distributes 90%+ of net income to the shareholders.

Confirmation: document stating the trade date, settlement date, and money due/owed for a securities purchase or sale. Delivered on or before the settlement date.

Consolidated Quotation System (CQS): system used for trading in the third market.

Consolidation: a stock trading in a narrow price range, trading "sideways."

Constant Dollar Plan: a defensive investment strategy in which an investor tries to maintain a constant dollar amount in the account, meaning that securities are sold if the account value rises and purchased if it goes down.

Constructive Receipt: the date that the IRS considers an investor to have put his grubby little hands on a dividend, interest payment, retirement plan distribution, etc. For example, IRA funds are not taxable until "constructive receipt," which usually starts somewhere between age 59½ and 70½.

Consumer Price Index (CPI): a measure of inflation/deflation for basic consumer goods and services. A rising CPI represents the greatest risk to most fixed-income investors.

Consumer: for purposes of Regulation S-P, a consumer is someone considering a financial relationship with a firm.

Contingency Offering: an offer of securities that will be canceled if a certain amount is not raised, with investor funds going into an escrow account from which they are returned if the offer is, in fact, canceled. A mini-max offering is an example of a contingency offering, as is an all-or-none offering.

Contingent Deferred Sales Charge: associated with B-shares, the sales charge is deducted from the investor's check when she redeems/sells her shares. The charge is deferred until she sells and is contingent upon when she sells—the sales charges decline over time, eventually disappearing after 7 years, at which point the B-shares become A-shares.

Continuing Commissions: the practice of paying retired registered representatives and principals commissions on business written while still employed with the firm, e.g., 12b-1 fees on mutual funds and annuities.

Continuous Net Settlement: method used by clearing agencies that involves the netting of all purchases and sales in a security or options contract for a member firm, as opposed to forcing firms to settle with the other side of each trade. After all trading ceases for the day, a member firm is either a net buyer or net seller of ABC common stock and either owes money or securities to the clearing corporation.

Contraction: phase of the business cycle associated with general economic decline, recession or depression.

Contribution: the money you put into a retirement plan subject to the limits imposed by the plan.

Control Relationship: for municipal securities, a situation in which a person is in a position of control both for the issuer and any underwriter. For broker-dealers, a situation in which the member executes a transaction in a security of an issuer related to the broker-dealer. Both situations require full disclosure of the nature of the conflict.

Conversion Ratio: the number of shares of common stock that the holder of a convertible bond or preferred stock would receive upon conversion. A bond "convertible at $50" has a conversion ratio of 20 (20 shares of stock per $1,000 par value).

Conversion/Exchange Privilege: a feature offered by many mutual funds whereby the investor may sell shares of one fund in the family and use the proceeds to buy another fund in the family at the NAV (avoiding the sales load). All gains/losses are recognized on the date of sale/conversion for tax purposes.

Convertible: a preferred stock or corporate bond allowing the investor to use the par value to "buy" shares of the company's common stock at a set price.

Cooling-off Period: a minimum 20-day period that starts after the registration statement is filed with the SEC. No sales or advertising allowed during this period, which lasts until the effective or release date.

Core Inflation: The CPI minus volatile items such as food and energy prices.

Corporate Financing Department or **CFD:** department of FINRA reviewing the terms of compensation for member firms involved with a securities offering.

Corporation: the most common form of business organization, in which the business's total value is divided among shares of stock, each representing an ownership interest or share of profits.

Correspondence: under FINRA rules = a communication sent to no more than 25 retail investors in a 30-day period.

Cost Basis: the amount that has gone into an investment and has been taxed already. For stock, includes the price paid plus commissions. For a variable annuity, equals the after-tax contributions into the account. Investors pay tax only on amounts above their cost basis, and only when they sell or take "constructive receipt."

Countercyclical: an industry or stock that performs better during bad economic times, e.g. employment placement agencies.

Counterparty Risk: the risk that the other party to a derivatives contract or repurchase agreement will not be able to meet its obligations upon exercise.

Coupon Rate: a.k.a. "nominal yield." The interest rate stated on a bond representing the percentage of the par value received by the investor each year. For example, a bond with a 5% "coupon rate" or "nominal yield" pays $50 per bond to the holder per year. Period.

Coverdell Education Savings Account: a tax-advantaged account whose earnings may be withdrawn tax-free for qualified education expenses.

Covered Call: a position in which an investor generates premium income by selling the right to buy stock the investor already owns, and at a set price.

CPI: Consumer Price Index, a measure of inflation/deflation for basic consumer goods and services. A rising CPI represents the greatest risk to most fixed-income investors.

Credit Agreement: document that must be signed by a margin customer in which all finance charges are explained in connection to the margin account.

Credit Enhancement: for example, an insured municipal bond backed by MBIA or AMBAC.

Credit Risk: a.k.a. "default" or "financial" risk. The risk that the issuer's credit rating will be downgraded, or that the issuer will default on a debt security.

Credit Spread: the different yields offered by bonds of similar maturities with different credit ratings, e.g. the spread between yields on Treasuries and junk bonds.

Cumulative Preferred Stock: preferred stock where missed dividends go into arrears and must be paid before the issuer may pay dividends to other preferred stock and/or common stock.

Cumulative Voting: method of voting whereby the shareholder may take the total votes and split them up any way he chooses. Said to benefit minority over majority shareholders. Total votes are found by multiplying the number of shares owned by the number of seats up for election to the Board of Directors.

Currency Exchange Risk: the risk that the value of the U.S. dollar versus another currency will have a negative impact on businesses and investors.

Currency Transaction Report (CTR): a reported submitted to the U.S. Treasury by a broker-dealer when a customer deposits more than $10,000 cash.

Current Refunding: refunding a bond issue where the existing bonds are redeemed within 90 days.

Current Yield: annual interest divided by market price of the bond. For example, an 8% bond purchased at $800 has a current yield of 10%. $80/$800 = 10%.

CUSIP Number: an identification number/code for a security.

Custodial Account: an investment account in which a custodian enters trades on behalf of the beneficial owner, who is usually a minor child.

Custodian: maintains custody of a mutual fund's securities and cash. Performs payable/receivable functions for portfolio purchases and sales. In an UGMA, the custodian is the adult named on the account who is responsible for the investment decisions and tax reporting.

Customer: a person who opens an investment account with a broker-dealer.

Customer Identification Program (CIP): requirements to probably identify customers when opening accounts and documenting how the customer's identity was verified by the broker-dealer, e.g. passport or other government-issued photo ID.

Cyclical Industry: a term of fundamental analysis for an industry that is sensitive to the business cycle. Includes: steel, automobiles, mining and construction equipment.

D

Dark Pools of Liquidity: large institutional orders for securities that are concealed from the public and executed typically on the fourth market.

Dated Date: the date on which interest begins to accrue on a new issue of bonds.

Dealer: a person who buys or sells securities for his/its own account, taking the other side of the trade. A dealer buys securities from and sells securities directly to a customer, while a broker merely arranges a trade between a customer and another party.

Death Benefit: the amount payable to the beneficiary of a life insurance (or annuity) contract, minus any outstanding loans and/or unpaid premiums.

Debenture: an unsecured bond backed by the issuer's ability to pay. No collateral.

Debit Balance: what the margin customer owes the broker-dealer in a long margin account.

Debt Limit: a self-imposed restriction on the total amount of general obligation debt that an issuer may have outstanding at any one time.

Debt per Capita: a measure that shows a bond analyst how much general obligation debt is outstanding divided by the number of residents of the municipality.

Debt Security: a security representing a loan from an investor to an issuer. Offers an interest rate in return for the loan, not an ownership position.

Debt Service: the schedule for repayment of interest and principal on a debt security.

Debt Statement: a statement in which a municipal issuer lists all of its outstanding debts.

Debt Ratio: a measure from the balance sheet showing how leveraged an issuer is. Found by comparing total liabilities to total assets. Similar to debt-to-equity ratio, another measure of long-term solvency.

Debt-to-Equity Ratio: a measure from the balance sheet showing how leveraged an issuer is. Found by comparing total liabilities to stockholders' equity.

Declaration Date: the date the Board declares a dividend.

Default: when the issuer of the bond is unable to pay interest or principal.

Default Risk: the risk that the issuer of the bond will not pay interest and/or principal. Measured by S&P and Moody's.

Defensive Industry: a company that can perform well even during rough economic times. For example, food and basic clothing represent two products purchased through both good and bad economic times; therefore, stocks of food and basic clothing companies would be "defensive" investments. a/k/a non-cyclical industry.

Deferred Annuity: an annuity that delays payments of income, installments, or a lump sum until the investor elects to receive it. Usually subject to surrender charges during the deferral period.

Deferred Compensation Plan: a non-qualified business plan that defers some of the employee's compensation until retirement. Usually for highly compensated employees.

Deficiency Letter: SEC notification of additions or corrections that an issuer must make to a registration statement before the offering can be cleared for distribution.

Defined Benefit Pension Plan: a qualified corporate pension plan that defines the benefit payable to the retiree.

Defined Contribution Plan: a qualified corporate plan that defines the contribution made on behalf of the employee, e.g., profit sharing, 401(k).

Deflation: a general drop in the level of prices across the economy, usually connected to an economic slump.

Delivery: the change in ownership of a security that takes place when the transaction settles. The seller delivers the securities purchased to the buyer.

Department of Enforcement: FINRA enforcers of the member conduct rules, a group you never want to hear from, especially by certified mail.

Depository Trust Company or **DTC:** centralized depository of securities involved with the final settlement process of a transaction in which securities and cash are moved to the appropriate parties.

Depreciation: spreading the cost of a fixed asset over its useful life by taking a series of non-cash charges on the income statement.

Depreciation Recapture: a tax collected when an asset that had been used for depreciation is sold for a capital gain.

Depression: a more severe version of a recession, e.g. America in the 1930s.

Designated Examining Authority: another name for an SRO or Self-Regulatory Organization, e.g., CBOE or FINRA.

Designated Market Maker: market participant charged with maintaining a fair and orderly market in the stocks they quote. DMMs must quote at the national best-bid-or-offer (NBBO) a specified percentage of the time, and facilitate price discovery throughout the day as well as at the open, close and in periods of significant imbalances and high volatility.

Developed Market: an international market that is more stable than an "emerging market," e.g. Japan as opposed to Brazil.

Developmental Program: an oil or gas drilling program in an area in which reserves are known to exist.

Diluted EPS: earnings per share after factoring in the dilution that would occur due to warrants and convertible securities.

Dilution of Equity: a reduction in the earnings per share of common stock, often due to convertible bonds or preferred stock being converted to common stock.

Direct Debt: the general obligation debt of a municipal issuer for which it is solely responsible.

Direct Participation Program (DPP): an investment in a limited partnership or similar pass-through entity in which the investor receives a share of income and expenses.

Direct Registration: a method of holding securities on the books of the transfer agent without the need for physical certificates to be issued to the investor.

Direct Transfer: moving the proceeds of a tax-deferred account to another custodian rather than the individual taking possession or control of the assets.

Discount: the difference between the (lower) market price for a bond and the par value.

Discount Bond: any bond traded below the par value, e.g., @97.

Discount Rate: interest rate charged by the 12 Federal Reserve Banks to member banks who borrow from the FRB.

Discretion: authority given to someone other than the account owner to make trading decisions for the account.

Discretionary: an order placed in which the agent/broker-dealer chose the asset or amount of shares to be purchased or sold.

Discretionary Income: the money left over after meeting all living expenses; what an investor has available for saving and investing based on his statement of cash flow.

Disintermediation: a situation in which money is being withdrawn from banks and savings & loans by depositors to reinvest the funds into higher yielding money market instruments (Treasury bills, certificates of deposit, money market funds). Disintermediation would occur when interest rates at savings banks are lower than money market instruments. The cause could be that the FRB is pursuing a "tight money policy," which is causing a rise in interest rates, creating a demand for the higher yielding money market securities.

Display Book: system of matching electronic orders automatically.

Distribution (Annuity) Stage: the period during which an individual receives payments from an annuity.

Distribution Expenses: the cost of distributing/marketing a mutual fund, including selling, printing prospectuses and sales literature, advertising, and mailing prospectuses to new/potential customers. Covered by sales charges/12b-1fees.

Distribution: the money you take out of a retirement plan.

Distributor: a FINRA member firm that bears distribution costs of a fund, profiting from the sales charges paid by the investors; a.k.a. "sponsor," "underwriter," "wholesaler."

Diversification: purchasing securities from many different issuers, or industries, or geographic regions, to reduce "nonsystematic risk."

Diversified Mutual Fund: an open- or closed-end fund hat complies with an SEC rule so that no more than 5% of assets are invested in a stock or bond and so that the fund does not own more than 10% of any issuer's outstanding stock. Often called the "75-5-10 rule," where the 75 means that only 75% of the assets must be diversified this way just to keep things nice and simple.

Dividend: money paid from profits to holders of common and preferred stock whenever the Board of Directors declares it.

Dividend Payout Ratio: the dividends paid divided by the earnings per share. Stocks with high dividend payout ratios are typically found in "equity income" funds.

Dividend Yield: annual dividends divided by market price of the stock. Equivalent to current yield for a debt security.

Dividend/Income Distributions: distributions from a fund to the investors made from net investment income. Typically, may be reinvested at the NAV to avoid sales charge.

DK notice: a notice sent to the other broker-dealer when a firm does not recognize a transaction.

Do Not Reduce (DNR): a buy-limit or sell-stop order that will not be reduced for the payment of a cash dividend.

Dollar Cost Averaging: investing fixed dollar amounts regularly, regardless of share price. Usually results in a lower average cost compared to average of share prices, as investors' dollars buy majority of shares at lower prices.

Donor: a person who makes a gift of money or securities to another.

Double Barreled: a municipal bond backed by both the issuer's full faith and credit and revenues.

Dow Jones Industrial Average (DJIA): an index comprised of 30 large cap stocks weighted by share price.

Due Bill: document sent by a broker-dealer when a dividend payment was sent to the wrong party and belongs to the broker-dealer's customer.

Due Diligence: meeting between issuer and underwriters with the purpose of verifying information contained in a registration statement/prospectus.

Durable Power of Attorney: authorizing another party to make legal, health-related, and financial decisions if the individual should become incapacitated.

DVP: a form of settlement in which payment will be made when the securities involved in the transaction are delivered and accepted.

E

Earned Income: income derived from active participation in a business, including wages, salary, tips, commissions, and bonuses. Alimony received is also considered earned income. Earned income can be used toward an IRA contribution.

Earnings Available to Common: net income after the preferred stock dividend is deducted. Used to find EPS.

Earnings per Share (EPS): the amount of earnings or "net income" available for each share of common stock. A major driver of the stock's price on the secondary market.

Eastern/Undivided Account: a syndicate account in which participants are responsible for a percentage of all bonds, even if they sell their allotment.

EDGAR: SEC repository for public company filings including annual reports and prospectuses. Stands for Electronic Data Gathering, Analysis, and Retrieval system.

Education IRA: earlier name for the Coverdell Education Savings Account in which after-tax contributions may be made to pay qualified education expenses for the beneficiary.

Effective Date: date established by SEC as to when the underwriters may sell new securities to investors; a.k.a. "release date."

Effective Tax Rate: a taxpayer's total tax divided by his taxable income, sometimes called an "average rate of tax."

Elective Deferrals: the amount of each paycheck a retirement plan participant directs the employer to deposit into his account, with that amount often matched in, for example, a 401(k) or SIMPLE plan up to a certain amount.

Electronic Communications Networks (ECNs): electronic trading platforms that allow institutional investors to buy and sell securities directly.

Eligibility: a section of ERISA that outlines who is/is not eligible to participate in a qualified plan. Those at least 21 years old who have worked "full time" for one year (1,000 hours or more) are eligible to participate in the plan.

Emerging Market: the financial markets of a developing country. Generally, a market with a short operating history, not as efficient or stable as developed markets. For example, Brazil, China, and India.

Employer's Contribution: the contributions to a retirement account made by the employer on behalf of an employee, whether matching or otherwise. As opposed to the participant's elective deferrals.

Endorsement: the process of signing over title of a security to another party due to a sale, gift, donation, etc.

Equipment Trust Certificate: a corporate bond secured by a pledge of equipment, e.g., airplanes, railroad cars.

Equity: ownership, e.g., common and preferred stock in a public company. In a margin account, the difference between the market value of stock held long and the debit balance.

Equity Funds: mutual funds that primarily invest in equity securities.

Equity Income Fund: a mutual fund that purchases common stocks whose issuers pay consistent and, perhaps, increasing dividends. The fund has less volatility than an equity fund with "growth" as an objective.

Equity-Indexed Annuity: an insurance product offering a minimum guaranteed rate and the opportunity to participate in some of the gains of an index, usually the S&P 500.

Equity Options: standardized options giving the holder the right to buy or sell the underlying stock at a set price (strike/exercise price).

Equity REIT: a Real Estate Investment Trust that owns and manages real estate, as opposed to a mortgage REIT.

ERISA: the Employee Retirement Income Security Act of 1974 that governs the operation of most corporate pension and benefit plans.

Escrow Account: an account held by an escrow agent/bank on behalf of, for example, investors subscribing to a contingent offer in which proceeds will be returned if the offer of securities is canceled. Also used by homeowners to automatically pay insurance and taxes.

Escrow Receipt: evidence that securities are held by an escrow agent, sometimes used when selling call options to show the broker-dealer that the underlying shares can be delivered if the contract is assigned.

Escrowed to Maturity: a municipal bond issue in which the issuer has deposited funds sufficient to retire the bonds on the original maturity date with an escrow agent/bank.

ESOP or an Employee Stock Option Plan: a benefit plan in which the company allows all workers to purchase company stock at a discount and through a payroll deduction. The stock and the dividends/cap gains generated on it grow tax-deferred, like a 401(k) plan.

Estate: a legal entity that represents all assets held by a deceased person at the moment he died—or the assets of a debtor-in-possession, known as the "bankruptcy estate."

Estate Tax: a tax on estates over a certain amount, often called the "death tax."

ETF: or "Exchange-Traded Fund," a fund that trades on an exchange, typically an index fund tracking the S&P 500, the Dow Jones Industrial Average, etc. Unlike an open-end index fund, the ETF allows investors to sell short, trade throughout the day, and even purchase shares on margin.

ETN: an exchange-traded note, an unsecured debt security with interest payments made at maturity and tied to an underlying benchmark.

European Style: an option that may be exercised at expiration only.

Excess Equity: the amount of equity above the Reg T requirement in a margin account.

Exchange-Listed Security: a security that has met listing requirements to trade on an exchange such as NYSE, AMEX, or NASDAQ.

Exchange Rate: a comparison of the relative strength between two currencies.

Exchanges: any electronic or physical marketplace where investors can buy and sell securities. For example, NASDAQ, NYSE, AMEX.

Exclusion Ratio: method of determining which part of an annuity payment is taxable, and which part represents the tax-free return of the annuitant's after-tax cost basis.

Ex-Date: two days before the Record Date for corporate stock. The date upon which the buyer is not entitled to the upcoming dividend. Note that for mutual funds, this date is established by the board of directors, usually the day after the Record Date.

Executing Broker: a firm that executes transactions for an introducing broker-dealer.

Execution Quality: for purposes of determining best execution, execution quality considers aspects other than price, such as a market maker's fill rate and speed of execution.

Exempt Security: a security not required to be registered under the Securities Act of 1933. Still subject to anti-fraud rules; not subject to registration requirements, e.g., municipal bonds and bank stock.

Exempt Transaction: a transactional exemption from registration requirements based on the way the security is offered and sold, e.g., private placements under Reg D.

Exercised: an option that the buyer has used to purchase or sell securities at the strike price.

Exercise Notice: notification sent by a firm to the OCC when a customer exercises an options contract.

Expansion: phase of the business cycle associated with increased activity.

Expected Return: the calculation of what a stock should return. When calculated by CAPM, involves the risk-free rate, the beta, and the overall expected return for the market.

Expense Ratio: a fund's expenses divided by/compared to average net assets. Represents operating efficiency of a mutual fund, where the lower the number the more efficient the fund.

Expiration: when an option contract ceases to trade.

Expiration Date: the final day of trading for an options contract.

Extension Risk: the risk that interest rates will rise, and the holder of a CMO or mortgage-backed security will have to wait longer than expected to receive principal.

F

Face Amount: the amount that a debt security pays out upon maturity.

Face-Amount Certificate: a debt security bought in a lump-sum or through installments that promises to pay out the stated face amount, which is higher than the investor's purchase price.

Face-Amount Certificate Company: one of the three types of investment company under the Investment Company Act of 1940. Issues face-amount certificates. Not a UIT or "management company."

Fail to Deliver: when a customer of a broker-dealer sells stock but fails to deliver by settlement.

Fair and Accurate Credit Transactions or FACT Act: federal legislation allowing consumers to monitor their credit reports and attempting to reduce identity theft.

Fair and Orderly Market: what the specialist at the NYSE is charged with maintaining.

FDIC (Federal Deposit Insurance Corporation): federal government agency that provides deposit insurance for member banks and prevents bank and "thrift" failures. Bank deposits are currently insured up to $250,000, a number that could have changed by the time you read this definition. A trip to your local bank will give you the updated number.

Feasibility Study: a study put together by a consulting firm analyzing the economic merits of a facility to be financed by revenue bonds.

Fed Funds Rate: interest rate charged on bank-to-bank loans. Subject to daily fluctuation.

Federal Covered: a security or an investment adviser whose registration is handled exclusively by the federal government (SEC) and subject only to notice filings at the state/blue sky level.

Federal Farm Credit System: organization of privately owned banks providing credit to farmers and mortgages on farm property.

Federal Open Market Committee (FOMC): council of Federal Reserve officials that sets monetary policy based on economic data. The money supply is tightened to fight inflation, loosened to provide stimulus to a faltering economy.

Federal Reserve Board: a seven-member board directing the operations of the Federal Reserve System.

Federal Reserve System: the central bank system of the United States, with a primary responsibility to manage the flow of money and credit in this country.

FEIN: or Federal Employer Identification Number, a tax identification number used by various entities including a corporation, estate, or trust.

FHLMC: a.k.a. "Freddie Mac." Like big sister Fannie Mae, a quasi-agency, public company that purchases mortgages from lenders and sells mortgage-backed securities to investors. Stock is listed on NYSE.

Fiduciary: someone responsible for the financial affairs of someone else, e.g., custodian, trustee, or registered rep in a discretionary account.

FIFO: first-in-first-out. An accounting method for valuing a company's inventory or for determining the capital gain/loss for an investor. Using FIFO, an investor indicates that, for example, the 100 shares of ABC that were sold at $55 are the first 100 shares that he purchased.

Filing Date: the date that an issuer files a registration statement with the SEC for a new issue of securities.

Final Prospectus: document delivered with final confirmation of a new issue of securities detailing the price, delivery date, and underwriting spread.

Financial Risk: another name for "credit risk," or the risk that the issuer of a bond could default.

Financial Statement: a report of a company's finances in terms of financial condition, profits, and cash flow, made public through a prospectus or 10K filing by a reporting company.

FinCEN: U.S. Treasury's "Financial Crimes Enforcement Network." Suspicious Activity Reports must be provided to FinCEN if a broker-dealer notices activity in accounts that appears suspicious or possibly related to fraud or money laundering activities.

FINRA (Financial Industry Regulatory Authority): the SRO formed when the NASD and the NYSE regulators merged.

Firm Commitment: an underwriting in which the underwriters agree to purchase all securities from an issuer, even the ones they failed to sell to investors. Involves acting in a "principal" capacity, unlike in "best efforts," "all or none," and "mini-max" offerings.

Firm Element: annual continuing education requirement for a registered representative.

Firm Quote: a quote by a dealer representing a price at which the dealer is prepared to trade.

First Market: another name for the exchange market, where the NYSE is the model.

First-In-First-Out (FIFO): an accounting method used to value a company's inventory or to determine capital gains/losses on an investor's securities transactions.

Fiscal Policy: Congress and President. Tax and Spend.

Fiscal Year: the twelve-month period used by an entity for preparing financial reports, e.g. income statements.

Fixed Annuity: an insurance product (not a security) in which the annuitant receives fixed dollar payments, usually for the rest of his or her life.

Fixed Exchange Rate: a system in which a country ties the value of its currency to a commodity—such as gold or silver—or to another currency, such as the peso or the dollar.

Fixed Income Clearing Corporation: a subsidiary of the Depository Trust Clearing Corporation that clears transactions in corporate, municipal, and government debt securities among member firms.

Fixed-Income Security: a security promising a stated stream of income to the investor, e.g., a bond as opposed to common stock.

Flat: term used for a debt security that trades without accrued interest, e.g. a zero coupon or a bond currently in default.

Flat Yield Curve: when interest rates for short-, intermediate-, and long-term bonds are similar.

Flexible Premium: a premium that is flexible. Characteristic of "universal" insurance. Allows the policyholder to adjust the premiums and death benefit according to changing needs.

Floating Rate Currency: a system in which a country allows the value of its currency to rise and fall with supply and demand and also influenced by central bank policies, e.g. the Federal Reserve Board's monetary policy.

Floor Broker: an individual who works for a member of the exchange filling orders for the firm and receiving a commission per-order. Present during open-outcry auctions to open and close each session.

Flow of Funds: a statement for a revenue bond issue showing the priority of payments to be made with revenue generated from the facility.

FNMA: a.k.a. "Fannie Mae." Like little brother Freddie Mac, Fannie buys mortgages from lenders and sells mortgage-backed securities to investors. A quasi-agency, a public company listed for trading on the NYSE.

FOMC: the Federal Reserve Board's Federal Open Market Committee. Sets short-term interest rates by setting discount rate, reserve requirement and buying/selling T-bills to/from primary dealers.

Foreign Currencies: the actual currencies of various nations traded through Forex.

Forex: an exchange for trading foreign currencies, e.g. British Pound, Swiss Franc, and Yen, etc.

Foreign Currency Options: standardized options in which the underlying instrument is a foreign currency, e.g., the yen, the euro, etc.

Foreign Exchange Risk: the risk to an American ADR holder that the American dollar will strengthen versus the currency used by the foreign corporation. For example, an American holding the Toyota ADR is at risk that the U.S. dollar will strengthen versus the yen.

Forward Pricing: the method of valuing mutual fund shares, whereby a purchase or redemption order is executed at the next calculated price. Mutual fund shares are bought and sold at the next computed price, not yesterday's stale prices.

Fourth Market, INSTINET: an ECN (electronic communications network) used by institutional investors, bypassing the services of a traditional broker. Institutional = INSTINET.

Fractional Share: a portion of a whole share of stock. Mutual fund shares typically are issued as whole and fractional shares, e.g., 101.45 shares.

Fraud: using deceit or manipulation to wrongfully take money/property from someone under false pretenses.

Free Credit Balance: the cash in a customer account that can be withdrawn.

Free-Look: period during which a contract or policyholder may cancel and receive all sales charges paid. Not a popular phrase among seasoned insurance and annuity salespersons.

Freeriding & Withholding: a violation in which underwriters fail to distribute all shares allocated in an offering of a "hot issue."

Front-end Load: a mutual fund commission or sales fee charged when shares are purchased (A-shares). The amount of the load is added to the NAV to determine the public offering price (POP).

Front-running: prohibited practice of taking advantage of a customer order by trading ahead and using the customer order to benefit the registered representative or firm at the expense of the customer.

Frozen Account: AKA "a frozen account," is an account in which purchase orders will be accepted only if the cash is in the account due to the customer's failure to comply with Reg T.

Full Faith and Credit: a phrase used to denote that there are no specific assets backing a bond issue, only the issuer's ability to repay the loan.

Fully Registered Bonds: bonds whose principal and interest payments are tracked/registered for purposes of taxation. A physical certificate with the owner's name, and interest payable automatically by the paying agent (no coupons).

Funded Debt: another term for corporate bonds backed by a sinking fund as opposed to collateral.

Funding: an ERISA guideline that stipulates, among other things, that retirement plan assets must be segregated from other corporate assets.

Fund of Funds: a mutual fund comprised of many funds within the same family.

Fund of Hedge Funds: a higher-risk mutual fund open to non-accredited investors that owns shares of hedge funds.

Fungible: interchangeable, e.g., $20 bills or shares of stock, where one is just as good as another.

G

GAN: Grant Anticipation Note, short-term debt obligation of a municipal issuer backed by funds to be received in a grant, usually from the federal government.

GDP: Gross Domestic Product, the sum total of all goods and services being produced by the domestic economy, regardless of nationality.

General Account: where an insurance company invests net premiums to fund guaranteed, fixed payouts.

General Obligation Bond: a municipal bond that is backed by the issuer's full faith and credit or full taxing authority.

General Partner: the manager of a DPP with unlimited liability and a fiduciary obligation to the limited partners.

General Securities Representative: an agent who passed the Series 99 and may sell virtually any security, unlike a Series 6 holder, who sells mutual funds and variable contracts only.

Generic Advertising: communications with the public that promote securities as investments but not particular securities.

Gift: the act of giving something of value or economic benefit and expecting nothing in return.

Gift Splitting: claiming a gift as coming from both husband and wife to avoid gift tax liability.

Gift Tax: a tax liability when a gift exceeds the current annual exclusion limit.

Global Fund: a mutual fund investing in companies located and doing business all across the globe, including the U.S.

GNMA: a.k.a. "Ginnie Mae," nickname for Government National Mortgage Association. A government agency (not a public company) that buys insured mortgages from lenders, selling pass-through certificates to investors. Monthly payments to investors pay interest and also pass through principal from a pool of mortgages. Recall that bonds pay interest and return principal only at maturity, while "pass-throughs" pass through principal monthly.

GNP or Gross National Product: the productivity of a nation's citizens, including those working overseas.

Good Faith Deposit: the deposit required by a municipal issuer for all syndicates submitting bids for an issue of bonds. Typically, 1–2% of par value.

Goodwill: an intangible asset listed on the balance sheet representing the amount paid for an acquired entity above its hard, tangible asset value.

Grantor: the party who establishes and funds a trust account.

Green Shoe Clause: an agreement allowing the underwriters to sell additional shares if demand is high for an offering of securities.

Gross Revenue Pledge: less common method used by revenue bond issuers in which debt service is paid even before operations & maintenance.

Growth: investment objective that seeks "capital appreciation." Achieved through common stock, primarily.

Growth & Income: a fund that purchases stocks for growth potential and also for dividend income. Less volatile than pure growth funds due to the income that calms investors down when the ride becomes turbulent. Also, a common investment objective that seeks both growth and income.

Growth Funds: mutual funds investing in stocks expected to grow faster than the overall market and trading at high price-to-earnings multiples.

GTC or Good-Til-Canceled: a stop or limit order that will remain open until either filled or canceled by the customer.

Guaranteed Bond: bond that is issued with a promise by a party other than the issuer to maintain payments of interest and principal if the issuer cannot.

Guardian: a fiduciary who manages the financial affairs of a minor or a person declared mentally incompetent by a court of law.

H

Hedge Fund: a private investment partnership open to accredited investors only. Illiquid investments that generally must be held one or two years before selling. Typically charge a management fee plus the first 20% of capital gains in most cases.

High-Yield: an investment whose income stream is very high relative to its low market price. A high-yield bond is either issued by a shaky company or municipal government forced to offer high nominal yields, or it begins to trade at lower and lower prices on the secondary market as the credit quality or perceived credit strength of the issuer deteriorates.

Holding Company: a company organized to invest in other corporations, e.g., Berkshire-Hathaway, which holds large stakes in other companies such as Coca-Cola, See's Candy, Dairy Queen, and Wells Fargo. Wells Fargo Corporation is, in turn, a bank holding company that owns a bank, a broker-dealer, and an investment adviser among other entities.

Holding Period: the period during which a security was held for purposes of determining whether a capital gain or loss is long- or short-term.

HOLDR: a financial product created by Merrill Lynch and traded daily on the American Stock Exchange that allows investors to buy and sell a basket of stocks in a sector, industry or other classification in a single transaction. Stands for Holding Company Depository Receipt.

Hold Recommendation: an explicit recommendation to refrain from selling a security currently held by an investor, subject to the agent's suitability obligations.

Howey Decision: a U.S. Supreme Court decision that defined an "investment contract" as "an investment of money in a common enterprise where the investor will profit solely through the efforts of others."

Hybrid REIT: a Real Estate Investment Trust that both owns operating real estate and also provides financing for real estate projects—a hybrid of an equity and a mortgage REIT.

Hybrid Security: another name for a convertible bond or convertible preferred stock, which starts as a fixed-income security but may be converted to common stock.

Hypothecate: to pledge securities purchased in a margin account as collateral to secure the loan.

Hypothecation Agreement: document that gives a broker-dealer the legal authority to pledge a margin customer's securities as collateral to secure the margin loan.

I

Identity Theft: the fraudulent use of another party's identity to make unauthorized purchases and other financial transactions.

IDR: "Industrial Development Revenue Bond," a revenue bond that builds a facility that the issuing municipality then leases to a corporation. The lease payments from the corporation back the interest and principal payments on the bonds.

Immediate Annuity: an insurance contract purchased with a single premium that starts to pay the annuitant immediately. Purchased by individuals who are afraid of outliving their retirement savings.

Income: investment objective that seeks current income, found by investing in fixed-income securities, e.g., bonds, money market, preferred stock. An equity income fund buys stocks that pay dividends; less volatile than a growth & income fund or a pure growth fund.

Income Bond: a bond that will pay interest only if the issuer earns sufficient income and the board of directors declares the payment; a.k.a. "adjustment bond."

Indenture: a contract that spells out the responsibilities and rights of an issuer in connection with a bond issue.

Index: a theoretical grouping of stocks, bonds, etc., that aids analysts who want to track something. The Consumer Price Index is a theoretical grouping or "basket" of things that consumers buy, used to track inflation. The Dow Jones Industrial Average is a theoretical grouping of 30 large-company stocks that analysts use to track the stock market. The S&P 500 index tracks the stock of 500 large companies and represents the overall stock market for many calculations, including beta.

Index Fund: a mutual fund or ETF providing investors a passive investment option seeking to match the performance of an index rather than "beating the market."

Index Option: a call or put option based on the value of an index, e.g., the Dow Jones Industrial Average or the S&P 500.

Indication of Interest: an investor's expression of interest in purchasing a new issue of securities after reading the preliminary prospectus; not a commitment to buy.

Individual Retirement Account (IRA): also called an "individual retirement arrangement." A tax-deferred account that generally allows an individual no older than 70 and with earned income to contribute 100% of earned income up to the current maximum contribution allowed on a pre-tax basis that reduces the current tax liability and allows investment returns to compound.

Inflation: rising prices, as measured by the Consumer Price Index (CPI). Major risk to fixed-income investors (loss of purchasing power).

Inflation-Adjusted: subtracting out the CPI or rate of inflation from an investor's return or from GDP calculations. Associated the word "real," e.g. "real rate or return" or "real GDP."

Inflation Risk: also called "constant dollar risk" or "purchasing power risk," it is the risk that inflation will erode the value of a fixed-income stream from a bond or preferred stock.

Initial Public Offering (IPO): a corporation's first sale of stock to public investors.

Inside Information: material information about a corporation that has not yet been released to the public and would likely affect the price of the corporation's stock and/or bonds. Inside information may not be "disseminated" or acted upon.

Insider: for purpose of insider trading rules, an "insider" is anyone who has or has access to material non-public information. Officers (CEO, CFO), members of the board of directors, and investors owning > 10% of the company's outstanding shares are assumed to possess and have access to inside information. As fiduciaries to the shareholders, insiders may not use inside information to their benefit.

Insider Trading and Securities Fraud Enforcement Act (ITSFEA) of 1988: an Act of Congress that addresses insider trading and lists the penalties for violations of the Act. Insider traders may be penalized up to three times the amount of their profit or their loss avoided by using inside information.

Institutional Communication: written communication made available only to institutional investors, e.g., banks and insurance companies.

Institutional Investor: not an individual. An institution is, for example, a pension fund, insurance company, or mutual fund. The large institutions are "accredited investors" who get to do things that retail (individual) investors often do not get to do.

Insurance: protection against loss of income due to death, disability, long-term care needs, etc.

Insurance Covenant: promise by a revenue bond issuer to keep the facility properly insured.

Integration: the final stage in the money laundering process.

Interdealer: among dealers. The "interdealer market" is the highest bid and lowest asked price for a security among all dealers/market makers.

Interest Rate Options: options based on the price or yield of U.S. Treasury securities.

Interest Rate Risk: the risk that interest rates will rise, pushing the market value of a fixed-income security down. Long-term bonds and preferred stock is most susceptible.

Interest Rates: the cost of borrowing money. To borrow money, borrowers pay a rate called an interest rate on top of the principal they will return at the end of the term.

Interest-Rate Sensitive: a security whose price rises and falls when interest rates change, e.g. a fixed-income security such as preferred stock, or a bond.

Internal Revenue Code (IRC): tax laws for the U.S. that define, for example, maximum IRA contributions, or the "conduit tax theory" that mutual funds use when distributing 90% of net income to shareholders, etc.

Internal Revenue Service (IRS): an agency for the federal government that no one seems to like very much. Responsible for collecting federal taxes for the U.S. Treasury and for administering tax rules and regulations.

International Fund: a mutual fund investing in companies established outside the U.S.

Interpositioning: unnecessarily inserting another party between the broker-dealer and the customer. A violation.

Interstate Offering: an offering of securities in several states, requiring registration with the SEC.

In-the-money: a call option allowing an investor to buy the underlying stock for less than it is worth or a put option allowing an investor to sell the underlying stock for more than it is worth. For example, if ABC trades @50, both the ABC Oct 45 calls and the ABC Oct 55 puts are "in-the-money."

Intrastate Offering: an offering of securities completed in the issuer's home state with investors who reside in that state, and, therefore, eligible for the Rule 147 Exemption to registration with the SEC. Intrastate offerings generally register with the state Administrator.

Intrinsic Value: the amount by which an option is in-the-money. For example, if ABC trades @50, an ABC Oct 45 call has $5 of intrinsic value, regardless of what the premium might be.

Introducing Broker: a broker that has a relationship with customers in which it makes recommendations to customers on how and what to trade, but lets another firm handle the execution of the trades.

Inverse Relationship: when one goes up, the other goes down, and vice versa. Interest Rates and Yields are inversely related to Bond Prices. Your rate of speed is inversely related to your travel time to and from the office.

Inverted Yield Curve: a rare situation in which short-term debt securities pay higher yields than longer-term debt securities.

Investment Adviser: a business or professional that is compensated for advising others as to the value of or advisability of investing in securities. The entity that manages mutual funds/separate accounts for an asset-based fee. Financial planners are also advisers.

Investment Adviser Representative or **IAR:** an individual representing an investment adviser for compensation.

Investment Banker: see "underwriter." A firm that raises capital for issuers on the primary market.

Investment Banking: the business of helping companies with mergers and acquisitions, performing IPOs and additional offerings. Investment bankers raise capital for issuers not by loaning money (like a traditional bank) but by finding investors willing to contribute to the cause.

Investment Company Act of 1940: classified Investment Companies and set rules for registration and operation.

Investment Company: a company engaged in the business of pooling investors' money and trading in securities on their behalf. Examples include unit investment trusts (UITs), face-amount certificate companies, and management companies.

Investment Grade: a bond rated at least BBB by S&P or Baa by Moody's. The bond does not have severe default risk, so it is said to be appropriate for investors, as opposed to the speculators who buy non-investment grade bonds.

Investment Objective: any goal that an investor has including current income, capital appreciation (growth), capital preservation (safety), or speculation.

Investment Profile: what an agent must learn through due diligence. Defined by FINRA as, "the customer's age, other investments, financial situation and needs, tax status, investment objectives, investment experience, investment time horizon, liquidity needs, risk tolerance, and any other information the customer may disclose to the member or associated person in connection with such recommendation."

Investment Risks: factors that may have a negative effect on a securities investment, e.g. interest rate or inflation risk.

Investment Style: an approach to investing, such as active, passive, or buy-and-hold.

IRA: Individual Retirement Account. A retirement account/arrangement for any individual with earned income. The Traditional IRA offers pre-tax contributions while the Roth IRA is funded with after-tax contributions.

Issued Shares: the number of shares that have been issued by a corporation.

Issued Stock: the shares that have been issued to investors by the corporation at this time. Often a lower number than the number of shares authorized.

Issuer: any individual or entity who issues or proposes to issue any security. For example, the issuer of Google common stock is Google.

Issuing Securities: raising capital by offering securities to investors on the primary market.

J

Joint Account: investment account owned by more than one individual. Account owners sign a joint account agreement that stipulates which % of the assets is owned by each individual. Joint accounts are either "tenants in common" or "tenants with rights of survivorship."

Joint with Last Survivor: a settlement/payout option on an annuity that requires the insurance company to make payments to the annuitants as long as they are alive.

JTIC (Joint Tenants In Common): account where the assets of the deceased party pass to the deceased's estate, not the other account owner(s).

JTWROS (Joint Tenants With Rights Of Survivorship): account where the assets of the deceased party pass to the other account owner(s).

Junk Bond: a bond backed by a shaky issuer. It was either issued by an entity with shaky credit, or is now trading at a low price on the secondary market because the issuer's credit has suddenly or recently been downgraded. Since the price is low, given the low quality of the debt, the yield is high. High-yield and junk are synonymous.

K

K-1: a tax form required of individuals who own direct participation interests (limited partnership, S-Corp).

Keogh: qualified retirement plan available to sole proprietorships.

Keynesian Economics: economic school of thought that advocates government intervention through fiscal policy to stimulate demand for goods and services.

L

Lagging Indicator: an economic indicator that shows up after-the-fact to confirm a trend, e.g. duration of unemployment or inventory.

Large Cap: a stock where the total value of the outstanding shares is large, generally greater than $10 billion. For example, GE, MSFT, IBM.

Last-In-First-Out (LIFO): an accounting method used for random withdrawals from an annuity. The IRS assumes that all withdrawals represent part of the taxable "excess over cost basis" first.

Late Trading: a violation in which select investors are allowed to buy or sell mutual fund shares after the NAV has already been determined.

Layering: the phase of money laundering in which the first attempt at disguising the source of the ownership of the funds is made by creating complex layers of transactions.

LEAPS: long-term standardized options.

Legal Opinion: the opinion of the bond counsel attesting to the municipality's legal authority to issue the bonds as well as the tax status of the bonds.

Legal Person: as opposed to a natural person—an entity including a trust, an estate, or a corporation.

Legend: box of text printed or stamped on a security certificate indicating restrictions on its transfer. Securities bought in a private placement frequently have such a legend, stamped usually on the back of the certificate.

Legislative Risk: the risk to an investor that laws will change and have a negative impact on an investment. For example, if municipal bonds lose their tax-exempt interest, their value would plummet.

Letter of Intent: LOI, a feature of many mutual funds whereby an investor may submit a letter or form expressing the intent to invest enough money over 13 months to achieve a breakpoint.

Level Load: an ongoing asset-based sales charge (12b-1 fee) associated with mutual fund C-shares. Appropriate for short-term investments only.

Leverage: using borrowed money to increase returns. Debt securities and margin accounts are associated with "leverage."

Leveraged Buyout: buying a company with the proceeds of a debt issue, frequently performed in private equity deals.

Liabilities: what an individual or corporation owes, e.g., credit card debt, bonds, mortgage balance, accounts payable.

LIBOR: short for the London Interbank Offered Rate, an average of the world's most creditworthy banks' interbank deposit rates for large loans with maturities between overnight and one year. LIBOR is the most frequently used benchmark for short-term interest rates.

Lifecycle Fund: an age-based portfolio whose asset allocation shifts automatically over time, e.g. a target retirement fund.

Life Only/Life Annuity: a payout option whereby the insurance/annuity company promises to make payments only for the rest of the annuitant's life.

Life with Joint and Last Survivor: a payout option whereby the insurance/annuity company promises to make payments to the annuitant for the rest of his life, then to the survivor for the rest of her life.

Life with Period Certain: a payout option whereby the insurance/annuity company promises to make payments to the annuitant for the rest of his life or a certain period, whichever is greater.

Life with Unit Refund: a payout option whereby the insurance/annuity company promises to make at least a certain number of payments to the annuitant or beneficiary.

Limit Orders: orders to buy or sell a security at a specified price or better.

Limited Liability: an investor's ability to limit losses to no more than the amount invested. Holders of common stock and limited partnership interests enjoy "limited liability," which means they can only lose 100% of what they invest.

Limited Partner: a person who owns a limited partnership interest. Has no managerial responsibility and is shielded from debts of—and lawsuits against—the partnership.

Limited Partnership: a form of business ownership in which income and expenses flow through directly to the partners rather than to a separate business entity.

Limited Representative: what one would be after passing the Series 6 and getting registered to represent one's broker-dealer.

Limited Tax Bonds: general obligation bonds backed by a tax whose rate may not be increased above a certain limit.

Limited Trading Authorization: an authorization for someone other than the account owner to enter purchase and sale orders but make no withdrawals of cash or securities.

Liquidation Priority: the priority of claims on a bankrupt entity's assets that places creditors (bondholders) ahead of stockholders and preferred stockholders ahead of common stockholders.

Liquidity: the degree to which an asset can be quickly converted to cash without having to sell at a discount. Also, the ability of a company to meet its short-term obligations as measured through, for example, their current or quick ratio.

Liquidity Risk: the risk of being unable to sell a security quickly for a fair price; a.k.a. "marketability risk."

Liquid Net Worth: a more stringent measure of net worth that excludes hard-to-liquidate assets such as real estate and limited partnerships.

Liquidity: ability to convert an investment to cash without taking a large hit to principal.

Limited Liability Company: a pass-through entity in which the owners are called members, and which provides protection to the owners against claims on their personal assets.

Loan Consent: a document that when signed gives the broker-dealer the permission to lend a customer's securities to short sellers.

Long: to buy or own.

Long-Term Gain: a profit realized when selling stock held for at least 12 months plus 1 day. Subject to lower capital gains tax rates than short-term gains.

Long-Term Liability: a debt to be repaid in the long-run, e.g., the principal value of an outstanding bond issue.

Long-Term Loss: a loss realized when selling stock held for at least 12 months plus 1 day. Used to offset long-term capital gains.

Long-Term Options (LEAPS): standardized options contracts with expiration terms of several years, unlike ordinary options, which expire in nine months or sooner.

Lump Sum Payment: a settlement/payout option for annuities or insurance where the annuitant or beneficiary receives a lump sum payment.

M

Maintenance Covenant: a promise of a revenue bond issuer to keep the facility properly maintained.

Maloney Act: An amendment to the Securities Exchange Act of 1934 creating the NASD as the self-regulatory organization (SRO) for the over-the-counter (OTC) market.

Management Company: one of the three types of Investment Companies, including both open-end and closed-end funds.

Management Fee: the % of assets charged to a mutual fund portfolio to cover the cost of the investment adviser's portfolio management services.

Manager's Fee: typically, the smallest piece of the spread, paid to the managing underwriter for every share sold by the syndicate.

Margin: amount of equity contributed by a customer as a percentage of the current market value of the securities held in a margin account. Or *profit* margin, showing the percentage of revenue left on various lines of the income statement—gross margin, net profit margin.

Marginal Tax Rate: the tax rate applied to the last dollar of income earned. AKA "marginal tax bracket."

Markdown: the difference between the highest bid price for a security and the price that a dealer pays an investor for her security.

Market Letter: a publication of a broker-dealer sent to customers or the public and discussing investing, financial markets, economic conditions, etc.

Market Maker: a dealer in the OTC market maintaining an inventory of a security and a firm Bid and Ask price good for a minimum of 100 shares. Acts as a "principal" on transactions, buying and selling for its/their own account.

Market Manipulation: the illegal process of using deception or collusion to move securities prices in favor of the conspirators.

Market Momentum: the ability of the market to sustain up or downswings in price.

Market-On-Close Order: a market order for a security filled on the closing trade for the session, or as close to the closing trade as possible.

Market-On-Open Order: a market order for a security placed before the opening of the next trading session and filled at the opening market price for the security.

Market Order: an order to buy or sell a security at the best available market price.

Market-Out Clause: a stipulation in an underwriting agreement allowing the underwriter(s) to back out of a securities offering if certain catastrophic events occur.

Market Risk: a type of "systematic risk," the risk inherent to the entire market rather than a specific security. The risk that the stock market may suffer violent upheavals due to unpredictable events including natural disaster, war, disease, famine, credit crises, etc. Market risk can be reduced by hedging with options or ETFs.

Market Sentiment: a judgment of the overall mood of the market, often found through the put/call ratio and option volatility.

Marketability Risk: the risk of being unable to sell a security quickly for a fair price; a.k.a. "liquidity risk."

Marketability: a.k.a. liquidity; the ease or difficulty an investor has when trying to sell a security for cash without losing his shirt. Thinly traded securities have poor marketability.

Mark to the Market: process of calculating margin requirements based on the most current market values for the securities in a margin account.

Markup: the difference between the lowest ask/offer price for a security and the price that a dealer charges.

Material Information: any fact that could reasonably affect an investor's decision to buy, sell, or hold a security. For example, profits and losses at the company, product liability lawsuits, the loss of key customers, etc.

Maturity Date: the date that a bond pays out the principal, and interest payments cease. Also called "redemption."

Mediation: informal process of dispute resolution that sometimes avoids arbitration claims.

Member Conduct Rules: FINRA rules that, when violated, subject associated persons and member firms to sanctions, fines, suspensions, etc.

Member Firm: a broker-dealer and/or underwriting firm that belongs to FINRA or another securities association (MSRB, CBOE).

Millage Rate: the property tax rate used to calculate a property owner's tax bill.

Mini-Max: a type of best efforts underwriting where the syndicate must sell a minimum amount and may sell up to a higher, maximum amount.

Minimum Death Benefit: the minimum death benefit payable to the insured, regardless of how lousy the separate account returns are in a variable policy.

Monetarists: officials who implement monetary policy designed to fight inflation or stimulate the economy, e.g. the Federal Reserve Board.

Minimum Maintenance Requirement: the minimum amount of equity that a margin customer must maintain on either a short or a long position.

Monetary Policy: what the FRB implements through the discount rate, reserve requirement, and FOMC open market operations. Monetary policy tightens or loosens credit to affect short-term interest rates and, therefore, the economy.

Money Laundering: the process of turning profits from illegal enterprises into seemingly legitimate assets.

Money Market Mutual Fund: a highly liquid holding place for cash. Sometimes called "stable value" funds, as the share price is generally maintained at $1. The mutual funds invest in money market securities.

Money Market Securities: the short-term (1 year or less) debt security market. Examples include commercial paper, bankers' acceptance, T-bills.

Money Purchase Plan: a retirement plan in which the employer must contribute a set percentage of the employee's salary.

Moody's Investors Service: one of the top three credit rating agencies for corporate and municipal bonds as well as stocks.

Moral Obligation Bond: type of revenue bond with a provision to seek emergency funding from the state legislature should the issuer run into financial problems.

Mortality Guarantee: a promise from an insurance company to pay out no matter how soon the insured dies, or to pay an annuitant no matter how long he lives.

Mortality & Expense Risk Fee: sometimes referred to as "M&E" expenses, annual charges levied by the annuity company to cover the cost of death benefits and any guaranteed income associated with an annuity.

Mortgage-backed Security: a debt security whose interest and principal is derived from a defined pool of mortgages, e.g. a FNMA security.

Mortgage Bond: a corporate bond secured by a pledge of real estate as collateral.

Mortgage REIT: a Real Estate Investment Trust engaging in the financing of projects as opposed to owning and managing properties.

Moving Average: an average found by regularly replacing the oldest data in the set with the most current information.

MSRB (Municipal Securities Rulemaking Board): the self-regulatory organization overseeing municipal securities dealers.

Multiplier Effect: the outsized effect that can occur when the FRB changes the reserve requirement.

Municipal Bond: a bond issued by a state, county, city, school district, etc., in order to build roads, schools, hospitals, etc., or simply to keep the government running long enough to hold another election.

Municipal Bond Fund: a mutual fund that invests in municipal bonds with an objective to maximize federally tax-exempt income.

Municipal Finance Professional: for purposes of rules on political contributions, the term includes principals, registered representatives, and any paid solicitors who help firms land underwriting deals.

Municipal Fund Security: a packaged product that is similar to, but not defined as, an investment company, e.g. a State 529 Plan.

Municipal Note: a short-term obligation of a city, state, school district, etc., backed by the anticipation of funds from revenues, taxes, or upcoming bond issues, e.g., TAN, RAN, BAN.

Mutual Fund: an investment company offering equity stakes in a portfolio that is usually managed actively and that always charges management fees and other expenses.

Mutual Fund Timing: a violation that occurs when a fund allows certain investors to redeem their shares frequently without being assessed any redemption fees.

N

Naked Call: a short call position that is not backed up by ownership of the shares the writer is obligated to deliver upon exercise. As opposed to a "covered call," wherein the writer already owns all shares he would be required to deliver upon exercise.

Narrow-based Index: an index focusing on an industry or geographic region, e.g., a transportation index.

NASD (National Association of Securities Dealers): former name of the SRO empowered with the passage of the Maloney Act of 1938. Regulates its own members and enforces SEC rules and regulations. Now called FINRA after a merger with the regulators from the NYSE.

NASDAQ: National Association of Securities Dealers Automated Quotation system. The main component of the OTC market. Stocks that meet certain criteria are quoted throughout the day on NASDAQ, e.g., MSFT, ORCL, and INTC.

National Adjudicatory Council: NAC, the first level of appeal for a party sanctioned by the DOE under FINRA's Code of Procedure.

National Securities Clearing Corporation: clearing agency for stock transactions that uses Continuous Net Settlement and guarantees the performance of all transactions between member firms.

Natural Event Risk: the risk that a weather-related or other catastrophic event will disrupt securities markets and have a material negative effect on an investor's holdings, e.g. a tsunami or a terrorist attack.

NAV or Net Asset Value: the liquidating value of an open-end mutual fund share. Found by taking Assets – Liabilities/Outstanding Shares.

Net Asset Value per Bond: a measure of asset coverage from the balance sheet showing the net tangible assets of the issuer divided by the number of bonds issued.

Negotiable: the characteristic of a security that allows an investor to sell or transfer ownership to another party. For example, savings bonds are not negotiable, while Treasury Bills are negotiable (able to be traded).

Negotiated Market: another name for the "second" or "over-the-counter" market.

Negotiated Underwriting: a municipal bond—usually a revenue bond—underwritten without a competitive, sealed bid.

Net Income: the "bottom line" of a corporation's income statement. Revenue minus all expenses. Also known as a "profit" or a "loss," depending on whether it's a positive or negative number.

Net Interest Cost: a measure of a municipal issuer's total cost of borrowing money by issuing bonds.

Net Investment Income: the source of an investment company's dividend distributions to shareholders. It is calculated by taking the fund's dividends and interest collected on portfolio securities, minus the operating expenses. Funds using the "conduit tax theory" distribute at least 90% of net investment income to avoid paying taxes on the amount distributed to shareholders.

Net Overall Debt: a municipal issuer's direct debt plus their overlapping debt.

Net Revenue: or "net operating revenue," represents revenue after accounting for any returns or discounting. Especially relevant for the retail sector.

Net Revenue Pledge: the more common method used by the issuer of a revenue bond in which operations & maintenance are covered before debt service.

Net Worth: the difference between assets and liabilities. The term can be applied to individuals and business entities, although for business entities the terms "shareholders' equity" or "stockholders' equity" are typically used instead.

New Account Form: the form that must be filled out for each new account opened with a broker-dealer. The form specifies, at a minimum, the name of the account owner, trading authorization, method of payment, and the type of investment securities that are appropriate for this account.

New Issue Market: the primary market, where securities are issued to investors with the proceeds going to the issuer of the securities. Initial public offerings (IPOs), for example, take place on the "new issue market."

NHA – New Housing Authority (bonds): revenue bonds issued by a municipal government but ultimately backed by the United States Government, who guarantees rental payments for the residents of the housing project.

Nolo Contendere: a Latin phrase meaning "no contest." If an agent or applicant has pled "nolo contendere" to any felony charge or specific misdemeanors, he is subject to statutory disqualification.

No-load Fund: a mutual fund sold without a sales charge, but one which may charge an ongoing 12b-1fee or "asset-based sales charge" up to .25% of net assets.

Nominal Quote: as opposed to a firm quote, an indication of what a market participant might be willing to pay or accept for a security. Nominal quotes must be clearly identified as such.

Nominal Yield: the interest rate paid by a bond or preferred stock. The investor receives this % of the par value each year, regardless of what the bond or preferred stock is trading for on the secondary market.

Non-accredited Purchaser: an investor who does not meet various SEC net worth and/or income requirements for accredited investors.

Non-Bank Qualified Municipal Bond: municipal bonds that do not allow banks to deduct 80% of the interest costs incurred to buy them.

Non-cumulative Preferred Stock: a type of preferred stock that does not have to pay missed dividends (dividends in arrears).

Non-Cyclical: an industry not as dependent on the business cycle as cyclical stocks. Also called defensive industries, including food, alcohol, and consumer staples in general.

Nondiscrimination Covenant: a promise by a municipal revenue bond issuer that all users of a facility must pay to use it, including VIPs of the municipality.

Non-diversified Fund: a fund that doesn't care to meet the 75-5-10 rule, preferring to concentrate more heavily in certain issues.

Non-equity Options: standardized options based on things other than equity securities, e.g., indexes or foreign currency options.

Non-NASDAQ OTC Securities: over-the-counter securities that do not meet the requirements of NASDAQ. For example, OTCBB securities.

Non-systematic Risk: the risk of holding any one stock or bond. Diversification spreads this risk among different issuers and different industries to minimize the impact of a bankruptcy or unexpected collapse of any one issuer.

Normal Yield Curve: the usual situation in which yields rise as maturities lengthen for debt securities.

Not Held (order): an order to buy or sell a specific number of shares of a stock that leaves the time of order placement up to the broker, e.g. "Buy 300 shares of ABC this afternoon."

Note: a shorter-term debt security.

Numbered Account: an account identified with a number rather than a name. Allowed if the owner files a statement with the broker-dealer attesting to ownership.

NYSE: New York Stock Exchange, an auction market where buyers and sellers shout out competitive bid and asked/offered prices throughout the day.

O

Obsolescence Risk: the risk that an issuer's products or services will become irrelevant.

Odd Lot: an order for less than the normal unit of trading in a security, e.g. 8 shares of stock.

Odd Lot Theory: theory used by some technical analysts that assumes odd-lot investors are typically wrong.

Offer: another name for "ask," or the price an investor must pay if he wants to buy a security from a dealer/market maker.

Offering Circular: offering document used when a prospectus is not required under the Securities Act of 1933.

Offer of Settlement: a respondent's offer to the disciplinary committee of FINRA to settle his or her recent rule violations.

Office of Foreign Asset Control (OFAC): federal government office that maintains a list of individuals and organizations viewed as a threat to the U.S., called Specially Designated Nationals.

Officers: high-level executives at a public corporation, e.g., the Chief Executive Officer (CEO), Chief Financial Officer (CFO), and the Chief Operating Officer (COO).

Official Notice of Sale: advertisement in the Bond Buyer in which a municipal issuer hopes to attract potential underwriters.

Official Statement: the document that discloses detailed information about a municipal bond issuer's financial condition.

OID: original issue discount. A bond purchased for less than the par value on the primary market, e.g., a zero-coupon bond.

Omitting Prospectus: an advertisement for a mutual fund that typically shows performance figures without providing (omitting) the full disclosure contained in the prospectus. Therefore, it must present caveats and encourage readers to read the prospectus and consider all the risks before investing in the fund.

Open-end Fund: an investment company that sells an unlimited number of shares to an unlimited number of investors on a continuous basis. Shares are redeemed by the company rather than traded among investors.

Open Market Operations: how the FOMC achieves monetary targets by buying and selling U.S. Treasury securities on the open market.

Operating Agreement: the agreement governing the structure and operation of an LLC.

Operating Expenses: expenses that a mutual fund deducts from the assets of the fund, including board of director salaries, custodial and transfer agent services, management fees, 12b-1 fees, etc.

Opportunity Cost: the return on the investment you could have made but didn't when you chose another one.

Option: a derivative giving the holder the right to buy or sell something for a stated price up to expiration of the contract. Puts and calls.

Option Volatility: a tool of technical analysis to measure market sentiment.

Order Audit Trail System (OATS): FINRA compliance system that captures order information reported by member firms and then integrates that order information with trade and quotation information from other systems.

Order Room: a.k.a. "wire room." The department of a broker-dealer that places trades.

Order Ticket/Trade Ticket: a ticket filled out by a registered representative when placing an order to buy or sell securities.

Ordinary Dividend: a dividend subject to the investor's marginal tax rate, not a qualified dividend. REITs, for example, distribute ordinary dividends to the unitholders.

Ordinary Income: virtually all income that is not a capital gain or a qualified dividend. Includes wages, tips, bonuses and commissions; profit from an ownership interest in a sole proprietorship, partnership, LLC or Subchapter S corporation; interest income; alimony; gambling winnings; taxable distributions from retirement accounts, pensions and annuities; and income from rents, royalties and trusts.

Ordinary Income Rate: tax rate paid on ordinary income, as opposed to the rate paid on capital gains.

OTC/Over-the-Counter: called a "negotiated market." Securities traded among dealers rather than on physical exchanges. Includes NASDAQ and Bulletin Board and Pink Sheet stocks, plus government, corporate, and municipal bonds.

OTC Options: exotic options traded on the over-the-counter market, where participants can choose the characteristics of the options traded.

Outstanding Shares: the number of shares a corporation has outstanding. Found by taking Issued shares minus Treasury stock.

Overallotment: allowing underwriters to sell additional shares of an offering, up to 15% more.

Overbought: a stock trading near resistance.

Oversold: a stock trading near support.

Overlapping Debt: the debt that a municipal issuer is responsible for along with a coterminous issuer.

P

PAC – Planned Amortization Class: a type of CMO (collateralized mortgage obligation) that provides more protection against extension risk vs. a TAC.

Packaged Security: a securities portfolio that pools capital from many investors and is typically managed by an investment adviser, e.g. an open-end or closed-end fund.

Painting the Tape: a form of market manipulation in which bogus trades are reported to affect the market price of a security. A violation.

Par, Principal: the face amount of a bond payable at maturity. Also, the face amount of a preferred stock. Preferred = $100, Bond = $1,000.

Parity: equal, e.g. when a convertible bond trades for exactly what the underlying shares are worth.

Partial Surrender: life insurance policyholder cashes in part of the cash value. Excess over premiums is taxable.

Participating Preferred Stock: preferred stock whose dividend is often raised above the stated rate.

Participation: provision of ERISA requiring that all employees in a qualified retirement plan be covered within a reasonable length of time after being hired.

Participation Rate: the percentage of the underlying index's increase credited to the account value of an equity indexed annuity.

Partnership Agreement: the agreement between the LPs and the GP for a direct participation program.

Passive Income: as opposed to "earned income," the income derived from rental properties, limited partnerships, or other enterprises in which the individual is not actively involved.

Pass-Through Certificate: a mortgage-backed security (usually GNMA) that takes a pool of mortgages and passes through interest and principal monthly to an investor.

Pattern Day Trader: anyone who trades in the same security 4 or more times in the same day over a 5-day period, and whose same-day trades account for at least 6% of his trading activity over that period.

Payable (or Payment) Date: the date that the dividend check is paid to investors.

Payroll Deduction IRA: retirement plan offered by some businesses in which employees direct the employer to deposit a certain amount of his paycheck into his IRA.

P/E or Price-to-Earnings Ratio: the market price of a stock compared to the earnings per share. Stocks trading at high P/E ratios are "growth stocks," while those trading at low P/E ratios are "value stocks."

Peak: the phase of the business cycle between expansion (good times) and contraction (bad times).

Pegging: a form of market manipulation in which parties illegally try to raise the price of a stock, often to force the put options the parties have written on the stock to go out-of-the-money. A violation.

Penny Stock Cold Calling Rules: rules to protect consumers receiving telemarketing pitches to buy risky stocks trading below $5 a share. Rules require special disclosure and investor signatures when selling penny stocks.

Pension Plan: a contract between an individual and an employer that provides for the distribution of benefits at retirement.

Performance Figures: total return for a mutual fund over 1, 5, and 10 years, and/or "life of fund." Only past performance may be indicated, and there must be a caveat that past performance does not guarantee future results.

Period Certain: a settlement option that promises to pay either the annuitant or his beneficiaries for at least a stated period, no matter how soon the annuitant passes.

Periodic-Payment Deferred Annuity: method of purchasing an annuity whereby the contract holder makes periodic payments into the contract. The pay-out phase must be deferred for all periodic payment plans.

Permanent Insurance: life insurance other than "term."

PHA – Public Housing Authority (bonds): another name for NHA/New Housing Authority municipal revenue bonds.

Physical Certificates: a method of owning securities in which paper certificates are issued to and in the name of the investor.

Pink Markets: a part of the OTC market where thinly traded, volatile stocks change hands. AKA "non-NASDAQ OTC."

Placement: the first stage in the cycle of money laundering in which illegally generated funds are placed into the financial system or are smuggled out of the country.

Placement Ratio: a statistic published in the Bond Buyer showing the dollar amount of municipal securities sold on the primary market out of the dollar amount offered the previous week; a.k.a. the "acceptance ratio."

Policyholder: the owner of an insurance policy who is responsible for paying premiums.

Political Risk: the risk that a country's government will radically change policies or that the political climate will become hostile or counterproductive to business and financial markets.

POP: public offering price. For an IPO, this includes the spread to the underwriters. For a mutual fund, this includes any sales loads that go to the underwriter/distributor.

Portfolio: the stocks, bonds, money market securities, or any combination thereof that an investor owns.

Position Limit: maximum number of options contracts that a trader can have on the same side of the market (bull/bear) and/or may exercise over a five-day period.

Power of Substitution: a document that when signed by the security owner authorizes transfer of the certificate to another party.

Precious Metals: metals with industrial uses or intrinsic worth including gold, silver, palladium, and platinum.

Precious Metals Funds: specialized mutual funds typically investing in the shares of mining/extraction companies.

Pre-dispute Arbitration Agreement: an agreement signed by the customer of a broker-dealer in which the customer agrees to use arbitration rather than civil court to settle disputes.

Pre-emptive Right: the right of common stockholders to maintain their proportional ownership if the company offers more shares of stock.

Preferred Stock: a fixed-income equity security whose stated dividends must be paid before common stock can receive any dividend payment. Also gets preference ahead of common stock in a liquidation (but behind all creditors).

Preliminary Official Statement: the official statement for a municipal bond issue subject to further additions and changes.

Preliminary Prospectus: a prospectus that lacks the POP and the effective date; a.k.a. "red herring." Used to solicit indications of interest.

Premium Bond: a bond purchased for more than the par value, usually due to a drop in interest rates.

Prepayment Risk: the risk that the mortgages underlying a mortgage-backed security will be paid off sooner than expected due to a drop in interest rates. Investors reinvest the principal at a lower rate going forward.

Preservation of Capital: an investment objective that places the emphasis on making sure the principal is not lost. Also called "safety."

Pre-Tax Plan: a retirement plan offering a tax deduction for the contribution made to the account.

Price-based Options: standardized interest rate options based on the price of various U.S. Treasury securities.

Price-to-Book: the market price of a stock compared to its book value per share.

Price-to-Cash: the market price of a stock compared to its cash-flow-from-operating-activities-per-share.

Price-to-Earnings: the market price of a stock compared to its earnings-per-share.

Price-to-Sales: the market price of a stock compared to its revenue-per-share.

Primary Market: where securities are issued to raise capital for the issuer.

Primary Offering: offering of securities in which the proceeds go to the issuer.

Prime Brokerage: a level of service provided to, for example, hedge funds requiring greater margin, securities lending, and other capabilities.

Prime Rate: interest rate charged to corporations with high credit ratings for unsecured loans.

Principal-Protected Fund: a mutual fund for people who want their principal protected. Involves holding the investment for several years, at which point the fund guarantees that the value of the investment will be equal to at least what the investor put in.

Private Company: a company not subject to reporting requirements under the Securities Exchange Act of 1934 and without securities trading on a secondary market.

Private Equity Fund: an alternative investment fund open to sophisticated investors and focusing on purchasing companies both public and private.

Private Placement: an exempt transaction under Reg D (Rule 506) of the Securities Act of 1933, allowing issuers to sell securities without registration to accredited investors, who agree to hold them for a required period.

Private Placement Memorandum or PPM: the offering document for a private placement of unregistered securities.

Private Securities Transaction: offering an investment opportunity not sponsored by the firm. Requires permission from the firm and any disclosure demanded; otherwise, a violation called "selling away."

Probate: the process of "proving" the will and distributing assets of the deceased.

Proceeds Transaction: using the proceeds from a sale of securities to buy other securities on the same day.

Producer Price Index or **PPI:** defined by the Bureau of Labor Statistics as "the average change over time in the selling prices received by domestic producers for their output. The prices included in the PPI are from the first commercial transaction for many products and some services."

Profit Sharing: a defined contribution plan whereby the company makes contributions at its discretion according to a prescribed formula.

Progressive Tax: a tax that increases as a percentage as the thing being taxed increases, including gift, estate, and income taxes. Not a flat tax.

Prospectus: a disclosure document that details a company's plans, history, officers, and risks of investment. It's the red herring plus the POP and the effective date.

Protective Covenants: promises from the issuer of a revenue bond to the bondholders designed to protect the bondholders against default.

Proxy Form: a form granting the power to vote according to a shareholder's instructions when the shareholder will not attend the meeting.

Proxy Statement: full disclosure document required by an issuer before soliciting votes by proxy at any annual or special shareholder meeting.

Prudent Investor Standards: guidance provided to fiduciaries investing on behalf of a third party, e.g., trustees or custodians of UTMA accounts.

PSA Model: a method of estimating the speed of prepayments on a CMO investment.

Public Company: a company with securities owned and traded by public investors.

Public Offering Price (POP): the price an investor pays for a mutual fund or an initial public offering. For a mutual fund, POP = NAV + the sales charge.

Public Offering: the sale of an issue of common stock, either an IPO or an additional offer of shares.

Purchase Payment: a payment made into an annuity contract, either periodically or in a single payment.

Purchasing Power: how much a dollar can buy relative to consumer prices.

Purchasing Power Risk: also called "constant dollar" or "inflation" risk, the risk that a fixed payment will not be sufficient to keep up with inflation (as measured through the CPI).

Put (n.): a contract giving the owner the right to sell something at a stated exercise price.

Put (v.): to sell.

Put/Call Ratio or **Puts-to-Calls:** a tool of technical analysis showing the ratio of puts purchased to calls, with a higher ratio a bearish indicator revealing that many stock investors have hedged by buying protective puts.

Put Feature: a feature of some bonds allowing the investor to sell the bond back for stated prices as of certain dates named in the indenture, protecting the investor from interest rate risk. AKA "puttable" bonds.

Put Spread: the act of buying and selling puts on the same underlying instrument where the two options are different in terms of strike price, expiration, or both.

Q

Qualified Dividend: a dividend that qualifies for a lower tax rate vs. ordinary income.

Qualified Institutional Buyers: investors meeting certain SEC criteria allowing them to participate in certain investment opportunities not open to the public.

Qualified Opinion: opinion by the bond counsel for a municipal issuer in which some doubt or reservations are expressed.

Qualified Plan: a retirement plan that qualifies for deductible contributions on behalf of employers and/or employees and covered by ERISA. For example, 401(k), defined benefit, Keogh. Must meet IRS approval, unlike more informal "non-qualified plans."

Quote, Quotation: a price that a dealer is willing to pay or accept for a security.

R

Random Withdrawal: a settlement option in an annuity whereby the investor takes the value of the subaccounts in two or more withdrawals, rather than one lump sum.

Rate Covenant: a promise that the issuer of a revenue bond will raise rates if necessary to cover the debt service.

Rating Service: e.g., S&P and Moody's; a company that assigns credit ratings to corporate and municipal bonds.

Realized Gain: the amount of the "profit" an investor earns when selling a security.

Real Rate of Return: an investor's return minus the rate of inflation as measured by the CPI. AKA "inflation-adjusted return."

Recession: a significant decline in economic activity spread across the economy, lasting more than a few months, normally visible in real GDP, real income, employment, industrial production, and wholesale-retail sales declines.

Reclamation: document sent by a broker-dealer when delivery of securities is apparently in error.

Recommendation: an affirmative statement or implication that an investor should consider buying, selling, or holding a security or pursuing an investment strategy.

Record Date: the date determined by the Board of Directors upon which the investor must be the holder "of record" in order to receive the upcoming dividend. Settlement of a trade must occur by the record date for the buyer to receive the dividend.

Reconciliation: process of matching bank records to the broker-dealer's own ledgers, or matching securities records from the DTC with the firm's stock record.

Recourse Note: an obligation of a limited partnership for which a limited partner is responsible personally.

Red Herring: a.k.a. "preliminary prospectus." Contains essentially the same information that the final prospectus will contain, minus the POP and effective date.

Redeemable Security: a security that may be redeemed or presented to the issuer for payment, e.g., open-end (but not closed-end) funds.

Redemption: for mutual funds, redemption involves the sale of mutual fund shares back to the fund at the NAV (less any redemption fees, back-end loads). For bonds, the date that principal is returned to the investor, along with the final interest payment.

Redemption Fee: a charge to a mutual fund investor who sells her shares back to the fund much sooner than the fund would prefer.

Refunding: replacing an outstanding bond issue by issuing new bonds at a lower interest rate. Also known as "calling" a bond issue.

Refunding Issue: the bonds being issued to replace a more expensive and existing issue of bonds when the issuer performs a refunding.

Reg A: a laid-back and predictable form of island music. Also, an exempt transaction under the Securities Act of 1933 for small offerings of securities ($5 million issued in a 12-month period).

Reg D: an exempt transaction under the Securities Act of 1933 for private placements.

Reg FD: legislation requiring that any material non-public information disclosed by a public corporation to analysts or other investors must be made public.

Reg NMS: SEC regulation concerned with the over-the-counter trading of stocks that trade on NYSE, NYSE Amex, and NASDAQ, as opposed to Over-The-Counter Bulletin Board (OTCBB) and Pink Quote stocks. Concerns over access to quotes and prompt and accurate trade reporting for NMS stocks.

Reg SHO: SEC rule to prevent abusive short selling with its locate requirement for broker-dealers executing short sales.

Reg S-K: provides guidance on forward-looking statements made by an issuer and lays out the information required in various types of securities registration statements.

Reg T: established by the FRB as the amount of credit a broker-dealer may extend to a customer pledging a security as collateral for a margin loan. In a margin account, customers must put down ½ of the security's value, or at least $2,000.

Reg U: established by the FRB as the amount of credit a bank may extend to a broker-dealer or public customer pledging a security as collateral.

Regulatory Element: continuing education requirement completed on second anniversary of registration and every three years thereafter. Failure to complete within 120 days of anniversary leads to "inactive" status.

Registered Options and Security Futures Principal: designation for the principal responsible for options firm communications and the allocation of exercise notices.

Registered as to Principal Only: a bond with only the principal registered. Interest coupons must be presented for payment.

Registered Representative: an associated person of an investment banker or broker-dealer who effects transactions in securities for compensation.

Registered Secondary: an offering of securities by persons other than the issuer. For example, the former CEO of a corporation may offer a large block of restricted (unregistered) stock to the public through a broker-dealer.

Registrar: audits the transfer agent to make sure the number of authorized shares is never exceeded.

Registration Statement: the legal document disclosing material information concerning an offering of a security and its issuer. Submitted to SEC under Securities Act of 1933.

Regressive Tax: a flat tax, e.g., gasoline, sales, excise taxes.

Regular Way Settlement: T + 2, trade date plus three business days. T + 1 for Treasury securities.

Regulated Investment Company: an investment company using the conduit tax theory by distributing 90% or more of net investment income to shareholders.

Regulation AC: legislation requiring research analysts to certify the accuracy and truthfulness of their research reports.

Reinstatement Privilege: a feature of some mutual funds allowing investors to make withdrawals and then reinstate the money without paying another sales charge.

Reinvestment Risk: the risk that a fixed-income investor will not be able to reinvest interest payments or the par value at attractive interest rates. Happens when rates are falling.

REIT (Real Estate Investment Trust): a corporation or trust that uses the pooled capital of investors to invest in ownership of either income property or mortgage loans. 90% of net income is paid out to shareholders.

Release Date: date established by the SEC as to when the underwriters may sell new securities to the buyers; a.k.a. "effective date."

REMIC: a Real Estate Mortgage Investment Conduit, another name for a CMO.

Reorganization Department: back office operation of a broker-dealer handling changes to securities ownership due to mergers, acquisitions, bankruptcies, bond calls, and tender offers.

Repurchase Agreement: an agreement in which one party sells securities to the other and agrees to repurchase them for a higher price over the short-term.

Required Minimum Distribution (RMD): the required minimum distribution that must be taken from a retirement plan to avoid IRS penalties. Usually must occur by April 1st of the year following the individual's 70½th birthday.

Research Analyst: associated person of a member firm who prepares research reports.

Research Report: a communication put out by a member firm that analyzes the investment merits of a security.

Reserve Requirement: amount of money a bank must lock up in reserve, established by the FRB.

Residual Claim: the right of common stockholders to claim assets after the claims of all creditors and preferred stockholders have been satisfied.

Restricted Person: a person who is ineligible to purchase an equity IPO, including members of the brokerage industry and their immediate family members.

Restricted Stock: stock whose transfer is subject to restrictions, e.g., a holding period. Stock purchased in private placements is an example of restricted stock.

Retail Communications: any written (paper or electronic) communication made available to more than 25 retail investors in a 30-day period.

Retail Investor: any investor who is not an institutional investor.

Retained Earnings: a balance sheet item reflecting profits not distributed to shareholders over the years but, rather, reinvested into the business. Accumulated net income of the company from which dividends are declared.

Revenue Anticipation Note (RAN): a short-term debt obligation of a municipal issuer backed by upcoming revenues.

Revenue Bond: a municipal bond whose interest and principal payments are backed by the revenues generated from the project being built by the proceeds of the bonds. Toll roads, for example, are usually built with revenue bonds backed by the tolls collected.

Reverse Repurchase Agreements: a repurchase agreement from the buyer's perspective, who resells the securities to the other side of the transaction at the agreed-upon price.

Rights of Accumulation: feature of many mutual funds whereby a rise in account value is counted the same as new money for purposes of achieving a breakpoint.

Rights Offering: additional offer of stock accompanied by the opportunity for each shareholder to maintain his/her proportionate ownership in the company.

Rights: short-term equity securities that allow the holder to buy new shares below the current market price.

Risk: the variability of returns an investment produces; e.g. standard deviation.

Risk-Averse: an investor who sacrifices potentially high returns for safety of income and principal, e.g., a T-Bond investor.

Risk Premium: the extra yield demanded by investors holding securities at greater risk of default, e.g. the difference in yield demanded by corporate bond investors versus Treasury security investors for securities of the same term to maturity.

Riskless Principal Transaction: transaction in which a broker-dealer chooses to act as a principal when they could have acted as an agent for the customer.

Risk Tolerance: an investor's ability to bear investment risk in terms of financial resources, liquidity needs, investment objectives, and psychological makeup. Risk tolerance is simply an investor's ability to tolerate risk.

Rollover: moving retirement funds from a 401(k) to an IRA, or from one IRA to another. In a "60-day rollover," the check is cut to the individual, who must then send a check to the new custodian within 60 days to avoid early distribution penalties.

Roth IRA: individual retirement account funded with non-deductible (after-tax) contributions. All distributions are tax-free provided the individual is 59½ and has had the account at least five years.

Round Lot: the usual or normal unit of trading. 100 shares for common stock.

RTRS: a trade reporting system used for transactions in municipal securities on the secondary market.

Rule (and Form) 144: regulates the sale of "control stock" by requiring board members, officers, and large shareholders to report sales of their corporation's stock and to adhere to volume limits. The form is filed as often as quarterly, no later than concurrently with the sale.

Rule 144a: rule that allows restricted securities to be re-sold to institutional investors including banks, insurance companies, broker-dealers, investment advisers, pension plans, and investment companies without violating holding period requirements.

Rule 145: rule that requires corporations in a proposed merger/acquisition to solicit the vote of the shareholders of both the purchasing and the acquired corporation.

Rule 147: exemption under the Securities Act of 1933 for intra-state offerings of securities.

Rumors: the illegal practice of trying to move a stock's market price by publishing unfounded allegations about the issuer.

Russell 2,000: a small cap stock index often used as a benchmark for small cap portfolios.

RVP: receipt versus payment, a method of settlement whereby payment on the transaction is made when delivery of the securities is received and accepted.

S

Safety: an investment objective that seeks to avoid loss of principal first and foremost. Bank CDs, Treasury securities, and fixed annuities are generally suitable.

Sales: another name for revenue, the top line of an income statement.

Sales Blotter: record of original entry showing "an itemized daily record of all purchases and sales of securities, all receipts and deliveries of securities (including certificate numbers), all receipts and disbursements of cash and all other debits and credits.

Sales Charge, Sales Load: a deduction from an investor's check that goes to the distributors/sellers of the fund. Deducted from investor's check, either when she buys (A-shares) or sells (B-shares).

Scheduled Premium: life insurance with established, scheduled premium payments, e.g., whole life, variable life. As opposed to "universal" insurance, which is "flexible premium."

S-corporation: a business entity providing flow-through to the shareholders and protection of personal assets, with a maximum number of owners.

Secondary Market: where investors trade securities among themselves and proceeds do not go to the issuer.

Secondary Offering/Distribution: a distribution of securities owned by major stockholders—not the issuer of the securities.

Sector Fund: a fund that concentrates heavily in an industry, e.g., the "Technology Fund." Higher risk/reward than funds invested in many industries.

Secured Bond: a corporate bond secured by collateral, e.g., mortgage bond, collateral trust certificate, equipment trust certificate.

Securities Act of 1933: regulates the new-issue or primary market, requiring non-exempt issuers to register securities and provide full disclosure.

Securities and Exchange Commission: SEC, empowered by passage of Securities Exchange Act of 1934. A government body, the ultimate securities regulator.

Securities Exchange Act of 1934: landmark securities legislation that prevents fraud in the securities markets. Created/empowered the SEC. Requires broker-dealers, exchanges and securities associations to register with SEC. Requires public companies to report quarterly and annually to SEC.

Securitization: the process of turning financial assets such as receivables or mortgages into securities that are packaged and sold to investors.

Security: an investment of money subject to fluctuation in value and negotiable/marketable to other investors. Other than an insurance policy or fixed annuity, a security is any piece of securitized "paper" that can be traded for value.

Security Index Future: futures contracts deriving their value from various indexes, often used to predict the movement of the stock movement when it opens.

Self-Clearing Broker: a/k/a "clearing broker," a member of the clearing agencies who clears trades for itself and other firms.

Self-Regulatory Organization: SRO, e.g., FINRA and the CBOE. An organization given the power to regulate its members. Not government bodies like the SEC, which oversees the SROs.

Self-Trades: transactions that unwittingly occur within the same firm due to electronic trading algorithms.

Seller's Option: a special type of trade settlement that is not to happen sooner than the fourth business day following execution and is to occur on a future date specified by the seller, alterable only with a one-day advance written notice to the buyer.

Sell Limit: an order to sell placed above the current market price that may be executed only if the bid price rises to the limit price or higher.

Sell Stop: an order to sell placed below the current market price, activated only if the market price hits or passes below the stop price.

Selling Away: a violation that occurs when a registered representative offers investment opportunities not sponsored by the firm.

Selling Concession: typically, the largest piece of the underwriting spread going to the firm credited with making the sale.

Selling Dividends: a violation where an investor is deceived into thinking that she needs to purchase a stock in order to receive an upcoming dividend.

Selling Group: certain broker-dealers with an agreement to act as selling agents for the syndicate (underwriters) with no capital at risk.

Semi-Annual: twice per year, or "at the half year," literally. Note that "bi-annually" means "every two years." Bond interest is paid semi-annually. Mutual funds report to their shareholders semi-annually and annually. Nothing happens "bi-annually" as a general rule of thumb.

Senior Security: a security that grants the holder a higher claim on the issuer's assets in the event of a liquidation/bankruptcy.

Separate Account: an account maintained by an insurance/annuity company that is separate from the company's general account. Used to invest customers' money for variable annuities and variable insurance contracts. Registered as an investment company under Investment Company Act of 1940.

SEP-IRA: pre-tax retirement plan available to small businesses. Only the employer contributes.

Series: e.g., a MSFT Nov 40 call. The standardized contracts available on the secondary market naming the underlying stock, the expiration, and the strike price.

Series EE Bond: a nonmarketable, interest-bearing U.S. Government savings bond issued at a discount from the par value. Interest is exempt from state and local taxation.

Series HH Bond: a nonmarketable, interest-bearing U.S. Government savings bond issued at par and purchased only by trading in Series EE bonds at maturity. Interest is exempt from state and local taxation.

Series I Bond: a savings bond issued by the U.S. Treasury that protects investors from inflation or purchasing power risk.

Settlement Options: payout options on annuities and life insurance including life-only, life with period certain, and joint and last survivorship.

Settlement: completion of a securities transaction wherein payment has been made by the buyer and delivery has been made by the seller.

Share Identification: a method of calculating capital gains and losses by which the investor identifies which shares were sold, as opposed to using FIFO or average cost.

Sharing Arrangement: as stated in the subscription agreement, the way in which income and capital contributions are to be allocated among the GP and the LPs.

Shelf Registration: registering securities that will be sold gradually on the primary market.

Short Sale: method of attempting to profit from a security whose price is expected to fall. Trader borrows certificates through a broker-dealer and sells them, with the obligation to replace them at a later date, hopefully at a lower price. Bearish position.

Short-Term Capital Gain: a profit realized on a security held for 12 months or less.

Short-Term Capital Loss: a loss realized on a security held for 12 months or less, deductible against Short-Term Capital Gains.

Signature Guarantee: an official stamp/medallion that officers of a bank affix to a stock power to attest to its validity.

SIMPLE Plan: a retirement plan for businesses with no more than 100 employees that have no other retirement plan in place. Pre-tax contributions, fully taxable distributions. Both employer and employees may contribute—through elective deferrals. Set up either as an IRA or 401(k).

Simple Trust: a trust that accumulates income and distributes it to the beneficiaries annually.

Simplified Arbitration: a method of resolving disputes involving a small amount of money.

Single-Payment Deferred Annuity: annuity purchased with a single payment wherein the individual defers the payout or "annuity" phase of the contract.

Single-Payment Immediate Annuity: annuity purchased with a single payment wherein the individual goes immediately into the payout or "annuity" phase of the contract.

Sinking Fund: an account established by an issuing corporation or municipality to provide funds required to redeem a bond issue.

SIPC: Securities Investor Protection Corporation, a non-profit, non-government, industry-funded insurance corporation protecting investors against broker-dealer failure.

SLGS: "State and Local Government Series" securities, special securities created by the U.S. Treasury to help municipalities do an advance refunding and comply with IRS rules and restrictions on such transactions.

Small Cap: a stock where the total value of all outstanding shares is considered "small," typically between $50 million and $2 billion.

Sole Proprietorship: a business owned as an individual with no protection provided for the owner's personal assets.

Solicited Order: an order placed for a customer pursuant to an agent's recommendation and subject to suitability requirements.

Solvency: the ability of a corporation or municipality to meet its obligations as they come due.

Sovereign Debt: bonds issued by a national government and payable in a foreign currency.

S&P 500: a market-cap weighted index of 500 large-company stocks that is used to represent the overall market for purposes of calculating beta.

Special Assessment Bonds: revenue bonds backed by an assessment on only those properties benefiting from the project.

Specially Designated Nationals: parties whose names are on a special list with the Office of Foreign Asset Control (OFAC) of persons that U.S. entities are not to do business with.

Special Memorandum Account (SMA): a line of credit in a margin account.

Special Tax: a tax on gasoline, hotel and motel, liquor, tobacco, etc.

Special Tax Bond: a revenue bond backed by taxes on gasoline, hotel and motel, liquor, tobacco, etc.

Specialized Fund: a mutual fund specializing its investment approach beyond just "growth, value, or growth & income." Specialized funds might write covered calls, focus on industry groups or geographic areas, provide age-based portfolios, or track indexes for passive investments, etc.

Specific Identification: method of determining cost basis on securities for purposes of capital gains/loss reporting.

Specified Program: a direct participation program in which the assets of the partnership are identified.

Speculation: an investment objective involving high-risk bets that an investment's market value will rise significantly. Associated with options, futures, and raw land investments.

Spin-Off: an offering of stock in a unit that is being divested from the issuer.

Sponsor: the party who puts together a direct participation program.

Spousal Account: an IRA established for a non-working spouse.

Spread: generally, the difference between a dealer's purchase price and selling price, both for new offerings (underwriting spread) and secondary market quotes. For underwritings the spread is the difference between the proceeds to the issuer and the POP.

Stabilizing/Stabilization: the surprising practice by which an underwriting syndicate bids up the price of an IPO whose price is dropping in the secondary market.

Stable Value Fund: a money market mutual fund attempting to keep the NAV at $1.

Stagflation: an unusual macroeconomic state associated with inflation *and* economic stagnation.

Standby Underwriting: a commitment by an underwriter to purchase any shares that are not subscribed to in a rights offering.

Standard & Poor's: a firm that analyses the credit quality of municipal and corporate bonds and puts together various indices to track the performance of the stock market and various segments thereof.

Statement of Additional Information or SAI: detailed registration document for an open- or closed-end management company providing further details than what is contained in the statutory prospectus.

Statute of Limitations: a time limit that, once reached, prevents criminal or civil action from being filed.

Statutory Disqualification: prohibiting a person from associating with an SRO due to disciplinary or criminal actions within the past 10 years, or due to filing a false or misleading application or report with a regulator.

Statutory Voting: method of voting whereby the shareholder may cast no more than the number of shares owned per candidate/item.

Step-Up Bond: a bond that pays higher interest payments to investors as time goes on.

Stochastics: a tool of technical analysts measuring the momentum of stocks and stock indexes.

Stock: an ownership or equity position in a public company whose value is tied to the company's profits (if any) and dividend payouts (if any).

Stock Dividend: payment of a dividend in the form of more shares of stock; not a taxable event.

Stockholders' Equity: from the balance sheet, the difference between assets and liabilities. AKA "net worth."

Stock Market: a physical or electronic facility allowing investors to buy and sell stock, e.g. the NYSE or NASDAQ.

Stock Market Data: the information of importance to technical analysts concerning pricing patters, volume, moving averages, etc. for common stock and stock indexes.

Stock Power: document used to transfer ownership of a stock.

Stock Record: a detailed list of the broker-dealer's holdings, separated by security, on an account by account basis. AKA "securities record."

Stock Record Break/Exception: a discrepancy between a broker-dealer's recorded positions in a security versus the actual positions in their DTC account.

Stock Record Department: department of a broker-dealer that performs regular reconciliations to ensure the accuracy of their books and records concerning securities positions held by the firm and its customers.

Stock Split: a change in the number of outstanding shares designed to change the price-per-share; not a taxable event.

Stop Loss: another name for a sell-stop order. So-named because an investor's losses are stopped once the stock trades at a certain price or lower.

Stop Order: an order that is activated only if the market price hits or passes through the stop price. Does not name a price for execution.

Stop-limit Order: a stop order that once triggered must be filled at an exact price (or better).

Stopping Stock: a courtesy in which the specialist will guarantee a price for execution and allow the participant to seek a better price.

Straight Life Annuity: a settlement option in which the annuity company pays the annuitant only as long as he or she is alive. Also called "straight life" or "life only."

Straight Preferred: a preferred stock whose missed dividends do not go into arrears, a.k.a. "non-cumulative preferred."

Street Name: in the name of the broker-dealer holding securities on behalf of customers.

Strike Price or Exercise Price: the price at which a call or put option allows the holder to buy or sell the underlying security.

STRIPS: Separate Trading of Registered Interest and Principal of Securities. A zero-coupon bond issued by the U.S. Treasury in which all interest income is received at maturity in the form of a higher (accreted) principal value. Avoids "reinvestment risk."

Subaccount: investment options available within the separate account for variable contract holders.

Subchapter M: section of the Internal Revenue Code providing the "conduit tax treatment" used by REITs and mutual funds distributing 90% or more of net income to shareholders. A mutual fund using this method is technically a Regulated Investment Company under IRC Subchapter M.

Subordinated Debenture: corporate bond with a claim that is subordinated or "junior" to a debenture and/or general creditor.

Subscription Agreement: what a potential Limited Partner/investor signs to invest into a DPP.

Subscription Price: the price that all buyers of a new issue will pay to buy the security being offered on the primary market.

Suitability: a determination by a registered representative that a security matches a customer's stated objectives and financial situation.

Supervision: a system implemented by a broker-dealer to ensure that its employees and associated persons comply with federal and state securities law, and the rules and regulations of the SEC, exchanges, and SROs.

Supplemental Liquidity Providers: specially designated off-floor members of the NYSE who play a unique role in the trading of securities on the secondary market. These participants use sophisticated computerized trading strategies to create high volume on exchanges to add liquidity to the markets. As an incentive to provide liquidity, the exchange pays the Supplemental Liquidity Provider (SLP) a fee/rebate.

Surrender: to cash out an annuity or life insurance policy for its surrender value.

Swaps: a private agreement in which two parties agree to pay each other various cash flows, e.g. a fixed interest rate for one side versus a floating rate for the other. As opposed to an actual principal amount, swaps use a notional value to calculate interest owed by each side of the agreement.

Sweep Program: method of holding customer cash in either FDIC-insured or SPIC-insured accounts.

Syndicate: a group of underwriters bringing a new issue to the primary market.

Syndicate Letter: another name for the agreement among underwriters. The document detailing the terms of operation for an underwriting syndicate.

Systematic Risk: another name for "market risk," or the risk that an investment's value could plummet due to an overall market panic or collapse. Other "systematic risks" include inflation and interest rate risk.

Systematic Withdrawal Plan: a plan to redeem mutual fund shares according to a certain time frame, monthly check amount, or number of shares, etc., until the account is exhausted.

T

T + 2: regular way settlement, trade date plus three business days.

TAC – Targeted Amortization Class: a type of CMO (collateralized mortgage obligation) that leaves the investor with greater extension risk as compared to a PAC (planned amortization class).

Target Funds: an age-based asset allocation fund that automatically rebalances to match the investors' time horizon, e.g. a "Target 2040" fund is designed for investors planning to retire in or around the year 2040.

Tax-Advantaged Account: an account that provides tax benefits for purposes of saving and investing for retirement, education, or healthcare expenses.

Tax and Revenue Anticipation Note (TRAN): a short-term debt obligation of a municipal issuer backed by future tax and revenue receipts.

Tax Anticipation Note (TAN): a short-term debt obligation of a municipal issuer backed by future tax receipts.

Tax Credit: an amount that can be subtracted from the amount of taxes owed.

Tax-Deferred: an account where all earnings remain untaxed until "constructive receipt."

Tax-Equivalent Yield: the rate of return that a taxable bond must offer to equal the tax-exempt yield on a municipal bond. To calculate, take the municipal yield and divide that by (100% – investor's tax bracket).

Tax-Exempt Bonds: municipal bonds whose interest is not subject to taxation by the federal government.

Tax Preference Item: certain items that must be added back to an investor's income for purposes of AMT, including interest on certain municipal bonds.

Tax Shelter: offsetting passive income with a share of passive losses from a direct participation program.

Tax-Sheltered Annuity (TSA): an annuity funded with pre-tax (tax-deductible) contributions. Available to employees of non-profit organizations such as schools, hospitals, and church organizations.

T-bills: direct obligation of U.S. Government. Sold at discount, mature at face amount. Maximum maturity is 1 year.

T-bonds: direct obligation of U.S. Government. Pay semi-annual interest. Quoted as % of par value plus 32nds. 10–30-year maturities.

Technical Analysis: a method of using stock market data concerning price and volume to spot buying and selling opportunities. For example, following chart patterns and short interest as opposed to following an issuer's profit margins or revenue.

Technical Analysts: stock traders who rely on market data to spot buying and selling opportunities.

Telemarketing: to market by telephone. Assuming you can get past the caller ID.

Telephone Consumer Protection Act of 1991: federal legislation restricting the activities of telemarketers, who generally may only call prospects between 8 a.m. and 9 p.m. in the prospect's time zone and must maintain a do-not-call list, also checking the national registry.

Tenants in Common: see Joint Tenants in Common, a joint account wherein the interest of the deceased owner reverts to his/her estate.

Tender Offer: an offer by the issuer of securities to repurchase the securities if the investors care to "tender" their securities for payment, or an offer to acquire the shares currently held by shareholders of another company in a merger or acquisition.

Term Life Insurance: form of temporary insurance that builds no cash value and must be renewed at a higher premium at the end of the term. Renting rather than buying insurance.

The Insured: the individual upon whose death a life insurance policy will pay out.

Third Market: exchange-listed stock traded OTC primarily by institutional investors.

Third-party Account: account managed on behalf of a third party, e.g., trust or UGMA.

Time Horizon: an investor's anticipated holding period, used to determine how much volatility can be withstood and how much liquidity is required.

Times Interest Earned: a measure of interest coverage for a bond. Found on the income statement by comparing EBIT to annual interest expense.

Time Value: the value of an option above its intrinsic value. For example, if XYZ trades @50, an XYZ Oct 50 call @1 has no intrinsic value but has $1 of time value.

Timing Risk: the risk of purchasing an investment at a peak price not likely to be sustained or seen again. Timing risk can be reduced through dollar cost averaging, rather than investing in a stock with one purchase.

Tippee: the guy who listened to the insider information.

Tipper: the guy who told him.

T-notes: direct obligation of U.S. Government. Pay semi-annual interest. Quoted as % of par value plus 32nds. 2–10-year maturities.

Tombstone: an advertisement allowed during the cooling-off period to announce an offer of securities, listing the issuer, the type of security, the underwriters, and directions for obtaining a prospectus.

Top-Down Analysis: fundamental analysis that starts with the overall economy, then moves down to industry groups and issuers to make buy or sell decisions.

Top-Heavy: a 401(k) plan, for example, where 60% or more of the benefits go to key, highly compensated employees.

Total Return: measuring growth in share price plus dividend and capital gains distributions.

Total Takedown: the additional takedown plus the concession.

Trade Confirmation: a document containing details of a securities transaction, e.g., price of the security, commissions, stock symbol, number of shares, registered rep code, trade date and settlement date, etc.

Trade Date: the date that a trade is executed.

Trade Reporting and Comparison Service (TRACS): system developed for ADF members, requiring them to report trades executed through the Alternative Display Facility within 10 seconds of execution.

Trade Reporting and Compliance Engine (TRACE): system used to report bond transactions in the secondary market.

Trading Authorization: a form granting another individual the authority to trade on behalf of the account owner. Either "limited" (buy/sell orders only) or "full" (buy/sell orders plus requests for checks/securities) authorization may be granted. Sometimes referred to as "power of attorney."

Trading Post: a group of monitors around which market participants communicate on the floor of the NYSE.

Traditional IRA: individual retirement account funded typically with tax-deductible contributions.

Tranche: a class of CMO. Principal is returned to one tranche at a time in a CMO.

Transfer Agent: issues and redeems certificates. Handles name changes, validates mutilated certificates. Distributes dividends, gains, and shareholder reports to mutual fund investors.

Transfer and Hold in Safekeeping: a buy order for securities in which securities are bought and transferred to the customer's name, but held by the broker-dealer.

Transfer and Ship: a buy order for securities in which securities are purchased and transferred to the customer's name, with the certificates sent to the customer.

Transfer on Death (TOD): individual account with a named beneficiary—assets transferred directly to the named beneficiary upon death of the account holder.

Treasury Bill: see T-bill.

Treasury Bond: see T-bond.

Treasury Note: see T-note.

Treasury Receipts: zero coupon bonds created by broker-dealers backed by Treasury securities held in escrow. Not a direct obligation of U.S. Government.

Treasury Securities: securities guaranteed by U.S. Treasury, including T-bills, T-notes, T-bonds, and STRIPS.

Treasury Stock: shares that have been issued and repurchased by the corporation. Has nothing to do with the U.S. Treasury.

True Interest Cost: a measure of a municipal issuer's total cost of borrowing money by issuing bonds. Unlike net interest cost, true interest cost factors in the time value of money.

Trust Indenture: a written agreement between an issuer and creditors wherein the terms of a debt security issue are set forth, e.g., interest rate, means of payment, maturity date, name of the trustee, etc.

Trust Indenture Act of 1939: corporate bond issues in excess of $5 million with maturities greater than 1 year must be issued with an indenture.

Trustee: a person legally appointed to act on a beneficiary's behalf.

Turnover: the frequency of trading within a portfolio.

Turnover Ratio: a measure of the frequency with which the investment adviser trades portfolio securities for an open- or closed-end fund.

Two-dollar Broker: an independent broker on the floor of the NYSE.

Type: option term used to separate a call from a put, the only two "types" of options.

U

U4: registration information for an associated person of a member firm. Used to apply for registration and subject to regular updating requirements.

U5: information provided to CRD when an associated person terminates employment with a member firm.

UGMA: Uniform Gifts to Minors Act. An account set up for the benefit of a minor, managed by a custodian.

UIT: Unit Investment Trust. A type of investment company where investments are selected, not traded/managed. No management fee is charged. Shares are redeemable.

Underwriter: see "investment banker." An underwriter or "investment banker" is a broker-dealer that distributes shares on the primary market.

Underwriting Spread: the profit to the syndicate. The difference between the proceeds to the issuer and the POP.

Unearned Income: income derived from investments and other sources not related to employment, e.g., savings account interest, dividends from stock, capital gains, and rental income.

Unfunded Pension Liabilities: obligations to retiring municipal workers that outweigh the funds set aside to pay them.

Uniform Practice Code: how FINRA promotes "cooperative effort," standardizing settlement dates, ex-dates, accrued interest calculations, etc.

Uniform Securities Act: a model act that state securities laws are based on. Designed to prevent fraud and maintain faith in capital markets through registration of securities, agents, broker-dealers, and investment advisers. Main purpose is to provide necessary protection to investors.

Unit of Beneficial Interest: what an investor in a Unit Investment Trust (UIT) owns.

Universal Life Insurance: a form of permanent insurance that offers flexibility in death benefit and both the amount of, and method of paying, premiums.

Unqualified Opinion: an opinion issued by the bond counsel expressing no doubts and requiring no qualifiers.

Unrealized Gain: the increase in the value of an asset that has not yet been sold. Unrealized gains are not taxable.

Unsecured Bond: a debenture, or bond issued without specific collateral.

Unsolicited Order: an order to buy or sell securities placed by the customer rather than recommended by the agent. Outside the agent's suitability obligations.

User Fee: a.k.a. "user charge," a source of revenue used to retire a revenue bond, e.g., park entrance fees, tolls, skybox rentals, etc.

Unsystematic Risk: an investment risk that is specific to an issuer or industry group, e.g. legislative or business risk.

UTMA: just like UGMA, only the minor typically must wait until 21 years of age to have the assets re-registered solely in his/her name. The "T" stands for "transfer."

V

Valuation Ratio: the comparison of a stock's market price to the EPS, book value, etc.

Value: as in "value investing" or a "value fund," the practice of purchasing stock in companies whose share price is currently depressed.

Value Funds: mutual funds investing in stocks currently out of favor with investors.

Variable Annuity: an annuity whose payout varies. Investments allocated to separate account as instructed by annuitant. Similar to investing in mutual funds, except that annuities offer tax deferral. No taxation until excess over cost basis is withdrawn.

Variable Insurance: insurance whose death benefit and cash values fluctuate with the investment performance of the separate account.

Variable Life Insurance: form of insurance where death benefit and cash value fluctuate according to fluctuations of the separate account.

Variable Universal Life Insurance: flexible-premium insurance with cash value and death benefit tied to the performance of the separate account.

Vesting: a schedule for determining at what point the employer's contributions become the property of the employee.

Viatical Settlement: a.k.a. "life settlement," the sale and purchase of a life insurance policy wherein the investor buys the death benefit at a discount and profits as soon as the insured dies.

Visible Supply: total par value of municipal bonds to be issued over the next 30 days, published in the Bond Buyer.

Volatility: the up and down movements of an investment that make investors dizzy and occasionally nauseated.

Volume: total number of shares traded over a given period (daily, weekly, etc.). Of interest to technical—but not fundamental— analysts.

Voluntary Accumulation Plan: a mutual fund account into which the investor commits to depositing amounts of money on a regular basis.

Voter Approval: the process of approving the issuance of a general obligation bond by referendum.

VRDO – variable rate demand obligation: a debt security whose interest rate is regularly re-set and which can be "put" or sold back to the issuer or a designated third party for the par value plus accrued interest.

W

Warrants: long-term equity securities giving the owner the right to purchase stock at a set price. Often attached as a "sweetener" that makes the other security more attractive.

Wash Sale: selling a security at a loss but then messing up by repurchasing it within 30 days and, therefore, not being able to use it to offset capital gains for that year. Also, a type of market manipulation in which a security is traded among the same or related parties without a "change in beneficial ownership" but only with the purpose of manipulating its market price.

Western/Divided Account: a syndicate account in which each participant is responsible for their share of the bonds only.

When-issued Confirmations: confirmations of a purchase on the primary market delivered before the securities have been issued.

Whole Life Insurance: form of permanent insurance with a guaranteed death benefit and minimum guaranteed cash value.

Withdrawal Plan: a feature of most mutual funds that allows investors to liquidate their accounts over a fixed time period, or using a fixed-share or fixed-dollar amount.

Wrap Account: an account in which the customer pays one fee to cover the costs of investment advisory services, execution of transactions, etc.

Wrap Fee: the fee charged in a wrap account to cover trade execution, portfolio management and other related services.

Written Supervisory Procedures (WSP): compliance manual/systems implemented by member firms and monitored regularly for adequacy.

Y

Yield: the income a stock or bond provides to the holder.

Yield-based Options: standardized options based on the yield of various U.S. Treasury securities.

Yield Curve: a graph showing securities of similar credit quality across various maturities. In a normal yield curve, yields rise with maturities. With an inverted yield curve, short-term securities yield more than longer-term securities.

Yield Spread: the difference in yields between debt securities of different credit quality and similar maturities. Also known as a "credit spread."

Yield to Call: the yield received on a bond if held to the date it is called.

Yield to Maturity: calculation of all interest payments plus/minus gain/loss on a bond if held to maturity.

Z

Zero Coupon Bond: a bond sold at a deep discount to its gradually increasing par value.

Index

Made in the USA
Middletown, DE
12 November 2018